Arnd Bauerkämper/Odd-Bjørn Fure/
Øystein Hetland/Robert Zimmermann (eds.)
From Patriotic Memory to a Universalistic Narrative?

KLARTEXT

Arnd Bauerkämper/Odd-Bjørn Fure/
Øystein Hetland/Robert Zimmermann (eds.)

From Patriotic Memory to a Universalistic Narrative?

Shifts in Norwegian Memory Culture after 1945 in Comparative Perspective

Titelabbildung:
Das Cover ist eines von zwei bekannten Bildern der Judendeportation aus Norwegen. Es wurde am 26. November 1942 am Osloer Kai vom Fotografen Georg W. Fossum aufgenommen und zeigt das deutsche Schiff »Donau«, das norwegische Juden nach Stettin transportierte. Von dort wurden sie direkt nach Auschwitz deportiert. Nur 30 von ihnen überlebten.
Foto: Georg W. Fossum
© picture alliance/NTB scanpix

Coverillustration:
The cover is one of only two known photos showing the deportation of Norwegian Jews. It was taken on 26 November 1942 in Oslo harbour by the photographer Georg W. Fossum. The ship »Donau« took the Jews to Stettin, from where they have been deported straight to Auschwitz.
Only 30 survived of the deportees survived.
Photo: Georg W. Fossum
© picture alliance/NTB scanpix

Gedruckt mit freundlicher Unterstützung des

E.ON Stipendienfonds
im Stifterverband für die Deutsche Wissenschaft

1. Auflage September 2014

Satz und Gestaltung:
Klartext Medienwerkstatt GmbH, Essen

Umschlaggestaltung:
Volker Pecher, Essen

Druck und Bindung:
Majuskel Medienproduktion GmbH, Wetzlar

ISBN 978-3-8375-1175-8
Alle Rechte vorbehalten
© Klartext Verlag, Essen 2014

www.klartext-verlag.de

Content

Steffen Bruendel
Preface: Historical Research and the Impact of Academic Cooperation –
Norway and Germany 9

Arnd Bauerkämper/Odd-Bjørn Fure/Øystein Hetland/
Robert Zimmermann
Introduction: From Patriotic Memory to a Universalistic Narrative?
Shifts in Norwegian Memory Culture after 1945
in Comparative Perspective 19

I. Between Patriotic and Universalistic Memory

Odd-Bjørn Fure
Developmental Societal Processes.
Changing Configurations of Memories The Case of Norway
in a Comparative Perspective 43

Arnd Bauerkämper
Beyond Resistance versus Collaboration:
The Twisted Road to a Universalistic Narrative in Norway 63

II. Towards a Universalistic Narrative: the Role of Holocaust Memory

Claudia Lenz
Linking Holocaust Education to Human Rights Education:
A Symptom of the Universalisation and Denationalization
of Memory Culture in Norway? 87

Jon Reitan
The Holocaust: Guilt and Apology in Norwegian Historical Culture 105

Iselin Theien/Bjørn Westlie
The Restitution Process and the Integration of the Jewish Minority
into the Norwegian Collective Memory of the Second World War 117

Ilse Raaijmakers
Between the »Particular« and the »Universal«:
Dynamics in Dutch Memory Culture 135

III. Narratives of the Past in Historiography, Education and Museums

Gunnar D. Hatlehol
In Command of History?
Historians, Memory Culture and German War Crimes
against Foreign Prisoners in Norway 153

Robert Zimmermann
From Captivity to the Classroom:
Educational Initiatives by former Political Prisoners' Associations
in Denmark and Norway since 1945 171

Doreen Reinhold
Exhibiting the Second World War Now and Then:
Narrative and Representation in *Norges Hjemmefrontmuseum*
and the *Senter for studier av Holocaust og livssynsminoriteter* 193

IV. Sites of Memory

Tor Einar Fagerland
Between Patriotism and Universalism:
Norwegian World War II Monuments and Memorials 1990–2014 from
a Transnational Perspective 215

Leiv Sem
The Eastern Front Revisited:
The Landscape of Memory in Norwegian Second World War Discourse .. 233

V. General Exclusion? Marginal Groups in Postwar Norway

Susanne Maerz
From Taboo to Compensation:
Krigsbarn in Public Discourse and Literature after 1945 253

Sigurd Sørlie
From Misguided Idealists to *Genocidaires:*
The Waffen-SS Volunteers in Norwegian Memory Culture 273

The Authors 297

Index of Names 301

Steffen Bruendel
Preface
Historical Research and the Impact of Transnational Academic Cooperation – Norway and Germany

On 8 May 1985, the President of the Federal Republic of Germany, Richard von Weizsäcker, gave a speech in West Germany's parliament, the *Bundestag*, which aroused significant interest. On the anniversary of the end of the Second World War, he introduced a new tone into the debate on the German culture of remembrance. Many peoples commemorated the day on which the Second World War came to an end in Europe, von Weizsäcker said, and he continued, »in line with its destiny, each people has its own feelings. Victory or defeat, liberation from unlawful and foreign domination or the transition to a new dependency, division, new alliances, enormous shifts in power – the 8th of May 1945 is a date of decisive historical significance in Europe.« The West German President emphasized that 8 May 1945 could not be uncoupled from 30 January 1933. Thus, the end of the war was inextricably linked to the beginning of the Nazi dictatorship, for Hitler's seizure of power abolished freedom and liberty, and ultimately caused tremendous violence, the war, defeat, flight and expulsion. Those who suffered under Nazi rule, including many Germans, were finally liberated in 1945.[1] The term »liberation« was employed for the first time in Germany in 1985, when it came to replace the notion of defeat. Undoubtedly, 8 May will always remain an ambivalent date for Germans, given that it signifies both liberation and defeat. At present, however, Germans agree that a notable change in German memory culture set in with von Weizsäcker's address to the *Bundestag*.

The term »memory culture« was introduced into scholarly vocabulary in the 1990s. Since then, it has become a guiding concept in modern research into cultural history.[2] Following a strict definition of the term, it serves as a generic con-

---

1 Richard von Weizsäcker: Speech 8 May 1985, in: Webarchiv des Deutschen Bundestages: <http://webarchiv.bundestag.de/archive/2006/0202/parlament/geschichte/parlhist/dokumente/dok08.html> (11.3.2013).
2 Cf. Christoph Cornelißen: Was heißt Erinnerungskultur? Begriff – Methoden – Perspektiven, in: Geschichte in Wissenschaft und Unterricht 54, 2003, 548–563.

cept »for the totality of the non-specifically scholarly usage of history in public life«.³ With regard to the developments in research over the past two decades, however, German historian Christoph Cornelißen has emphasized that »on the whole it is more sensible to understand ›memory culture‹ as a formal generic concept encompassing all conceivable forms of conscious remembrance of historical events, personalities and processes, whether they be of an aesthetic, political or cognitive nature.«⁴ Thus, the term comprises all modes of representation of history, including debates among historians and private recollections, insofar as they have left traces in public life. The bearers of this »collective memory« (Maurice Halbwachs) are individuals, social groups or even nations.

In that deeply symbolic year of 1985, which was to become so decisive for German historical culture, a German-Norwegian history project was initiated, a programme for historical scholarship under the auspices of the Ruhrgas Scholarship Fund, a foundation established in 1983. Establishing the fund, the Ruhrgas AG entered a new domain, since the task of promoting scientific scholarship beyond the company's own research and development had primarily been regarded as a mission for the state to fulfil. Since the 1950s, moreover, Norway had increasingly been leaning towards the United States. After concluding the first German-Norwegian natural gas supply contracts in 1977, the Norwegian government strove to internationalise its scientific research and practices and to renew former academic relationships, in particular with Germany. Ruhrgas AG seized that opportunity. Since the beginning of the 1970s, the company, originally founded in 1926 in Essen by Ruhr Mining to use coking plant gas, had established itself as the largest German gas network company. As was to emerge later, Ruhrgas AG had contributed to easing East-West tensions thanks to the celebrated gas-for-pipe deal with the Soviet Union signed in 1970.⁵

---

3 Hans Günter Hockerts: Zugänge zur Zeitgeschichte. Primärerfahrung, Erinnerungskultur, Geschichtswissenschaft, in: Konrad H. Jarausch/Martin Sabrow (eds.): Verletztes Gedächtnis. Erinnerungskultur und Zeitgeschichte im Konflikt, Frankfurt a. M. 2002, 39–73, at 41.
4 Christoph Cornelißen: Erinnerungskulturen, in: <http://docupedia.de/zg/Erinnerungskulturen_Version_2.0_Christoph_Corneli%C3%9Fen#cite_ref-0> (11.3.2013).
5 See Ruhrgas AG (ed.): Schlaglichter. Die ersten 75 Jahre. Essen 2001; Karsten Rudolph: Wirtschaftsdiplomatie im Kalten Krieg: Die Ostpolitik der westdeutschen Großindustrie 1945–1991. Frankfurt a. M./New York 2004; Manfred Pohl: Geschäft und Politik. Deutsch-russisch/sowjetische Wirtschaftsbeziehungen 1850–1988. Mainz 1988; Claudia Wörmann: Osthandel als Problem der atlantischen Allianz. Erfahrungen aus dem Erd-

With the renowned *Stifterverband für die Deutsche Wissenschaft* (Donors' Association for the Promotion of Sciences and Humanities in Germany), likewise located in Essen, Ruhrgas AG chose a partner that had gained considerable experience in promoting science since its foundation in 1920. Moreover, close collaboration with precursors of today's Research Council of Norway assured that Norway's policy objectives in research would also be taken into account. The selection committees for the new scholarship fund were composed of renowned experts. Moreover, it was supported by a German-Norwegian advisory council consisting of selected representatives from scientific and business circles along with members of civil society in order to anchor the new foundation and its programmes in Norwegian society and politics. At the same time, Ruhrgas was eager to supplement academic collaboration with cultural exchanges, for instance, by sponsoring art exhibitions.[6]

At its meeting of 18 September 1985, the advisory council decided to set up a history programme. »In the view of the Research Council for the Humanities«, it read in the proposal to establish a German-Norwegian scholarship scheme for history, »closer collaboration and more contacts between Norwegian and West German historians should be encouraged, as Norwegian historians tend to focus on Anglo-Saxon history in Norwegian memory culture.«[7] This scholarship programme for historians eventually enabled Norwegian students, young researchers and university lecturers to undertake research at German universities and archives and/or to attend conferences. After the initial scheme for economists, the history scholarship programme was the second such initiative to consolidate academic ties between Norway and Germany.

German-Norwegian energy business grew and intensified considerably following the initial distribution of Norwegian natural gas to Germany in 1977. New contracts signed in 1986 established Norway – along with the Soviet Union – as a

---

gas-Röhren-Geschäft mit der UdSSR. Forschungsinstitut der Deutschen Gesellschaft für Auswärtige Politik. 31. Januar 1986.

6 See Museum Folkwang/Kunsthalle Rostock (ed.): Norske Profiler. Aktuelle Kunst aus Norwegen. Bonn 1997; Munch-Museet (ed.): 1905–1935 Ekspresjon! Edvard Munch – Tysk og norsk kunst i tre tiår. Oslo 2006; Munch Museum (ed.): Munchs Laboratorium. Der Weg zur Aula. Oslo 2011 (English version: Munch's Laboratory. The Path to the Aula. Oslo 2011).

7 Proposal to establish a German-Norwegian Scholarship Scheme for History, 6 September 1985, 1 (Archives of the E.ON Ruhrgas Scholarship Fund).

decisive partner for German energy security.⁸ Relations between Scandinavia and Germany have often been characterized in terms of an elective affinity (*Wahlverwandtschaft*).⁹ Until the mid-twentieth century, this view was seen as particularly characteristic of the relationship between Norway and Germany. The Second World War, however, was to provoke a rupture. Thus, West German support for Norwegian historians within the framework of the Ruhrgas scholarships was not without risk because the German occupation during the Second World War still played a critical role in the Norwegian memory culture. Historical issues arising out of events in the twentieth century had to be approached with sensitivity. »Despite some misgivings about the historians' programme, we set something in motion that could possibly produce more conflict than reconciliation. There were no relationships between Norwegian and German historians.«¹⁰ This was soon to change.

How did this transformation come about? As with all the Ruhrgas programmes, acknowledged experts from both countries, including the likes of Jarle Simensen and Christian Meier, were appointed to the selection committee of historians.¹¹ Simensen was then a professor of history at the University of Trondheim, and was appointed to head the committee until 1990. From the outset, he was convinced of the significance of this programme because »up until 1945 every Norwegian historian learnt German as their first foreign language, and our most important academic connections were with our German colleagues.« Also with regard to research policy, the programme in Norway was established just at the right time: »Already at the beginning of the 1980s, we had come to the conclusion that we needed to broaden our perspectives,« Simensen said. »Hence internationalisation became a central aim of the Norwegian Research Council, which fitted well in with this new binational programme.«¹²

---

8   Klaus Liesen: Partnerschaft mit Zukunft, in: Deutsch-Norwegische Gesellschaft (ed.): 1949–1989. 40 Jahre deutsch-norwegische Beziehungen, second edition, Oslo 1990, 276–291.
9   Bernd Henningsen/Janine Klain/Helmut Müssener/Solfrid Söderlind (eds.): Wahlverwandtschaft. Skandinavien und Deutschland 1800 bis 1914. Ausstellungskatalog Deutsches Historisches Museum. Berlin 1997.
10 Former Chairman of the Board of Ruhrgas AG, Dr. Klaus Liesen, quoted in E.ON Ruhrgas Scholarship Fund (ed.): Bericht. Die ersten 25 Jahre/Rapport. De første 25 årene. Essen 2009, 23 f.
11 Ibid., 23–25.
12 Quoted in ibid. 23.

The programme remained in place for 15 years. After its termination in 2000, it was replaced by a programme for political scientists. In retrospect, all those who participated in the history programme regard it as a success, since not only Norwegian, but also German historians took into consideration all branches of their discipline, discussed various methodological approaches and engaged critically on a variety of topics. Thus, it had been important »to also admit candidates in the history of art and of architecture«, Anneken Tue recalled some years ago as she looked back on her service on the selection committee. The art historian and former museum director in Bergen stressed the major links between both countries, especially in the artistic sphere: »Bauhaus and the German Werkbund had a strong impact here. At that time, anyone artistically talented in our country went to Germany, and nowadays they are going there once again.«[13] The contacts Anneken Tue had established during her collaboration with German researchers and museums also helped her to organise the momentous *Brücke* exhibition in Bergen in 2009.[14] Interestingly, the proposal to set up a scholarship programme for historians was made by a Norwegian, Johan B. Holte, then director of Norsk Hydro and a member of the foundation's advisory council. After some initial misgivings on the German side, agreement was quickly reached with the Norwegian Research Council in Oslo, and the programme started in 1985.[15] Ten years later, Jarle Simensen wrote in Norway's most prestigious historical journal, *Historisk Tidsskrift*, about the positive effects of the programme with regard to internationalisation.[16] Between 1985 and 2000, a total of ten historians' conferences took place. The results have been published. During the same period, around 260 scholarships were awarded to carefully selected students and scholars. Their work covered a broad range of topics from the German *Hanse* to Norway's energy legislation.[17]

---

13 Quoted in ibid. 24.
14 Bergen Kunstmuseum (ed.): Brücke. Tysk Ekspresjonism 1905–1913. Verk fra Brücke-museet i Berlin. München 2009.
15 Jarle Simensen: Das Ruhrgasprogramm 1984–2005, in: Bernd Henningen (ed.): Hundert Jahre deutsch-norwegische Begegnungen. Nicht nur Lachs und Würstchen. Begleitbuch zur Ausstellung. Berlin 2005, 134–137, at 135.
16 Jarle Simensen: Internasjonalisering i Historiefaget: Det Tysk-Norske Stipendienprogrammet for Historie (Ruhrgas), 1985–1995, in: Historisk Tidsskrift, Vol. 75, No. 1/2, 1996, 158–184.
17 E.ON Ruhrgas Scholarship Fund, Report, 24. See also Deutsch-Norwegisches Stipendienprogramm für Geschichtswissenschaften (Ruhrgas-Stipendium) (ed.): Bericht über das 9. deutsch-norwegische Historikertreffen in Meißen/Dresden, Mai

»At that time the programme soon became widely known among students and professors«, recalled Norwegian historian Hans Otto Frøland in 2009. He was twice awarded a scholarship and currently teaches German history at the NTNU Trondheim. The Ruhrgas scholarships awakened his interest in Germany. To the present day, Frøland says, these scholarships have had a considerable impact on Norwegian historians.[18] Norwegian politicians, too, were persuaded of the benefits of the Ruhrgas scholarships. »Without doubt, the Ruhrgas scholarship programme has contributed to significantly to improving our knowledge of Germany and the German language,« as former Prime Minister, Kjell Magne Bondevik, put it.[19]

The scholarly exchange between Norwegian and German historians pertained to all epochs and aspects of German-Norwegian relations.[20] Moreover, German-Norwegian collaboration among historians contributed towards their getting to know and understand each other better. »Initially, we were unsure as to the extent« of the reservations and objections that still existed about us,« recalled German historian Christian Meier in the mid-1990s. He regards the dismantling of these reservations over time as »a very important achievement of this programme.«[21] Furthermore, the historians' programme was to gain considerable significance for internationalising Norwegian historiography, which had hitherto been preoccupied almost exclusively with national topics.[22] Since the 1980s, however, the German historians' debates over how to deal with dictatorship, war and the Holocaust, which had a strong impact on memory culture in Germany, struck a chord among their Norwegian colleagues. The intensive expert engagement with historical issues that were discussed in Germany also had an impact on Norwegian memory culture over time. If up until the 1990s the narrative of a collective resistance during the German occupation had been cultivated, younger Norwe-

---

1998: Universitäts-, Wissenschafts- und Intellektuellengeschichte. Bericht über das 10. deutsch-norwegische Historikertreffen in Bergen, Mai/Juni 2000: Bilanz eines Jahrhunderts. Oslo 2001.
18 E.ON Ruhrgas Scholarship Fund, Report, p. 24 (Frøland quotation ibid.).
19 Kjell Magne Bondevik, Norwegian Prime Minister 1997–2000 and 2001–2005, quoted in DNF-Magazin. Zeitschrift der Deutsch-Norwegischen Freundschaftsgesellschaft e. V., Issue 4, 2008, 2.
20 Cf. Jarle Simensen (ed.), Deutschland – Norwegen. Die lange Geschichte. Oslo 1999.
21 Christian Meier: Stellungnahme zum deutsch-norwegischen Stipendienprogramm, 14 September 1995, Essen (Archives of the Scholarship Fund).
22 Simensen, Ruhrgasprogramm,135.

gian historians started to deal with problematic aspects of their twentieth-century past in the late 1980s. Examples of such work include those of Odd-Bjørn Fure, an alumnus of the Scholarship Fund, Hans Fredrik Dahl and Øystein Sørensen.[23]

What had for so long seemed inconceivable has now become normal academic exchange. Those attending German-Norwegian expert conferences (self-) critically discuss how to come to terms with defeat as well as the experiences of occupation, collaboration and resistance, identity, inclusion as much as exclusion. German-Norwegian collaboration in the project network Transnational Constructions of Societies in 20th-Century Europe offers further evidence of this achievement.[24] This co-operation began in 2009 as Arnd Bauerkämper and Jarle Simensen got to know each other at a history workshop on the occasion of the Scholarship Fund's alumni meeting in Berlin. Even though the history programme had terminated in 2000, selected German-Norwegian history projects have also been supported in the last decade. Thus, two joint conferences on memory culture organized by the Free University of Berlin and the Holocaust Center in Oslo were held in June 2011 in Berlin and in March 2013 in Oslo. Both conferences were highly relevant with regard to the history of Second World War and the politics of remembering.[25]

Following the exhibition »National Myths. 1945 – Arena of Memories« (*Mythen der Nationen. 1945 – Arena der Erinnerungen*) at the German Historical Museum in Berlin in 2004,[26] numerous studies on the European politics of remembering after 1945 have been published in the last few years. Apart from comprehensive

---

23 Odd-Bjørn Fure: Mellomkrigstid: 1920–1940, in: Norsk utenrikspolitikks historie, Vol. 3, Oslo 1996; Hans Fredrik Dahl: Vidkun Quisling. En fører blir til. Oslo 1991; Øystein Sørensen: Hitler eller Quisling – ideologiske brytninger i Nasjonal Samling 1940–1945. Oslo 1989.

24 Project »Transnational Constructions of Societies in 20th-Century Europe. Concepts and Socio-Political Practices«: <http://www.geschkult.fu-berlin.de/en/e/fmi/arbeitsbereiche/ab_bauerkaemper/Projektverbund/index.html> (30.11.2013).

25 Vgl. Tagungsbericht *Das umstrittene Gedächtnis. Transnationale und innergesellschaftliche Erinnerungskonflikte in Europa nach 1945*. 17.6.2011–18.6.2011, Berlin, in: H-Soz-u-Kult, 27.7.2011, <http://hsozkult.geschichte.hu-berlin.de/tagungsberichte/id=3746> (30.11.2013); Tagungsbericht *From Patriotic Memory to a Universalistic Narrative: Shifts in Norwegian Memory Culture after 1945 in Comparative Perspective*. 15.3.2013–16.3.2013, Oslo, in: H-Soz-u-Kult, 18.6.2013, <http://hsozkult.geschichte.hu-berlin.de/tagungsberichte/id=4864> (30.11.2013).

26 Monika Flacke (ed.): Mythen der Nationen. 1945 – Arena der Erinnerungen. Ausstellungskatalog Deutsches Historisches Museum Berlin. Mainz 2004.

studies, many East European countries along with Germany and Scandinavia have also been investigated in detailed studies.[27] In 2009, the twentieth anniversary of the fall of the Berlin Wall was of particular interest not only for historians, but also for political scientists. Norwegian and German scholars thus held a conference in Oslo supported by the Scholarship Fund.[28] However, a new overview on *Das umstrittene Gedächtnis. Die Erinnerung an Nationalsozialismus, Faschismus und Krieg in Europa seit 1945* (Disputed Memory. Recollections of National Socialism, Fascism and War in Europe since 1945), which goes back to the Berlin conference on memory culture of 2011, might well be regarded as one of the most comprehensive accounts of the politics and culture of memory in Europe.[29]

Comparative studies of European states have demonstrated that a unified European memory culture is not yet on the horizon because commemoration policies have been nationally framed. Moreover, they remain a »politically contested terrain« in all countries.[30] In order to work out similarities and peculiarities in the various memory cultures, it is indispensable to adopt a comparative perspective. Applied to a period spanning several decades, it can be shown how specific patriotic cultures of remembrance have gradually yielded to a more transnational embedding of one's own national history in a European or universal context, although this overriding trend has by no means yet abolished national variants. This has also been demonstrated by the manifold contributions to the conference on »Shifts in Norwegian Memory Culture after 1945 in Comparative Perspective«

27 Cf. Kerstin von Lingen (ed.): Kriegserfahrung und nationale Identität in Europa nach 1945. Erinnerung, Säuberungsprozesse und nationales Gedächtnis. Paderborn 2009; Regina Fritz/Carola Sachse/Edgar Wolfrum (ed.): Nationen und ihre Selbstbilder. Postdiktatorische Gesellschaften in Europa. Göttingen 2008; Robert Bohn/Christoph Cornelißen/Karl Christian Lammers (ed.): Vergangenheitspolitik und Erinnerungskulturen im Schatten des Zweiten Weltkriegs. Deutschland und Skandinavien seit 1945. Essen 2008.
28 Elisabeth Bakke/Ingo Peters (eds.): Twenty Years after the Fall of the Berlin Wall. Transitions, State Break-up and Democratic Politics in Central Europe and Germany. Berlin 2011.
29 Arnd Bauerkämper: Das umstrittene Gedächtnis. Die Erinnerung an Nationalsozialismus, Faschismus und Krieg in Europa seit 1945. Paderborn 2012.
30 Wolfram Pyta: Politisch umkämpftes Terrain. Europa konnte nach dem Zweiten Weltkrieg keine einheitliche Erinnerungskultur hervorbringen, in: *Frankfurter Allgemeine Zeitung*, 18.2.2013. Also see Ortrun Huber: Das umstrittene Gedächtnis. Forscher am Friedrich-Meinecke-Institut der Freien Universität Berlin untersuchen Erinnerungskonflikte in Europa nach 1945, in: *Tagesspiegel*-Beilage, 10.12.2011.

held on 15 and 16 March 2013 in Oslo. This volume presents the findings of the conference.

Three decades of privately sponsored promotion of research by the Ruhrgas scholarships have led to an increase in academic exchanges amongst students and researchers. Scholarly knowledge has been generated, extended and deepened. At the same time, the philanthropic engagement by Ruhrgas AG – which was re-named E.ON Ruhrgas after having been integrated into E.ON, Germany's largest energy company in 2003 – has not encroached on the freedom to teach and undertake research. Due to the special role of the company's non-profit scholarship fund[31], a separate article was devoted to the »Ruhrgas Programme« in the catalogue for the exhibition on one hundred years of German-Norwegian relations published in 2005.[32] Thus, the Scholarship Fund's history programme, too, has contributed to academic exchanges between Germany and Norway that have become increasingly intensive. The preferred cooperation has proved to be fruitful for historians from both countries. Ultimately, the exchange facilitated Norwegian historians' efforts to develop and gain a transnational perspective on their history.

---

31 After E.ON had taken over Ruhrgas in 2003, the Ruhrgas Scholarship Fund was renamed into E.ON Ruhrgas Scholarship Fund. Since the merger of E.ON Ruhrgas with E.ON Global Commodities in 2013, the foundation's name changed to E.ON Scholarship Fund.

32 Simensen, Ruhrgasprogramm, 134–137.

Arnd Bauerkämper/Odd-Bjørn Fure/Øystein Hetland/
Robert Zimmermann
Introduction: From Patriotic Memory to a Universalistic Narrative?
Shifts in Norwegian Memory Culture after 1945 in Comparative Perspective

I. General Approach and European Context

Over the last two decades there has been a marked upsurge of exploration and analysis of memories of the Second World War, the impact of Nazi occupation, different forms of collaboration and the Holocaust in European historiography. Some historians have even bemoaned a »commemorative excess« since the 1990s.[1] Yet transnational entanglements between memories of Nazi and fascist rule, the Second World War and the Holocaust have hitherto received scant attention. In a similar vein, comparative perspectives have largely been neglected. This book is expected to contribute in filling this lacuna in historical research. It will situate Norway in a transnational perspective in order to identify the specifics of the country's memory culture.

National paradigms have to date prevailed in political debates as well as in historiography. Especially in the first few decades after 1945, patriotic memory predominated memory cultures in Western and Central Europe. In Norway, it highlighted armed and to a lesser degree civil resistance (including sabotage) against the German occupiers and their collaborators in Vidkun Quisling's fascist *Nasjonal Samling* (NS).[2] Scholars, on the whole, have emphasised the persistence of national frameworks in the memorising process. In Eastern Europe, in particu-

---

1 Geoff Eley: Foreword, in: M. Evans/K. Lunn (eds.): War and Memory in the Twentieth Century, New York 1997, VII–XIII, VIII.
2 For an overview of Norway, see Synne Corell: The Solidity of a National Narrative. The German Occupation in Norwegian History Culture, in: H. Stenius/M. Österberg/J. Östling (eds.): Nordic Narratives of the Second World War, National Historiographies Revisited, Lund 2011, 101–125.

lar, popular support and enthusiasm for the nation-state was even reinforced in the wake of the collapse of communism between 1989 and 1991. Although the national paradigm had largely coalesced with communist internationalism in countries like Poland before 1989, the collapse of the dictatorships has lent memories of national history a new lease of life. In the east European states that had been subverted to Soviet rule following the advances by the Red Army in 1944 and 1945, the end of the Nazi occupation had largely been perceived as a new occupation by a new power, in this case the USSR. After 1989–91, memories of the Gulag have therefore given risen rise to a sense of national self-victimisation in these countries, though by no means universally.[3]

By contrast, a shift from a patriotic narrative of heroic resistance to more self-critical memories of responsibility and guilt has been identified in recent historiography and public discourse, especially in Western and Central Europe. Norway has furnished tangible proof for this observation. On the occasion of the International Holocaust Remembrance Day on 27 January 2012, for instance, Prime Minister Jens Stoltenberg publicly apologised for the participation of Norwegians in the mass murder of the European Jewry during the Second World War, without, however, linking it to those members of the NS who had participated in the arrests and deportation of the Jews in 1942–43. And yet, he lauded those citizens who had abstained from participation in these deportations or had even opposed the Holocaust in Norway.[4]

His public statement has been hailed as a landmark in the change of tack toward a self-critical memory based on universalistic notions of human rights that have increasingly characterised memory cultures in other West European countries, too. Over the last three decades, heroic narratives have gradually ebbed

---

3 Richard Ned Lebow: The Memory of Politics in Postwar Europe, in: idem/W. Kansteiner/C. Fugo (eds.): The Politics of Memory in Postwar Europe (London 2006), 1–39; Stefan Troebst: ›Was für ein Teppich?‹ Postkommunistische Erinnerungskulturen in Ost (Mittel) Europa, in: V. Knigge/U. Mählert (eds.): Der Kommunismus im Museum. Formen der Auseinandersetzung in Deutschland und Ostmitteleuropa, Cologne 2005, 31–51.

4 See Spiegel Online, 27 January 2012 (<http://www.spiegel.de/politik/ausland/holocaust-gedenktag-norwegen-entschuldigt-sich-fuer-deportation-der-juden-a-811918.html>). For the text of Stoltenberg's speech, see <http://www.norway.org.il/News_and_events/Jewish-History-and-Culture-in-Norway/Norwegian-PM-Jens-Stoltenbergs-Speech-on-the-International-Holocaust-Remembrance-Day-27-January-2012/#.UtvSvhAweUk> (last access: 29 January 2014).

in national memory cultures in favour of more sceptical and self-critical remembrances that concentrate on the plight of victims. This »negative memory« has gradually emerged in Western and Central Europe. In those states that were once occupied by Nazi Germany, deeply entrenched and enduring taboos have been broken. The *krigsbarn*, the Norwegian children of the war, for example, have now not only started to inquire about their German fathers – soldiers with the occupying forces garrisoned in Norway during the Second World War –, but some of them have also acquired dual citizenship in Germany and been able to meet their relatives in their fathers' homeland. Not least, these victims have established transnational organisations that testify to the growing leverage and expanding role of civil society in cross-border interaction on memorialisation.[5]

The transition from the leitmotif of national heroism or patriotic sacrifice to the innocent victim has been crucial in the emergence of a more self-critical memorial culture in Western and Central Europe. As a corollary, demands for a transnational, European, cosmopolitan or even universal memory culture have increasingly struck a chord in public discourse over the last few years, at least in the western hemisphere. Against the backdrop of the on-going economic and social crises across the European Union (EU), even a shared common memory culture has been proposed as a panacea for European integration.[6] Thus, German political scientist Claus Leggewie has identified seven »circles« of European memory: the Holocaust, the Gulag, ethnic cleansing, wars and crises, colonial crimes, the history of migration and European integration itself.[7] Similarly, Aleida Assmann

---

5   K. Olsen: Under the Care of Lebensborn. Norwegian War Children and their Mothers, in: K. Ericsson/E. Simonsen (eds.): Children of World War II. The Hidden Enemy Legacy, New York 2004, 15–34. For background information, see the contributions to Ingvill C. Mochmann/Sabine Lee/Barbara Stelzl-Marx (eds.): Children Born of War: Second World War and Beyond, Historical Social Research, Vol. 34, No. 129/2009.
6   Klaus Eder, Remembering National Memories: The Formation of a Transnational Identity in Europe, in: idem/W. Spohn (eds.): Collective Memory and European Identity. The Effects of Integration and Enlargement, Aldershot 2005, 197–220, 199, 218.
7   Claus Leggewie: Der Kampf um die europäische Erinnerung. Ein Schlachtfeld wird besichtigt, Munich 2011, 15–47, idem: Schlachtfeld Europa. Transnationale Erinnerung und nationale Identität, in: Blätter zur deutschen und internationalen Politik 64 (2009), No. 2, 81–93.

has reconstructed three layers of European memory: the Holocaust, the Gulag and the Second World War.[8]

Occasionally, even an explicit commitment to a self-critical memory has been demanded of accession states in order to gain access to the European Union.[9] Yet a unified memory culture has proven to be an illusion. Memory cultures, in the main, are by no means homogeneous and united throughout Europe, but often ambiguous, dynamic and a constant source of dispute. As constructions, moreover, memories are selective and fractured. They must be distinguished from historiography which is influenced by memory cultures. Although they defy verification or falsification, memories can – and should – be decoded and analysed, for instance, as regards their objectives and whom and/or what they are promoting. This book takes up this research agenda.[10]

In particular, the contributions to this publication investigate if, and to what extent and how a shift from a patriotic memory to a more universalistic narrative has occurred in Norway in a comparative perspective with several other European countries. In order to tackle this central question, distinct levels of memory cultures need to be differentiated at the outset. In general, »memory culture« designates all forms of explicit remembrances of historical events, personalities and processes, irrespective of their aesthetic, political and cognitive nature. Beyond this broad definition, however, scholars have not reached a consensus on the concepts which memory studies are based upon. Arguably, disagreements on the terminology are due to a lack of international exchange on conceptual issues.[11] According to John Bodnar, however, at least three variants of memory cul-

---

8   Aleida Assmann: Auf dem Weg zu einer europäischen Gedächtniskultur? Vienna 2012, 21.
9   Tony Judt: Postwar. A History of Europe Since 1945, New York 2005, 803. Also see p. 35 in this introduction.
10 Jürgen Straub, Psychology, Narrative, and Cultural Memory: Past and Present, in: A. Erll/A. Nünning (eds.): A Companion to Cultural Memory Studies, Berlin 2010, 215–227, 217–222; Vita Fortunati/Elena Lamberti: Cultural Memory: A European Perspective, in: Erll/Nünning (eds.), Companion, 127–137, 127f., 132; Cornelißen, Erinnerungskulturen, 168f., 175.
11 Christoph Cornelißen: Was heißt Erinnerungskultur? Begriff – Methoden – Perspektiven, Geschichte in Wissenschaft und Unterricht 54 (2003), 548–563, 555. See also Heike Bungert, Memory and Migration Studies, in: H.-J. Grabbe/S. Schindler (eds.), The Merits of Memory. Concepts, Contexts, Debates, Heidelberg 2008, 197–219, 197; Christoph Cornelißen, Erinnerungskulturen, in: Frank Bösch (ed.): Zeitgeschichte. Konzepte und Methoden. Göttingen 2012, 166–184, 166; idem/Lutz Klinkhammer/

ture need to be differentiated: (1) vernacular memory, (2) official memory, and (3) public memory. Whereas vernacular memory is anchored in small communities and intimate groups like the family, official memory serves to legitimise political rule and the nation-state. In fact, outright memory politics by state institutions aims to enhance and underpin the official views of the past by promoting public representations – in particular myths – and rituals. Re-enacting memories has invariably been an integral element of campaigns to legitimise the nation-state. As the individual chapters of this volume amply demonstrate, however, vernacular and official memory often clash and are at cross-purposes. In Norway, various actors such as politicians, journalists or scholars have attempted to dissolve the tensions between official and vernacular memory in the arena of public memory.[12]

Small communities and groups have shared a similar vernacular memory in that Nordic country, as Sigurd Sørlie, Leiv Sem and Robert Zimmermann demonstrate in this volume. Doreen Reinhold and Tor Einar Fagerland deal with more institutionalised official memories. Claudia Lenz, Susanne Maerz, Odd-Bjørn Fure and Jon Reitan investigate how memories have been imposed, created or employed in public spaces.[13]

Conflicts, power struggles and diverse actors have to be taken into account in the studies of the transformation of Europe's multiple memory cultures.[14] European states have been riven by disagreements over memory. The Cold War, in particular, resulted in a magnetic field for conflicting memories. In their efforts to gain predominance in the memories of French citizens, for instance, the followers of General Charles de Gaulle and the Communists competed in the first few decades after 1945. Similarly, the Italian Christian Democrats took issue with

---

Wolfgang Schwentker, Nationale Erinnerungskulturen seit 1945 im Vergleich, eadem (eds.): Erinnerungskulturen. Deutschland, Italien und Japan seit 1945, Frankfurt am Main, 2nd edition, 2004, 9–27, 12–14.

12 On the concepts of »official«, »vernacular« and »public memory«, see John E. Bodnar, Remaking America: Public Memory, Commemoration, and Patriotism in the Twentieth Century, Princeton 1992, 13 f.

13 See their chapters in this book.

14 Helmut König: Das Politische des Gedächtnisses, in: Christian Gudebus/Arianne Eichenberg/Harald Welzer (eds.), Gedächtnis und Erinnerung. Ein interdisziplinäres Handbuch, Stuttgart 2010, 115–125; Astrid Erll: Kollektives Gedächtnis und Erinnerungskulturen. Eine Einführung, Stuttgart 2005, 53–55, 81, 86 f.; Aleida Assmann: Der lange Schatten der Vergangenheit. Erinnerungskultur und Geschichtspolitik, Bonn 2007, 30.

the memories of the Italian Communists. In other European states, too, where different political and social actors have striven for recognition and legitimacy, contrasting memories of resistance have led to fierce conflicts.[15]

Apart from these internal disputes, differing and often even contrasting official national memories have sundered European nations from one another. In particular, citizens of those states that had been occupied by Nazi Germany were averse to the Germans and to a lesser degree the Austrians – whom they stigmatised as foes, at least until the 1960s. This elementary antagonism has even been interpreted as an initial stage in the »Europeanisation« of memory cultures. Moreover, the confrontation between the two major power blocs in the Cold War physically separated Europeans from one another. At the same time, it enforced co-operation between the West European member-states of NATO and the European Economic Community. To a lesser extent, member states of the Warsaw Pact collaborated with the German Democratic Republic.[16]

In recent years, historiography has demonstrated the coalescence of national and more universalistic variants of memory. References to human rights have increasingly shaped memories of the Holocaust and called the nation-state's hegemonic role in the memorising process into question.[17] Yet the transformation has been multi-faceted, ambivalent and by no means linear. Despite the »de-territorialisation of Holocaust memories«[18], national institutions still vigorously shape memories throughout Europe. In fact, nationhood and national memories have been redefined and reconfigured rather than replaced by more cosmopolitan values that concentrate on human rights. They can be conceived as a »thin« culture

---

15 Siobhan Kattago: Memory and Representation in Contemporary Europe. The Persistence of the Past, Farnham 2012, 97–121.
16 Henning Grunwald: Nothing more Cosmopolitan than the Camps? Holocaust Remembrance and (de-)Europeanization, in: M. Conway/K.K. Patel (eds.): Europeanization in the Twentieth Century. Historical Approaches, Houndmills 2010, 253–270, at 263.
17 Daniel Levy: Cosmopolitization of Victimhood. Holocaust Memories and the Human Rights Regime, in: A. Weinke/N. Frei (eds.): Toward a New Moral World Order? Menschenrechtspolitik und Völkerrecht seit 1945, Göttingen 2013, 210–218; Daniel Levy/Natan Sznaider: The Institutionalization of Cosmopolitan Morality. The Holocaust and Human Rights, in: Journal of Human Rights 3 (2004), No. 2, 143–157.
18 Daniel Levy/Natan Sznaider: The Holocaust and Memory in the Global Age, Philadelphia 2006, 28.

impregnating national memories. The gradual transformation of Norway's memory culture testifies to this complex and even ambiguous development.¹⁹

In the following sections, the multi-layered evolution of Norway's memory culture will be dealt with in greater detail. As Norway's memory culture has lastingly been shaped by resistance, its multiple variants and actors during the Second World War merit an overview. Furthermore, the account deals with another major narrative that has enduringly imprinted on vernacular, official and public memory: the Holocaust. This introduction will conclude with an introduction to the individual contributions to this volume.

II. Resistance in Norway in Comparative Perspective

With the notable exception of Denmark, all continental Western European states north of the Pyrenees were overrun and occupied by Nazi forces during the period between 9 April and 22 June 1940. Denmark avoided a large-scale invasion and occupation because the Danish government bowed to the German ultimatum and surrendered after a symbolic fight that lasted only a brief few hours. The defence battles by the others nations lasted somewhat longer – from four days in the Netherlands to two months in Norway – and all culminated in unprecedented and crushing defeats. The conquered nations of Western Europe were then to experience two different types of occupying regimes. Belgium and the German occupied territories in France were ruled by military authorities, whereas the Netherlands and Norway were governed by civilian authorities – *Reichskommissariate* – led by prominent Nazi officials. In spite of differences between the various systems of occupation rule, these four countries were subject to the identical form of Nazi political domination. All decisions of any importance were taken by the Nazi leadership in Berlin. The long and complex processes of gaining and securing national independence, democratic governance and rule of law, which often were characterised by alternating advances and setbacks, were abruptly reversed and replaced by foreign dominance and totalitarian rule. The physical presence of the occupying forces – whether in the guise of the *Wehrmacht* and/

---

19   This has been demonstrated by Claudia Lenz. See her contribution to this volume. On the concept of a »thin« culture of human rights, see K. Cmiel: The Emergence of Human Rights in the United States, in: Journal of American History 86 (1999), 1231–1250, 1233, 1248 f.; Michael Walzer: Thick and Thin: Moral Argument at Home and Abroad, Notre Dame 1994, 6.

or the repressive and terrorising units of the SS – caused widespread humiliation, fear, and insecurity.

Occupation also brought with it economic plunder, hardship and suffering. After the Germans suffered their first major defeats at El Alamein in October 1942 and at Stalingrad in February 1943, ushering in a new stage of total war, the German war industry desperately needed labour. This growing demand could no longer be met by forced labour from Eastern Europe alone, and labour conscription was consequently extended to the occupied territories in Western Europe as well. For those countries that became entangled in this desperate hunt for manpower – Belgium, France and the Netherlands –, it had enormous individual and societal impact and constituted one of the most traumatic experiences of the entire occupation ordeal. Most importantly, labour conscription was to trigger resistance on a scale hitherto unknown. After February 1943, some 650,000 young men were subject to conscription in France and forcibly transferred to Germany. Both Denmark and Norway escaped this measure; Denmark due to the exceptional form of political dominance exercised by the Nazi state and Norway due to the hesitant attitude to this campaign by the *Reichskommissariat* and to the widespread and effective Norwegian resistance against it.

Reactions, in the main, by the populace of those occupied countries in Western Europe displayed complex and varying constellations of different forms and degrees of accommodation, collaboration and resistance, and whose centre of gravity changed significantly during the occupation. There was an inextricable connection between the nature of the occupying regime, the evolution of its occupation politics, and the character of resistance. The main determinant for the various modes of resistance and non-resistance was the status accorded to the respective indigenous population in the Nazi racial hierarchy. Where the majority of the population were not exposed to mass killings and the occupying authority was hesitant – as was the case in all the occupied Western European countries in 1940 and 1941 –, radical and large-scale resistance was unlikely to emerge. It only surfaced after the decisive turning point in the war in 1942 and 1943 and when the Nazi state suffered major defeats and the need for labour in the German war industry led to forced conscription. On a general level, it may be argued that the character and mode of resistance emerged as the result of interaction between the populace's reaction, societal predispositions and the occupation policies.

The resistance that gradually emerged after the German defeats comprised a wide scope of activities ranging from setting up escape routes, intelligence gathering, secret military units and sabotage as the main forms of armed struggle, as well as general civilian resistance. The significance of the illegal press, in particular, is a central feature in accounts of civilian resistance in north-western Europe. In Pieter Lagrou's synopsis, it represented »a powerful counterweight and a demonstration of the continuing independence of mind.«[20] It demonstrated that the supremacy of Nazi power structures had its limits, and that the road from domination to political submission in societies permeated by democratic culture before the occupation was not necessarily to be taken for granted. Besides, Hitler had a deep distrust of the small and insignificant Nazi parties in this region, and consequently blocked their access to state power.[21] The sole exception to this rule was Norway's tiny *Nasjonal Samling*, which was allowed to form a puppet government as late as February 1942. Moreover, it was subordinate to the *Reichskommissariat* and therefore had no effect on the power structure of the occupying regime. This Norwegian exception could not be attributed to a particularly strong standing by the indigenous Nazi party, but rather to the special relationship between Vidkun Quisling and several top Nazi leaders in Berlin, namely Hitler, Alfred Rosenberg and Erich Raeder. Although Quislings »government« had no autonomous basis, the mandate it was given by *Reichskommissar* Josef Terboven and the conditions set for maintaining this position forcefully contributed to shaping relations between the occupying authorities and the Norwegian population for the remainder of the war.

Norway clearly illustrates that the position accorded to its population in the Nazi racial hierarchy, the structure of the occupying power, and the predispositions of reactions – emanating from profound traits of the Norwegian mentality[22] – were decisive factors in shaping the character, form, and course of the resistance. In Norway, the triple power structure of *Wehrmacht, Reichskommissariat* and *Höhere SS- und Polizeiführer* was supplemented by an ideologically motivated collaborative regime. This was a unique configuration in the occupation history of the Second World War, and it was probably the key reason the Nazification advances in Norway started earlier, were far more comprehensive and accorded more prestige than those in the Netherlands. Although military priorities and considerations weighed utmost for the occupying authorities in Norway as elsewhere in Western Europe, the Nazification project was also considered of great political importance by the National Socialist occupiers who were planning an Aryan empire in Europe. In the short and medium term, they also wanted

---

20 Pieter Lagrou: Belgium, in: Bob Moore (ed.): Resistance in Western Europe, Oxford 2000, 39.
21 Bob Moore: Comparing Resistance and Resistance Movements, in: idem (ed.): Resistance, 251.
22 See Odd-Bjørn Fure's contribution in this volume.

to consolidate politically the nations they conquered according to their National Socialist principles.

For their ideological collaborators, a successful outcome to this racially driven project was of crucial significance. It was a precondition for gaining legitimacy among the Norwegian populace and for demonstrating to the Germans the fascist party's ability to build up and expand its power base in order to transform a hitherto democratic society into one adhering to National Socialism.

The peculiar constellation of a puppet government without popular support assaulting the fundamental values of the overwhelming majority of Norwegians ended in an abject failure for the project of ideological and political Nazification. It is interesting to note that the occupying power had supported this thrust but had not resorted to large-scale repression to break the will of the resistance fighters. The determined civilian struggle by a comprehensive front of athletes, artists, teachers, parents, clergy, bishops and numerous other civic groups could not fundamentally alter the core of the occupier's power structure, but it did manage to preserve social cohesion and the value system of these groups while at the same time avoiding any political and ideological submission. The outcome of the struggle made it possible – in spite of the constant harassment, and experiences of humiliation and trauma – to live alongside the occupiers and their collaborators with some sense of dignity. The constellation of an unchallenged domination by the occupying power and successful resistance to attempts at political and ideological submission – including conscription – characterised Norwegian national consciousness during the occupation and its aftermath.[23]

There is good reason to assume that the achievements of civilian resistance, supported by armed fighters towards the end of the war, strengthened the position of those who were involved in the prevalent system of pragmatic collaboration. Ministerial bureaucratic bodies and economic elites, in particular, were engaged in this kind of non-ideological collaboration with representatives of *Reichskommissariat*.[24] The defining features of this collaboration were an awareness of the political differences between occupiers and occupied; a desire to keep Norwegian Nazis out of prominent positions and a recognition that there were elements of common interest between both parties in some areas. These ministerial bureaucrats were generally deeply entrenched in the democratic political culture. They had a good

---

23 See Odd-Bjørn Fure's contribution to this publication.
24 Robert Bohn: Reichskommissariat Norwegen. Nationalsozialistische Neuordnung« und Kriegswirtschaft, Munich 2000, 460 f.

standing in society, and several of them were even clandestinely engaged in the resistance.

Ultimately, Norway was subject to the most comprehensive attempt at Nazification ever attempted in Western Europe. It was a massive assault aimed at utterly destroying the political and moral basis upon which civic society was built. The main function of the civilian resistance – the *holdningskamp* – that emerged from the late autumn of 1940 onwards was to reaffirm, strengthen and revitalise democratic values, attitudes, the vision of political and personal freedom, human compassion and the central role of truth and individual conscience. On the whole, these values were prevalent among resistance movements throughout Western Europe. But it was only in Norway, with its particular constellation of a Nazi occupation power and an ideologically motivated collaborative puppet government, where these values were the main target of a series of frontal assaults that triggered a mass movement in their defence. In spite of the great achievements by the Norwegian civilian resistance, these chains of events were at the forefront of the collective memory for only a limited timespan after the war. Yet they survived as a form of tacit knowledge in the sub-stratum of the national remembrance of the wartime ordeal.[25]

The contrasting nature of the collaborative regimes in Denmark and Norway determined the choice of strategy and tactics of the resistance movements in both countries. The Danish resistance fought against a non-ideological collaboration based on a national strategy involving all democratic parties; they succeeded to terminate it on the political level in 1943. The key issue behind the battle was more Denmark's position in the world war rather than a question of humanistic values. A further result of the attempts by the resistance movement was a sense of national reintegration and ultimately a transition whereby the nation shifted from being associated with the Axis partners and re-directed itself toward the Allies.

Norway's resistance movement was unable to topple the ideological collaborating regime, despite the NS's lack of support among the population. The regime was supported by the enormous resources of the German occupation power, which ruled according to instructions from Hitler. The Germans could therefore not abandon the regime without severe loss of prestige. Aside, however, from steps taken against local self-government and the police in the autumn of 1940, attacks on most societal institutions and sectors of civic society were blocked by civilian resistance. The series of defeats for the Norwegian National Socialists left them

---

25 See Odd-Bjørn Fure's contribution to this volume.

little room for political manoeuvre. It is interesting to note that this failure was evident ever before the great German military setbacks in 1942–43.

The key feature of the resistance fighters' attitude was a definite emphasis on individual decisions and choices and of the will and determination demonstrated in joining and persevering with the resistance. Such a step implied ideological non-cooperation and a refusal to endorse the various programmes promoted by the occupying power and their ideological collaborators. Resistance, in this sense, was firmly rooted in honour, values, and ethics. These dispositions gave the resistance fighters an indelible imprint. It was these dimensions of the resistance fighters' actions that entitled them to impart a lesson and transmit a message to future generations.[26]

In Norway's case the extent of ideological non-cooperation on the political level was unique in the Western European sphere. In no other country in this region did all branches of the constitutional state power abstain from this kind of co-operation with the enemy. The fact that they all either went into exile to continue the struggle – King Haakon VII and the Cabinet –, resigned collectively – High Court judges and bishops of the Church of Norway –, or severed negotiations – the President of the *Storting* – conveyed strong signals of resistance and non-cooperation. The combination of these clear signals from above and the inextricable link between democratic attitudes of the population and the nation were the basic conditions that ensured the achievements of the civilian resistance.

In the period when the patriotic memory predominated until the early 1960s,[27] there was a strong societal need for the lessons and example of those who had resisted, and according to Pieter Lagrou, especially in the form of a patriotic epic: »The liberated societies of Europe were traumatised, and their now fragile national consensus was in urgent need of the kind of patriotic epic which only the resistance could deliver.«[28]

But the message of the resistance fighter was not merely confined to repairing traumatised national habitus and rebuilding national consensus. The resistance narrative was also charged with the task of being a powerful symbol of rebirth and societal renewal: »The resistance was the vigorous element of the nation's moral

---

26 Francois Bédarida: Résistants, in: Jean Pierre Azéma Francois Bédarida (eds.): 1938–1948 Les Années de Tourmente. De Munich à Prague. Dictionnaire Critique, Paris 1995, 703.
27 Pieter Lagrou: The Legacy of Nazy Occupation. Patriotic Memory and National Recovery in Western Europe, 1945–165, Cambridge 2000, 15.
28 Ibid. 2.

health; it was the symbol of rebirth, of the fundamentally new. This role it occupied not only in the political discourse of the post-war years, but to an important degree also in historical and memorialist writing [...].«[29]

III. From German Barbarity to a Shared Crime – Views of the Holocaust in Norway from a Comparative Perspective

In 1945, the Norwegian government produced a preliminary report for use during the Nuremberg trials of prominent Nazi criminals.[30] The report catalogues German crimes perpetrated in Norway and against Norwegian citizens during the occupation. It states, »as a crime against humanity, special mention must be made of the cruelties and miseries which were inflicted upon Norway's Jewry. The ›Jewish problem‹ was one of the staple policies of the Nazi programme and the ›execution‹ of this policy has cost the lives of millions of innocent human beings.« Then, however, to underline the absurdity of linking the Holocaust with Norway, the report adds, »no ›Jewish problem‹ has ever existed in Norway, and the Jews constituted only a small minority of the population.«

The report could serve as an illustration of several tendencies regarding the manner in which the topic of the Holocaust was handled in the aftermath of the war. First of all, as Jon Reitan points out in his contribution, the reality of the Holocaust was not ignored in Norway. The horror of the extermination camps was by no means unknown, even if not completely understood and realised. Secondly, the report recognises the special place the Jews held in Nazi policy and it duly acknowledges their suffering as the worst amongst all Norwegians, while simultaneously including them in the »national register of victims« and using their fate to illustrate the overall extent of German brutality in Norway. Thirdly, the blame, and thus the guilt, for what happened are laid squarely with the Nazis. The report merely states that the Norwegian Jews »were arrested« – without mentioning that the arrests were undertaken by Norwegian policemen, and not all of them were dedicated National Socialists. Fourthly, traces of some scepticism towards the Jews are evident in the report through the presumed possibility of a »Jewish problem«.

---

29 Ibid. 22.
30 Finn Palmstrøm/Normann Torgersen: Preliminary Report on Germany's Crimes against Norway, Oslo 1945.

So while it would be ill-judged to dispute that the Holocaust was ignored or unknown to the Norwegian public, the tendencies towards ignoring or underplaying Norway's role in it and the latent scepticism towards the Jews, as evidenced in the post-war report, mirror the way the issue was treated in some post-war trials and compensation settlements. In their contribution, Iselin Theien and Bjørn Westlie point to several legal cases, notably the accusations against Knut Rød, where such sentiments could be said to have played a significant role in the trial's outcome, along with the inability of the existing system to grasp and cope with the uniquely destructive and comprehensive character of the Holocaust. Tore Pryser has shown that the arrests of Jews were accorded little weight at the post-war trials against police officers in the areas in which he researched, while other charges took precedence and were decisive.[31] This tendency to focus on the »nationally memorable« and to ascribe guilt to the Germans also had, as Theien and Westlie as well as Claudia Lenz point out, an indispensable function during the post-war reconstruction process. Instead of harking back to the past, this positive narrative could unite the nation for the future and the task of rebuilding the country. But, as Odd-Bjørn Fure argued in 1999 and as Jon Reitan also points out, the »unmediated« issues regarding the war, including the issue of Norwegian responsibility during the Holocaust, were not forgotten, but subsisted in a »substratum« of the public debate, generating friction and dissatisfaction with mainstream narratives of the war.[32]

In his article, Jon Reitan argues that it was Per Ole Johansen's 1984 book *Oss selv nærmest* that first truly opened the eyes of the Norwegian public to the role of the Norwegian state apparatus and its adherents during the Holocaust, initiating a process that gradually paved the way for the mass murder of the Jews becoming a cardinal issue in the Norwegian debate about the occupation. Above all else, the so-called »restitution case«, where the journalist Bjørn Westlie, the historian Bjarte Bruland and the psychologist Berit Reisel played critical roles, would illustrate the transformation which had taken place in Norwegian public opinion over the course of the 1980s and 1990s. As Theien and Westlie remark, the Skarpnes commission majority's view of Norwegian guilt and responsibility – one that mirrored that of the immediate post-war period – was now seen as obsolete. The Norwegian

---

31 Tore Pryser: Holocaust i innlandsregionen, in: Per Ole Johansen (ed.): På siden av rettsoppgjøret, Oslo 2006, 93–129.
32 Odd-Bjørn Fure: Norsk okkupasjonshistorie. Konsensus, berøringsangst og tabuisering, in: S. U. Larsen (ed.): I krigens kjølvann. Nye sider ved norsk krigshistorie og norsk etterkrigstid. Oslo 1999, 31–46.

parliament, by virtue of the compensation payments it authorised to the Jewish minority, accepted that Norwegians had a moral responsibility for the deportations of Jews from Norway. Ever since the Holocaust has retained a prominent and unquestionable place in the Norwegian discourse on the war, with numerous memorial sites, a research centre (*HL-senter*) and a range of scholarly works commissioned in order to fully uncover the history of the Holocaust in Norway and to ensure that it retains a central position within Norwegian memory culture. This goal enjoys broad popular support: in the *HL-senter*'s report on Norwegian anti-Semitism, 92 per cent of respondents wanted school children to learn about the fate of the Norwegian Jews during the war. The majority of those who agreed to this proposition also considered that learning about this particular chapter was indispensable, citing, inter alia, reasons such as »because it is an important part of Norwegian history«; »in order to prevent it from happening again«; »it shows us what racism can lead to«; and »it shows us the importance of defending vulnerable groups even today«.[33]

While Norwegian memory culture has its own »landmarks« marking changes in how the Holocaust has been perceived, the general trend bears similarities with developments on continental Europe. As Ilse Raaijmakers argues in her article, the overall pattern is that of the initial focus on the nation as a whole, with a narrative of patriotism, heroism, national unity and externalisation of guilt, useful for the task of post-war reconstruction; this also characterised the immediate post-war memory culture in the Netherlands. As in Norway, this narrative gradually gave way to a more pluralist version, with a special place reserved for the Holocaust. But as Raaijmakers confirms, the focus on the Holocaust began earlier in the Netherlands; this was likely the consequence of the comparatively much greater impact of the extermination of the Jewish minority in that country, both regarding the percentage of Dutch Jews killed and the overall number of war victims – more than 100,000 Jews in the Netherlands, compared with less than eight hundred in Norway – which also entailed that the Holocaust in the Netherlands directly affected the lives of a wider segment of that populace than was the case in Norway.

While local events and historical facts have had a decisive role to play in determining when and how the Holocaust gained prominence in a country's memory culture, common developments in Western countries also represented a driving force towards the true recognition of the scale of the Holocaust. One notable

---

33 HL-senteret: Antisemittisme i Norge? Den norske befolkningens holdninger til jøder og andre minoriteter, Oslo 2012, 29.

factor has been international events such as the Eichmann trial or the American TV-series »Holocaust«. But the increasing role of the Holocaust also reflected common intellectual and social tendencies within most of the Western world, with the focus shifting from the collective and the nation to the individual and smaller groups. Arguably, heightened focus on the Holocaust has been both a catalyst for and a result of this development. The Holocaust represents, as Claudia Lenz points out, a »negative starting point« for a new identity based on a critical attitude towards exclusionary collective identities. Above all else, the Holocaust has shown, as Lenz puts it, »the pitfalls of the identitarian discourse«. Insofar as ethics only relate to a specific group, another holocaust is possible. Only a truly universal framework, with guaranteed rights for all groups and individuals, could profess to be a safeguard against it happening again.

Controversial but influential contributions to the societal debate by Theodor Adorno, Raul Hilberg, Hannah Arendt, Stanley Milgram, Philip Zimbardo and later Christopher R. Browning all closely connected or seemed to connect the Holocaust to more universal characteristics of modernity and humanity, rather than just traits unique to Nazi Germany, thus underlining the argument that the potential for evil is a universal human trait.[34] Sociologist Zygmunt Bauman made the connection explicit – to him, holocausts were always a latent possibility in modern society. The acceptance of such ideas had drastic consequences, necessitating a constant awareness and rejection of contemporary ideas and practices that could potentially lead to another holocaust. Such a broadening of the potential for evil also meant that the earlier externalisation of guilt – blaming everything on the evil Nazis – was to become less acceptable and plausible. This line of thought would, in turn, prompt an inward-looking process, examining the role of petty bureaucrats, »ordinary men« and other »cogs in the wheel«, including non-Germans, in allowing the Holocaust to happen.

Such general trends towards seeing the Holocaust both as a »shared« crime and a »warning from history«, requiring the adoption of certain universalistic policies today in order to ensure that it never happens again, both result in and are further strengthened by policies and institutions designed to synchronise remembrance and policies on an inter- and transnational level. One of the strongest manifesta-

---

34 For an introduction and discussion of the changing interpretations of the Holocaust and the problems of these interpretations, see Christopher R. Browning: Revisiting the Holocaust Perpetrators. Why Did They Kill? The Raul Hilberg Memorial Lecture 2011, uvm.edu, last access: 6 February 2014, <http://www.uvm.edu/~uvmchs/documents/HilbergLectureBrowning2011.pdf>.

tions of this trend was, as Jon Reitan argues, the establishment of the Task Force for International Cooperation on Holocaust Education, Remembrance and Research (ITF) in 1999 – now called the IHRA. Fittingly and not coincidentally, Norway held the chair of the ITF in 2009–10. As both Tor Einar Fagerland and Claudia Lenz point out, the EU has also taken an active role in promoting knowledge and remembrance of the Holocaust. As Fagerland puts it: »Throughout Europe today people are being asked to remember what they formerly were taught to forget«.[35] Quoting Tony Judt, Reitan argues; critical self-examination of the history of the Holocaust is now an »entry ticket« to the European community.

This internationalisation of memory, however, has not rendered irrelevant the nation-state as a frame of reference. Since the 1990s, Norway has experienced a turn towards a more »pluralist«, yet nonetheless a »national« discourse. The discussion retains a distinctly national character, but now also open up for a wider variety of more complex stories, and, in turn, allows for the recognition of new groups and distinctions. Nowadays, we more readily acknowledge the interests and stories of groups and individuals previously neglected due to the country's material or psychological needs during the immediate post-war period. As Claudia Lenz reveals in her analysis, national identities are being redefined, with »having learned the lessons of the Holocaust« – which entails being able to recognise one's own historical guilt and accepting the need for guaranteed human rights for individuals and minority groups – now being considered as an indispensable part of the identity of a modern state. This, in turn, has the advantage, however, of enabling one state to make moral demands on other states. Being seen as ignoring or disregarding the »lessons of history« carries an onerous diplomatic and moral cost, as both Iran and Turkey have experienced through their failure to recognise the Holocaust and the Armenian genocide, respectively. In other words – true recognition of the lessons of the Holocaust could now also be in a country's self-interest in the narrow sense of the word.

In many ways, Norway's Minister of Foreign Affairs Jonas Gahr Støre's opening speeches at *HL-senter* and *Falstad-senter* in 2006 serve as excellent illustrations of what has transpired since 1945. Støre's speeches incorporate all of the elements discussed above; he explicitly links the Holocaust to contemporary crimes and problematic tendencies; he accepts that evil can be committed by »ordinary people with ordinary lives«; he accepts Norway's guilt for what happened, and uses the premise of having learned from history as a moral basis for current policies,

---

35 See p. 218.

ultimately justified by the moral imperative that mankind never again experience another Holocaust.

IV. The Chapters of the Volume

Each contribution to the volume individually highlights the transformation in the Norwegian memory culture landscape since the end of the Second World War. The process of coming to terms with history is examined from various angles and perspectives and within a wider pan-European framework. Hence many chapters explicitly integrate a transnational dimension. In the first of five thematic sections Odd-Bjørn Fure and Arnd Bauerkämper provide introductions to the postwar memory culture and its European setting. Both authors describe the area of memory conflicts between patriotic and universalistic tendencies from different perspectives. In the opening chapter, Odd-Bjørn Fure introduces the development of the Norwegian culture of remembrance and its specifics. The author argues that notions of the Norwegian nation and democracy have been strongly interlinked. Collective memory, in Fure's view, has not only been shaped by the experience of the occupation during the Second World War, but also by the development of parliamentarianism and the emergence of a democratic political culture in nineteenth-century Norway. Attempts to sever this connection by fringe movements on the left and the right of the political spectrum, have invariably failed. Hence, memories of the war continue to be nationally framed and coexist with transnational and universalistic schemes of thinking.

In his chapter, Arnd Bauerkämper explains how the twists and turns in Norway's memory culture after 1945 must be understood as a process of frequently asymmetrical interchange and negotiation between specific actors who have pursued particular aims in order to advance their respective vested interests. He outlines how the dichotomy of resistance and collaboration splintered, giving rise to a more pluralistic and self-critical memorial culture in the 1980s. Bauerkämper describes this development as a shift that can be traced in many Western European countries. He identifies this change of tack as a turn to a more universalistic narrative, triggered by the recognition of the plight of passive, helpless victims. This development, which has resulted from the growing recognition of human rights, has consequently diminished the focus on national martyrs without, however, completely obliterating the national framework.

The book's second section tackles trends towards a universalistic narrative on one of the two main strands in the post-war memory culture in Norway: the

Holocaust. Claudia Lenz focuses on the teaching of history as a part of the memory culture of the Holocaust. In her chapter, the author reflects on the recent linkage between Holocaust education and concern for human rights education, asking whether the trend can be conceived as a symptom of the universalisation and de-nationalisation of memory culture in Norway, or rather as an incentive to develop a different concept to explain Norwegian history related to the Second World War and the Holocaust. As a case study, she analyses the speeches made during the opening ceremonies at two contemporary Norwegian institutions, both profoundly connected with the legacy of the Second World War and the Holocaust: *Falstad senter* and *HL-senter*. The latter institution also figures prominently in Doreen Reinhold's analysis in this publication's third section. Jon Reitan's contribution commences with the official apology on the International Holocaust Remembrance Day in 2012 by the former Norwegian Prime Minister Jens Stoltenberg for Norway's role in the murder of the Jews. The chapter identifies a guilt discourse as the main factor shaping Holocaust consciousness in contemporary Norway. Reitan argues that external forces and transnational processes, in particular, have shaped the trend, but it must also be seen in the light of specific national developments such as the restitution process, which started with a newspaper article published in 1995.

Iselin Theien and Bjørn Westlie explore how this restitution process of Jewish survivors in Norway worked as a catalyst for integrating the wartime experiences of the Jewish minority into the national memory culture. They reason that a transformation of the moral and political judgement of the post-war treatment of Holocaust survivors in Norway was of central importance for this process, as it allowed for a more pluralist understanding of Norwegian losses and suffering during the Second World War.

The fourth and final contribution to this section contrasts the respective developments in how Norway and the Netherlands came to terms with their Holocaust history. Ilse Raaijmakers portrays the dynamics of the Dutch memory culture by focusing on the form and content of the Dutch national commemoration days for the Second World War – 4 and 5 May. She argues that a tension has characterised Dutch post-war memory culture: a contrast between the »particular« and the »universal«, between exclusion and inclusion of various actors, and between well-defined groups of victims and more universal meanings linked to the war.

The third section of the book concentrates on the various agents, who have impacted on memory culture in Norway and beyond. First, Gunnar Hatlehol examines how and when Norwegian historians became aware of foreign prisoners of war including the thousands of forced labourers in Norway in general and the war crimes committed against them by the German occupying forces in particular. He seeks to establish whether scholarship has had any impact on public commemoration practices. Second, Robert Zimmermann analyses the educational and outreach initiatives undertaken by post-war associations of former Norwegian and Danish political prisoners in the light of the increasing obliviousness to history among younger generations. Zimmermann demonstrates how their educational activities altered their resistance-centred narrative to one in which their victimhood was more strongly emphasised. The Norwegian associations in particular have thereby presented themselves not only as advocates of their own life-stories, but also as representatives of universalistic values such as democracy and human rights. Hence, former political prisoners are portrayed as a group, which has adapted to the new trends towards universalistic narratives. Third, Doreen Reinhold deals with the representation of the Second World War and the Holocaust in Norwegian museum culture. She investigates exhibitions at *Norges Hjemmefrontmuseum* (Norwegian Resistance Museum) and the *HL-senter*. As Reinhold suggests, museums should not only be interpreted as products of collective memory, but also as tools that are actively involved in shaping it.

The fourth section deals with memorial sites, in the broadest sense of the term, in Norway as well as in Eastern Europe. Tor Einar Fagerland analyses a series of Norwegian monuments and memorials that have been built or planned since 1990. Commemorating events and historical personages, they have addressed issues connected to the Second World War. Fagerland discusses some of the complexities involved in representing and interpreting the war in public spaces in post-Cold War Norway by placing these examples into a broader international and theoretical framework. He argues that an example, such as the unresolved issue of dealing with the buried fascist monument at Stiklestad, reflects Norway's hidden – and subsequently excavated – memory of the Second World War. Leiv Sem turns towards the Eastern Front of the Second World War and its representation in Norwegian commemorative culture. He probes autobiographies and memoirs by former Norwegian Waffen-SS volunteers and demonstrates the influence of this literature on present-day remembrances of the fight on the Eastern Front.

The book's final section deals with marginal groups in post-war Norway. Sigurd Sørlie's chapter analyses the Norwegian Waffen-SS volunteers as one particular group of collaborators and their role in the country's memory culture. Not only does the author integrate the scholarly work about the *frontkjempere* (front fighters), but he also highlights the various forms of public perception and representation, ever before historians engaged with that subject. Sørlie thereby traces the narrative of this particular group. According to his findings, former Norwegian Waffen-SS volunteers faced less public scorn than other collaborators in the post-war years, because they have generally been perceived as young and unselfish idealists who had been victims of social pressure and circumstances. Contrary to the predominant interpretations of memorialisation of the Second World War in Norway in the first few decades after 1945, there was no universal silence surrounding Norwegian supporters of the Nazi war.

The final contribution aims at another marginal group placed outside of the Norwegian consensus: *krigsbarn*, the offspring of German soldiers and Norwegian women. Susanne Maerz shows how paternal origins and the treatment of wartime children quickly became a taboo in post-war Norwegian society. It was only addressed for the first time in the 1980s. Analysing literary works that deal with this topic, Maerz reconstructs the difficult process of coming to terms with the wartime fate of these children. She argues that the rupture of the late 1980s resulted in a new narrative of their personal suffering and also in changing attitudes towards this group among a wide segment of the population. Herbjørg Wassmo's book »The House with the Blind Glass Windows« (1981) and Jostein Gaarder's novel »The Solitaire Mystery« (1990) are examples of the universalisation of narratives about the Second World War in general, and about the wartime children in particular.

All contributions to this volume have been presented at one of two workshops, which took place in Berlin on 17–18 June 2011[36] and in Oslo on 15–16 March 2013[37]. We would like to thank *E.ON Stipendienfonds im Stifterverband für die Deutsche Wissenschaft* for their generous financial support for both those events and towards the publication of this book. Moreover, the volume could not have been published without John Barrett's meticulous editorial work. We are also grateful to Ane Ingvild Støen, Christoph Meißner, André Keil, Elke Stadelmann-Wenz and Ann Elisabeth Mellbye for their help in organising and realising the events.

---

36   André Keil/Christoph Meißner: Das umstrittene Gedächtnis. Transnationale und innergesellschaftliche Erinnerungskonflikte in Europa nach 1945. 17–18 June 2011, Berlin, conference report, in: H-Soz-u-Kult, 27 July 2011, <http://hsozkult.geschichte.hu-berlin.de/tagungsberichte/id=3746>.

37   Ane Ingvild Støen: From Patriotic Memory to a Universalistic Narrative: Shifts in Norwegian Memory Culture after 1945 in Comparative Perspective. 15–16 March 2013, Oslo, conference report, in: H-Soz-u-Kult, 18 June 2013, <http://hsozkult.geschichte.hu-berlin.de/tagungsberichte/id=4864>.

The editors owe particular thanks to the institutions, which hosted the events: the *Freie Universität Berlin* and the *HL-senter*, especially its Director, Guri Hjeltnes.

I.
Between Patriotic and Universalistic Memory

Odd-Bjørn Fure
Developmental Societal Processes
Changing Configurations of Memories.
The Case of Norway in a Comparative Perspective

The title of this book advances the sweeping proposition of a process of profound historical reorientation in the field of memory in Norway and elsewhere in Western Europe after the Second World War. What does this mean? And how could the thesis be theoretically established and elaborated in order to expose it to empirical testing? The concept of memory – in this context – could be fruitfully clarified in two dimensions: its scope and its intrinsic value system. A patriotic memory privileges a frame of reference confined to a nation's basic experiences and history, and tends to operate within a hierarchy of national cultures, placing its own at the pinnacle. It might be more or less open to broader horizons and be based on varying political values of democratic or authoritarian character. The tacit assumption of the concept of patriotic memory is that it will favour events that are memorable from a national perspective and that its parameters for moral judgments are distorted. This archetype of memory has dominated the memorial landscape of Europa from the emergence of the nation-state to the early post-war period.

From that time onwards, a patriotic memory with these specific attributes has been in universal decline across Western Europe. It has collided against – or run counter to – three interconnected macro-processes over the past thirty to forty years: the devolution of the nation-state; the interconnected processes of the growing ascendancy of supranational integration and regionalisation; and the upgrading of universal human rights procedures.

Furthermore, the growing distance in time has contributed to a more balanced view of wartime experiences. What has happened in the field of memory after the gradual erosion of the patriotic memory in Norway and elsewhere in Europe? In the introduction to a recent publication entitled »Nordic Narratives of the Second World War«, the editors submit the following sweeping thesis: »... as a general rule the leitmotifs of the national narratives of the Second World War have undergone a fundamental change in the last decades, shifting from patriotism to universalism, or at least shifting from outright methodological nationalism.«¹ This proposition is neither conceptually resolved nor empirically substantiated. In the same anthology, Synne Corell, the author of an article with the revealing title »The Solidity of a National Narrative«, paints another picture of the development of war-related memory processes in Norway. Although challenged in several ways and exposed to pressure from various angles, her conclusion is that a national horizon is still predominant: »A nationally framed understanding appears consistent over time, but ought to be conceived of as relying on changing contexts …«²

One of these contexts is obviously of a transnational character, offering opportunities both to explore experience-based memories that transcend national arenas and borders and to compare them with different nationally framed memories. This perspective is obviously an extension of scope and not a change of character, and has the advantage of playing down the obsession with national peculiarities.

On the basis of this brief outline of patriotic, nationally-framed and transnational memories, which may coexist with or define different memorial stages in a long-term development, we can approach the concept of universal memorial narratives. How could we fruitfully elaborate on the concept of a universalistic informed memorial narrative?

A universalistic memory knows no geographical, political or cultural boundaries; its horizon is humanity and it is informed and impregnated by universal human rights. It should be recognised that fully universalistic narratives only exist as ideals and as rather small segments of complex and compound memorial cultures. No general or comprehensive shift to a universalistic narrative is discernible in any European memory culture. In accordance with the persistence of the nation-state, nationally framed memories linger on everywhere. It would be reasonable to assume that universalistic-based memories presuppose that these narratives are disconnected from particular needs of nations. Today, this is certainly a utopian thought, but it reminds us that the concept of universal memorial narratives could not be fruitfully used without strong qualification. Since we are discussing a culture of memory that does not exist as a dominant strand, or perhaps not even as a strong tendency within national configurations of memories, we should conceive of a universalistic narrative as a model that contains parameters for evaluating institutions, mentalities and political cultures, as represented

---

1   Henrik Stenius/Mirja Østerberg/Johan Östling (eds.): Nordic Narratives of the Second World War. An Introduction. Lund 2011, 16.
2   Synne Corell in Henrik Stenius/Mirja Østerberg/Johan Östling, 2011, 119.

and communicated in complex systems of memories. As we will see, a shift from prioritising heroic deeds to grievous and painful experiences has taken place. We should, however, be careful not to interpret this as a development in a universalistic direction. The crucial question concerns not only content and the themes, but also the perspectives and values from which these are perceived and evaluated.

What were the characteristics of the Norwegian variant of patriotic memory and the societal processes upon which it was built? What were its main political substance and message? The development of national habitus in Europe in the second half of the 19th and the first half of the 20th centuries was strongly influenced by political ideologies and practices on the right wing of the political spectrum. This tendency also included Nordic countries such as Finland and Sweden, but not Denmark and Iceland. Where was Norway positioned in this grand scheme? What were the strengths and weaknesses, seen from a democratic point of view, of the Norwegian national configuration? And most importantly: what challenges did it encounter during the war and interwar periods?

I. Norway's Democracy: Political Developments from the 1880s to the 1920s

Political development in Norway in the 19th century and in the first two decades of the 20th century was characterised by early and steady democratisation, with no reversals in an authoritarian direction. The introduction of parliamentary government and modern political parties in 1884, universal male suffrage in 1898, which was subsequently extended to women in 1913, and a proportional electoral system in 1919, are the most significant milestones in the democratisation of the state, which gained depth through the establishment of local self-government in 1837 and an emerging civil society from the 1840s. The driving force and hegemonic power in this broad process of democratising institutions in state and society between 1880 and 1920 was *Venstre*, a social-liberal party, along with a vast complex of social movements associated with it. The practices and values that were shaped by this constellation of societal forces and the broad participation in a number of social movements laid the foundation for an inextricable connection between the nation and a democratic ethos. This bond has been an enduring feature of the Norwegian national habitus. In some situations, it has – as we will see – been challenged, but never broken or profoundly shaken. Because the project of this social-liberal party was primarily of a political nature, and due to the constant friction with Sweden about the content and scope of the union with

Norway between 1814 and 1905, political issues predominated over cultural and ethnic aspects of Norwegian nationalism up until 1920.[3]

While the struggle for and against parliamentarian rule in the 1880s was fiercely – albeit legally – fought for years, with little room for compromise, the broader process of modernisation, the transformation of the aristocratic estates and the abolition of the corresponding hereditary privileges was a protracted and rather smooth process based on broad alliances encompassing prominent liberal conservatives. The reason for this exceptional transition – from a comparative perspective – is to be found in the peculiar social structures that prevailed, marked by a dominance of relatively small self-governing peasants and the absence of a strong nobility rooted in pre-industrial modes of production, which in turn were conditioned by a particular topography. The modernising forces had thus the privilege of enjoying an almost unimpeded path into modernity.

At the centre of the modernisation process was the industrialisation of Norway, which started late – in the 1890s – and was comprehensive, occurred at an accelerated pace, and led to processes of social and political polarisation, disintegration, and fragmentation. In this new constellation, *Venstre* lost its hegemonic position and, consequently, much of its integrative power. From 1917 to the mid-1930s, the dynamic political activity no longer took place at the political centre or centre-left, but rather on the two flanks. The Labour Party went through a process of radicalisation that was unparalleled in labour parties mustering a majority of workers in the democratic states in Europe. The radicalisation culminated in the Norwegian Labour Party's accession to Comintern in 1919. This development entailed a double break with the dominant national configuration of the previous period, firstly by attempting to replace allegiance to the nation with a class-based horizon of identification, a proletarian internationalism with Comintern as the institutional frame of reference; and secondly, by aiming to replace the universal suffrage of the existing state by extending democracy to the economic sphere and by proposing to narrow the franchise in the political realm to those classified as working people. In short, the liberal democratic state based on the principles of equal rights and

3   See, for example, Rolf Danielsen: Demokratiseringen av de politiske systemer i de nordiske land 1870–1920, in: Geir Atle Ersland/Edgar Hovland/Ståle Dyrvik (eds.): Festskrift til Historisk institutts 40-års jubileum. Bergen 1997, 203–220. Cf. Odd-Bjørn Fure: Mellomkrigstid 1920–1940, vol. 3, Norsk utenrikspolitikks historie. Oslo 1996, 16, 25–27. See also Øystein Sørensen: Hegemonikamp om det norske. Elitenes nasjonsbyggingsprosjekter 1770–1945, in Øystein Sørensen (ed.): Jakten på det norske. Perspektiver på utviklingen av norsk nasjonalisme på 1800-tallet. Oslo 1998, 30–36.

obligations of citizens was to be replaced by a state based on one social class and a council constitution.[4] Bringing this programme to fruition would have led to a glaring regression of the process of democratisation.

The idea of a proletarian internationalism influenced the Labour Party's politics in several respects, but the announced break with liberal democracy was confined to the programmatic level and to verbal incantations. In fact, the Norwegian Labour Party never engaged in practical actions to destroy democratic institutions. Although the road back to the nation and to liberal democracy was twisted, it was more or less arrived at by the end of the 1930s. However, the attitudes and practices that finally merged with the state and the nation were indeed different from those from which the party had departed. One of Norway's greatest historians, Jens Arup Seip, famously said that the liberal Western European societies had an immense ability to successively digest their rebels.[5] The fate of the attempt by the biggest social force in Norway to transcend the national democratic order – mobilising more than 30 per cent of the population at the elections in 1915, and more than 40 per cent in 1933 – confirms this proposition. The thrust to transform the Norwegian society, nation and state comprehensively was entangled in a vast complex of democratic institutions and cultural practices that permeated most of society. The Labour Party was split into three political parties between 1921 and 1927 and the labour movement lost popular support over the same period. Only after a consolidation of forces and an adaptation to democratic governance was the Labour Party able to resume an offensive position.

When clashes arise between mentalities or deeply rooted cultures and ideologies, the former will generally prevail. The case of the peculiarly Norwegian labour radicalism in the interwar period is no exception to this historical rule.

The processes of disruption and disintegration of societal relations caused by the rapid industrialisation, combined with the threat from the revolutionary labour movement, resulted in a shift of the centre of gravity of national discourse to the right of the political spectrum. In some cases, the reactions from right-wing formations and groups aimed to break the traditionally close connection between the nation and democratic culture and institutions. This right-wing authoritarian challenge spanned a spectrum ranging from traditional anti-democratic ideas to National Socialist ideology. The establishment of *Fedrelandslaget* (The Fatherland

---

4 Odd-Bjørn Fure: Mellom reformisme og bolsjevisme. Norsk arbeiderbevegelse 1918–1920. Teori Praksis, Bergen 1983, 110–160.
5 Jens Arup Seip: Fra embetsmannsstat til ettpartistat og andre essays. Oslo 1963, 40.

League) in 1925 was a reaction to the divisions and alleged weakness and appeasement of the political right in the face of the revolutionary threat from the left. Its key message was to unite forces to resist and overcome the socialist scheme of transforming the existing state into a Soviet republic, combined with a dream to return to the pre-parliamentary regime that existed before 1884. *Fedrelandslaget* managed to recruit some well-known and respected public figures, such as Fridtjof Nansen, but no active politician of any significance joined the organisation. As an instrument for mobilising the bourgeois electorate, it played a certain role, particularly in the decisive election of 1930, but by the 1930s its influence was waning, at the same time as it was drifting toward fascism. The organisation was dissolved in 1940.[6]

The National Socialist Party (NS), founded in 1933 with the NSDAP as its model, lay at the other extremity of this right-wing spectrum. It had totalitarian features right from the start, and gradually became characterised by the same racist and anti-Semitic worldview as its German prototype. By 1936, the party was marked by factional conflicts, resignations, expulsions, and the virtual collapse of the organisation.[7] The authoritarians and totalitarians on the right had followers in some state institutions: the army, the police force, and sections of the state bureaucracy. They also enjoyed the sympathy and support of several conservative newspapers. Yet they failed to muster significant endorsement in their efforts to mobilise popular support for severing the traditional connection between the nation and democratic values. They managed neither to win representation in parliament nor to secure more than 2.3 per cent of the popular vote in general elections. By the last general election before the war, in 1936, the party won only 26,577 votes.[8] The Norwegian people rejected overwhelmingly the vision of linking the nation to a totalitarian, national socialist political configuration, and the democratic state institutions remained intact. By the end of the 1930s, the NS was haunted by factional strife and discord, and was reduced to a political sect by the time of the German invasion in 1940.[9]

The fact that the democratic institutions were so deeply rooted in Norwegian society that they were able to resist totalitarian challenges from both left and right in the interwar period is a basic feature of the political development in Nor-

---

6 Odd-Bjørn Fure: Mellomkrigstid. 1920–1940. Oslo 1996, 25–45.
7 Hans Olav Brevig/Ivo de Figueiredo: Den norske fascismen. Nasjonal Samling 1933–1940. Oslo 2002, 111.
8 Oddvar Høidal: Quisling – en studie i landssvik. Oslo 2002, 183.
9 Ibid., 173–240.

way in the 20th century. It is nevertheless far from the whole story of Norwegian democracy in this period. Between 1870 and 1950, the Norwegian state pursued a heavy-handed assimilation policy toward its minorities. This was rooted in a belief system that was based on the ideal of an ethnically and culturally homogeneous society. This was seen as a precondition for a fully developed and strong nation-state. This belief system and its corresponding policy of assimilation and nation- building dominated the policy pursued toward minorities all over Europe in this period, though there were variations and differences. Norway started this period as probably the most ethnically homogeneous country in Europe. This was mainly due to geo-political conditions, which, because of its position on the North-western periphery of Europe, had kept it out of all the major European wars, from the religious conflicts of the 16th century to the Second World War. Consequently, Norway was not affected by the waves of forced migration that had accompanied these wars elsewhere. This extreme ethnic homogeneity obviously underpinned a strong predisposition for a heavy-handed policy of assimilation of the minorities. With the exception of the Sámi, they consisted of tiny groups: The Romani and the Rom, who like the Sámi were nomadic; the Kvens and the Jews. Assimilation policies were aimed at forcing minorities to abandon their respective cultural heritage, such as language, customs, clothing, and way of life, and to adapt to society's overarching cultural pattern.[10] The group that was exposed to the harshest measures was the Romani. The Jews were least affected by this policy, because their economic basis and lifestyle did not differ significantly from those of the Norwegian majority. The most notable exception was the parliamentary ban on *Shechita*, the traditional Jewish method of slaughter, in 1929. Nonetheless, the Jews were the only group that managed to improve their living conditions during the thirties. The policy towards minorities exposed the limits of Norwegian democratic culture. It demonstrated a poor awareness of the rights and vulnerabilities of the most marginal groups in Norwegian society. Although this was indeed the case all over Europe, the differences should nonetheless not be underestimated. The assimilation policy toward minorities was less heavy-handed in Sweden, especially after 1900.[11] Whereas this was a difference in terms of degree, a comparative view

10 The standard work dealing with the politics of assimilation of the Sámi and the Kvens is Knut Einar Eriksen/Einar Niemi: Den finske fare. Sikkerhetsproblemer og minoritetspolitikk i nord 1860–1940. Oslo 1981.
11 Eriksen/Niemi. Oslo 1981, 346–348.

of the racial state in Germany in the thirties shows differences in nature.¹² The case of Norway and some other democratic states in Europe in this period demonstrate that democratic institutions and processes alone were unable to safeguard the rights of minorities.

They could only have been secured by a strong democratic culture, permeated by the values and norms of universal human rights. A political culture of this type did not exist in Norway or elsewhere at that time.

II. The Impact of Norway's Political Development on Memory Culture

What can be said about the character of the collective memory of political development in Norway in the 20th century, and especially about the democratisation process and the treatment of minorities? Although little research has been conducted in this field, it is possible to identify the basic underpinnings of this remembrance, as manifested in scholarly works, literature, newspapers and expositions, in particular. At the end of the interwar period, the narratives displayed the characteristic features of a patriotic memory in a democratic state. They were heavily concentrated on nationally memorable events and developmental traits, and stories about the nation-building process: the winning and securing of national freedom; the processes of democratisation and endeavours as well as achievements in the fields of science and culture, especially the spectacular expeditions and discoveries in the Arctic and Antarctic. The traumatic elements in Norway's national memory, the perceived inadequate national, cultural heritage due to its long subordinated position in the union with Denmark, and the fear of increasing social and political tensions and cleavages were overcome or were at least in the process of being overcome. The great exhibition in Oslo in 1938 – *Vi kan* (»We can do it«) – testified to a self-confident and optimistic society that was on the rise, but with an inadequate awareness of the impending catastrophe that lay ahead. Norwegian society's search for what Robert W. Moeller has called »a usable past« did not include the fate of the minorities.¹³ They were generally placed either on

---

12 Michael Burleigh/Wolfgang Zimmermann: The Racial State. Germany, 1933–1945. Cambridge 1991.
13 Robert W. Moeller: The Search for a usable Past in the Federal Republic of Germany, in: American Historical Review 101 (1996), 1008–1048.

the periphery of or outside the collective memory. Insofar as the minorities featured in the collective memory of society at all, they were regarded as problems.

How did the Norwegian state and society engage with the totalitarian, German occupying power? Similarities and differences in the reactions of the occupied countries were conditioned by a wide spectrum of factors. In this connection, the main emphasis is placed on the position of the majority population in the Nazi race hierarchy, and in this respect, we can distinguish between three main positions:

1. Those at the bottom of the Nazi racial hierarchy: certain groups of Slavs who were to be exterminated or deported (Poland, Western Soviet Union).
2. Those in the middle, who were to be heavily exploited, territorially fragmented and deprived of the resources of a great power (France).
3. Those at the top of the racial hierarchy: the Nordic peoples (Denmark, the Netherlands and Norway) who were considered to have equal or even superior racial qualities in comparison to the Germans. The attitudes, norms, values and institutions of these societies were to be brought in line with Nazi ideology and policies; the people were to merge with the Germans.

The countries belonging to the first and third categories were all meant to cease to exist, both as states and as nations; those in the first group through force and by the physical elimination of the greater part of the population; those in the third category by being merged with the Germans by means of ideological propaganda, persuasion and coercion.[14]

In the first category, the occupiers were interested in the territories, the natural resources and a small portion of the population that could be transformed into slaves. This model did not imply any restraint of violence on the part of the occupier. Because the administrative systems and much of the infrastructure were destroyed in these countries, there were few arenas for collaboration. The dominant reaction therefore consisted of armed resistance and guerrilla warfare, but in Poland there was also a strong and widespread civilian resistance. The occupying power closed all schools above the elementary level, but illegal organisations organised school courses for almost 100,000 pupils at all levels. It is estimated that about 18,000 pupils passed their baccalaureate with the help of these underground

---

14 Philippe Burrin: Vichy et les expériences étrangères: esquisse de comparaison, in Jean-Pierre Azéma/François Bédarida (eds.): Vichy et les Français. Paris 1992, 649–661.

teaching agencies.[15] In the second category, that of France, the Germans were interested in gaining geo-strategic positions, access to national resources, and the population as workers and producers. This was to exert some restraint on the behaviour and policies of the occupiers.[16] In the third case, the occupation of the Netherlands and Norway started off with geo-strategic aims as the prime objective, and this consideration weighed heaviest throughout the whole occupation period. But in these two countries, and especially in Norway, the aim of winning the population over to Nazi ideas was also given a high priority. This goal put some restraint on the measures taken by the German rulers at the beginning of the occupation. Although the occupying regimes in both countries showed basic similarities, there were also significant differences. Unlike Norway, the Netherlands had no government of National Socialist collaborators. In order to acquire legitimacy and to expand its weak position in the population, the collaboration authorities in Norway launched a campaign aimed at Nazifying important sectors of the society, notably the whole spectrum of trade organisations, professional associations, non-governmental organisations, and the state bureaucracy. The result of the combined assault by the Germans and the Norwegian collaborators on Norwegian state and social institutions and organisations is concisely summed up in Robert Bohn's important book on the *Reichskommissariat*:

1. As early as the autumn of 1940 – after some months of confusion and permissiveness on the part of parliamentarians over the question of a seemingly legal collaborative government – it became clear that Norwegian state institutions would remain loyal to the Constitution and reject the Nazi rearrangement thrusts. Bohn places particular emphasis on the message of non-cooperation given by the Supreme Court judges, who collectively resigned in December 1940 because of political interference.
2. The massive Nazification offensive toward organisations from 1941 onwards completely failed. After this experience, Terboven concluded that it was impossible to Nazify Norway in line with the German model. The NS lacked both people with competence to implement the Nazi programme and support in the population.

---

15 Jacques Sémelin: Unarmed against Hitler. Civilian Resistance in Europe, 1939–1943. London 1993, 78–80.
16 Philippe Burrin: Vichy et les expériences étrangères: esquisse de comparaison, in: Jean-Pierre Azéma/François Bédarida (eds.): Vichy et les Français. Paris 1992, 649–661.

3. The failed attempts to steer Norwegian society in the direction of National Socialism and to use the new politically homogenised state and society to exploit the country's resources for the benefit of German warfare led to a partial strategic reorientation. The preferred, and at least partially successful, strategic line was to induce the ministerial bureaucratic bodies and the economic elites to pragmatic collaboration.[17]

The large-scale and intensive offensive by the German and Norwegian SS to transform the police according to the German model obtaining a fusion of an imagined superior race and a de-civilised SS behaviour had some success. Eventually, however, there was left a narrow field of action between the *Reichskommissar*'s inclination for realpolitik and the resistance of the robust democratic culture of Norwegian society.[18]

The combination of massive civilian resistance and struggle for democratic norms and values, on the one hand, and of non-ideological, comprehensive, pragmatic collaboration in the economic and administrative sectors of Norwegian society, on the other, were predominant traits of the Norwegian responses to the German occupation.[19] Other factors that shaped the course of the German occupation of Norway were: the determination of the Norwegian government and King to fight the invaders; their decision to leave occupied Norwegian territory and to continue the struggle in exile in the United Kingdom against Nazi-Germany; their rejection of the thrust for an apparently legal government; and the outcome of the lengthy »negotiations« between representatives of the Parliament and Terboven in June 1940 in which the former accepted – under heavy pressure – to submit to the German demand to establish a system of authoritarian rule based on a political collaboration of Norwegian elites. However, after occupying France and now preparing for an attack on Great Britain, Hitler was too preoccupied with the grand strategy to reap the fruits of Terboven's victory over the Norwegian parliamentarians. When »negotiations« resumed in early September, the overall mood in influential

---

17 Robert Bohn: Reichskommissariat Norwegen. »Nationalsozialistische Neuordnung« und Kriegswirtschaft. Munich 2000, 254–255.
18 Terje Emberland/Matthew Kott: Himmlers Norge. Normenn i det stortyske prosjekt. Oslo 2012, 204 ff.
19 A brilliant contribution to the modest body of international literature dealing with the Norwegian civilian resistance is the recently published book by Arne Hassing: Church Resistance to Nazism in Norway 1940–1945. Seattle 2014. While the main emphasis is on the resistance by the Church, the book covers most aspects of civilian resistance.

segments of the population had changed. The King and the government's resolute rejection in early July of the call by the presidency of the parliament to abdicate and of any collaboration at political level – which was widely circulated among Norwegians and broadcasted by the BBC – had a strong impact on ordinary people and the remnants of the political elite in Oslo. At the beginning of the ensuing negotiations, however, the parliamentarians continued to yield to new demands by Terboven's representatives, who persevered with even greater determination to ensure that the new, seemingly legal government would serve the interests of the occupying power. But eventually a more realistic understanding of the German scheme emerged. In a meeting on September 18, faced with fresh demands from the Germans, the Norwegian negotiators decided to stop yielding any further. Both sides concluded that the negotiations had failed.[20] It also marked the final attempt to achieve political goals through governing bodies that were to be given legitimacy by constitutional institutions. This represented a clear defeat for Terboven and Hitler, because the prioritised strategy of establishing Nazi domination of Norway through apparently constitutional institutions had failed.

Terboven's coup on 25 September 1940 deposed the King and the government, banned all political parties except the *Nasjonal Samling*, avoided all reference to the Parliament, and installed a system of *Kommissarische Staatsräte*. Although all *Staatsräte* were Norwegian, it was a German institution whose members were directly subordinate to the *Reichskommissariat*.[21] The majority of them were members of the National Socialist Party, whose leader was Vidkun Quisling, though he held no formal position. Terboven's announcement of 25 September 1940 and the subsequent implementation represented a profound change of the political regime in Norway. It was a total break with democratic rule on the state level.

The final factor was the supreme position in the Nazi racial hierarchy assigned to Norwegians. Initially, this afforded some level of protection to Norwegians who did not engage in any kind of resistance. Gradually, however, the realisation that there was no hope of winning the population over to Nazi politics, combined with the growing resistance, meant that this status ceased to offer much advantage, and Terboven increasingly resorted to harsher persecution and terror. The only factor that had any restraining effect on this brutal rule was the possibility that

---

20 Hans-Dietrich Loock: Quisling, Rosenberg und Terboven. Zur Vorgeschichte und Geschichte der nationalsozialistischen Revolution in Norwegen. Stuttgart 1970, 395–540.
21 Robert Bohn: Reichskommissariat Norwegen. »Nationalsozialistische Neuordnung« und Kriegswirtschaft. Oldenburg 2000, 46.

an escalation in civil disobedience might harm the pragmatic collaboration and destabilise the occupying administration.

The civilian struggle against attempts to Nazify a wide spectrum of organisations and important sectors of the state and to abolish the state of law involved a protest by forty-three organisations nationwide and counting some 700,000 members in the spring of 1941. The action was also supported by a large number of individuals at a local level. The outcome of this struggle in 1941 and 1942 reaffirmed the conception of nation and democratic culture as inextricably intertwined in Norway.[22]

In spite of those comprehensive changes imposed on the institutional landscape, the political culture remained intact and, when placed under heavy pressure, was even revitalised. The range of shared fundamental values became broader, regardless of the respective goals of the political parties. This is the main reason why the German occupation left almost no enduring traces on the structure of Norwegian state and society. Its lasting impact has been in the field of experience and collective memory.

Some destructive assaults, however, were of such a radical nature that their results were in different ways irreparable: the confiscation of all Jewish property; the destruction of Jewish institutions; the deportation and killing of 43 per cent of Norway's Jewish population, and the scorched-earth policy in northern Norway in 1944, with the expulsion of the local population and the utter destruction of every kind of building as well as quays, boats, tools, equipment, and works of art. The rampage in Finnmark was carried out by the Wehrmacht and SS units. The assault on the Jews was ordered by German authorities, coordinated and executed by the Norwegian political police, and supported by paramilitary units and ordinary Norwegian police units.

The Jewish community never recovered from this catastrophe. Finnmark was rebuilt and repopulated after the war, but continuity in terms of its tangible culture was completely broken. The key difference between these events was that the assault on the Norwegian Jewry was directed at the lives, property, culture, and memory of a tiny minority. By contrast, the destruction of Finnmark aimed to render the territory useless to the enemy rather than to kill its population. Both events had a European dimension, manifested in the genocide of the European Jews and the enormous extent of the scorched-earth policy in the western Soviet Union.

---

22 Thomas Chr. Wyller: Nyordning og motstand. Organisasjonenes politiske rolle under okkupasjonen. Oslo 1958, 23 ff.

It is interesting to note that these two important ruptures were not readily recorded in the collective memory during the post-war period. The Holocaust has, however, increasingly shaped memorial processes from the second half of the 1990s, whereas the destruction of Finnmark never became an important part of the national memory.

III. Conclusion

In her article »The Solidity of a National Narrative«, Synne Corell presents a thorough and critical discussion of the polarised grand narrative of the occupation, representing strong opposition between the Home Front, the King and government in exile, on the one side, and the German occupying forces, the NS party and the NS authorities, which pursued an ideologically based collaboration, on the other. Two of her central propositions are that the grand narrative proved durable but that it was nevertheless modified and changed as a result of changing societal configurations.[23] On the basis of the evidence and arguments presented above, there are reasons to claim that the changes over the two last decades had a somewhat broader scope than assumed in Corell's text.

By way of conclusion, and rather than reiterating Corell's sound arguments, I will approach the post-war collective memory from slightly different angles and propose some other perspectives and propositions. Taking the Holocaust as the point of reference, the war experiences generated a new consciousness among some politicians, state bureaucrats, academics, and Sámi activists, resulting in the view that the policy of assimilation had to be reconsidered. A stronger emphasis on pluralism and the need to protect the rights of the Sámi people gained ground. However, the reorientation in the following years was marked by ambiguity. A governmental committee submitted far-reaching proposals in 1959 and a majority of deputies in the Parliament favoured comprehensive changes in policy. Yet the implementation of concrete measures was hampered by disagreement and conflict between local politicians and within the Sámi community itself. Nevertheless, the changes implemented in this area in the 1960s and 1970s were considerable. A series of measures was taken to promote the Sámi language, and several institutions were established to maintain and develop the culture of this minority. A comprehensive and critical assessment of the assimilation policy finally took

---

23 Synne Corell in Henrik Stenius/Mirja Østerberg/Johan Östling, 2011, 102, 119.

place around 1980, and in 1990 Norway ratified Convention No. 169 of the International Labour Organisation, which gave the Sámi an international legal status as an indigenous people. The Kvens benefitted far less from this new sensitivity to the rights of minorities. They continued to be scrutinised and subjected to the entrenched suspicion of questionable patriotic attitudes, due to their perceived loyalty to Finland, their ancestral homeland. The Framework Convention for the Protection of National Minorities, ratified by Norway in 1999, eventually paved the way for more harmonious relations between the Kvens and society at large.[24] Nevertheless, the tendency at the time was to omit this field from public memory. The continuity from the 1930s was obvious.

Events and phenomena, which aroused painful or traumatic associations from a national point of view, were either placed at the periphery of the collective memory or became taboo subjects. Notable examples are the Waffen-SS volunteers; the arrest and transport of Norwegian Jews to Oslo harbour for deportation executed by Norwegian personnel; the treatment of Norwegian women who engaged in relationships with German soldiers and of the children born out of such relationships; and the liquidation of particularly dangerous collaborators and informers by the resistance movement.[25]

Not only were events which were considered harmful to the nation-building process left out of the remembrances in Norway, the same applied to whatever fell outside the general national framing and was thus considered irrelevant to national consolidation processes. The most conspicuous example is the fate of some 117,000 POWs from the Soviet Union, Poland, and Yugoslavia who were brought to Norway by the Germans as slave labour.[26] About 16,700 of them were either killed by German guards or perished because of the inhumane working conditions, brutality and inadequate nutrition. They were used to build fortifications and infrastructure for the occupying power, but they also worked in factories that

---

24   I am deeply grateful to Professor Einar Niemi at the University of Tromsø for providing me valuable information from an ongoing project on the relationships between the Sàmi and Kven peoples, the local political elites in Finmark, and the state.
25   Odd-Bjørn Fure: Norsk okkupasjonshistorie. Konsensus, berøringsangst og tabuisering, in: Stein Ugelvik Larsen (ed.): I krigens kjølvann. Oslo 1999, 31–46. For the break-down of a situation where the fates of the four latter groups were treated with silence to their integration into open memorial processes, see Susanne Maerz: Die langen Schatten der Besatzungsmacht. »Vergangenheitsbewältigung« in Norwegen als Identitätsdiskurs. Berlin 2007, 219–277.
26   Fure, Norsk okkupasjonshistorie, 37–38.

produced important items for the German war effort, and contributed greatly to modernising Norwegian infrastructure by building railways, roads, tunnels, and airports.[27] The existence and fate of these slave labourers figured positively in the national consciousness immediately after the war, but they disappeared when the weighty ramifications of the Cold War made its impact on public discourse.

Within the spectrum of resistance in Norway, the civilian struggle for defending, confirming, and revitalising democratic values, norms and procedures loomed large in terms of its widespread mobilisation – unparalleled in any other occupied country – and of its consequences. Within the overall framework set by the occupying power, it shaped the course of the occupation in Norway.[28] The civilian struggle could, of course, not change the core of the power relations between the occupiers and the occupied. But it demonstrated that popular support for the civilian front was so strong that any attempt to break it with brutal force would have to be paid for at a very high price. Terboven's persistently hesitant attitude toward the challenges posed by teachers, bishops, priests, and other groups is striking and interesting. Such reticence does not correspond with his typical behaviour.

Milorg, the military branch of the resistance movement, became operative much later, in 1944, while communist groups, who were pioneers in this kind of struggle, started acts of sabotage as early as 1941. After a period of tension between Milorg, the British Special Operations Executive, and the exile government in the first years of the war, an increasingly well-coordinated system of operations was gradually developed which also implied a unified leadership of the civilian and armed wings of the Home Front.[29] The armed wing of the Norwegian resistance movement played a key role in two respects. First, intelligence gathering from about fifty observation posts and radio transmitters along the entire coastline was of vital importance for the British naval warfare in this theatre.[30] The most spec-

---

27   Marianne Neerland Soleim: Sovjetiske krigsfanger i Norge 1941–1945. Antall, organisering og repatriering. Oslo 2009.
28   The best scholarly presentation in English of the civilian resistance movement in Norway during the German occupation is the recently published book by Arne Hassing.
29   Arnfinn Moland: Norway, in: Bob More (ed.): Resistance in Western Europe. Oxford 2000, 233 ff. The standard work on the making of a unified leadership of the civilian and military wings of the Home Front is, Ole Kristian Grimnes: Hjemmefrontens ledelse. Norge og den 2. Verdenskrig. Oslo 1979.
30   Olav Riste: »London-regjeringa«: Norge i krigsalliansen 1940–1945, in: 1940–1942: Prøvetid. Oslo 1973, 109.

tacular achievement of this activity was the identification and close surveillance of the battleship *Tirpitz* off the southwest coast of Norway in January 1942 until she was sunk by RAF bombers in northern Norway in November 1944. The approximately 40,000 members of the Home Front, who were eventually armed in 1944, secured the smooth handover of power from the Wehrmacht to the Norwegian authorities in May 1945.

How did the collective memory record the activities of the resistance movement in the post-war period? Initially, the civilian resistance – the struggle for civic norms and democratic values – was assigned a position that corresponded with its actual scope and significance during the occupation. Thomas Christian Wyller's classic monograph on this topic laid the foundation for this realistic reception.[31] Subsequently, however, the remembrance of the war displayed a recasting of the relationship between the two forms of struggle; armed resistance and sabotage came to the forefront in the narratives of the occupation while civilian struggle faded into the background. There were many reasons for this change: the activities of the saboteurs were generally more dramatic and spectacular than those of the operatives in the civilian field, working painstakingly to boost and revitalise democratic attitudes. Furthermore, many of the saboteurs wrote books about their actions, which immediately touched a nerve with the public with their narratives of the war. But the most important explanations are found in the deep structure of society or, more precisely, in the connecting tissue between a democratic society and a nation. This linkage was so deeply rooted in Norwegian culture that in the aftermath of the occupation, the democratic mobilisation was perceived as normal or self-evident, even in an abnormal situation. It could safely be referred to as tacit knowledge.

In the 1970s and 1980s, the pillars of the patriotic memory began to erode, some earlier, some later. This was not an exclusively Norwegian phenomenon. The macro-processes mentioned in the introduction undermined this particular culture of national remembrance. This constellation of forces, combined with new experiences and perceptions created the impression that the old selective way of remembering no longer corresponded to the basic values and needs of society. A fundamental reorientation in the memory culture in Norway and elsewhere in the Western world was emerging.

---

31 Thomas Chr. Wyller: Nyordning og motstand. Organisasjonenes politiske rolle under okkupasjonen. Oslo 1958.

The mid-1990s saw a profound transformation of memory culture in Norway. It was still, to a great extent, nationally framed, but it differed significantly from the previous patriotic memory and was strongly informed by universal human rights thinking. The policy of assimilation – with all its catastrophic consequences – was gradually abandoned in the 1960s and 1970s. Universal rejection came even later, in the 1980s.

A less tense attitude to the national community led to greater openness toward problematic, traumatic, and painful events and behaviour. Over the past fifteen years, the neglected themes (mentioned above) have been thoroughly researched and subjected to critical appraisal. There seems to be a growing understanding that a politically healthy nation cannot cultivate a memory that is confined solely to what has traditionally been considered as nationally memorable actions. The painful, traumatic, and tragic events should also be recorded in and integrated into the collective memory. Moreover, it has been recognised and increasingly taken for granted that the conditions and cultures of the minorities should be part of a broad and complex mosaic of memories. The fact that the Norwegian Parliament has voted unanimously to establish institutions like the Center for Studies of the Holocaust and Religious Minorities and the Falstad Centre indicates that this conception has now sound political backing.

Susanne Maerz asserts that over the past two decades the earlier practice of covering complex relationships with undifferentiated statements has been increasingly replaced by an approach that treats difficult aspects of the past with more differentiated concepts. A growing propensity for critical reflection of difficult themes – *Aufarbeitung der Geschichte* – is now seen as an integral part of the same process, though several areas still need to be assessed.[32]

Today, the fate of the Norwegian Rom before, during and after the war is the most conspicuous example of what has been left outside the broader and more inclusive process of critical remembrance. This field is still not researched. In the Aliens Act of 1927, foreign Roma were forbidden to enter Norwegian state territory.[33] It was the only group of people ever to be banned from Norway by democratic authorities.

Alongside this long-term development of more comprehensive, inclusive and complex collective memories, with differentiated propositions and a potential for critical assessments of the past, a new tendency has evolved in recent years that

---

32   Maerz, 300–304.
33   Odd-Bjørn Fure: Mellomkrigstid 1920–1940. Oslo 1996, 48–49.

negates all these features. It appears as an inverted image of an extreme version of the patriotic memory of the early post-war period. It has nothing to say about the invasion, the bombing of Norwegian cities and the rule of terror by the occupation authorities, or the arrest, torture, killing, and deportation of resistance fighters to the concentration camps in Germany. Nor does the massive thrust of Nazification of nearly all societal sectors, one of the dominant traits of the occupation policy, feature in this recollection of the war. The same applies to the mass mobilisation of civilian resistance that blocked the advancement of Nazification, and thus greatly influenced the outcome of the occupation. While this current has almost nothing to convey about the resistance as such, one of its main priorities is to ironise about its presentation in broader streams of remembrance in a way that denies its historical significance altogether. The favoured theme of this recollection is the presentation of a considerable proportion of the Norwegian population as willing henchmen for the German occupying authorities. While resistance is treated in an ironic discourse, the collaborators are presented in a strongly moralistic and condescending way – though with one exception; the Norwegian National Socialists. All other collaborators are treated without any differentiation.

This is a remembrance based on an extremely relativistic mode of thinking, presenting accounts of the occupation that mention neither the occupier nor the occupied. This approach presumes that it was possible to live a relatively normal life under utterly abnormal conditions. Its proponents advocate studies related to grey zones without understanding that the existence of such zones are dependent on the existence of dark and bright ones.

This relativistic scheme loses sight of the basic question of what was at stake during the occupation of Norway, and elsewhere in countries occupied by the Nazi state. One extreme example of this mode of thinking is the equation of those Norwegians who volunteered to join the Waffen-SS and participated in a racial war of extermination in the Soviet Union with those who fought for regaining national liberation, democracy and a state of law.[34] Since this current is characterised by a relativistic mode of thinking, it remains virtually unaffected by the otherwise growing influence of the universalistic way of assessing past events.

---

34 See, for instance Kjetil Østli: En historie om helter, *Aftenposten*, Magasinet no. 20, 21 May 2010, Arvid Bryne: Vi sloss for Norge – Frontkjemper og motstandsmann – fiender i krig – venner i fred, Oslo 2007; and Erling Fossen: Motstand glorifiseres, *Aftenposten*, 21 May 2010.

Today's memorial landscape in Norway is more than ever characterised by diversity. A master-narrative of the old type is not readily discernible, only its remnants linger on and they just appear under certain circumstances. The patriotic memory has definitely diminished. Memories of the war are still – though to varying degrees – nationally framed in Norway, and they coexist with transnational and universalistic modes of thinking. Human rights thinking in this field is operative both as an undercurrent with considerable scope and as a separate, alternative current to nationally framed versions. A comprehensive or full shift to universalistic narratives is unthinkable as long as the nation-state maintains its current status and functions.

Arnd Bauerkämper
Beyond Resistance versus Collaboration
The Twisted Road to a Universalistic Memory of the Second World War in Norway

Across national borders, the shift to memory studies has been fuelled by generational change, the increasing political integration of Europe, and the emergence of a universalistic memorial culture that has started to transcend national narratives and focused on the Holocaust. Politicians as well as historians, for instance, have argued that intensified coordination and co-operation between European states should be based on a discursive and reflexive memorial culture that is to encompass self-criticism and empathy.[1]

Yet holistic concepts like »collective memory« (Maurice Halbwachs), »memorial culture« (Christoph Cornelißen) as well as »cultural memory« (Aleida and Jan Assmann), the »politics of history« (Edgar Wolfrum) and the »politics of the past« (Norbert Frei) have reinforced rather than undermined the widely-held notion that memories of National Socialism, Fascism, collaboration, and the Holocaust have been largely homogeneous and tied to the individual European nation-states. Research along these lines has also strengthened national master-narratives like myths of united resistance against German occupation authorities and the large-scale rejection of their collaborators. These narratives had been shaped by ruling elites, but responded to the broader needs of post-war societies shaken by the experience of German occupation. As a corollary, fissures, tensions and ambiguities

---

1   Heidemarie Uhl: Schuldgedächtnis und Erinnerungsbegehren. Thesen zur europäischen Erinnerungskultur, in: Transit 35 (2008), 6–22, 9f., 13, 15; Kerstin von Lingen: Kriegserfahrung und die Formierung nationaler Identität in Europa nach 1945: Eine Einführung, in: ead. (ed.): Kriegserfahrung und die Formierung nationaler Identität in Europa nach 1945. Erinnerung, Säuberungsprozesse und nationales Gedächtnis, Paderborn 2009, 11–26, 16; Reinhart Koselleck: Formen und Traditionen des negativen Gedächtnisses, in: V. Knigge/N. Frei (eds.): Verbrechen erinnern. Die Auseinandersetzung mit Holocaust und Völkermord, Munich 2002, 21–32.

in memories persisted. Even the more recent distinction between »national basic narratives« (*nationale Basisnarrative*) and »family memory« (*Familiengedächtnis*) has reinforced rather than superseded the national paradigm in historiography. Thus, studies of memorial cultures that have transcended the confines of one nation-state are usually mere compilations of national studies of remembering Nazi and fascist rule, resistance, collaboration, and the Holocaust. Moreover, conflicts of different and often competing memories have been neglected in favour of investigations of supposedly homogeneous memorial cultures in the individual European nation-states that, however, have lastingly shaped memorial cultures in Europe.[2]

By contrast, recent research has highlighted the role of actors and conflicts over memories, as the following conceptual considerations explain. They are based on the distinction between »official«, »vernacular« and »public memory«.[3] This contribution will also demonstrate the dynamics of remembrances that have been related to or even shaped by needs of the present. In the following, the gradual, protracted and twisted turn from a heroic narrative to a more self-critical and universalistic narrative of the Second World War in Norway will be traced. »Heroic« and »universalistic« are to be conceived as types that need to be differentiated. Heroic narratives predominated in the European countries in the first few decades, though to varying degrees. In Norway, for instance, historiography has not unequivocally supported popular tales of heroism against the German occupiers. Even autobiographies of resistance fighters have not merely been self-congratulatory. By contrast, many Norwegian films have glorified – and thus magnified – the civic and armed resistance of Norwegians against the Germans in the Second World War. In the Federal Republic of Germany, the German Democratic Republic and (to a lesser extent) in Austria, heroic narratives of the war were largely subdued in the public spheres. These successor nations of the Third Reich had lost the war and could not officially claim heroic narratives of combat or resistance. As memories of heroism were closely tied to the nation, they were only employed in order to demand the reunification of a divided Germany. In vernacular memory,

---

2 Arnd Bauerkämper: Das umstrittene Gedächtnis. Die Erinnerung an Nationalsozialismus, Faschismus und Krieg in Europa seit 1945, Paderborn 2012, esp. 11–50; Heidemarie Uhl, Vom Nachkriegsmythos zur Ethik der Erinnerung: Transformationen der Erinnerungskultur in Europa von 1945 bis zur Gegenwart, in: Revue d'Allemagne et des Pays de langue allemande 44 (2012), No. 2, 189–197, 193 f.
3 For a more detailed explanation, see the introduction.

however, heroic memories were by no means suppressed or tabooed. By contrast, universalistic narratives are a »negative« memory.[4]

They respect memories of other (national) communities and do not serve easily as tools of identity construction. They are not self-congratulatory and affirmative, but self-critical. A »negative memory« is not primarily geared to the nation, but more cosmopolitan and related to humanity.[5] In Western and Central Europe, in particular, a gradual shift to more universalistic memory cultures has been identified by scholarly, journalistic and political observers, especially since the 1980s. Yet this process has not been uniform. In particular, »official« and »vernacular« memory needs to be distinguished.[6] As will be explained in this chapter, the content and forms of memories of the Second World War have shifted in Norway since 1945, though by means of a complex process. Following an overview of this change, the transformation of Norwegian memory culture will be placed in its European context.

I. Conceptual Considerations and Memorialisation in Nordic Countries

Processes of remembering Nazism, Fascism, occupation, and the Holocaust have resulted from continuous reconfigurations of relationships between specific social and political groups and actors. Yet they have usually been asymmetrical and shaped by political power. In fact, party politicians and social groups as well as leaders and members of political and civic associations have harboured and proposed different memories of the recent past. Even veterans of resistance groups have partially disagreed on the merits and achievements of their respective struggles against Nazism, Fascism, and occupation. Although Communists were largely marginalized in the Cold War, political differences and debates both reflected and exacerbated conflicting memories. These controversies need to be investigated in

---

4 On »negative« memory, see R. Koselleck, Formen und Traditionen des negativen Gedächtnisses, in: Volkhard Knigge/Norbert Frei (eds.): Verbrechen erinnern. Die Auseinandersetzung mit Holocaust und Völkermord, Munich 2002, 21–32; H. Uhl, Die Transformation des »österreichischen Gedächtnisses« in der Erinnerungskultur der Zweiten Republik, in: Geschichte und Region 13 (2004), 23–54, 25.
5 Uhl, Nachkriegsmythos, 191–193.
6 Laurence van Ypersele: Mourning and Memory, 1919–1945, in: J. Horne (ed.): A Companion to World War I, Oxford 2012, 576–590, 576.

studies of memorialisation in Norway. With regard to this dimension, however, scholars are to differentiate between democracies, where citizens have publicly debated these issues, and post-war communist and authoritarian dictatorships. Their rulers sought to suppress memories that did not comply with the official glorification of »anti-fascist« resistance and national resurgence, respectively. However, different memories lived on and persisted even under these regimes, as the emergence of new national narratives of National Socialism, fascism, occupation, and the Holocaust in the transformation process in east European states has demonstrated. Altogether, memories proposed by specific actors in societies therefore merit a separate and close scrutiny. In dictatorships as well as in democracies, remembering National Socialism, Fascism, occupation and the Holocaust in small groups like families and civic associations have frequently differed from the dominant narratives that governments and leading politicians attempted to impose. Concepts like »resistance«, »collaboration« and »treason« have not only been contested in the political realm, but also within and between European societies. In fact, controversies over the diverse modes of behaviour under Fascism, National Socialism and occupation regimes have continually decided on the social inclusion and exclusion of specific individual and collective actors. Ultimately, memories are contested and thus strongly shaped by power relations. They are specific and usually selective representations of history according to particular aims and vested interests. In particular, they reflect different and often contradictory quests for identification and legitimation.[7]

In order to explain the twists and turns in memorial cultures, historians are to investigate memorialisation as a process of (frequently asymmetrical) interchange between specific actors who pursue particular aims, not least according to their vested interests. Moreover, memories cannot be uncoupled from history,

---

7 Wulf Kansteiner: Finding Meaning in Memory. A Methodological Critique of Collective Memory Studies, in: History and Theory 41 (2002), 179–197; Katherine Hodgkin/Susannah Radstone: Introduction. Contested Pasts, in: K. Hodgkin/S. Radstone (eds.): Contested Pasts. The Politics of Memory, London 2003, 1–21; Anita Kasabova: Memory, Memorials, and Commemoration, in: History and Theory 47 (2008), 331–350; Jörn Rüsen: Interpreting the Holocaust. Some Theoretical Issues, in: K. G. Karlsson/U. Zander (eds.): Holocaust Heritage. Inquiries into European Historical Cultures, Malmö 2004, 35–62, 40–44; Frederick Whitling: Damnatio Memoriae and the Power of Remembrance. Reflections on Memory and History, in: M. Pakier/B. Stråth (eds.): A European Memory? Contested Histories and Politics of Remembrance, New York 2010, 87–97.

even though they are constructions. In fact, practices of remembrance of National Socialism, fascism, the Second World War and the Holocaust have been shaped by the specific historical experiences in the various nations. In Northern Europe, Finland had been beaten by the Soviet army in the Winter War of 1939–40. In June 1941, the country's forces joined the Third Reich in the attack on the USSR in order to regain its lost territories. After severe military setbacks, however, Finland's President Carl Mannerheim conceded a ceasefire to the Soviet Union. After 1944, the concept of a »separate war« was to disentangle Finland from the military defeat and political stigmatisation of a defeated and discredited Germany.[8]

In Sweden, official memory highlighted the country's status as a neutral power during the Second World War, irrespective of the concessions that the government had made to the seemingly victorious Third Reich, for instance in the ›mid-summer crisis‹ of 1941 when Sweden had allowed German troops to be brought across its territory to the Eastern Front.[9] In Denmark, which had surrendered to the superior German forces within a few hours on 9 April 1940, official memories highlighted the end of the collaborationist government in August 1943 when the government rejected German demands to introduce a curfew and the death penalty for sabotage. As a consequence, the Danish government that had refused to relent to pressure resigned. It was finally dissolved by the German authorities that also imposed martial law. Apart from this break with collaboration on the political level between governments, many Danes emphasized their contribution to the rescue of the Jews in late 1943. However, plans for the deportation of the Danish Jews had been leaked by the German diplomat Georg Ferdinand Duckwitz to the Social Democratic politician Hans Hedtoft, among others, who then passed the information on to politicians who had close contacts with the Danish resistance movement. Official post-war memories also ignored that the rescue of the Jews

---

8   Matti Klinge: Finland and the Experience of War, in: S. Ekman/N. Edling (eds.): War Experience, Self-Image and National Identity. The Second World War as Myth and History, Södertälje 1997, 114–129.
9   Kristian Gerner: The Holocaust and Memory Culture: The Case of Sweden, in: H. Bjerg/C. Lenz/E. Thorstensen (eds.): Historicizing the Uses of the Past. Scandinavian Perspectives on History Culture, Historical Consciousness and Didactics of History Related to World War II, Bielefeld 2011, 91–106; Johan Östling: The Rise and Fall of Small-State Realism. Sweden and the Second World War, in: H. Stenius/M. Österberg/J. Östling (eds.): Nordic Narratives of the Second World War. National Historiographies Revisited, Lund 2011, 127–147.

was less due to the strength of the resistance movement than a result of civic disobedience.[10]

Norway had been attacked on 9 April 1940, but held out until 10 June when the country's troops surrendered to Germany. However, the government-in-exile and King Haakon VII, who had escaped to London, refused to abdicate. An Administrative Council, which had been appointed by the Norwegian Supreme Court on 15 April 1940, merely had consultative and administrative functions. The German occupiers aimed at full-fledged political collaboration by the leading Norwegian politicians who lacked knowledge of Nazi rule in the Third Reich. Yet German attempts to win over established Norwegian politicians to self-Nazification encountered strong reservations and foundered in early September 1940. This failure was also due to an intervention by Alfred Rosenberg who competed with Joachim von Ribbentrop in Germany's foreign policy. Rosenberg had introduced Vidkun Quisling, the leader of Norway's fascist party, the *Nasjonal Samling*, to Hitler in 1939, and he opposed efforts to entrust moderate Norwegian politicians with governing the occupied country. In the end, German authorities had to rely on the Norwegian fascists, thereby initiating ideological collaboration. At the same time, pragmatic co-operation continued between more moderate and liberal Norwegians, although they were fully aware of the ideological differences. As efforts to initiate a full-fledged political collaboration had failed, Nazi functionary Josef Terboven established a *Reichskommissariat* on 24 September.[11]

In the course of the war, the German occupation authorities were increasingly confronted with active resistance. Even more significantly, civic defiance, the *hold-*

---

10 Matthias Bath: Danebrog gegen Hakrenkreuz. Der Widerstand in Dänemark 1940–1945, Neumünster 2011, 128; Mete Zølner: Remembering the Second World War in Denmark: The Impact of Politics, Ideology and Generation, in: B. Stråth (ed.): Myth and Memory in the Construction of Community. Historical Patterns in Europe and Beyond, Brussels 2000, 351–373.

11 For the attempts by the German occupation authorities to establish an officially recognised government in Norway, see Hans-Dietrich Loock: Quisling, Rosenberg und Terboven. Zur Vorgeschichte und Geschichte der nationalsozialistischen Revolution in Norwegen, Stuttgart 1970. For an overview, cf. Robert Bohn: Die Errichtung des Reichskommissariats Norwegen, in: ibid. et al. (eds.): Neutralität und totalitäre Aggression. Nordeuropa und die Großmächte im Zweiten Weltkrieg, Stuttgart 1991, 129–148; ibid.: Die Instrumentarien der deutschen Herrschaft im Reichskommissariat Norwegen, in: idem (ed.): Die deutsche Herrschaft in den »germanischen« Ländern 1940–1945, Stuttgart 1997, 71–108, 71–75.

ningskamp, became a cornerstone of Norway's memory culture after 1945. Like all formerly occupied states, for example the Netherlands, official remembrances of the Second World War glorified non-compliance and resistance in the first few decades after 1945, whereas conformity, fraternization and collaboration with the German occupiers were largely silenced. The latter narratives contrasted with the official memory politics. All in all, national histories and the specific post-war conditions enduringly influenced remembrances of the recent past.[12]

II. The Heroic Narrative: a Nation in Resistance

After the Second World War a broad, but fragile consensus emerged in Norway. Leading officials and entrepreneurs who had collaborated with the Nazi occupiers (though to varying degrees) claimed to have protected Norway from civil repression and terror. However, this self-portrayal did not remain without its detractors. Representatives of the military resistance, in particular, highlighted the compromises that co-operating Norwegians had been ready to make with the Germans, not least in order to alleviate the burden of occupation. Moreover, they held Norway's pre-war elites responsible for the lack of military preparedness that had supposedly encouraged the German attack and facilitated the advance of the *Wehrmacht*. Yet any attempt to establish an apparently legal government had been impossible after 5 September 1940. Leading conservative, liberal and socialist politicians had abandoned political co-operation or gone into exile, where the Norwegian government gradually gained control over the »home front« (*hjemmefront*) of resistance fighters in Norway. This common front against the German invaders laid the ground for a broad agreement on the occupation and a compromise between the elites. Einar Gerhardsen's first unity government of June 1945 reflected that wide-ranging consensus between pre-war politicians and the diverse representatives of the resistance movement. Former Norwegian exiles co-operated with their compatriots who had remained in the occupied country. This government also included former inmates of concentration camps like Prime Minister Gerhardsen. Labour, Conservative and Liberal politicians co-operated

---

12 Henrik Stenius/Mirja Österberg/Johan Östling, Nordic Narratives of the Second World War. An Introduction, in: ead. (eds.): Narratives, 9–30. See also Odd-Bjørn Fure's contribution to this volume.

with their colleagues in the Agrarian Party and with Communists.[13] Whereas the former resistance fighters glorified their actions against the Germans, traditional elites claimed to have shielded Norway from the worst excesses of occupation. Despite this slight difference, the two groups shared a profound antipathy towards the Germans and the members of the *Nasjonal Samling* who had challenged the strong connection between national independence and democracy as hallmarks of Norway's political culture.[14]

The consensual narrative of a unified nation in active or passive resistance deeply shaped Norway's political culture after 1945. It stabilised and legitimised the post-war political order in the Scandinavian country that had been shaken by the traumatic turmoil of the German invasion and occupation. According to this narrative that dominated official memory in the first three decades after the Second World War, the liberation of the state ultimately led to a national revival. Thus, it was highly symbolic that King Haakon VII returned to Norway on 7 June 1945, exactly forty years after the country had achieved its full national independence from Sweden and five years after the king had to escape into British exile. The general concept of the *holdningskamp* represented the consensus on Norway's recent past. The notion emphasized civic resilience and large-scale obstruction of German orders in occupied Norway as much as opposition to the Nazifica-

---

13 As in some other European states like Austria and Italy, however, Communists were excluded from high office with the onset of the Cold War.
14 Ole Kristian Grimnes: Occupation and Collective Memory in Norway, in: Ekman/Edling (eds.): War Experience, 142; Susanne Maerz: Landesverrat versus Widerstand. Stationen und Probleme der »Vergangenheitsbewältigung« in Norwegen, in: Nordeuropa-Forum 15 (2005), 43–73, 46; id.: Die langen Schatten der Besatzungszeit. »Vergangenheitsbewältigung« in Norwegen als Identitätsdiskurs, Berlin 2008, 280, 293; Claudia Lenz: »Das ist ein deutsches Problem«. Das Wehrmachtsbild und die Rezeption der Ausstellung »Vernichtungskrieg« in Norwegen, in: Michael Th. Greven/Oliver von Wrochem (Hg.): Der Krieg in der Nachkriegszeit. Der Zweite Weltkrieg in Politik und Gesellschaft der Bundesrepublik, Opladen 2000, 255–270, 265 f.; Rolf Hobson: Die weißen Flecken in der norwegischen Geschichtsschreibung über die deutsche Besatzung, in: Robert Bohn/Christoph Cornelißen/Karl Christian Lammers (eds.): Vergangenheitspolitik und Erinnerungskulturen im Schatten des Zweiten Weltkriegs. Deutschland und Skandinavien seit 1945, Essen 2008, 95–103, 98; Bo Stråth: Geschichtspolitik und Gründungsmythen in den nordischen Ländern. 1989 im Rückblick, in: Etienne François et al. (eds.): Geschichtspolitik in Europa seit 1989. Deutschland, Frankreich und Polen im internationalen Vergleich, Göttingen 2013, 427–448, 430, 438.

tion efforts of the NS. The fascist party was strongly rejected by the majority of the Norwegians who stigmatised Quisling and his adherents as »traitors«.[15] The very vagueness of *holdningskamp* lent it considerable appeal and utility in postwar public discourse. As military resistance had remained weak und ineffective until 1944, the *holdingskamp* on the home front received particular attention and acclaim. The heroic narrative has been paradigmatically represented by the *Norges Hjemmefrontmuseum* that was opened on the eve of the 25th anniversary of Norway's liberation on 7 May 1970.[16]

Public memories of the occupation bordered on a foundational myth that enabled the vast majority of Norwegians to identify themselves with their homeland. Although resistance was glorified, Norwegian elites and large sections of society accepted pragmatic collaboration after the war. As most post-war Norwegian historians understandably shared concerns about the fractures, divisions and confrontations of the recent past, they indirectly supported efforts to retrospectively unify Norway's memorial culture by highlighting ideological co-operation, on the one hand, and resistance, on the other. Thus, proposals to establish a memorial fund that would promote mutual understanding between Norwegian youth and young people from other European countries (including West Germany) met strong opposition in Norway's parliament, the *Storting*, as late as 1970.[17]

---

15 Grimnes: Occupation, 130–148, 131, 134, 138 f.
16 Ivar Kraglund: Norway's Resistance Museum in Oslo – An Integral Part of Collective Memory, in: R. Bohn/Chr. Cornelißen/K. Chr. Lammers (eds.): Vergangenheitspolitik, 181–184. See also Doreen Reinhold's chapter in this volume.
17 Katharina Pohl: »Eine unbehagliche Geschichte«. Norwegische Vergangenheitsdebatten und der Holocaust, in: H. Schmid (ed.): Geschichtspolitik und kollektives Gedächtnis. Erinnerungskulturen in Theorie und Praxis, Göttingen 2009, 229–248, 233; Synne Corell: The Solidity of a National Narrative. The German Occupation in Norwegian Historical Culture, in: H. Stenius/M. Österberg/J. Östling (eds.): Narratives, 101–125, 105, 107; Clemens Maier: A Victory Celebrated. Danish and Norwegian Celebrations of the Liberation, in: M. Pakier/B. Stråth (eds.): A European Memory?, 147–159, 149 f.; Claudia Lenz: Strengthening Narrative Competence by Diversification of (Hi)stories, in: H. Bjerg/C. Lenz/E. Thorstensen (eds.): Historicizing, 257–280, 258, 265 f.; Maerz: Probleme, 265 f.; Lenz: »Das ist ein deutsches Problem«, 265 f.; Armin Lang: Die Besetzung Norwegens in deutscher und norwegischer Sicht. Eine Typologie des Umgangs mit Invasion und Okkupation, in: Wolfgang Michalka (ed.): Der Zweite Weltkrieg. Analysen, Grundzüge, Forschungsbilanz, München 1989, 138–154, 146; Hobson: Flecken, 95, 97, 101 f.

On the other side of the dualistic memory culture, the indigenous fascists as well as Norwegians tainted with close contacts with the German occupiers were excluded from the Norwegian national community. In particular, openly ideological collaboration was condemned. Thus, members of the *Nasjonal Samling* were excluded from the national community and public remembrance. In fact, Norway's post-war coalition government excluded the ardent adherents of the Third Reich from civil service. After the administration had been cleansed of committed Norwegian democrats, 44.3 per cent of the remaining high-ranking and 13.9 per cent of the ordinary state officials had joined the NS during the war. These groups were closely scrutinised by special denazification committees. Some of the accused officials defended their co-operation with the occupiers by the need for realpolitik and referred to Count Wedel, who had been praised as a patriot after his compromised peace with Sweden in 1814. Yet they were unable to resist the pressure of the accusations. Veterans of the resistance movements as well as politicians who had half-heartedly co-operated with the Germans stigmatised Norwegian Nazis as traitors and opportunists. As many positions in the civil service had been staffed with members of the NS, especially between 1942 and 1944, 60.0 per cent of the high-ranking state officials and 7.8 per cent of the lower ranks of the bureaucracy were dismissed in the first few months after the end of the war. Not least, the experiences of Norwegian soldiers of the Waffen-SS and spouses of German soldiers were excluded from the political consensus that underpinned the memory politics of Norway's post-war governments. All in all, as many as 93,000 Norwegians were interned in the first few months after the war, frequently in former Nazi camps.[18] Even though the vast majority was soon released, their symbolic exclusion from the national community was to stabilise the national identities of the majority of Norwegians. As a corollary, symbols of NS power like the monument at Stiklestad were destroyed in 1945.[19]

However, »passive« members of the NS as well as soldiers of the Waffen-SS were later allowed to return to their positions if they had joined the resistance

---

18 Jon Reitan: The Nazi Camps in the Norwegian Historical Culture, H. Berg/C. Lenz/ E. Thorstensen (eds.): Historicizing, 57–65, 63f.; Stein U. Larsen: Die Ausschaltung der Quislinge in Norwegen, in: Klaus-Dietmar Henke/H. Woller (eds.): Politische Säuberung in Europa. Die Abrechnung mit Faschismus und Kollaboration nach dem Zweiten Weltkrieg, Munich 1991, 241–280, 270–273, 280.
19 Tor Einar Fagerland/Trond Risto Nilssen: The Norwegian Fascist Monument at Stiklestad 1944–45, in: Helle Berg/Claudia Lenz/Erik Thorstensen (eds.): Historicizing, 77–90. See also Tor Einar Fagerland's contribution to this volume.

movement in the latter stages of the war. Norwegian Nazis, who were considered loyal compatriots, were also re-admitted to the national community. More generally, the official memory narrative largely ignored everyday collaboration. In particular, Norwegian entrepreneurs who had worked for the Germans by constructing fortifications, shelters and airfields were exempted from trials and reprisals. Norway's industries had participated in Germany's war effort by producing weapons and other vital armaments. Even some aspects of the resistance fight remained on the sidelines of official memory. Thus, the role of female resistance fighters was downgraded vis-à-vis their male compatriots. Furthermore, there was widespread silence on the liquidation of »traitors« and »collaborators« by members of the resistance movement. Not least, Communist resistance to the Nazis and to the Norwegian fascists received little recognition from the late 1940s onwards. All in all, public remembrances largely ignored the ›grey zones‹ between resistance and collaboration. Yet pragmatic co-operation was accepted.[20]

By contrast, memories were more ambivalent or even ambiguous in small-scale communities like villages and families. Personal bonds and networks secured former fellow-travellers of the Germans and ex-Nazis some protection and immunity at a local level. Emotional attachments took precedence over public condemnations. Moreover, some villagers continued to harbour fond memories of individual Germans. Altogether, official narratives partially contrasted with everyday experiences of pragmatic or even amicable co-operation with the German occupiers.[21]

It was the large-scale marginalisation of the specifics of the Holocaust, however, that ultimately splintered Norway's memory culture. Up to the 1970s, the Jewish victims of the Holocaust had largely been ignored. The concentration on

---

20 Claudia Lenz: Haushaltspflicht und Widerstand. Erzählungen norwegischer Frauen über die deutsche Besatzung 1940–1945 im Lichte nationaler Vergangenheitskonstruktionen, Tübingen 2003, 92 f.; Lenz, »Das ist ein deutsches Problem«, 268; Lenz, Strengthening, 365 f.; Einhart Lorenz: Die Deportation der norwegischen Juden und ihre verspätete Aufarbeitung, in: R. Bohn/Chr. Cornelißen/K. Chr. Lammers (eds.): Vergangenheitspolitik, 104–121, 118.

21 Claudia Lenz: Vom Widerstand zum Weltfrieden. Der Wandel nationaler und familiärer Konsenserzählungen über die Besatzungszeit in Norwegen, in: Harald Welzer (ed.): Der Krieg der Erinnerung. Holocaust, Kollaboration und Widerstand im europäischen Gedächtnis, Frankfurt/Main 2007, 41–75; Ruth Sindt: Okkupanten und Okkupierte in Kirkenes – Kriegsalltag, Kriegserinnerungen und Erinnerungsmuster, in: R. Bohn/Chr. Cornelißen/K. Chr. Lammers (eds.): Vergangenheitspolitik, 217–225, 222.

the *Holdningskamp* and the exclusion of the ideological collaborators of the *Nasjonal Samling* and their supporters had exempted the majority of the population from responsibility and guilt. From the 1980s onwards, however, the erosion of the consensus narrative gave rise to more self-critical memories that were to supersede the entrenched dichotomy of »resistance« as against »treason« – a term that had faded out in the 1960s. Yet, ideological collaboration continued to be condemned in official memory politics, at least until the 1980s.[22]

III. Towards a Self-Critical Memorial Culture: the Central Role of Holocaust Remembrance and Concern for Human Rights

In the 1970s, the consensus narrative that had juxtaposed resistance and collaboration started to erode. Triggered off by a controversy about former members of the *Nasjonal Samling* in the *Storting* and the partial espousal of the Nazi doctrine by the eminent writer Knut Hamsun, many Norwegians became aware of their half-hearted or even uninhibited collaboration during the Second World War. The NBC production »Holocaust«, in particular, turned public attention to the plight of the Norwegian Jews during the war. About 1,100 of the 2,100 Norwegian Jews managed to escape to Sweden, whereas at least 771 were murdered. Due to the co-operation by the police, para-police units and the higher echelons of the administration that had been staffed with many members of the NS, a comparatively high percentage of Norwegian Jews fell victim to the Holocaust[23]. In the course of the 1980s, it also emerged that anti-Semitic policies like the restrictions of access to specific professions like medicine and law (passed in 1940) as well as the enforced registration of Jews in 1942 had been imposed by the Germans

---

22 Lorenz, Deportation, 105, 113–118.
23 Whereas 80 of the Dutch Jewry and 45 per cent the Belgian Jews were murdered, 75 per cent of French Jews managed to escape and hide. See Jacques Semelin, Persécutions et entraides dans la France occupée. Comment 75 % des juifs en France ont échappé à la mort, Paris 2013, III f., 852–855. On Norway, see Katja Happe: Einleitung, in: id. (ed.): Die Verfolgung und Ermordung der europäischen Juden durch das nationalsozialistische Deutschland 1933–1945, Vol. 5, Munich 2012, 27 f., 54; Maerz, Schatten, 149–165, 284; id., Probleme, 275. Different figures in Oskar Mendelsohn: Norwegen, in: W. Benz (ed.): Dimensionen des Völkermords. Die Zahl der jüdischen Opfer des Nationalsozialismus (Munich 1991), 187–197, 187, 196.

but endorsed by Norwegian officials in order to create the semblance of a home grown initiative. In the ensuing debate, Jews complained about Norway's refusal to provide financial support for the return of the deportees. Political prisoners, too, were aghast at the revelations of Norway's willing collaborators that pointed to indigenous roots of anti-Semitism.[24]

It took another fifteen years, however, before the debate about the dispossession of Norwegian Jews in the Second World War ignited another fierce controversy that raised new doubts about the long-standing heroic national memorial narrative. Against the backdrop of debates on plunder and Jewish accounts in Switzerland and Jewish property that had been transferred as gold to Swiss banks, Norway's government established an enquiry commission. Its mission was to trace property that had been seized in the country during the Second World War. In its final report of 1997, the commission equivocally demonstrated that the Norwegian authorities and some citizens had enriched themselves by seizing Jewish property. Although the majority of commission members did not hold Norway's police forces accountable for the plundering and thus denied any obligation for restitution, the minority, consisting of the two Jewish representatives on the commission, demanded some compensation. This conflict reflected a clash of recollections. Whereas the majority of Norwegians did not see the specificity of plundering the Jews, the offspring and representatives of these victims endorsed the view that the dispossession of the Jews was singular. The controversy called the fixation on resistance in Norway's memorial culture into question, at least implicitly. Against the majority vote of the commission, the *Storting* ultimately decided to grant a compensation of 450 million Norwegian crowns. Deputies earmarked some of this fund for Holocaust education that was to prevent or at least restrict anti-Semitic stereotyping. This has also been the mission of the *HL-senter* (Center for Studies of Holocaust and Religious Minorities) that was officially established in 2001. After the millennium, the participation of Norwegian policemen and their commander in Oslo, Knut Rød, in the deportation of the Jews from the Norwegian capital in November 1942 and February 1943, too, once more gave rise to memories of collaboration.[25] On 27 January 2012 (Holocaust Remembrance Day), the rising awareness of Norwegians' participation in the Holocaust finally resulted in Prime

---

24   As an instructive autobiographical source, see Ruth Maier: »Das Leben könnte gut sein«. Tagebücher 1933–1942, ed. by Jan-Erik Vold, Munich 2008.
25   Maerz, Schatten, 303 f.

Minister Jens Stoltenberg's public apology to the Jews for the participation of Norwegians in the deportation of their innocent and helpless compatriots.[26]

Apart from the Jewish victims, some other hitherto neglected groups have gradually been integrated into Norway's official memorial culture. As early as 1980s, members of the *Nasjonal Samling* were given a public voice. Thus, the TV documentary series *I solkorsets tegn* (›In the Sign of the Suncross‹) broadcast in Norway in 1981 included interviews with former members and supporters of the NS. Although some Norwegians conceded some former political collaborators were motivated by patriotic reasons, the majority continued to regard them as undemocratic. As a consequence, most Norwegians demanded to maintain the normative distinction between opposition and the *Holdningskamp*, on the one hand, and the pro-Nazi activities and collaboration of the *Nasjonal Samling*, on the other. Former functionaries and leaders of the Norwegian Nazis were not to be retrospectively endorsed in their wartime self-portrayal as »patriots«.[27]

Moreover, the important role of women in the resistance groups was increasingly acknowledged. Thus, Queen Sonia highlighted their contribution during a celebration on the occasion on the fiftieth anniversary of Norway's liberation in Trondheim on 7 May 1995. On top of that, the plight that former spouses of German soldiers and their offspring had suffered after the Second World War entered Norway's official memory culture. On 1 January 2000, prime minster Kjell Magne Bondevik asked these women and their offspring to pardon Norwegians for the repression and humiliation to which they had been subjected. As early as 1987, the government had allowed Norwegian children of the war to obtain information on

---

26 Pohl, »Eine unbehagliche Geschichte«, 239–242; Maerz, Probleme, 278–280; id., Landesverrat, 62–65; Uffe Østergård: Der Holocaust und europäische Werte, in: Aus Politik und Zeitgeschichte, B 1–2 (2008), 25–31, at 25. On the »Holocaust Remembrance Day, see Harald Schmid: Europäisierung des Auschwitzgedenkens? Zum Aufstieg des 27. Januar als »Holocaustgedenktag« in Europa, in: J. Eckel/C. Moisel (eds.): Universalisierung des Holocaust? Erinnerungskultur und Geschichtspolitik in internationaler Perspektive, Göttingen 2008, 174–202.

27 Fagerland/Nilssen: 81; Claus Bryld: »The Five Accursed Years«. Danish perception and usage of the period of the German Occupation with a wider view to Norway and Sweden, in: Scandinavian Journal of History 32 (2007), 86–115, 104; Maerz, Probleme, 275–277; Maerz, Landesverrat, 57–65; Lenz, »Das ist ein deutsches Problem«, 255, 261–263.

their fathers. The authorities thereby legalised the activities of an association that the sons and daughters of German soldiers had founded in 1986.[28]

Altogether, the turn to a more self-critical, pluralist memorial culture has eroded the post-war national consensus and given rise to a wide scope of more differentiated memories. Thus, Norwegians had by no means universally condemned all German soldiers whom they had met during the occupation. Interviews, in particular, have revealed that some Norwegians distinguished between German soldiers who had been forced to come to Norway and those who had volunteered to join the occupying forces. Similarly, even some former Norwegian members of the Waffen-SS who had returned to their homeland after the end of the war, were pardoned by their neighbours.[29] Whereas the patriotic narrative of resistance had predominated in the public in the first few decades after 1945, more positive and even apologetic memories of accommodation and collaboration had persisted in local communities and small groups like families.[30]

Conversely, patriotic memories of resistance by no means dissolved in the course of the 1980s and 1990s. Yet the tide turned against memories that were geared to the stabilisation of the Norwegian state. Whereas critical voices had been marginalized in the 1970s, more self-critical remembrances were advanced in public discussions. Beyond the dichotomy of resistance and collaboration as well as »heroes« and »traitors«, a more nuanced memorial culture that inter-relates recollections in small-scale communities (like families) and public, official memory culture has emerged. In a similar vein, the recognition of helpless victims like the Jews has complemented, if not replaced sacrificial notions of active resistance. It has also given rise to universalistic narratives that have led Norwegians to fight

---

28   Østergård, Holocaust, 26; Christine Gundermann: Leiden ohne Täter? Deutsch-niederländische Kommunikation über die nationalsozialistischen Verbrechen, in: B. Hofmann/K. Wetzel (eds.): Diktaturüberwindung in Europa. Neue nationale und transnationale Perspektiven, Heidelberg 2010, 132–150, 133; Bjarte Bruland: Norwegen. Wie sich erinnern? Norwegen und der Krieg, in: M. Flacke (ed.): Mythen der Nationen. 1945 – Arena der Erinnerungen, Vol. 1, Mainz 2004, 453–480, 464–471; Lenz, Strengthening, 259. For background information see, the contributions to Ingvill C. Mochmann/Sabine Lee/Barbara Stelzl-Marx (eds.): Children Born of War: Second World War and Beyond (Historical Research, Vol. 34, No. 129/2009); Ericsson/Simonsen (eds.), Children of World War II.

29   Arvid Bryne, Vi sloss for Norge – Frontkjemper og motstandsmann – fiender i krig, venner i fred (Oslo 2007).

30   See Sigurd Sørlie's chapter in this book.

racism, promote human rights as well as democracy and commit themselves to a tolerant civil society and peace. National remembrances have by no means completely vanished in Norway. In fact, they have persisted, albeit in a different guise, and been related to more universal memorial narratives that have been geared to national political aims in Norway – a paradox that merits detailed investigation, also in memorial cultures in countries like Sweden. As in some other European states like Austria, Poland and the Federal Republic of Germany, a »reflexive particularism« has emerged in Norway. It has been characterised by an »ongoing negotiation between variable modes of national belonging and cosmopolitan orientations toward the supranational or pan-European.«[31]

All in all, a gradual shift from patriotic towards a more universalistic narrative has made headway in Norway from the 1970s onwards, though not as a clear sequence and as a linear development. Thus, small-scale memories in local communities as well as national memory cultures continue to co-exist with more universalistic narratives. Nation-states still provide indispensable resources for creating, reconfiguring, disseminating and institutionalising memories. For instance, Norway's national government supports institutions such as schools and museums that strongly influence the prevailing memory culture. Moreover, the Norwegian nation-state still frames the memories of its citizens.[32] As universal human rights have received increasing attention, however, national heroism has receded in favour of more self-critical reappraisals of the plight of the victims of Nazi occupation and Norwegian collaboration. Yet this reorientation has reframed rather than abolished national narratives, establishing a dialectical relationship between denationalisation and renationalisation. Self-reflective memories even continue to coexist with outright nationalist heroism. The success of Thomas Nordseth-Tiller's film »Max Manus« in Norway during 2008 and 2009, for instance, highlights the persistence of this narrative. The film still glorifies the resistance fight of Max

---

31   Daniel Levy/Michael Henlein/Lars Breuer: Reflexive Particularism and Cosmopolitanization: The Reconfiguration of the National, in: Global Networks 11 (2011), 139–159, 139 (quote). More generally on the coalescence of national and cosmopolitan narratives, cf. Daniel Levy/Natan Sznaider: The Holocaust and Memory in the Global Age, Philadelphia 2006, 28, 35, 38, 200; Daniel Levy: Cosmopolitization of Victimhood. Holocaust Memories and the Human Rights Regime, in: A. Weinke/N. Frei (eds.): Toward a New Moral World Order? Menschenrechtspolitik und Völkerrecht seit 1945, Göttingen 2013, 210–218, 211.
32   See Doreen Reinhold's chapter in this volume. More generally, cf. Uhl, Nachkriegsmythos, 193.

Manus and his comrades against the German occupiers. Moreover, a specifically Norwegian pride in a more self-critically reappraisal of the country's past has emerged. In fact, the on-going transformation of its memory culture corresponds to Norway's self-image as a beacon of peace and understanding, as testified by the Oslo Accords of 1993 and 1995 as well as the Nobel Peace Prize that is awarded in the Norwegian capital every year. Not least, the moderate reactions to Anders Breivik's terrorist attacks on 22 July 2011 have served to reinforce Norway's self-image as a peaceful, resilient and civic-minded nation.[33]

As regards historiography, here, too, a price had to be paid for the emergence of a self-critical, pluralist and universalistic memorial culture in Norway. Apart from leveling moral distinctions, the emphasis on Norwegian collaborators might downplay the specific and unique role of German perpetrators. The members of the *Nasjonal Samling* had joined the party in the 1930s in the context of a stable democratic tradition, whereas ardent German Nazis had been influenced by the authoritarian political culture of Imperial Germany and what they perceived as the succession of crises in the Weimar Republic. Historians surely need to uncover hitherto hidden aspects of Norway's recent past and break down the taboos that have impeded or even obstructed processes of memorialisation. At the same time, they have to accentuate the specific historical context in Norway during the Second World War, highlight different roles during the occupation and acknowledge normative distinctions in memorial cultures.[34]

---

33 Lenz, »Das ist ein deutsches Problem«, 264–266; Lenz, Strengthening, 268–275; Reitan: Nazi Camps, 66; Lenz, Widerstand, 67; id.: Erinnerungskultur und Geschichtspolitik – Politische Autorisierung, Hegemoniebildung und Narrationen des Widerstandes in Norwegen, in: C. Fröhlich/H. A. Heinrich (eds.): Geschichtspolitik. Wer sind ihre Akteure, wer ihre Rezipienten?, Stuttgart 2004, 81–94, 93 f.; Bruland: Norwegen, 464–472. For a different interpretation, see Stråth, Geschichtspolitik, 440, 447.

34 Ole Kristian Grimnes: Norwegian Resistance and Postwar Politics, in: Robert Bohn/Jürgen Elvert (eds.): Kriegsende im Norden. Vom heißen zum kalten Krieg, Stuttgart 1995, 173–187, 175, 183–187; Pohl, ›Eine unbehagliche Geschichte‹, 245–247; Katrin Steffen: Der Holocaust in der Geschichte Ostmitteleuropas, in: Anna Kaminsky/Dietmar Müller/Stefan Troebst (eds.): Der Hitler-Stalin-Pakt 1939 in den Erinnerungskulturen der Europäer, Göttingen 2011, 489–517, 515 f.

IV. The European Context

Like the prevalence of a nationalist and affirmative memorial culture in the first few decades following the war, the increasing awareness of the Holocaust has by no means been restricted to Norway. In fact, it has also led to soul-searching all over Western and Central Europe. Thus, the dualistic memory politics of resistance versus collaboration gradually fell asunder in states like France, Italy and Austria in the course of the 1980s and 1990s. Influential politicians in these states came to acknowledge that some of their citizens had sympathised with or even assisted in Nazi policies of repression, persecution, terror and annihilation in these countries.[35] Although under the conditions of occupation, fellow travellers and supporters of the national socialists had participated in Nazi crimes. Politicians of various European states therefore asked Jewish victims for pardon in the 1990s. In 1993, for instance, Austrian Chancellor Franz Vranitzky abandoned the established view that Austrians had been exclusively the first victims of the Third Reich. In fact, he acknowledged guilt and responsibility during his state visit to Israel. In 1995, French President Jacques Chirac conceded that policemen of the Vichy regime had assisted the German occupation authorities in the deportation of Jews.

The turn to a more self-critical universalistic memory is no longer restricted to crimes committed under the Nazi dictatorship, fascist rule or occupation regimes during the Second World War. In fact, it includes citizens that had been repressed and often severely punished after the Second World War, as Prime Minister Kjell Magne Bondevik's appeal to Norwegian children of war to pardon Norwegians for the discrimination and stigmatisation and marginalisation they were subjected to after the Second World War demonstrates.[36]

Universalistic memories overlap with more nationalist ones in states like Norway, and remembrances of the occupation are still disconnected from memories of the mass murder of the Jews. Similarly, the death of Soviet prisoners of war who were forced to work under the command of the Germans in Norway has received

---

35 Oliver Marchart/Vrääth Öhner/Heidemarie Uhl: Holocaust Revisited – Lesarten eines Medienereignisses zwischen globaler Erinnerungskultur und nationaler Vergangenheitsbewältigung, in: Tel Aviver Jahrbuch für deutsche Geschichte 31 (2003), 307–334; Reitan, Nazi Camps, 64, 70.
36 Kåre Olsen: Under the Care of Lebensborn: Norwegian War Children and their Mothers, in: Kjersti Ericsson/Eva Simonsen (eds.): Children of World War II. The Hidden Enemy Legacy, New York 2004, 15–34.

scant attention[37]. Recent investigations have also provided detailed evidence for the transformation of memory cultures in Austria, France, Poland and the Federal Republic of Germany. Universalistic narratives had already started to influence discussions of the Holocaust in the first post-war years, but narratives of heroism met the predominant need to stabilise the formerly occupied European states after the Second World War. Since the 1980s, however, national narratives been gradually transformed by more universalistic notions of victimhood and human rights norms. For example, the debate about atrocities committed by the Polish inhabitants of the village of Jedwabne against their Jewish neighbours in July 1941 sparked off a fierce controversy in Poland in 2000, as the findings of historian Jan Tomasz Gross had called the established narrative of heroic sacrifice into question.[38]

All in all, the mass murder of the Jews has emerged as a universalistic reference point for human rights, democracy, civil society and reconciliation in the western world. Thus, the »Stockholm International Forum on the Holocaust« of January 2000 passed a resolution that emphasised the unique place of the annihilation of Jews in recent European history. In the conference resolution, the assembled European statesmen committed themselves »to remember the victims who perished, respect the survivors still with us, and reaffirm humanity's common aspiration for mutual understanding and justice«. A commitment to openly condemn genocide has unofficially become part of the *acquis communautaire* (the rules of accession to the European Union). On 4 April 2009, the European Parliament even decided to officially and annually commemorate all victims of totalitarian and authoritarian dictatorships on 23 August. This resolution that had been demanded by the new member-states of the EU in East Central Europa has aroused fierce controversies because of its tendency to lump together victims of Nazi, fascist and Communist rule. Nevertheless, it testifies to a strong urge to self-critically evaluate

---

37 Maerz, Schatten, 37f. Robert Bohn: Zwangsarbeiter und Zwangsarbeiterinnen im Reichskommisariat Norwegen, in: Dieter Pohl/Tanja Sebta (eds.): Zwangsarbeit in Hitlers Europa. Besatzung, Arbeit, Folgen, Berlin 2013, 293–300.
38 Daniel Levy/Natan Sznaider: The Institutionalization of Cosmopolitan Morality. The Holocaust and Human Rights, in: Journal of Human Rights 3 (2004), No. 2, 143–157; Uhl: Transformation, 48; Levy/Henlein/Breuer, Particularism, 139, 153; Lenz, Strengthening, 278.

and recognize guilt and responsibility for political crimes as a precondition for reconciliation and European unification.[39]

Yet the relationship between the collective memory of the Holocaust and European identity had been complex and ambivalent. Although memories of the genocide have tied Europeans together, the common antagonism towards Germany rather than high-flying visions had been the most important driving force of Europeanisation in the first few decades after the end of the Second World War. It was only in the 1970s (more than twenty years after the European Convention on Human Rights had been signed) that universalistic memories of the Holocaust became vital components of transnational human rights regimes in Europe. Thus, 21 out of 24 member states of the International Task Force for Holocaust Education, Remembrance and Research that was founded in 1998 following an initiative by Swedish Prime Minister Göran Persson are European. Although national memory frames have persisted in the post-communist states of Eastern Europe as well as among West Europeans, they have increasingly been questioned by external institutions and actors.[40]

---

39 Quote taken from Birgit Schwelling: Auf dem Weg zu europäischen Erinnerungsorten? Gemeinsame und trennende Erinnerungen in Europa, in: B. Majerus et al. (eds.): Nationale Erinnerungsorte hinterfragt. Methodologische Innovationen, vergleichende Annäherungen, transnationale Lektüren, Brussels 2009, 175–188, 183. For detailed accounts, see Jens Kroh: Transnationale Erinnerung. Der Holocaust im Fokus geschichtspolitischer Initiativen, Frankfurt/Main 2006; id.: Europäische Innenpolitik? Die Stockholmer »Holocaust-Konferenz« und die diplomatischen Maßnahmen der »EU der 14« gegen Österreich, in: K. Hammerstein et al. (eds.): Aufarbeitung der Diktatur – Diktat der Aufarbeitung?, Göttingen 2009, 204–214; Jan-Werner Müller: On ›European Memory‹. Some Conceptual and Normative Remarks, in: M. Pakier/B. Stråth (eds.): A European Memory?, 25–37, 31. On the relationship between the debates of human rights and memories of the war and the Holocaust since 1945, see Tom Buchanan: Human Rights, the Memory of War and the Making of a »European« Identity, 1945–75, in: Martin Conway/Kiran Klaus Patel (eds.): Europeanization in the Twentieth Century. Historical Approaches, Houndmills 2010, 151–171; J. Eckel: Utopie der Moral, Kalkül der Macht. Menschenrechte in der globalen Politik seit 1945, in: Archiv für Sozialgeschichte 49 (2009), 437–484, 461, 475.

40 Henning Grunwald: »Nothing more cosmopolitan than the camps?« Holocaust Remembrance and (de-)Europeanization, in: Conway/Patel (eds.): Europeanization, 253–270, 254f., 263, 267; Christoph Cornelißen: Vom Schreiben einer Geschichte Europas im 20. Jahrhundert. Perspektiven und Herausforderungen, in: F. Bösch/M. Sabrow (eds.): ZeitRäume, Potsdam 2013, 65–87, 84; Steffen, Holocaust, 489, 514.

V. Conclusion

As this chapter has demonstrated, memories of the Second World War were contested in Norway immediately after Germany's defeat in May 1945 and the ensuing formation of a coalition government. Yet a broad consensus glorified the Norwegian resistance fighters, whereas the leading functionaries and members of the Norwegian Nazis, the *Nasjonal Samling*, were punished or at least stigmatised and marginalised. At the same time, female members of the resistance movement, too, fell into oblivion. Moreover, the dominant memory politics largely ignored the suffering that spouses of German soldiers and their children had to endure in Norway after 1945.[41] Most importantly, the prevailing narrative downplayed the central role of the Holocaust. From the 1980s onwards, however, the dichotomy of resistance and collaboration broke up in favour of a more pluralistic memorial culture. As has been argued, this turn to a more universalistic narrative was triggered off by the recognition of the plight of »passive«, helpless victims at the expense of the national martyrs. Yet the pluralisation of Norway's memorial culture has tended to blur and underrate important distinctions and differences (for instance, between Germans and Norwegians). More generally, historians are to contribute to a universalistic memorial culture of the Second World War without ignoring specific historical contexts – a tightrope walk that is by no means restricted to accounts of memorialisation in Norway, but also in Europe. Scholars should neither fall into the trap of politically legitimising the European Union nor ignore specific contexts and constellations at the expense of a hurried universalisation of memories. At the same, however, they will have to bear Hannah Arendt's widely known insight in mind that historical objects have to change in order to stay with us in the present.[42]

The relationship between heroic memories that have served to rebuild nations after 1945 and more cosmopolitan narratives is intricate and complex. In Norway, universalistic orientations towards the recent past have emerged within the entrenched national memory culture. Instead of a clear succession, national and more universalistic memories have been intertwined, overlapped and renegotiated since the 1970s. Although exclusionary forms of glorifying the Norwegian resistance movement have receded and the responsibility of Norwegians for the repression and deportation of Jews have been acknowledged, scepticism vis-à-vis

---

41 Susanne Maerz elaborates on the details in her chapter.
42 Hannah Arendt, Vita Activa, Munich 1960, 87 f.

a common European memory still prevails. Yet the contours of a »shared mnemonic inventory« are visible in Norway: a commitment to a multi-perspectival, pluralist memory culture that recognises the recollections of other Europeans. Notwithstanding disagreements about the specific content of memories of the Second World War and life under German occupation, a »particular shared mode of engaging with the past« may pave the way for a memory culture that has to be based on empathy as much as on precise historical knowledge. It is the emergence of cosmopolitan orientations and the concern for the victims rather than a universalistic narrative that has characterised the evolution of Norway's memory culture since the 1980s.[43]

---

43   Levy/Henlein/Breuer, Particularism, 153.

II.
Towards a Universalistic Narrative: the Role of Holocaust Memory

Claudia Lenz
Linking Holocaust Education to Human Rights Education
A Symptom of the Universalisation and Denationalisation of Memory Culture in Norway?

I. Introduction

In this article recent developments in Norwegian public memory culture and memory politics related to World War II and the Holocaust will be explored. The main focus will be on the discourse that accompanied the establishment and opening of two Norwegian institutions, namely, the Center for Studies of Holocaust and Religious Minorities in Oslo, and the Falstad Centre – Memorial and Human Rights Centre. Furthermore, it will be discussed whether the tendency to interpret the Norwegian history related to World War II and the Holocaust within a universalist, human rights oriented framework points to a denationalisation of memory culture and the memory politics related to it.

Why does a Norwegian Foreign Minister attend the official opening of two institutions related to the history of World War II and the Holocaust within a very short period as one of the main speakers? And, how can we interpret his speeches at these events, in which he explicitly acknowledges national guilt and the suffering of those who hitherto had not been regarded as part of the national community during and after the war? What kind of signals does his presence and words convey within the national context, and in which ways are international developments reflected in them?

II. »Discover the Past for the Future«

I want to start the exploration of these questions by highlighting one crucial event within the international context. In 2010, a report bearing the title »Discover the Past for the Future« was published by the Fundamental Rights Agency.[1] This document is an interesting hybrid of »genres«: It is a research report with a strong educational outlook and yet a highly politicised document. The report is the result of a study that had been conducted in several EU member states. The starting point for the study was the question of how the Holocaust can remain a topic of interest and relevance for younger generations. After all, nearly seventy years after the end of the Second World War the Holocaust is less and less part of people's individual experience, which also means it is decreasingly part of family memory and increasingly transmitted by cultural representations. This means that what the cultural scientist Aleida Assmann calls the »communicative memory« about World War II and the Holocaust is about to fade away. It might be replaced by another mode of collective maintenance of historical references: the transmission of historical meaning *exclusively* by means of cultural symbols and practices (communicative memory is also transmitted by cultural media, but constantly connected to and moderated by the direct communication of those who have personal memories of historical events or who were directly affected by their consequences). Assmann calls this »mode« that replaces communicative memory over time »cultural memory«.[2] This is the mode in which coming generations will assume responsibility for the legacy and memory of the Holocaust.

Without affective connections to »living memories«, why should young people still be interested in such historical events? Through focus group interviews with young people visiting memorial sites and interviews with memorial educators and scholars, a research group investigated these questions. The challenge is to find out how young people can relate to and make sense of a historical event that is no longer part of the experience of those they encounter. The suggestion made by the

---

1 The European Union Agency for Fundamental Rights (FRA) is one of the EU's decentralised agencies. These agencies are set up to provide expert advice to the institutions of the EU and its member states on a range of issues. The FRA helps to ensure that the fundamental rights of people living in the EU are protected. Source: European Union Agency for Fundamental Rights: About the FRA, FRA, last access: 7. January 2013, <http://fra.europa.eu/en/about-fra>.
2 Aleida Assmann: Erinnerungsräume. Formen und Wandlungen des kulturellen Gedächtnisses, München 1999.

Fundamental Rights Agency is quite blunt: human rights, as a normative framework and as a value system which is relevant for today's situation, could serve as an interpretative framework for the encounter with Holocaust history and memory. Human rights education could serve as a sort of matchmaker, allowing young people to relate to past experiences in a way that is meaningful to their own lives.

One could ask all kinds of critical questions about this report and its recommendations.[3] I will not delve further into these critiques, but instead focus on the impact of the report, which has been significant. In fact, one could say that »Discover the Past for the Future« puts the issue of linking Holocaust education to human rights education »officially« on the agenda – although it did not present completely new ideas. Still, having been made public by an expert group under the auspices of the FRA, it generated a different kind of attention and political impact in the EU member states. The signal sent out by the report points in the direction of a universalisation of Holocaust education in a double sense:

Broadening the focus when it comes to historical traumatic events from the singularity of the Holocaust to a range of genocides and systematic human rights violations.

Underlining a tendency that Holocaust education already represents within history education: to transcend national frameworks and »patriotic« narratives and replace them with a focus on transnational processes and interdependencies.

I will not go any further in discussing the ramifications of this FRA report and the general tendency to link Holocaust and human rights education to educational practice »on the ground«. Instead, I interpret the report as an intervention in history politics at a transnational level, and will explore history politics and memory culture at a national level – and will use Norway as a case study. Can we observe a shift of memory politics and memory culture related to the Second World War and the Holocaust towards universalist frameworks? If so, where are the links and »relays« between the politics and memory culture? To search for those »relays« in ritualised events in memory culture, in which politicians play a key role, in the various memorial days, the unveiling of monuments and the opening of memorial sites would seem to be obvious examples. In this article, I will focus on two such events, the opening of the Center for Studies of Holocaust and Religious Minorities in Oslo and the opening of the Falstad Centre – Memorial and Human Rights Centre in Ekne, both in the autumn of 2006. Critical attention will be paid to

---

3 In fact, there has been a debate around the report which focused on methodological issues (the validity of the findings) and its recommendations.

two noteworthy speeches by the former Norwegian foreign minister. But before proceeding with this case study, one might ask: What are we talking about when using the concepts of universalism in this context? What qualifies as a universalist historical interpretation and narrative? And, in which way does it relate to national(ist) interpretations and narratives – do they diverge or converge? A first step in exploring this question is a reflection on the semantics. In order to understand the idea of universalism in the context of historical narratives, it us useful to explore the meaning of the concept through its opposite: particularism. The following quote succinctly demonstrates that universalism and particularism pertain to opposing claims regarding the possible outreach or validity of any kind of human order:

> »*Particularism* […] *forms the basis of all theories of international law which assert that true public order is only possible within a homogeneous community.* […] *In contrast, universalism* […] *underlies all positions which assert that truly public order is in principle possible on a global scale.*«[4]

Even if the focus of this quote is international law, it points to the crux of the matter: The opposition between the assumption that any human order is in its validity and outreach limited to homogenous communities, on the one hand, and the assumption that human order can be established validly and effectively on a global scale, on the other. This polarity is highly important in the field of history and memory culture. Is there any alternative to historical narratives always being accounts of »our« past as opposed to »theirs«, built upon contrasting and hostile claims of honour and victory, or, as portrayed in more recent times of suffering and victimhood?

---

4 Armin von Bogdandy/Sergio Dellavalle: Universalism and Particularism as Paradigms of International Law. IILJ Working Paper 2008/3, New York 2008.

III. Universalist versus Patriotic Narratives

The FRA report is very clear in stating that a human rights-based framework could provide a universalist narrative that transcends the quite problematic consequences of nationalism and nationalist memories. But what is a universalist narrative, and what are the distinctive features of a memory culture built around that type of narrative? The basic questions here seem to be:
- Who is the addressee of the narrative?
- Who is the agent of the narrative?

When talking about historical narratives we need to ask: Who is remembered and who is remembering; who is the agent to base future actions on this remembrance?

In the wake of 1945 distinct forms of patriotic narratives about the Second World War emerged in all the countries that had been occupied by Nazi Germany.[5] In these emerging narratives in academic history writing as well as in all channels of memory culture and memory politics, »the nation« – or rather the collective of patriots – served both as the addressee and as the agent. These versions of the past offered post-war societies a highly integrative framework for creating common national virtues in a time of physical and mental recovery from the disasters of the war. But the flip side of the coin was the exclusion of a number of groups that were either branded »un-national« due to their complicity and collaboration with the occupying forces, or who simply were not considered to be an integral part of the national community due to the fact that they were minority groups in society. When the FRA report addressed these problematic aspects of the nationalistic interpretations of the Second World War history in 2010, it contributed to an on-going international trend.

Further evidence of the emergence of the critical discourse on patriotic narratives related to World War II was the exhibition »Myths of the Nations«, which was opened to the public in Berlin in 2004. The exhibition and the subsequent two-volume publication explored memory cultures in a wide range of European countries, Russia and the USA.[6] It constituted a kind of mental stocktaking of

---

5   Monika Flacke: Mythen der Nationen. 1945 – Arena der Erinnerungen. Katalog zur Ausstellung im Deutschen Historischen Museum Berlin, Mainz 2004; Claudia Lenz; Harald Welzer: Opa in Europa. Erste Befunde einer vergleichenden Tradierungsforschung. In: Harald Welzer (Hg.) Krieg der Erinnerung. Krieg der Erinnerungen. Holocaust, Kollaboration und Widerstand im europäischen Gedächtnis. Frankfurt am Main: S. Fischer 2007, S. 7–41.
6   Flacke: Mythen der Nationen.

the narratives and representations of the war, which also partly highlighted some of the »forgotten« or only reluctantly integrated memories. Four years after the Stockholm conference on Holocaust education, which resulted in the foundation of the Task Force on Holocaust Education, the »Myths of the Nations« exhibition still depicted the Holocaust as a rather marginalised part of national memory cultures, while by that juncture the subject was well on its way to becoming incorporated into national memory politics and syllabi across many Western European countries. One reviewer called the publication a step towards the Europeanised master-narrative about the war.[7] In other words, over recent decades, supranational narratives have emerged, which concur with denationalised and universalistic interpretations. It is within this broader context that the FRA report points to human rights education as the possible source of a universalist narrative that would place mankind both as addressee and as agent.

I have far argued that the universalist narrative has emerged alongside a critical discourse highlighting the excluding effects of the patriotic narrative. However, I would still argue that the national or patriotic and the universalist narratives do not necessarily mutually exclude or replace each other, but rather mutually inform each other. New »intermediate« forms are emerging.

In this context, the new significance of the local level as a reference point in memory cultures needs to be considered. Without doubt, local history culture (which experienced an upsurge in interest in the 1970s with many local lay historians starting to generate knowledge and cultural representations about the past, in the form of exhibitions and public presentations) has strongly been influenced by the hitherto established interpretations of the national »master-narrative«.

However, local history can at times take the form of a subversive counter-narrative. Through local history aspects of the wartime experience, which are under-communicated in the patriotic narrative, can be highlighted – but on the whole local history doesn't challenge the overall narrative logic. A case in point: there are many books on and by local resistance heroes in Norway, which readily integrate the national narrative. Stories that shed positive light on the collaboration between Norwegians and Russian partisans, however, represented more of a challenge to the master-narrative of the Cold War period. Thus, local mem-

---

7   Rainer Eckert: Rezension zu: Flacke, Monika (Hrsg.): Mythen der Nationen. 1945 – Arena der Erinnerungen. Katalog zur Ausstellung im Deutschen Historischen Museum Berlin. Mainz 2004, H-Soz-u-Kult, last access: 23. January 2014, <http://hsozkult.geschichte.hu-berlin.de/rezensionen/id=8206>.

ories offer a wide range of »particularities« which tend to be related to but not fully determined by the national master-narrative. This relative openness enables »inscribing« the concrete and particular memory into the abstract and universalist narrative of humanity. As indicated in the FRA report, memorials – which are geographically linked to a local dimension of history – can serve as »mediating spaces« between these two interpretative frameworks. I will later return to this point, exemplifying it with a Norwegian case study.

IV. Holocaust Memory as a Matrix of a Universalist Narrative?

If one historical event has transcended patriotic memories during recent decades, it is the Holocaust. The murder of six million Jews from all across Europe, the way it was master-planned and executed, is supranational by nature. Even if German responsibility for this crime undoubtedly exceeds that of any other country, recent years have seen a process in which European societies have confronted and tried to come to grips with issues of anti-Semitism, collaboration in the deportation of Jews from their respective countries and a lack of interest in the fate of the Jews after 1945. This development has created a historical discourse and an interpretative framework that seems hard to reconcile with traditional »patriotic memories« that focus on heroes and villains.

Daniel Levy and Natan Sznaider see a new »cosmopolitan« memory culture emerging – with the Holocaust as its nexus – that transcends the national. Their analysis is based on the observation that the globalised Holocaust memory is a *mediated* memory. This memory is constructed around cultural products (films like »Schindler's List« or books like »The Diary of Anne Frank«) that circulate internationally and allow people in a broad variety of contexts to relate to and identify with the morality that addresses good and evil as issues *mankind* has to face at all times and in all places. The price for this, as postulated by Levy and Sznaider, is the decontextualisation and dislocation of memory. The icons of memory no longer point to a specific time or a place where it happened but to a universal message. The motto »never again« points to a future, in which »a Holocaust« could happen at any time and everywhere, and where everyone is held responsible to prevent this from happening. The Holocaust is no longer about the

Jews being exterminated by the Germans; rather, it is about human beings and the most extreme violation of human rights.[8]

The implicit promise of the universalisation of Holocaust memory is that we are going to overcome the pitfalls of patriotic memory; we are going to prevail over its exclusionary effects. By focusing on mankind, we can include all kinds of injustice, and not only injustices against ourselves. But, this endeavour can be superficial and hollow, and even without consequence. It could potentially be instrumentalised for other purposes. In other words, the on-going universalisation of the Holocaust memory and the formation of a cosmopolitan identity is a double-edged sword.

Before moving on to my case study, I wish to introduce one more theoretical concept, which is extremely useful when analysing the ramifications of the emerging universalist narrative about the Second World War. As I have indicated, not only interpretations concerning the past, but also expectations and visions regarding a possible and desirable future are changing with this shift from the nation-state to »mankind« as object of historical accounts. Reinhart Koselleck has coined the conceptual pair of »realm of experience« (*Erfahrungsraum*) and »horizon of expectation« (*Erwartungshorizont*).[9] If applied to the topic of this article, one could say that national, nationalised or patriotic memory patterns have framed or have constituted a specific horizon of expectation. In the immediate post-war years national narratives of heroism, suffering and victory served as a focal point for positive national identity and as a constitutive cultural element in times of reconstruction. In the Norwegian case, the patriotic narrative was linked to the expectation of progress and to the notion of a well-deserved share in the national wealth. In this way, it was linked to the legitimisation of the welfare state.

Cosmopolitan memory, in contrast, starts with a negative identification, originating in the idea of *Zivilisationsbruch*, the breakdown of civilisation. One of the first to express this idea and link it to education was Theodor Adorno. After witnessing the horrors of the Holocaust which took place in the very cradle of enlightenment and master-minded and executed by people who were proud of their education and cultivated manners (*Bildungsbürger*), he was of the opinion that nothing in this enlightened culture could serve as a guarantee against barba-

---

8 Daniel Levy/Natan Sznaider: The Holocaust and Memory in the Global Age, Philadelphia 2006.
9 Reinhart Koselleck: »Erfahrungsraum« und »Erwartungshorizont« – zwei historische Kategorien, in: R. Koselleck: Vergangene Zukunft. Zur Semantik geschichtlicher Zeiten, Frankfurt am Main 1989, 349–375.

rism. By learning from the past in order to prevent such horrors ever happening again, we come to realise that we cannot build on tradition but need to start from the experience of a radical rupture. Only radical doubt and scepticism towards *positive* identifications (which lead to the violent and potential eliminatory exclusion of the other) can fulfil the credo that »Auschwitz should not repeat itself« (»*dass Auschwitz sich nicht wiederhole*«). It constitutes a negative reference point for all historical meaning.[10]

Still, there is a kind of future project emerging from it. If the Holocaust reveals the potential of human evil, which is a result or a consequence of the breakdown of the regulating force of critical thinking and self-reflection, then learning from the Holocaust implies the need to create a regulatory mechanism, a distance between the subject and its ambitions, ideas and identifications. Consequently, a universalist narrative about the Holocaust cannot allow itself to offer any non-ambivalent identification with any collective other than mankind itself, and even here the consideration of the potential of evil in human nature needs to be built in as a security mechanism. The universalist claim for a self-reflective, radically critical position towards any construction or re-enforcement of closed and separatist identitarian discourse seems to be the core of the universalist memory, which places humanity itself and not the nation-state or other particular entities as the subject of remembrance. That said, this does not imply that the narratives and pedagogic strategies that try to »teach« the lessons of the Holocaust – including those based on human rights – are free from the pitfalls of the identitarian discourse. I will return to this point in the forthcoming paragraphs while discussing my case study.

V. Case Study –
Nationalising the Universalist Memory in Norway

Is Norway, then, taking the road of a denationalised, universalist memory with respect to the Holocaust? For sure we have seen the widespread introduction and institutionalisation of Holocaust remembrance and Holocaust education. The establishment of the Center for Studies of Holocaust and Religious Minorities (*HL-senter*) in 2006 and the annual celebration of the Holocaust Remembrance

---

10 Adorno, Theodor W.: Erziehung nach Auschwitz. In: T. W. Adorno: Erziehung zur Mündigkeit. Vorträge und Gespräche mit Hellmut Becker 1959–1969, Frankfurt am Main 1971, 88–104.

Day are symbols of this development. But, in which way is the Holocaust conveyed and taught? Where can we position Holocaust education and Holocaust remembrance in Norway in that expanse between particularist and universalist memory?

My case study is based on events in 2006, when two Norwegian institutions dealing with the legacy of the Second World War and the Holocaust were established. The *HL-senter* was opened on 24 August 2006 in Oslo, followed by the Falstad Memorial and Human Rights Centre on 6 October 2006 in Ekne (Mid-Norway). The official speeches given during the opening ceremonies on both sites furnish highly interesting empirical data in the context of this article, since these speeches indicate how both these newly opened institutions were perceived within official memory politics at that juncture. In this article, I will concentrate on three separate speeches which the former Foreign Minister Jonas Gahr Støre gave at the opening ceremonies in Oslo and at Falstad.[11]

First, however, I wish to make some remarks on the establishment of these two institutions and their stated objectives to link past and present. The establishment of the HL-senter is a consequence of the political restitution process regarding Jewish property that had been confiscated by the Norwegian state in 1942, as part of its persecution of Norwegian Jews and its efforts to ensure their »economic liquidation«.[12] The Centre's mandate combines information, education and research related to the Holocaust and to contemporary issues:

> »*The Norwegian chapter in the history of the Holocaust plays a key role in research and educational activities at the Center. The Norwegian story is placed in a wider European context. Research at the Center covers historical and contemporary anti-Semitism as well as studies of genocide and violations of human rights. The Center also focuses on the historical and current situation of Norwegian minorities and their roles within a multi-cultural society.*«[13]

---

11 Opening speech at the *HL-Senter*, 24 August 2006; speech at the inauguration of the memorial in the Falstad forest and the opening speech at the Falstad Centre, both on 7 October 2006.
12 See: The Reisel/Bruland Report on the Confiscation of Jewish property in Norway during World War II (June 1997).
13 *HL-senter*: About the Center, HL-senteret, last access: 4 January 2013, <http://www.hlsenteret.no/english/about/index.html>.

It is interesting to note that the scope of issues is not primarily directed *outwards*, as in the broader studies of genocide[14], but *inwards*, linking the focus on the fate of the Norwegian Jews to the situation of minorities in Norway today. This opens the way for self-critical reflection on the past and present.

The Falstad Centre has a somewhat different mandate. It is a memorial site housing a human rights centre, situated on the premises of a former concentration camp. The Centre has, of course, a national mission, but with a very strong local focus. The way the Centre connects the local with the national can be seen in how it illuminates a particular »blind spot«: the fate of Russian and Yugoslavian prisoners of war, an issue which had been an under-communicated aspect of the history of the German occupation in Norway until the beginning of the 2000s. But when it came to a contemporary topic, the interpretation of the human rights orientation caused a fierce struggle about the power of definition. Should the building's pre- and post-war history – it was a home for so-called difficult children – be included in this critical reflection, given that severe abuses of these children have been documented? Wouldn't this be a »natural« human rights issue to address in this setting? The memorial was also meant to include this aspect of local history in the permanent exhibition, but a strong coalition uniting politicians and former concentration camp prisoners managed to prevent this. This conflict reveals the kind of power struggle that emerges when the universalist framework is linked to national and local history. The concentration camp survivors felt it would devalue their sufferings were they presented alongside the sufferings of deviant children – even if under the heading of human rights abuses.

In my next step, I will examine the public addresses by Gahr Støre with a special focus on which of the narrative frameworks are included, how they manifest themselves and if there is any dominating narrative present.

The opening of the *HL-senter* might seem at first sight to represent quite a challenge to a representative of the Norwegian government. How could the aspect of Norwegian co-responsibility for and involvement in the persecution, deportation and murder of 772 Norwegian Jews be acknowledged and yet integrated into a discourse of memory politics that offers positive identification? Gahr Støre managed to defuse this tension by linking the acknowledgment of this »dark chapter« in Norwegian history to the moral legitimisation of contemporary Norwegian foreign policy. Above all else, however, he needed to find an expression for the Norwegian involvement in the Holocaust:

14 Even if academic work at the Center also covers the field of genocide studies.

»*The Holocaust was no natural disaster. It was an atrocity perpetrated by people. And its horrors were perpetrated in our country as well, by ordinary people with ordinary lives. [...] This happened under German occupation. But the people who deported the Jews, who drew up the lists, who kept them in line, and who drove them to the quayside – they were all Norwegians. [...] And these were not isolated deeds. They arose from motives found at a deeper level – in the people themselves, in the culture, in history, in the spirit of the time.*«[15]

The term »ordinary people« seems to allude to the international academic discourse on Holocaust perpetrators, notably Christopher Browning's concept of »ordinary men«.[16] This choice of expression shows that he sees the responsibility for the Holocaust in Norway as not limited to a small elite of fanatic Norwegian Nazis who collaborated with the German occupier, but extends to »ordinary Norwegians«. At the same time he creates a distance between these crimes and the audience by pointing to the »spirit of the time«. So, is there any legacy to concern ourselves about if the »spirit of our time« is completely different? Yes, because the contemporary spirit which Gahr Støre formulates and represents is exactly one that acknowledges and assumes responsibility for the crimes of the past. And evidence for this spirit is, according to Gahr Støre, to be found in Norwegian foreign policy:

»*The currents that led to the Holocaust have not gone away. They raise their heads and find expression; they rise up in new forms and in new places. New place names have been added to a dark list: Srebrenica, Rwanda, Darfur. [...]A head of state has publicly denied that the Holocaust took place. Minorities are openly discriminated against and persecuted – sometimes to death. Behind the scenes, prejudices are growing that will find expression in the public arena. [...] It is in these grey zones that the fight must be fought – against anti-Semitism, against all ideologies that exclude groups of people and spread hatred.*«[17]

15   Jonas Gahr Støre: Opening Ceremony – The Center for Studies of Holocaust and Religious Minorities, regjeringen.no, last access: 10 December 2013, <http://www.regjeringen.no/en/archive/Stoltenbergs-2nd-Government/Ministry-of-Foreign-Affairs/taler-og-artikler/2006/opening-ceremony---the-center-for-studie.html?id=420864>.
16   Christopher Browning: Ordinary Men. Reserve Police Battalion 101 and the Final Solution in Poland, New York 1992.
17   Støre, Opening ceremony speech.

Here, it seems that the distance from Auschwitz to Srebrenica and Darfur is very short and the bridge leading from one point to the other is the subject of Norwegian responsibility. Having learned from one's own past implies taking responsibility and ensuring that racist ideologies do not lead to the persecution of minorities and genocides elsewhere. Here, we find almost the ideal type of a universalist interpretation of the past. Yet it is not accompanied by denationalisation of the historical-political discourse. Quite the opposite: we are reminded of the idea of Norway being a moral superpower in the global context. Having come to terms with the darker sides in one's own national history provides moral legitimacy and leverage during international conflict resolution. This brings to mind Elazar Barkan description of how the acknowledgement of historical guilt has become a kind of admission ticket into the good society of nations that can make political claims on the basis of their moral integrity.[18] How, then, did the foreign minister link past, present and future some weeks later, at the opening of the Falstad Centre?

VI. From Falstad to the Balkans – Local War Memories and a Foreign Policy Narrative

In both his speeches at the Falstad Centre, Jonas Gahr Støre once again links the past, which is commemorated at that site, to current Norwegian foreign policy. Here, however, the historical point of reference is not (primarily) the Holocaust but the fate of the prisoners of war, primarily those from the former Yugoslavia. The following excerpt from his speech at the unveiling of a memorial for murdered Yugoslavs displays the narrative operations that build a bridge between local war histories, on the one side, and national foreign policy, on the other:

> »*The Yugoslav POWs in Norway underwent extraordinary suffering. But many of them received help from Norwegian citizens – not least here in this area – and from neighbours, too, and a close friendship developed between the POWs and the Norwegians who helped them. [...] This was the seed for Norwegian-Yugoslavian bonds of friendship and city twinning. Many of these bonds of friendship are still active. Close and personal relations have developed among people in Norway and the Western Balkans. There is also close contact between the*

---

18 Elazar Barkan: The Guilt of Nations. Restitution and Negotiating Historical Injustices, New York 2002.

partnered cities and regular visits take place to the twin cities. [...] These tight bonds contributed to the establishment of a close friendship between Norway and Yugoslavia. [...] This has continued with those countries that now form the Western Balkans. The Norwegian government attaches great importance to the good relationship with these countries – and history counts as a dimension of its own in the humanitarian engagement we still have in this region.«[19]

Gahr Støre here presents a narrative that spans from the support of POWs by the local community and the positive personal relationships that resulted thereof, to the good Norwegian-Yugoslavian relations during the Tito era and to the Norwegian humanitarian engagement in the emerging nation-states after the breakup of Yugoslavia. He elegantly links local history and »big politics« in order to construct a historical continuity transcending ruptures. Despite radical changes in the political systems and the geo-political landscape, continuity is found in the good relations, based on Norwegian solidarity. But, as in Oslo, Gahr Støre in his opening ceremony speech acknowledges the shades of grey and darker spots in the historical image:

»Cruelty and brutality are not limited to nationality, ethnicity, religion, gender or age. The so-called Serb camps in northern Norway remind us of that. The camp guards were Norwegian. Humans were humiliated and tortured. The death rates were among the highest among the prison camps in Norway. [...] And we have to remind each other about this. It happened during an occupation by Nazi Germany. But Norwegians were not passive. Norwegians were eager and skilful at finding and expelling Norwegian Jews during the war. And there were Norwegians among the workforce here at Falstad.«[20]

Some paragraphs later, this acknowledgement of historical national guilt is transformed into praise for contemporary national responsibility:

---

19   Jonas Gahr Støre: Innvielse av minnestein med navn på henrettede jugoslaviske fanger [translation by the author], regjeringen.no, last access: 1 December 2013, <http://www.regjeringen.no/nb/dokumentarkiv/stoltenberg-ii/ud/taler-og-artikler/2006/innvielse-av-minnestein-med-navn-pa-henr.html?id=273549>.
20   Jonas Gahr Støre: Åpning av Falstadsenteret [translation by the author], regjeringen.no, last access: 23 January 2014, <http://www.regjeringen.no/nb/dokumentarkiv/stoltenberg-ii/ud/taler-og-artikler/2006/apning-av-falstadsenteret.html?id=273548>.

»*International and national standards and guarantees of the rule of law have been developed over a long time to protect against haphazard treatment and to protect human lives, health and dignity, regardless of the abhorrent deeds a person might be suspected of. [...] The Norwegian government is therefore still in pursuit of those who encourage atrocities and demand that they be held responsible. Many of those responsible for the crimes at Srebrenica and in Rwanda have been persecuted. Many have been imprisoned and are serving their sentences. [...] Norway, together with many other countries, has contributed to this.*«[21]

And finally, this praise, which undoubtedly reinforces a strongly national frame of reference – even if the authority of *international* juridical instruments invariably diminishes full national sovereignty – is followed by a quote that takes the full step into the universalistic framework:

»*Today, we have some instruments of utmost importance: Universal human rights and international humanitarian law. These constitute a common, basic protection of human integrity and dignity. They stand like a shield between civilisation and barbarism.*«[22]

At this point, Gahr Støre's line of argumentation is the same as it had been in his opening speech at the *HL-senter* in Oslo: The involvement of the Norwegian government in the international persecution of crimes against humanity is neither based on nor legitimised by the absence of responsibility for such crimes in Norway's recent history. Quite the opposite: the acknowledgement and the process of coming to terms with this responsibility is regarded as the basis for a moral integrity that allows Norway to insist that other countries elsewhere in the world do likewise. This in itself could still form the basis for an arrogant neo-colonialist model, were it not for the call for supranational institutions to safeguard human rights and enforce humanitarian law – which, as a matter of fact, would diminish full national sovereignty. The lesson learned here seems to be an insight into the need for a regulatory mechanism that would deny the nation-state the ability to exercise unlimited power over human beings.

One last aspect of the foreign minister's speech is remarkable in this context. He systematically addresses »difficult« aspects of the past, naming the silenced

21 Ibid.
22 Ibid.

layer of the history of the Falstad building and acknowledging the suffering of the victims of cruel treatment there during the periods before and after Falstad was used as a concentration camp:

> »Many people associate Falstad with powerful symbols. This includes those who experienced a stay here when the buildings housed an institution for ›deviant boys‹ as they were called back then. For this reason, a representative from the ›Stiftelsen for Tapere‹[23] is present today. [...] I remember that I visited Falstad when it was being renovated. I could see boys' drawings on the walls. These spoke to us, too.«[24]

Gahr Støre thus pleads for the integration of the different layers of history, and the acknowledgement of various forms of suffering – without placing them in a hierarchy. As mentioned previously, the presentation of this aspect of Falstad's history had been prevented by fierce protests by the Second World War veterans. Where Gahr Støre saw human suffering, they feared relativisation and the diminishing of the uniqueness of their suffering in the name of national defence and resistance.

In summing up the analysis of his public speeches on both memorial sites, it can be said that Gahr Støre covers a broad spectrum of the rhetoric of memory politics by linking local, national and inter- and transnational frames of reference. Interestingly, these seem to fit into the same rationale for Norwegian foreign policy, in its constructed humanitarian continuity throughout the whole post-war era until today. Remarkably, Gahr Støre argued in both Centres that this positive national self-image of humanitarian engagement is not weakened, but strengthened, by acknowledging historical guilt.

VII. Conclusion

The memory of the Second World War and the Holocaust, including education at memorials and museums, has absorbed international perspectives and outlooks, and is compatible with a universalist and human rights oriented framework. Yet simultaneously it still serves as a strong building block of national identity. Rather

---

23   Translation: »Association for Losers« – a focus group for, among others, former inmates of the institution.
24   Støre, Åpning av Falstadsenteret.

than mere denationalisation, one might observe the interplay of de- and renationalisation in memory culture and memory politics. Perhaps the best way to describe the shift towards a universalist framework would be to call it a process of »modernisation« of the national self-image and self-interpretation in a globalised world. With respect to the teaching of history, this means a shift away from the traditional notion of educating patriots and obedient subjects. A modernised education project – especially history teaching – in a democratic society needs to prepare young people for life not alone within a nation-state but also in a globalised world. Perhaps, the programmatic speeches by Gahr Støre point to this interplay between national realities and transnational and globalised ones. Can the universalist orientation towards humanity and the indivisible rights of every human being be reconciled with the particularist orientations and interests of the nation-state?

I will finish this essay with a somewhat sceptical outlook by referring to Adorno once again: The inclusion of Holocaust memory in the national narrative in itself is insufficient if it is not connected to a self-reflective attitude, which is prepared to confront its blind spots even in the future. All over Europe, impacted by the on-going economic crisis, the tendency towards a re-enforcement of nationalistic orientations can be observed, including in the field of history politics, memory culture and history education. In some countries, such as Hungary, this has led to a more or less blunt rejection to face the dark sides and grey zones of its national history, favouring heroic and even military patriotic narratives. More complex are the cases of Western European countries like the Netherlands, in which a universalist orientation towards history and linked to the idea of »Western« liberal values, has become a building block in a nationalist, right-wing populist rhetoric. Here, the interpretation of these values serves as a means to position and regard minorities, especially Muslims, as outsiders and even as a threat to the national community.[25] If universalistic frameworks of historical narratives fail to build in a mechanism for reflection, they might just become another type of master narrative, contributing to »othering« and cultural domination. Given this background, the path from patriotic to universalist narratives should not be taken for granted as a one-way process, nor be simply seen as a story of progress.

---

25 See also the chapter by Ilse Raaijmakers in this volume.

Jon Reitan
The Holocaust: Guilt and Apology in Norwegian Historical Culture

I. Introduction

On International Holocaust Remembrance Day in 2012, the Norwegian Prime Minister Jens Stoltenberg (Labour Party) characterized the deportations of Norwegian Jews as »the voyage of shame«. He continued: »Without taking responsibility away from the Nazis, it is about time to face the fact that Norwegian policemen and other Norwegians participated in arresting and deporting Norwegian Jews. Today, I find it necessary to express our deepest apologies for the fact that this could happen on Norwegian soil.«[1]

Commemorating the deportations of 70 years ago, the Norwegian police authorities publicly apologised on 26 November 2012 for having taken part in the arrests of the Jews in Norway. In a statement, the Head of the Police Directorate, Odd Humlegård, stated: »On behalf of the Norwegian police and those who were involved in the deportations of Norwegian Jews to concentration camps, I would like to apologise.« The leader of Oslo's Jewish community, Ervin Kohn, responded positively to this apology, but stressed at the same time the importance of taking contemporary acts of anti-Semitism in Norway seriously.[2]

Since the 2012 anniversary, public discussions of Norwegian guilt, shame and co-responsibility have continued – relating among other matters to the involvement of the Norwegian State Railways and sections of the Norwegian state bureaucracy. Furthermore, apologies for the deeply regrettable involvement of the Norwegian police were repeated on a political level on Holocaust Remembrance Day in 2013, this time by the Minister of Justice and Public Security, Grete Faremo

---

1 Jens Stoltenberg: Tale ved minnemarkeringen på Holocaustdagen [translation by the author], regjeringen.no, last access: 23 January 2014, <http://www.regjeringen.no/nb/dokumentarkiv/stoltenberg-ii/smk/taler-og-artikler/2012/minnemarkering-pa-holocaustdagen.html?id=670621>.
2 Dagsavisen: Historisk unnskyldning [translation by the author], dagsavisen.no, last access: 16 December 2013, <http://www.dagsavisen.no/samfunn/historisk-unnskyldning/>.

(Labour Party).³ In brief, it seems that a discourse on guilt constitutes an important factor in the shaping of Holocaust consciousness in contemporary Norway.

In this chapter, I wish to discuss the genesis of these cultural and political trends. To what extent might the public apologies from the Norwegian authorities reflect longer-term developments and patterns in the national historical culture? And, to what extent have external forces and transnational processes shaped this culture of regret? My working hypotheses will be that the current wave of Norwegian expressions of regret and apologies is primarily a reflection of the latter, but that it cannot be separated from specific national developments. At the outset, I would like to stress that this article reflects a work in progress, as part of an on-going PhD study of the cultural afterlife of the Holocaust in the Norwegian public sphere.⁴

In the programme folder of the Oslo conference, which initiated the making of this anthology, it was argued that the official speech by the Norwegian Prime Minister on 27 January 2012 represented a paradigmatic shift from a patriotic to a universal narrative, in which the Holocaust gradually has gained a pivotal cultural and political function in Norway. This is a pattern that can be traced and identified in large parts of the global community. Saul Friedländer writes that the presence of the Holocaust since the end of the Cold War »resembles that of some sort of lava rising ever closer to the surface and blazoned by ever stronger eruptions«.⁵

It is not hard to find empirical examples of such eruptive movements and incidents. As I write, Paraguay is inaugurating its first national Jewish Museum with a separate Holocaust Studies Center.⁶ Over the last two decades, a vast number of Holocaust museums, monuments, memorial sites and research centres have been established around the world. Holocaust remembrance has become a major

---

3   Grete Faremo: Tale av justis- og beredskapsminister Grete Faremo på den internasjonale Holocaustdagen 2013 ved minnesmerket over deporterte norske jøder på Akershuskaia i Oslo, regjeringen.no, last access: 16 December 2013, <http://www.regjeringen.no/nb/dokumentarkiv/stoltenberg-ii/jd-2/taler-og-artikler/2013/den-internasjonale-holocaustdagen-2013.html?id=713399>.
4   My theoretical framework for this article and my PhD thesis is inspired by the theories of history didactics and historical culture, developed by Klas-G. Karlsson.
5   Saul Friedländer: History, Memory and the Historian: Dilemmas and Responsibilities, in: New German Critique, No. 80 (2000), 6–7.
6   IHRA: Jewish Museum opens in Paraguay, holocaustremembrance.com, last access: 17 December 2013, <http://www.holocaustremembrance.com/media-room/news-archive/jewish-museum-opens-paraguay>.

political issue, at the highest possible national and transnational levels. This development has been accompanied by an intensive scholarly and educational examination of the genocide of European Jewry. Given that I completed lower secondary school in 1989, I belong to that last generation of Norwegian school pupils that did not travel in great numbers to Auschwitz. Twenty years later, the number of visitors to the Auschwitz-Birkenau Memorial Museum reached a peak, exceeding 1.3 million people, of whom approximately 820,000 were pupils and students.[7] In that intervening period, former Nazis, collaborators and even Holocaust deniers were put on trial; meanwhile, public attention and interest towards survivors led Anette Wieviorka to label the period »the era of the witness«.[8]

These various trends and developments are all crucial in both framing and understanding the speech by our Prime Minister on Holocaust Remembrance Day in 2012. In the following pages, I will pay particular attention to one network, which in some respects reflects a transcending of geographical, political, intellectual and cultural levels in recent years.

II. Norway and the International Holocaust Remembrance Alliance (IHRA)

On 7 May 1998, the Swedish Prime Minister, Göran Persson, invited US President Bill Clinton and British Prime Minister Tony Blair to Stockholm for »a meeting on the Holocaust«, together with diplomats and historians who were engaged in the already on-going Holocaust restitution and compensation processes in the international community. Even though isolated Swedish incidents led Persson to establish the Living History Forum in Stockholm in 1997, his ambitions at the time stretched far beyond the borders of the former »bystander« state – targeting a binding, transnational co-operation on governmental level. It was within this framework that the so-called Task Force for International Cooperation on Holocaust Education, Remembrance and Research (ITF) was conceived and created in Washington, D.C. in 1999. One of the academic experts involved in the process, Stuart Eizenstaat, wrote about the historical character and implications of

---

7   Memorial and Museum Auschwitz-Birkenau: The attendance record – 1.3 million visitors at Auschwitz Memorial in 2009, Auschwitz.org, last access: 16 December 2013, <http://en.auschwitz.org/m/index.php?option=com_content&task=view&id=728&Itemid=8>.
8   Anette Wieviorka: The Era of the Witness, Ithaca 2006.

this gathering in the American capital: »For the first time, heads of government agreed to co-operate directly with other countries, through diplomatic and other channels, to strengthen Holocaust education efforts on both sides of the Atlantic and beyond.«[9]

Over 15 years, the International Holocaust Remembrance Alliance or the IHRA (the institution changed its name to the IHRA in 2012) has grown rapidly into a global institution with 31 member states.[10] Besides member and so-called observer countries, the IHRA has several affiliated transnational organisations, such as the European Union, the European Council, the United Nations, the OSCE and the Conference on Jewish Material Claims Against Germany. Within the IHRA, governmental representatives and academics from Non-governmental organisations annually meet to discuss and promote research, education and commemoration of the Holocaust within the global community.

One of the milestones in the short history of this institution was the Stockholm International Forum on the Holocaust in January 2000. Sixteen countries were represented at the first conference (of a total of four consecutive conferences 2000–2004), which concluded with the launching of an official charter: the Stockholm Declaration. In this document, consisting of eight articles, one binding principle stands out as fundamental and formative to the work and ideology of the IHRA, as formulated by the Swedish hosts in 2000:

»Today, we know that the Swedish authorities failed in the performance of their duty during the Second World War. The Swedish government deeply regrets that we have to make such an observation. The moral and political responsibility for what Swedish society did – or failed to do – during the war will always be with us.«[11]

In official IHRA documents we will find several other examples of the importance of this ethical standard, for instance related to membership criteria and founding principles for research and educational activities within member countries:

---

9   Aleida Assmann: The Holocaust – a Global Memory? Extensions and Limits of a New Memory Community, in Aleida Assmann/Sebastian Conrad (eds.) Memory in a Global Age. Discourses, Practices and Trajectories, Basingstoke 2010, 102.
10 IHRA: About us, holocaustremembrance.com, last access: 23 January 2014, <http://www.holocaustremembrance.com/about-us>.
11 Göran Persson: Opening Address, Stockholm International Forum, last access: 14 July 2014, <http://www.d.dccam.org/Projects/Affinity/SIF/DATA/2000/page900.html>.

»Another basic principle developed over the last ten years is the demand made on all member governments to examine their own past history regarding actions or inaction during the Holocaust. It can be said without exaggeration that nobody comes out clean in considering their past, and that without social and collective self-criticism it would be hypocritical to indulge in public declarations and statements decrying the Holocaust. Governments that are not willing to engage seriously in this self-examination cannot become members of the ITF.«[12]

»Nobody comes out clean in considering their past.« According to Tony Judt, this kind of critical self-examination, set against a background of negative memories, injustice, shame and fatal collaboration with Nazi Germany, has, in practice, functioned as an »entry ticket« into the integrated European community.[13] In these processes, the IHRA and its affiliated organisations have arguably had a critical impact. First and foremost, they have in parallel managed to establish new forms of transnational infrastructures that have gradually made it possible to coordinate and strengthen educational and political agendas across geographical borders. One of the most important arenas for this work is the annual International Holocaust Remembrance Day on 27 January, the date marking the liberation of Auschwitz-Birkenau. All member countries of the IHRA have committed themselves to officially celebrate this particular remembrance day. In 2005, in close co-operation with the IHRA, 27 January was also inaugurated as an official day of commemoration, both by the European Parliament in Brussels, and the United Nations in New York.

To what extent has the IHRA contributed in standardising a kind of international morality, based on guilt and collaboration, regarding the memory of the Holocaust?[14] It is difficult to trace these developments exclusively to the IHRA, partly because the same issues were at stake prior to the organisation's establishment in the 1990s, during the international restitutions for the losses of Holocaust victims. It is also evident that a global discourse on guilt not only concerns the history of the Holocaust, but also other historical episodes of injustice. The sheer

---

12 History of the ITF, Holocaust Task Force, last access: 28 April 2014 <http://www.holocausttaskforce.org/about-the-itf/history-of-the-itf.html>.
13 Tony Judt: Post-War. A History of Europe since 1945, London 2010.
14 See, for instance, Helmut Dubiel: The Remembrance of the Holocaust as a Catalyst for a Transnational Ethic?, in: New German Critique, No. 90 (2003), 59–70. See also: Assmann/Conrad.

number of restitution processes since the end of the Cold War marks, according to Elazar Barkan, a global trend labelled »the guilt of nations«:

> »*This universe is studded with abundant contradictions but increasingly subscribes to a shared political culture, which pays greater attention to history as a formative political force [...] the need for restitution to past victims has become a major part of national politics and international diplomacy.*«[15]

Still, it seems evident that the IHRA network, for instance, through its membership criteria and infrastructures, represents an arena where shared values and memories can be communicated. Belgium, for example, actively used its IHRA chairmanship in 2012 to express an official apology for its participation in implementing the genocide of European Jewry. Under the heading »IHRA Chair Condemns anti-Semitic Imagery at the Aalst, Carnival«, Belgium made the following official statement in February 2012:

> *The Belgian Chair of the IHRA is deeply shocked by the parade featuring a fake Nazi railcar during the Aalst Carnival. The representation of a float with ›officers‹ drinking champagne and stereotyping a Jewish victim is a despicable act and an insult to the memory of the victims of the Holocaust. Especially during the year of its chairmanship of the International Holocaust Remembrance Alliance, when Belgium has recognised the state's responsibility in the deportation of its Jewish citizens by the Nazi occupiers and their collaborators, the Holocaust must not be trivialised for the purposes of a local political situation.*«[16]

In what ways can we identify similar political and cultural patterns in Norwegian historical culture? Norway became a formal member of the IHRA in 2003 in Washington, D.C., and held the chair of the organisation in 2009 and 2010, arranging two conferences and meetings in Oslo and Trondheim, respectively. The Norwegian delegation to the IHRA is led by representatives from the Ministry of Foreign Affairs.

---

15 Elazar Barkan, The Guilt of Nations. Restitution and Negotiating Historical Injustices, London and Baltimore: The John Hopkins University Press, 2000, foreword.
16 IHRA Chair Condemns Antisemtic Imagery at the Aalst Carnival, holocaust remembrance.com, last access: 14 July 2014, <https://www.holocaustremembrance.com/media-room/news-archive/ihra-chair-condemns-antisemitic-imagery-aalst-carnival-0>.

From my perspective, there are some interesting links between the speech by our Prime Minister in 2012, the decade-long Norwegian membership of the IHRA and the multitude of ethical imperatives nurtured and developed within this global Holocaust memory community. When Norway applied for membership of the IHRA prior to the meeting in Washington, D.C. in 2003, the critical Norwegian self-examination, as it was so thoroughly communicated and debated in the public eye during the national restitution processes in the late 1990s, had an important position and function. And when Norway chose to seek the chair of the organisation in 2009, the Norwegian sense of guilt and co-responsibility was then articulated as *the* main motivating factor and explanation. In his opening address to an international audience in Oslo on 24 June 2009, the then Foreign Minister, Jonas Gahr Støre (Labour Party), explained:

»Let me turn to Norway and share with you some reflections on why we have chosen to engage actively with the ITF. Sixty-seven years ago, the mass arrests of Norwegian Jews got underway in occupied Norway and in this city. Today, we know – and we need to spell it out loudly however painful it may be to some: The decision was taken elsewhere, but the arrests were carried out by uniformed Norwegian police, Norwegian men, who handed over the Norwegian Jews to the German Sicherheitspolizei ...«[17]

In 2010, as the Norwegian chair was drawing to a close, representatives from all member countries gathered in Stockholm to mark the tenth anniversary of the Stockholm Declaration. Here, our Foreign Minister chose to repeat his message of 2009:

»Membership comes with commitments. To qualify for membership, countries are required to scrutinise all aspects of their history with regard to the Holocaust, both actions and omissions. No one comes out clean from this painful, but vital self-scrutiny and soul-searching.«[18]

---

17   Jonas Gahr Støre: Holocaust Task Force – tale i anledning Norges formannskap Oslo, 24 June 2009, regjeringen.no, last access: 14 December 2013, <http://www.regjeringen.no/nb/dokumentarkiv/stoltenberg-ii/ud/taler-og-artikler/2009/itf_formannskap.html?id=569323>.
18   Jonas Gahr Støre: Ten Years with the Stockholm Declaration, Stockholm, 26 January 2010, regjeringen.no, last access: 14 July 2014, <http://www.regjeringen.no/nb/doku-

III. The Question of Guilt prior to the Trans-Nationalisation of Holocaust Remembrance

While Norway has been linked to a supranational upsurge in Holocaust awareness, I also believe the subject of guilt and collaboration needs to be discussed within a national framework, and over a broader time span than just the last decade. In international studies of the *Wirkungsgeschichte* of the genocide, there seems to exist a consensus that the Holocaust was neglected and ignored in the initial postwar decades, at least until the 1960s and 1970s, for a variety of interrelated reasons: from a widespread desire to forget; a social and political need for narratives based on heroic resistance; ancient traditions of commemorating soldiers rather than civilian victims; the inability to understand the very nature of genocide and even to the virulent anti-Semitism in Europe after 1945.

In Norway's case, I do not necessarily find this transnational scheme fully compatible. The Holocaust (of course, a nameless crime at the time) was discussed and employed as a rhetorical tool for various purposes after 1945, also within the framework of a dominant, patriotic historical culture. The extermination of the Jews was, for instance, often used and referred to in public debates about the enormous European refugee problem after the war, the newly founded state of Israel, anti-Semitism and the post-war trials, as well as in the reception of the first wave of publications in which survivors gave their accounts. Some books on Auschwitz were already translated into Norwegian just a few months after its liberation. The translation of Anne Frank's diary in 1952 and the Norwegian theatre adaptations that ensued became huge successes nationwide throughout the 1950s. Furthermore, there are numerous examples of how the Holocaust and Auschwitz were portrayed and understood as something particular within the larger scheme of World War II suffering, or as an »event at the limits«.[19]

Within this cluster of historical products, debates and public negotiations about the Holocaust, the issue of Norwegian co-responsibility was subordinate to the one-dimensional image of the German perpetrators, and subordinate to the history of Norwegians helping Jews to flee from the Nazis. Still, it was a topic that circulated repeatedly in the public sphere in post-war Norway. In the sum-

---

mentarkiv/stoltenberg-ii/ud/taler-og-artikler/2010/stockholm_declaration.html?regj_oss=1&id=592282>.

19 Jon Reitan, Norwegian Encounters with the Holocaust. The Historical Culture of the Endlösung, NTNU, 2014 (forthcoming).

mer of 1948, during the trial of Knut Rød, the infamous assistant chief of police, a newspaper article discussed in detail the co-responsibility of the Norwegian police, and called for a public investigation into the role of the police during the actions against the Jews. This call was – not surprisingly perhaps – dismissed by the police authorities at the time. It is, however, interesting that the topic featured in the daily press, which was arguably the most powerful agent in the shaping of a national historical culture after five years of war and occupation.[20]

Norwegian co-responsibility was also discussed in conjunction with the Eichmann trial in Jerusalem in 1961, an affair that, according to David Cesarani, »electrified the world«.[21] The trial received massive media attention in Norway. Most articles preferred to present and discuss the Holocaust through the lens of the patriotic narrative. The daily newspaper *Aftenposten*, for instance, labelled the Norwegian actions to help the Jews as a »ray of light« in an otherwise dark picture. Nevertheless, other and more critical voices were present. An article published in June 1961, entitled »Eichmann and his Norwegian helpers«, called for a collective Norwegian self-scrutiny with regard to the fate of its Jewish population. And as in most other Western European countries, the same issue rose to the surface following the broadcast of the popular American television-series »Holocaust« in 1979.

It was not until the mid-1980s, however, that attention towards this historical trauma really reached its first monumental peak in Norway. This was provoked by the book, *Oss selv nærmest*, by the criminologist Per Ole Johansen in 1984. This was the first academic work in Norway dedicated specifically to discussing the active role of the national police force in anti-Jewish policies prior to, and during, the Second World War. The book received massive media attention, creating headlines and articles on an unprecedented scale. One of Norway's most widely circulated tabloids, *Dagbladet*, commented on 11 September 1984: »Embarrassing to be Norwegian. [...] This is a story so terrible that no heroic resistance fight can wash it away.« The following day another newspaper *Morgenbladet* expressed its views on the book with the comment »shocking to read«, while *Agderposten* published an article with the headline »The Destiny of the Jews and our Co-responsibility«.[22]

20 Reitan 2014 (forthcoming).
21 David Cesarani: Becoming Eichmann. Rethinking the Life, Crimes and Trial of a »Desk Murderer«, Da Capo Press 2006.
22 Reitan 2014.

IV. Conclusion

The public shock and sense of confrontation articulated in the aftermath of this publication was, however, to diminish over time. It was to take yet another decade before the Norwegian guilt became subject to a paradigmatic shift from a position in public memory into official memory politics. Put briefly, this process started with the now famous newspaper article »*Det norske jøderanet*« (»The Robbery of the Norwegian Jews«), published in *Dagens Næringsliv* in conjunction with the 50th anniversary of the liberation in 1995. It continued with the Norwegian restitution process over the following years, which significantly exposed the role of Norwegian society during the Holocaust, and culminated with the first Norwegian manifestation of the global trend of institutionalising Holocaust memory: the establishment of the research institution the *HL-senter* (the Center for Studies of the Holocaust and Religious Minorities) in Oslo.[23]

In some respects, the Center's opening ceremony in Oslo in 2006 might symbolise and illustrate several important lines of development at the same time: Firstly, how scholarly agendas and interpretations of the Holocaust met with a political resonance among the Norwegian public. In their respective speeches, both the Director of the Center, Odd-Bjørn Fure, and the Norwegian Foreign Minister, Jonas Gahr Støre, stressed the responsibility of Norwegian perpetrators before their international audience. Secondly, the Center's inauguration might illustrate how the Holocaust has shifted from a communicative and transitory memory to a cultural and lasting one, placing more responsibility on such institutions to nurture the legacy of the witnesses. The transnational wave of restitutions and apologies for historical injustices and historical traumas might be interpreted as a »last-minute attempt« during an on-going generational shift. And finally: When the *HL-senter* opened its doors to the public in 2006, it had for three years already been part of the official Norwegian delegation to the IHRA, as such contributing as a national agent in developing a transnational network of research, education and remembrance, aiming at creating a shared memory of the Holocaust.

To conclude, one might note that several important issues remain to be discussed in the light of current historic-cultural trends and patterns. What are the various arguments for and against creating unified or standardised historical narratives and memories, including those based on guilt, apologies and making up for historical injustices? And, what would be the various arguments for and against

---

23 See also the chapter by Iselin Theien and Bjørn Westlie in this volume.

if the aim is to oppose movements in the globalised community: to stimulate and nurture the multi-perspectivity of locally, regionally and nationally framed Holocaust narratives, emphasising the many differences between countries and events?

Iselin Theien/Bjørn Westlie
The Restitution Process and the Integration of the Jewish Minority into the Norwegian Collective Memory of the Second World War

I. Introduction

It was only after the 50th anniversary of the end of the Second World War that the economic dimensions of the Shoah emerged as a central topic of historical investigation. As Avi Beker of the World Jewish Congress asserted in 2001, the question of Jewish property had »unexpectedly surfaced from the past and opened a hitherto almost unknown dimension to the discussion of the Shoah«.[1]

The reasons advanced for the recent international outburst of interest in the wartime plundering of the European Jews are complex. Avi Beker has pointed to the end of the Cold War as a catalyst for the creation of the World Jewish Restitution Organization in 1992, originally designed to deal with privatisation claims in Eastern Europe. Their action was contingent upon international backing, and in 1995 the diplomatic groundwork secured the support of the Clinton administration.[2] President Clinton duly appointed the US Ambassador to the European Union, Stuart Eizenstat, as a special emissary for Jewish property claims in Europe, broadening the scope and the public interest in the inquiry beyond former communist countries.

In his account of the mission he had headed, Eizenstat, too, raised the question of why it had taken so long before the restitution claims had been articulated. The answer he provided pointed, like Beker's, to the impact of the Cold War, which had

---

1 Avi Beker (ed.): The Plunder of Jewish Property During the Holocaust. Confronting European History, Houndmills 2001, 1.
2 Beker, 7.

»diverted Allied attention from the victims and threw up impenetrable barriers for those behind the Iron Curtain to trace their looted property«.[3]

While the Cold War explanation indicates international strategic considerations for the repression of potentially divisive processes of restitution within the Western bloc, Beker also points to the relevance of selective national memories in Europe.[4] Elie Wiesel has suggested a dynamic of repression that could explain the shaping of such selective national memories in Europe. One aspect of this repression has been the self-imposed silence of the victims, who, according to Wiesel, had long hesitated to articulate claims that might somehow seem unworthy. A former president of the Norwegian parliament, Jo Benkow (Conservative), hinted at such an explanation when he said, »there were other aspects of the war that concerned us more than earthly goods«.[5] As a Jew, he had been forced to flee Norway in 1942, while his mother and other close family members had been arrested, deported and subsequently murdered in Auschwitz.

Wiesel attributes a more active form of repression of the economic aspects of the Shoah to the fact that »the banks and governments, which ought to have opened up the inquests, had chosen to remain forgetful of past crimes«.[6] To the last category, Peter Hayes has added the damning verdict that in every country formerly occupied by Nazi Germany, »[t]he non-Jewish majority both prioritized recompense for its own suffering and clung to any gains that the persecution of the Jews had offered«.[7]

In their edited collection on the social history of silence, »Shadows of War«, Jay Winter, Efrat Ben Ze'ev and Ruth Ginio evoke silence as one possible response to violent events. However, they contend that »[t]he unsayable and the unsaid rarely stay fixed«, suggesting an inquiry into how »the transformation of moral and political judgements over time can lead to the breaking of silences or to the changing of their boundaries«.[8]

---

3 Stuart Eizenstat: Imperfect Justice. Looted Assets, Slave Labour, and the unfinished Business of World War II, New York 2003, 3.
4 Beker, 4.
5 »Få krav fra norske jøder etter '45«, *Aftenposten*, 11 January 1996.
6 Elie Wiesel's foreword in Eizenstat, x.
7 Peter Hayes: Plundering and Restitution, in: P. Hayes/J. K. Roth (eds.): The Oxford Handbook of Holocaust Studies, Oxford 2010, 548.
8 Jay Winter: Thinking about Silence, in: E. B. Ze'ev/R. Ginio/J. Winter (eds.): Shadows of War. A Social History of Silence in the Twentieth Century, Cambridge 2010, 22–23.

Antero Holmila and Karin Kvist Geverts have recently argued that there never was a total silence surrounding the Shoah in Scandinavia, but »more a kind of uneasiness to talk about it«. However, they find that systematic historical research on the subject only began in the 1990s, coinciding with what has elsewhere been described as the moral turn in Nordic historiography on the Second World War. They place the restitution processes, which occurred in Norway and Sweden in the second half of the 1990s, within the wider framework of a »cosmopolitanisation of Holocaust remembrance«, entrenching the Scandinavian understanding of the Shoah in its European context.[9]

In this article, we will explore how the restitution process in Norway worked as a catalyst for integrating the wartime experiences of the Jewish minority into the national memory of the war. Central to this process was a transformation of the moral and political judgement of the post-war treatment of the surviving members of the Jewish community, allowing for a more pluralist understanding of Norwegian losses during the war.

II. The Norwegian Road to Restitution

In Norway, the economic liquidation of the Jewish minority had been surrounded by silence for fifty years until the business daily *Dagens Næringsliv* in 1995 published an article on how Norwegians had collaborated in the robbery of property and belongings owned by the Norwegian Jewry.[10] The article was followed up by an interview with Berit Reisel, the deputy leader of the Jewish Community in Oslo. She pioneered the view that Norway ought to open up for a settlement over the wartime liquidations.[11]

These articles prompted the then leader of the parliamentary Standing Committee on Scrutiny and Constitutional Affairs, Petter Thomassen (Conservative), to demand a public inquiry into the confiscation of Jewish wartime assets. In a let-

---

9   Antero Holmila and Karin Kvist Geverts: On Forgetting and Remembering the Holocaust in Scandinavia. Introduction to the special issue on the histories and memories of Holocaust in Scandinavia, in: Scandinavian Journal of History 5 (2011), 520–535. The term »moral turn« comes from Henrik Stenius, Mirja Österberg and Johan Östling: Nordic Narratives of the Second World War. National Histriographies Revisited, Lund 2011.
10 Bjørn Westlie: Nordmenn ranet de norske jødene, *Dagens Næringsliv*, 27 May 1995.
11 Bjørn Westlie: Oppgjør i skyggen av Holocaust, Oslo 2002, 19–20.

ter addressed to Grete Faremo, the Minister of Justice in the Labour government, Thomassen wrote, »the issues raised by the two [...] articles in *Dagens Næringsliv* are of such a nature that the Norwegian state cannot ignore them«. He further contended that the authorities ought to reach for a settlement that could »close this dark chapter of the war history in a dignified manner«.[12]

But it was only after the case had made an interesting international loop that it made its way onto the political agenda in Norway. In January 1996, the Institute of the World Jewish Congress published a report based on the original *Dagens Næringsliv* article: »Still No Peace for the Jews of Norway: The Unresolved Restitution Claims.«[13] News of this publication reached Norwegian media through Reuter's New York office, and the liberal daily *Dagbladet* was among the newspapers that aired the view that it was high time the authorities now addressed the question of what had happened to the Jewish wartime property.[14]

On 31 January 1996, the parliamentary leader of the Christian Democrats, Kjell Magne Bondevik, raised a question in parliament to the Minister of Justice on how she intended to proceed in order to investigate what had happened to the Jewish property in Norway before and after the war. »This can never be made good again,« he said, »but neither can we leave things as they are now«.[15] Rather than conducting a meticulous financial survey, Bondevik called for the government to open up for a broad moral and ethical settlement.

Faremo replied that the Ministry of Justice had established, and hoped to continue, cooperation with the Jewish community in Norway. As regards Bondevik's question of how broad the restitution process ahead would be, she stated that it was too early to define the mandate and the composition of the commission which would be appointed to carry out the investigations. She signalled that the investigation would take at least one year to carry out, requiring the involvement of scientific experts.[16]

Under the heading »Debt of Honour«, the conservative daily *Aftenposten* criticised the slow and intricate approach signalled by Faremo. Supporting Bondevik's interpellation, the *Aftenposten* asserted that it was more important to settle an

---

12 Bjørn Westlie: Ber Faremo granske jødeboene fra krigen, *Dagens Næringsliv*, 14 June 1995.
13 Westlie, Oppgjør, 98 ff. Westlie was the author of the report published by the Institute of the World Jewish Congress.
14 »Hvem stjal fra jødene?« in *Dagbladet*, 13 January 1996.
15 Stortingstidende 1996, 2159.
16 Ibid.

account that was fifty years overdue rather than to check all the details in that account. In order to settle what amounted to a debt of honour, the state should without further delay pay out a »more than generous« restitution to the Jewish community.[17]

While the promised commission was still being put together, a new incentive was launched in parliament in the form of a motion by the representative Roy Wetterstad (Independent – formerly of The Progress Party). In addition to a full economic restitution, Wetterstad proposed that the parliament should offer a clear apology »for the injustice which has been committed against the Jews who have not received reparation for property and valuables confiscated during the war«.[18]

Wetterstad thus clearly shifted attention to the responsibility of the democratic institutions in post-war Norway. The incomplete and unjust reparation policies towards the surviving members of the Jewish minority after the Shoah »ought to cause political shame«, Wetterstad contended.[19] Similar expressions of the political feeling towards the Jewish community had been voiced in the media by other members of parliament. Jon Lilletun, a Christian Democrat, also referred to the lack of a settlement as a shame, while Per-Kristian Foss of the Conservative Party described it as an embarrassment that the Jews had not received a restitution settlement. Foss pointed to the faults of the post-war historians who, as he saw it, had silenced this aspect of Norwegian history, while Lilletun declared, »we have known about this injustice, but have pushed it to the background«.[20]

In parliament, however, Wetterstad's proposal was only supported by Erling Folkvord of the Red Electoral Alliance on the far-left wing of the party political spectrum, the political antipode of the Progress Party to which Wetterstad originally belonged. Folkvord's support was dictated by a wish for parliament to display »a minimum of common decency« and demonstrate a firm stand against all forms of anti-Semitism.[21] The lack of further support did not stem from any political disagreement over the need for a restitution process. On the contrary, Olav Akselsen (Labour) believed that all members of parliament shared Wetterstad's conviction, and regretted that the debate might »give an impression of a disagreement which

17 »Æresgjeld«, *Aftenposten*, 1 February 1996.
18 Stortinget: Dokument 8:59 (1995–96): Forslag fra stortingsrepresentant Roy N. Wetterstad om å yte rettferdighet overfor jøder i Norge – erstatning for konfiskerte verdier og krigspensjon, 29 February 1996.
19 Stortingstidende 1996, 3429 (13 May).
20 »Ut mot fortielse av jøders skjebner«, *Aftenposten*, 13 January 1996.
21 Stortingstidende 1996, 3429.

does not exist«.[22] Anders Sjaastad of the Conservative Party voiced a similar concern that this was a matter that engaged all members of parliament, but along with the majority he would prefer to wait for the Ministry of Justice to deliver the investigation it had promised before taking action. Failing to attract further support, Wetterstad then agreed to withdraw his proposal.[23]

While Wetterstad's proposal thus came to nothing, it nevertheless brought to light an ambition to reach a restitution settlement that cut across party political lines in parliament. As had also been demonstrated by Bondevik's interpellation and the media statements by Foss and Lilletun, the source of this ambition was a moral unease imbued with shame over how the Jewish minority had been treated after the war.

The mandate and the composition of the commission promised by the Ministry of Justice were established on 29 March 1996. County Governor Oluf Skarpnes was appointed chair of the commission consisting of professor of law Thor Falkanger, professor of history Ole Kristian Grimnes, district court judge Guri Sunde, Anne Hals (later replaced by Eli Fure) from the National Archives Services of Norway, historian Bjarte Bruland, and psychologist Berit Reisel. Their mandate was to present a report of what had happened to Jewish property during the war, and further to present a survey of how and to what extent the property was returned to the Jewish survivors after the war, and of what had happened to the estates of the Jewish families who had been annihilated in the extermination camps. »The commission can also treat other matters of relevance to the case,« the Ministry stated.[24]

It soon became evident that the two commission members representing the Jewish community, Bruland and Reisel, interpreted the mandate for their investigation differently to the majority of the commission. In May 1997, the commission openly split into a minority group consisting of Bruland and Reisel, and a majority headed by Skarpnes.[25] While the majority of commission members pursued a more narrow calculation of the losses and compensations established by the bureaucracy of the immediate post-war period, Bruland and Reisel interpreted their mandate as a call for a broader historical investigation and approached the economic liquidation of Norway's Jewry as an integral part of the »Final Solution«. In June 1997, the Skarpnes commission thus presented two separate reports to

---

22   Ibid., 3431.
23   Ibid., 3430.
24   St prp nr 82 (1997–98): Et historisk og moralsk oppgjør med behandlingen i Norge av den økonomiske likvidasjonen av den jødiske minoritet under den 2. verdenskrig, 8.
25   Westlie, Oppgjør, 104 ff.

the government, consisting of a majority report delivered by Skarpnes, Falkanger, Grimnes, Fure and Sunde, and a minority report delivered by Bruland and Reisel.[26]

III. The Dual Liquidation

The property of Norwegian Jews had been seized in the autumn of 1942, in connection with the arrests and subsequent deportations of 772 Jews from Norway to Auschwitz. Before the war, the Jewish minority had counted nearly 2,200 members in Norway. The majority survived by escaping to Sweden. Of the 772 who had been deported, only 34 survived.

The Quisling government issued an edict dictating the confiscation of all property belonging to the Jews on the same day that all Jewish men were arrested in Norway, on 26 October 1942. In the beginning of November, the so-called Liquidation Board for the Confiscation of Jewish Property was created under the auspices of the Ministry of Finance. The Liquidation Board employed more than sixty official receivers responsible for the management of the Jewish estates.[27] According to the first official guidelines for the Liquidation Board, it was desirable that the official receivers hold a law degree.[28] Given the large number of accomplices required, the Liquidation Board, however, soon amended this rule, and in the standard letter sent out to several local authorities asking for suggestions as to new appointments, it was specified that a law degree was not required of the official receivers, as long as they were »conscientious and had a business sense«.[29]

Part of the conflict between the majority and the minority on the Skarpnes commission stemmed from two diverging readings of the source materials from the Liquidation Board, which largely rested upon the registrations made by the

---

26 NOU 1997:22: Inndragning av jødisk eiendom i Norge under den 2. verdenskrig.
27 Riksarkivet (Norwegian national archives): S-1564: Justisdepartementet, Tilbakeføringskontoret for inndratte formuer: Box J-b 1046, file »Lister over jødeboer med mer«: List of official receivers appointed by the Liquidation board, receivers for Jewish estates marked »J«, undated.
28 Riksarkivet, S-1564: Justisdepartementet, Tilbakeføringskontoret for inndratte formuer: Box Dd 0049, file »Instrukser og rundskriv vedrørende jøder«: Forskrifter i medhold av lov av 26. oktober 1942 vedrørende inndragning av formue som har tilhørt jøder, paragraph 2.
29 Riksarkivet, S-1564: Justisdepartementet, Tilbakeføringskontoret for inndratte formuer: Box Dd 0049, file »Kopier av bobestyreroppnevnelser«.

official receivers. The majority on the commission noted that such registrations were steeped in uncertainties, yet they questioned whether one should distrust these accounts »simply because the Liquidation Board was an NS-institution«.[30]

By contrast, the minority group based their investigation on the premise that »the physical and economic liquidation of the Jews must be regarded as two facets of the same crime«.[31] In treating the economic liquidation of the Jews not as a consequence, but as an integral part of the monstrous crime, the minority report presented a qualitatively different picture of the losses incurred. This approach bore the imprint of the work of Raul Hilberg, who had also inspired the US historian Martin Dean's recent treatise on the robbing of the European Jews as one of the few earlier »detail-oriented historians who did not underestimate the role of property confiscation in the destruction process«.[32]

The link between Raul Hilberg's scheme for understanding the Shoah as presented in »The Destruction of the European Jews« and the minority report presented to the Norwegian government in 1997 runs through a master thesis submitted by the historian Bjarte Bruland in 1995. Together with Berit Reisel, Bruland formed the commission minority in 1996–97, and his master thesis on »The Attempt to Annihilate the Norwegian Jews« was a pioneer academic treatment of the economic liquidation in Norway. Bruland explicitly modelled his thesis upon Hilberg's analysis of the destruction process, tracing the steps of the annihilation from the official definition of the Jews to their arrest and deportation – each step followed by economic expropriation decrees.[33]

The methodological insights stemming from Hilberg's original work thus led the Reisel and Bruland to approach the economic liquidation as a series of criminal acts, dictating a more critical reading of the source materials than demonstrated by the majority of commission members. The aim of the Liquidation Board was not, as some of its members claimed in their own defence at the post-war trials, to look after the possessions of the Jews, but rather to annihilate the Jewish minority also in a material sense. As an illustration of how intimately the liquidation of economic assets was linked to the total annihilation of the Jewish minority in Norway, the minority report cites a letter from the Liquidation Board to one of

30 NOU 1997: 22, 37.
31 NOU 1997: 22, 131.
32 Martin Dean: Robbing the Jews. The Confiscation of Jewish Property in the Holocaust, 1933–1945, Cambridge 2008, 8.
33 Bjarte Bruland. Forsøket på å tilintetgjøre de norske jødene, Master thesis (University of Bergen) 1995, 2–3.

the official receivers, providing instructions as to what to do with what was left of a family home: »As regards the old rubbish you mention, where it has no sale value, we would prefer it to be burned. Particularly such things as old photographs, family albums, etc. are of very little interest for the rising generation in the new Norway.«[34]

While the majority on the Skarpnes commission underlined that the principal administrative guidelines for the liquidation dictated a detailed registration of the estates, and thus arguably treating such corruption as an exception to the norm, the minority considered corruption as the norm in a criminal apparatus. Corruption involved failing to register the property to the estate of the original owner, making it possible for personal belongings to change hands in an improvised manner – and making it impossible to recuperate the property after the war.

IV. Post-War Justice and the Creation of a Patriotic Memory Culture

Accusations of corruption were incriminating for accomplices of the Liquidation Board in post-war trials. If the liquidators had caused the personal belongings of the Jews to disappear, it would render their claim that they were merely looking after the property (or even safe-guarding it from the Germans) improbable.

In the post-war trials, one of the more high profile official receivers, Helge Schjærve, was confronted with potentially damaging photographic evidence from a wartime goldsmith, displaying a silver tray made with melted down silver cutlery confiscated from a Jewish estate. Schjærve had also removed a fridge from another Jewish home, taking it into his own kitchen to replace an older model, which he had then sold on at an auction.

These two cases are on record because the victims' estates filed compensation claims against Schjærve after the war. However, and despite very concrete evidence, the Oslo police ultimately chose to believe in the accused's »good intentions«, acquitting him of the charges of theft. The reason the police displayed such trust in this particular accomplice of the Nazi régime was that Schjærve had used his connections to help several so-called »good Norwegians« get out of prison during the war. Such a man simply could not be evil, the Oslo police concluded,

---

34 NOU 1997: 22, 119.

and they therefore found no reason to distrust his explanation that he was only trying to look after the property of the Jews.[35]

The legal reasoning in the Schjærve case echoes that of the far more prominent case against Assistant Chief of Police Knut Rød, who had headed the arrests and subsequent deportation of the Norwegian Jews to Auschwitz in the early hours of 26 November 1942. Rød was arrested a week after the liberation in May 1945, on suspicion of treason. Rød's defence was that he had merely carried out technical police work during the deportations, and that his membership of Quisling's NS party had in reality been a cover for assisting the resistance movement. After several rounds in the Norwegian court system, Rød was finally acquitted of the charge of treason on the grounds that he had only carried out orders, and that it was »with great reluctance« that he had participated in the »actions against the Jews«.[36] In 1952, Rød was reinstated in his wartime position as Assistant Chief of Police with the Oslo police, and remained in this post until he retired in 1965.

The Rød case has not, however, been allowed to rest. In 2010, the Norwegian law journal *Lov og Rett* reopened the debate surrounding Rød's acquittal. In a detailed criticism of the 1945–48 court case against Rød, the lawyer Christopher S. Harper noted how the presiding judges used phrases such as »good Norwegians« and »the protection of Norwegian interests« in Rød's defence, quite evidently excluding the Jewish minority as belonging to the national community.[37] A former attorney general, Georg Rieber-Mohn, argued against Harper that the legal reasoning behind acquitting Rød was defensible; had Rød declined to participate in the actions against the Jews, it would only have weakened the resistance at large.[38] Professor and dean of the Faculty of Law at Oslo University, Hans Petter Graver, contested Rieber-Mohn's claims on legal as well as ethical grounds. Not just any action would or could be offset by services to abet the resistance movement, Graver argued, and the deeds Rød stood accused of »were genocide then, and are genocide now, even without the gas chambers«.[39]

---

35 Iselin Theien: Sonja Wigert. Et dobbeltliv, Oslo 2010, 179–182.
36 Knut Sveri: Landssvikoppgjørets merkeligste rettssak, in: A. Bratholm et. al. (eds.): Lov og frihet. Festskrift til Johs Andenæs, Oslo 1982.
37 Christopher S. Harper: Landssvikoppgjørets behandling av jødeforfølgelsen i Norge 1940–45, in: Lov og rett 8 (2010), 469–89.
38 Georg Fr. Rieber-Mohn: Landssviksakene mot Knut Rød, in: Lov og Rett (1–2) 2011, 94–107.
39 Hans Petter Graver: Mer om Rød-saken in: Lov og Rett (3) 2011, 171–173.

The successful defence in the cases against Knut Rød and Helge Schjærve suggests that the post-war legal system created a hierarchy ranking Norwegian resistance above Jewish victims. A similar process took place elsewhere in Europe, as noted by Pieter Lagrou: »Persecuted for something they had not chosen, for the simple reason of being born Jews, they were placed at the bottom of the hierarchy of martyrs,« he writes of the Shoah survivors.[40]

Ingjerd Veiden Brakstad has conducted a study of how the press in the immediate post-war period presented the persecution of the Jews in Norway. Brakstad finds that the persecutions were overwhelmingly portrayed as a German policy, alien to Norwegian culture and disposition. »The deep collapse of culture which fosters anti-Semitism has fortunately not yet been experienced in Norway. In this country, a human is still a human,« the *Dagbladet* asserted in 1947.[41]

Synne Corell has analysed how the persecution of the Jews has been treated in Norwegian post-war historiography. Her findings and analysis could also be seen to reflect Brakstad's in the sense that Norway escapes responsibility for the persecutions. Indeed, Corell argues, post-war historians have »made the Jews responsible for their own destiny, and for not having appreciated the efforts of the police and the Home Front army to rescue them«.[42]

One could thus identify several mechanisms working to supress the wartime history of the Jewish minority. One was associated with the ways in which the legal system constructed a hierarchy of the persecuted, whereby support for the »good Norwegians« and the resistance movement trumped any complicity in the crimes against the Jews.

Secondly, the sharp focus on the monstrous German war crimes let important nuances of Norwegian collaboration slip out of view. In the case of the economic liquidations, Martin Dean has recently demonstrated how »[r]ipples of complicity spread throughout Europe propelled by the universality of human greed« as consumers, firms and government agencies started to compete for the Jewish property even before the deportations began.[43]

---

40 Pieter Lagrou: Victims of Genocide and National Memory. Belgium, France and the Netherlands 1945–65, in: Past and Present 154 (1997), 222.
41 Ingjerd Veiden Brakstad: Jødeforfølgelsene i Norge. Omtale i årene 1942–1948, Master thesis (University of Oslo) 2006.
42 Synne Corell. Krigens ettertid. Okkupasjonshistorien i norske historiebøker, Oslo 2010, 157.
43 Dean, 377.

The Skarpnes commission majority repeatedly referred to the discontinuity between the German occupation regime and the post-war government as an argument why the Norwegian state bore no responsibility for compensating the losses of the Jewish minority. In this respect, 1945 appeared as a year zero, and what mattered to the then Norwegian Labour government was reconstruction. In such a context, the Skarpnes majority contended, »there was a widespread feeling that the nation as a whole had suffered, and a certain reluctance to compare suffering. ›Everybody‹ had been ›in the same boat‹.«[44]

V. Restitution Subordinate to Reconstruction

In May 1945, the first Jews returned to Norway from their exile in Sweden. In the autumn, the few who against all odds had managed to survive the extermination camps also made it back. It was only upon their return that survivors and refugees alike became aware that all they had left behind had gone missing. The impact of this shock was not mitigated when they discovered that it was an arduous process to recuperate their property.

It was evident to the Norwegian political authorities that a large proportion of the Jewish property had vanished, as already admitted by a parliamentary proposition in 1945. Here, the government stated that the belongings of the Jews had in part been destroyed or taken out of Norway, and »the rest has been scattered to the winds domestically, and could hardly be traced«.[45]

Nevertheless, there was a marked unwillingness to make special provisions for the Jewish survivors in post-war Norwegian society. The ideological resilience of this principle is evident in the Skarpnes majority report, which defended the bureaucratic principles of equal treatment guiding the post-war settlement. »While there had been special rules for the Jews during the war, the rules after the war were the same for everybody«, the majority report contended.[46] Leora Auslander has remarked how the French Fourth and Fifth Republics in a similar vein »largely abandoned the question of the expropriation of the Jewish population under Vichy«.[47] She partly ascribes this to the universal aspirations of French

---

44 NOU 1997:22, 44.
45 Records of the Norwegian Storting: Ot. prop. 137. 1945.
46 NOU 1997: 22, 68.
47 Leora Auslander: Coming Home? Jews in Postwar Paris, in: Journal of Contemporary History 40 (2005), 256–7.

republicanism that professed blindness to religious and racial difference. In Norway, the egalitarianism of the post-war Labour government was primarily linked to an ideology of social equality, but the results for the Jewish minority were very similar.

Equal treatment within the boundaries of the national state was designed to promote the Labour government's dual programme of production-oriented reconstruction and social equality. Individual claims for compensation were measured against what the bureaucracy judged to be objective needs and potential for social usefulness. These principles were expressed in the so-called »sliding scale« principle for war damage reparation. The sliding scale dictated that moveable property belonging to one household was compensated in full only up to a value of 3,000 Norwegian crowns (increased by 1,000 crowns for each extra household member). For additional amounts, the compensation was gradually reduced to a compensation grade of 50 per cent of the original insurance value.

As the minority on the Skarpnes commission argued, these redistributive regulations discriminated negatively against the Jewish minority after the war due to the collective character of the dual physical and material liquidation they had suffered. The sliding scale ensured that those who had lost most had their compensation correspondingly reduced. Moreover, the principle of reconstruction was designed to benefit productive members of society, implying that compensation for the assets of those deceased would be sharply reduced. In addition, a number of regulations pertaining to inheritance procedures and compensation reductions where more than one family member had been killed during the war hit the decimated Jewish minority unduly hard. Peter Hayes' observation that a German bureaucrat could not possibly envisage paying out restitution »*ohne Beleg*«[48] also applies to the Norwegian case, where the lack, for instance, of a death certificate from Auschwitz proved an obstacle for surviving family members to obtain compensation.

The Skarpnes commission majority defended the redistributive principles of the post-war restitution on the grounds that it was financially impossible to make up for the wartime losses of any group in Norwegian society. »After all«, the majority report stated, »the nation as a whole had suffered losses. Individual

---

48 Center for Advanced Holocaust Studies. US Holocaust Memorial Museum: Confiscations of Jewish property in Europe 1933–45. New Sources and Perspectives. Symposium Proceedings, Washington D.C. 2003, 145.

citizens therefore had to accept that they would emerge from the war bearing economic losses and reduced welfare«.[49]

An example of how survivors were treated is illustrated by what happened to Bernard Plesansky.[50] The eldest son of Isak Plesansky, who had run a clothes shop in the small town of Tønsberg, Bernard managed to escape to Sweden before the mass arrests because he went to school in Oslo. He returned to his hometown in June 1945. Back in Norway and Tønsberg he learned that his entire family was dead and that he was the sole survivor. He decided to try to reopen the shop. He went to see the local bank manager, but was told, »you must remember that you are not your father«. He did not get a loan or any help to start over again.

Bernard Plesansky then went through the accounts of his father's estate, and quickly spotted that a rival firm, Emil Kjølner A/S, had bought stock from the Plesansky shop for a pittance. He wanted to raise a private compensation claim, but abandoned the idea. Some money, however, was still left in the estate. Of the original 33,000 Norwegian crowns which the Liquidation Board had registered to the estate of the late-Isak Plesansky, Bernard Plesansky had 68 per cent, or about 21,000 crowns, returned to him in 1947. That he only got 68 per cent and not the full amount that had been registered to the estate was the standard return rate regulated by law. The remaining 32 per cent was deducted to cover administrative costs of the Liquidation Board and the Reparations Office.

Another case that surfaced in the mid-1990s was that of Kai Feinberg. Feinberg had lost thirty close family members in Auschwitz, including his parents and siblings. He returned alone to Oslo in October 1945. In his memoir he describes his experience of returning to his family home: »The next day I walked to my childhood home on Kirkeveien 123. But when I got there, it was inhabited by complete strangers. I did, of course, understand that they were Nazis who had taken over the flat in the belief that the original owners would never return. But I didn't want any trouble, and calmly told them my name. That turned out to be more than enough. Baffled, the couple standing in front of me said: ›We understand. By tomorrow the flat will be vacated.‹ And it was.«[51]

Feinberg's condensed description of his homecoming has made an impact on Norwegian historiography as one of rare testimonies of this kind.[52] Feinberg's

---

49   NOU 1997: 22, 8.
50   »Det norske jøderanet«, *Dagens Næringsliv*, 27 May 1995.
51   Kai Feinberg/Arnt Stefansen: Fange nr 79108 vender tilbake. Oslo 1995, 142.
52   It is included in Kristian Ottosen's standard work on the deportation of the Norwegian Jews: I slik en natt. Historien om deportasjonen av jøder fra Norge, Oslo 1994, 286.

homecoming was also brought up in the heated public debate surrounding the Skarpnes commission, when it was argued that one shouldn't overlook the fact that Feinberg had recuperated his apartment.[53]

This argument missed the point that the apartment had been plundered of everything that had made it a family home. The case illustrates that the forms and procedures of the post-war bureaucracy simply were not suited to deal with the losses of the Norwegian Jews. Upon his return to Oslo, Feinberg was asked to describe »the nature and extent of damage« on a compensation form to the Ministry of Justice. »Lost everything,« he wrote.[54]

After a year of bureaucratic processing, Feinberg was given an *ex gratia* payment of 705 Norwegian crowns for the loss of personal effects and clothing in the extermination camps. It took two more years for him to receive partial compensation for the goods that had gone missing from the family apartment. The Office for War Damage to Buildings and Movable Property eventually paid Feinberg back about one third of the original insurance value of the family property, making reductions for books and other items categorised as luxuries, and for the personal belongings of the four dead family members.[55]

VI. Towards a Pluralist National Memory

In the context of bureaucratic stonewalling and fears of continued anti-Semitism, many of the Shoah victims simply chose to be silent about their economic losses. Social scientist Irene Levin has conducted a study of the wartime Norwegian Jewish refugees in Sweden, suggesting that they even lacked a language for talking about the Shoah, for the same reasons of the sheer extremity of the situation which had made the Jews elsewhere in Europe reluctant to raise their voices. The survivors did not talk about the war, not even within their own families. Levin has interpreted this partly as a strategy to avoid uncomfortable memories or thoughts, and partly as a silence imposed upon them by their social surroundings.[56]

---

53 Ole Kolsrud in Dagbladet, 29.6.1997, discussed in Westlie, Oppgjør, 115.
54 Riksarkivet: S-1056, Justisdepartementet: Oppgjørsavdelingen, Series Jbf – Political prisoners, Box 0012, File »Feinberg«: Application form filled out by Kai Feinberg on 29 November 1945, approved on 27 August 1946.
55 Riksarkivet: S-1548: Krigsskadetrygdene for bygning og løsøre. Løsøresaker. Forsikret. Box 1199: L-nr 92656–92696: Folder 92693.
56 Irene Levin: Taushetens tale, in: Nytt Norsk Tidsskrift 4 (2001), 371–382.

The social disinterest in the wartime memories of the Jews could be compared to the mechanisms that Peter Novick has noted for refugees to America. »It is said that survivors' memories were so painful that they repressed them,« he has argued. »No doubt this was often true, but there is considerable evidence that many were willing, indeed anxious, to talk of their experiences but made a deliberate choice not to do so, except amongst themselves.«[57] Rather than dealing with the pluralism of wartime experiences, the language of reconstruction had encouraged the construction of a common history of shared hardships, or, as the Skarpnes majority put it, of a nation having been in the same boat.

Anne Sender, a former chair of the Jewish community in Oslo, has reported that fears of fuelling anti-Semitism was a decisive factor in maintaining a silence about economic losses up until the restitution process of the 1990s. Kai Feinberg, who had moved on to become the chair of the Jewish community, was amongst those who refused to comment on the articles in *Dagens Næringsliv* out of fear of stirring up the underlying currents of anti-Semitism.[58]

The minority report by Berit Reisel and Bjarte Bruland broke this silence by spelling out the consequences of the fact that the Jewish community had been on a very different boat to the majority during the occupation. Their dissent broke the tacit post-war reluctance to compare the suffering reported by the Skarpnes majority, by articulating the »extremely unfortunate consequences for the Norwegian Jews due to their special situation« in the post-war settlements.[59] Treating the physical and economic liquidation of the Jews as parts of the same crime, the minority report sought to illuminate the total magnitude of the losses and the resulting inadequacy of the post-war government to provide justice for the victims. By contrast, the Skarpnes majority contended »there was a good and thorough settlement and restitution process after the war«.[60]

When the Skarpnes commission delivered its divided report in June 1997, the majority group failed to attract support for their verdicts on the post-war settlements. Instead, newspapers and politicians from across the party-political spectrum embraced the premises and conclusions drawn by the minority group on

---

57 Peter Novick: The Holocaust and Collective Memory. Bloomsbury 1999, 83.
58 Anne Sender: Vår jødiske reise. Oslo 2013, 79.
59 The Reisel/Bruland Report on the Confiscation of Jewish property in Norway during World War II, Part of Official Norwegian Report 1997: 22 (English version, June 1997), Oslo 1997, 5–6.
60 NOU 1997: 22, 8.

the committee.⁶¹ Prime Minister Thorbjørn Jagland stated that the 1997 Labour government had come to regard the settlement as a moral responsibility. Reflecting the integrated approach of Reisel and Bruland, Jagland said, »[t]he losses of the Jewish population cannot be limited to an assessment of material sacrifice. The organized arrests, the deportation and liquidation of Jews amount to genocide and the elimination of an entire cultural community«.⁶² The Ministry of Foreign Affairs made it patently clear that the character of genocide placed the Jews in a special situation among the many Norwegian victims of Nazism. »The economic measures which were carried out against the Jews in Norway can only be understood properly in this broad context,« the Ministry stated in its English-language press release.⁶³

In October 1997, a new coalition government was formed under the premiership of Bondevik of the Christian Democrats. The conclusions of the minority report also answered to the moral and ethical restitution settlement, which he had called for in parliament early in 1996. The heading of the government proposal to the parliament clearly stated their support for the ambition of a »historical and moral settlement pertaining to the treatment in Norway of the Jewish minority during the Second World War and of their economic liquidation«.⁶⁴ In parliament, the acting Minister of Justice Dagfinn Høybråten (Christian Democrat) underlined the government's endorsement of the premise in the minority report that the physical and economic liquidation of the Jews formed two aspects of the same crime.⁶⁵

Erik Solheim of the Socialist Left Party, who supported the work of the minority commission since they had split from the majority in May, described the work of the Skarpnes majority in similar terms he employed to explain what had gone wrong after 1945: The experts had lost sight of the moral, political and ethical aspects of the case in their pursuit of formal judicial accountancy. The majority group had thus endangered the deeper historical meaning of the restitution pro-

---

61 Westlie, Oppgjør, 98.
62 Press release no. 77/97, 23 June 1997. »A moral responsibility to clarify and settle the terrible crimes against the Jewish people,« says Norway's Prime Minister«, regjeringen.no, last access: 23 January 2014, <http://www.regjeringen.no/en/dokumentarkiv/Regjeringen-Jagland/smk/Nyheter-og-pressemeldinger/1997/-et_moralsk_ansvar_a_klargjore.html?id=237875>.
63 Ibid.
64 St prp nr 82 (1997–98): Et historisk og moralsk oppgjør med behandlingen i Norge av den økonomiske likvidasjonen av den jødiske minoriteten under den 2. verdenskrig.
65 Stortingstidende 1999, 2320 (11 March).

cess, and Solheim praised the current and the previous government for having chosen a different course than the one suggested by Skarpnes.[66]

While the Progress Party initially dissented from the standardised reparation sum proposed by the government for individuals affected by the economic liquidation, there was no disagreement in principle over the suggested historical and moral restitution settlement. Parliament thus unanimously passed the government proposal for a settlement of 200 million crowns in compensations to individuals. In addition, the government proposal for a 250 million crown collective restitution settlement aimed at supporting Jewish culture and to establish the Center for Studies of Holocaust and Religious Minorities was passed by a majority against a dissenting proposal from the Progress Party.[67]

VII. Conclusion

The broad political support for the premises of the minority report marked a turning point in collective memory of the Second World War in Norway. While the premise of the Skarpnes majority report that all Norwegians had undergone identical experiences and sufferings could perhaps most easily be understood in the trajectory of a patriotic memory culture, the minority on the commission integrated experiences such as those of Kai Feinberg, who had lost everything, into a more pluralist national memory of the war.

The broadening scope of the Norwegian collective memory of the Second World War could be seen as part of the new international emphasis of morality »characterised not only by accusing other countries of human rights abuses but also by self examination«, as noted by Elazar Barkan.[68] The Norwegian restitution process was driven by an unequivocal political support for a moral settlement. The failure to understand that the Jews had been in a special position after the war came to be regarded as a responsibility that weighed upon the nation. While it was impossible to make amends for the injustices committed to the Jewish people during the war, the government wished that the settlement could at last bring a dignified closure to the economic restitution process.[69]

66 Stortingstidende 1999, 2318 (11 March).
67 Stortingstidende 1999, 2322; Innst. S. nr. 108 (1998–99).
68 Elazar Barkan: The Guilt of Nations. Restitution and Negotiating Historical Injustices. Baltimore and London, 2000, xvi.
69 Stortingstidende 1999, 2320. (Høybråten); St prp nr 82.

Ilse Raaijmakers
Between the »Particular« and the »Universal«
Dynamics in Dutch Memory Culture

I. In the Small Town of Vorden

On 4 May 2012 – the Dutch Remembrance Day of the Second World War – a light aircraft flew over the Dutch village of Vorden, towing a banner that read: *Vorden is fout* (Vorden is bad).[1] For half an hour the plane circled over the small village of 7,500 inhabitants, situated in the eastern Netherlands, just thirty kilometres from the German border. Only hours later, the official commemoration of the war dead was to start, as in all other parts of the country. The local commemoration in Vorden, however, had become the topic of a heated national debate. The airplane banner was the preliminary climax of this dramatic negotiation over Dutch war memory.

The crux of the controversy was the question of whether the commemoration on 4 May should include references to German war victims. The organising committee in Vorden planned to do so, by walking past the graves of ten German *Wehrmacht* soldiers, who were buried in the cemetery where the commemoration would take place.[2] This plan caused a storm of protest that was soon picked up by national media. The discussion truly escalated when a Dutch Jewish organisation started proceedings against the mayor, who was to attend the commemoration.[3] It considered it unlawful and a slight against the victims of the Nazi régime for a Dutch mayor to commemorate the former enemy on 4 May. Only a few hours

---

1 All quotes are translated by the author, unless otherwise noted.
2 The commemoration in Vorden takes place at a cemetery where victims of the Second World War are buried. Besides British allied soldiers and Dutch civilians, there are also ten graves of German Wehrmacht soldiers, who had died in action during the final months of the war. They have their own memorial stone.
3 Henk Aalderink, mayor of the township of Bronckhorst to which the village of Vorden belongs.

before the commemoration was about to start, a judge in summary proceedings agreed with the plaintiffs and prohibited the mayor and other municipal officials to walk past the German graves.[4] Nevertheless, another Jewish interest group went ahead with their plan for the airplane banner *Vorden is fout*.[5]

This court intervention was unique in the history of Dutch war commemorations, but tumultuous discussions are far from new. Since 1945, the Dutch seized countless opportunities to discuss which war victims they wanted to remember in public. Many of these debates have centred on Remembrance Day. Starting in 1946, guidelines have been provided to local authorities nationwide, which spell out in exact detail who is to be remembered and how the commemoration should be organised. In this article, I will analyse some important dynamics in Dutch memory culture on the basis of these guidelines. By following in detail how the wording and phrasing have changed over several decades, major shifts in cultural memory at large can be traced.

Recent discussions in the Netherlands about 4 May reflect an uncertainty that has been simmering for some time. The banner *Vorden is fout* referred to a widely recognised trope in Dutch memory culture of the Second World War: *goed* (good) and *fout* (bad). These terms were used to differentiate Dutch behaviour in the war as either resistance (*goed*) or collaboration (*fout*), and more generally to distinguish victims from perpetrators. In the early decades after 1945, this was an important political and moral framework to interpret the war, both by historians and the wider public. From this perspective, the war came to serve as a »moral touchstone« in Dutch society, »the basis of a clear distinction between moral and immoral, good and bad«.[6] However, the comfortable certainty that this framework offered has crumbled.

---

4   In February 2013, this judgment was reversed on appeal, but no officials did in fact walk past the German graves on 4 May that year.
5   The airplane banner was ordered by the Jewish interest group Tradition is Our Future (TOF). The proceedings against the mayor were started by the Jewish organisation Joods Federatief Nederland (Jewish Federative Netherlands). These small organisations are by no means the most representative organisations of the Dutch Jewish community. By contrast, many inhabitants of Vorden – as private citizens not bound by the judgment – did in fact decide on 4 May to pass by the graves of the German soldiers. No judge in the Netherlands can prescribe how individual citizens are supposed to remember.
6   J. C. H. Blom: Suffering as a Warning. The Netherlands and the Legacy of a War, in: Revue Canadienne d'Etudes Néerlandaises/Canadian Journal of Netherlandic Studies 16 (1995), no. 2, 64.

Since the 1980s the dichotomy of *goed* and *fout* has come under scrutiny from historians, and the criticism started to reach a wider public in the 1990s.[7] Many intellectuals, politicians and people from post-war generations wanted to cut across this black and white view in a more self-critical way. They questioned, for example, the dichotomy of evil and guilty Germans versus the good and innocent Dutch. However, the introduction of more nuanced perspectives on the war – which in commemoration politics correspond with broader definitions of who can or should be remembered on 4 May – is often at odds with the rhetoric of national commemoration days, where it is desirable to draw clear moral lessons from the past. In memorial discussions such as in Vorden, we can discern a wish to once again reinstate clear boundaries: to clarify which war victims are included and which are excluded on Remembrance Day. In this article, I argue that in Dutch memory culture of the Second World War, such tensions between the »particular« and the »universal« have always existed. With the former, I mean the effort to draw boundaries, to define who can be the in-group in the Dutch war narrative and who does not belong to the memorial community. With the latter, I refer to more inclusive tendencies in memory culture and more universal meanings attached to the war, like the general value of human rights. Remembering the war in a democratic society is a pendulum that moves back and forth between those poles.

II. Oppression and Resistance

The Second World War in the Netherlands lasted from 10 May 1940 until 5 May 1945. On 10 May 1940, about a month after Germany had invaded Norway, German troops crossed the Dutch-German border. Both the Netherlands and Norway had hoped to stay out of the military conflict by reiterating their strategy of neutrality in international affairs, which had kept them out of the First World War. After the German attack, the government and the head of state in both countries – the Norwegian King and the Dutch Queen – fled to London. In the Netherlands the fighting lasted only five days, whereas it continued for almost two months in

---

7   Most famously this criticism was launched by Dutch historian J. C. H. Blom in his inaugural lecture in 1983. In his view, public opinion was (regrettably) under the spell of *goed* and *fout*: J. C. H. Blom: In de ban van goed en fout? Wetenschappelijke geschiedschrijving over de bezetting in Nederland, in: ibid. (ed.): Crisis, bezetting en herstel. Tien studies over Nederland 1930–1950, Den Haag 1989 [1983], 102–120; ibid: Nog altijd in de ban van goed en fout, in: De Volkskrant, 20 April 2007, 11.

Norway. Both countries were placed under a civil occupation régime, a *Reichskommissariat*, but with important differences in its execution. The war damage inflicted differed between the two countries, too. The southern provinces of the Netherlands were already liberated in September 1944, but the northern parts of the country had to wait for their liberation until April and May 1945. The winter of 1944–1945 was particularly tough for Dutch citizens in the big cities – Amsterdam, Rotterdam – and came to be known as the »hunger winter«. After the German capitulation in May 1945, the Netherlands found itself in dire straits. The nation had suffered more from the Second World War than other Western European countries. In particular, it experienced severe damage, economic and social chaos, and above all large numbers of casualties. The Netherlands lost comparatively many lives: 225,000 citizens. The largest group of victims were the Jews. Almost 75 per cent of the Dutch Jewry, about 102,000 of them, were murdered. Numerous Dutch citizens also died in the former colony of the Dutch East Indies, which constitutes another significant difference with Norway. The colony had been overrun by the Japanese army in early 1942 and remained under occupation until 15 August 1945. Immediately following the Japanese capitulation, a new war erupted: the Dutch-Indonesian war of decolonisation that lasted until the end of 1949.

These various war experiences were only selectively remembered in public after 1945. The *national* suffering played an important role in the narrative about the war: the Dutch nation as a collective victim of German aggression. The other essential patriotic element in this narrative was that of the resistance, which became the foundation myth of post-war Dutch society. According to the official narrative, *resistance* was glorified as the distinguishing attitude or mentality of the entire population: the Dutch people as a nation had defied the Germans. In public memory, the war thus became the paragon of national unity. Many Dutch people identified with this image of the Second World War as a period of »oppression and resistance«. It supported both the post-war reconstruction and the morale of the populace; one could be proud of the past.

This national myth in many cases compensated for the humiliating and shocking experience that had characterised the actual war experience. »National impotence« was demonstrated by the quick military defeat in 1940, the degrading occupation, and the liberation by foreign armies in 1944–1945.[8] In order to reconstruct national self-esteem, a meaningful patriotic narrative of national suf-

---

8   Pieter Lagrou: The Legacy of Nazi Occupation. Patriotic Memory and National Recovery in Western Europe, 1945–1965, Cambridge 2000, 2.

fering and resistance was constructed and disseminated with great success.⁹ In official speeches, war films, museums or schoolbooks – almost everywhere this image of the Second World War was reproduced. Consequently, the heroic death of resistance fighters and Dutch and Allied soldiers were at the centre of attention in the annual celebrations on 4 May.

The Netherlands owes the institution of its Remembrance Day, 4 May, to one individual: Jan Drop. This former resistance fighter from The Hague was the architect of the national commemoration. He wanted to honour the victims in a dignified ritual, observed nationally in a uniform way. For this purpose, he established the *Commissie Nationale Herdenking 1940–1945* (CNH, National Commemoration Commission 1940–1945), founded in late 1945. In the beginning, the CNH was merely a façade: the only members were Drop, his wife and a friend. Under the name of this commission, Drop drafted guidelines that spelled out exactly who was to be remembered, and how the commemorations on 4 May were to be held. The former resistance fighter gave his guidelines an official guise, with a formal letterhead and stilted language, and dispatched it to all municipalities nationwide. Most interpreted the initiative as originating from or at least sanctioned by the government. Neither was true. The prime minister had been informed of the initiative but was not further involved. Nevertheless, in 1946, Drop's ideas for commemorating the dead were copied throughout the Netherlands. The commemorations of those deceased during the Second World War on 4 May proved such a success that in 1947 the government asked the CNH to write a national manual for the remembrance of the dead. Thus, Drop's grassroots initiative was quickly institutionalised.

The first guideline specified those that were to be remembered on 4 May: »the Dutch soldiers, sailors and resistance fighters as well as the Allied soldiers, who died for the liberation of our country«.¹⁰ The national remembrance discourse of the immediate post-war period was very exclusive. Soldiers and resistance fighters were mentioned, but victims such as Jews, Roma, Sinti or other civilians had no specific place in the public commemorations.

This situation was not unique to the Netherlands, as at the time in many European countries cultural memory of the Second World War concentrated on *active*

---

9   Blom: Suffering as a Warning, 64–68; Frank van Vree: Auschwitz and the Origins of Contemporary Historical Culture. Memories of World War II in a European Perspective, in: A. Pók/J. Rüssen/J. Scherrer (eds.): European History. Challenge for a Common Future, Hamburg 2002, 202–220.

10 National Archives, The Hague (henceforth NL-HaNA), Ministry of the Interior, 2.04.87, 10448, guidelines CNH 1947.

victims, individuals who had died because of their (heroic) actions. Their deaths could not be interpreted as in vain; they had made sacrifices for the national community. By contrast, *passive* victims had not died through something they had *done*, but because of who they *were*.[11] Their deaths, as such, were useless to the post-war community. The national foundation myth of the resistance had no place or use for them. As Tony Judt has put it: »[W]hereas liberation, resistance and deportees [...] could all be put to some service in compensatory national myth-making, there was nothing ›usable‹ about the Holocaust.«[12] Moreover, there was silence about private memories and individual suffering in public memory. Resistance fighters and soldiers were not remembered as individual victims, but as heroic groups. The ideals for which they had fought – such as freedom, unanimity, independence or peace – were recalled during the commemorations of 4 May. Their legacy offered solace and was presented as a binding legacy for the present period of reconstruction as well as for the future. In this way, a meaningful relationship was established between the past, present and future.[13]

Throughout the 1950s, the guidelines provided by the CNH remained roughly unchanged. A first major alteration was implemented in 1961. From this year on, the commemorations of 4 May were dedicated to all victims, »either civilian or soldier«, who had »fallen since 10 May 1940, anywhere in the world, in the interest of the Kingdom [of the Netherlands]«.[14] In comparison to the earlier guidelines, clearly defined groups of active victims – such as resistance fighters and Allied soldiers – were not included anymore. Instead, the guidelines explicitly mentioned civilians for the first time in 1961. Yet they still mainly referred to active victims. The phrasing »in the interest of the Kingdom« hinted at soldiers and resistance fighters – the latter mainly being civilians – who had been part of the »good« side during the war. The commission wanted to avoid inadvertently including collaborators such as SS volunteers.

A more far-reaching change in the revised formulation of 1961 is hidden in the use of the words »since 10 May 1940«. In veiled terms, this implied that the

---

11 Aleida Assmann: Der lange Schatten der Vergangenheit: Erinnerungskultur und Geschichtspolitik, München 2006, 73–74.
12 Tony Judt: Postwar: a History of Europe since 1945, New York 2005, 809.
13 Frank van Vree: In de schaduw van Auschwitz. Herinneringen, beelden, geschiedenis, Groningen 1995, 43–44; Van Vree: Auschwitz and the Origins, 204.
14 NL-HaNA, Prime minister's Cabinet, 2.03.01, 2338, guidelines CNH 1962. In 1961, the national commemoration was already dedicated to all victims who died for the Kingdom since 10 May 1940, but only in 1962 was this printed in the guidelines.

Dutch soldiers who had died since the end of the Second World War would also be commemorated on 4 May. In concrete terms – which, however, were not specified – this concerned the soldiers who had died during the Indonesian War of Independence (1945–1949) as well as during the Korean War (1950–1953). Early in the 1950s a group of Dutch East Indies veterans had started to claim the right for their fallen comrades to be included in the national commemoration on 4 May. These soldiers had given their lives for the country and were therefore to be remembered on this day as well. This was eventually achieved in 1961, after intensive lobbying efforts that had lasted many years.

As 4 May had highlighted active victims, the category of soldiers who died in Indonesia and Korea fitted well into the patriotic remembrance discourse. Yet their status was not undisputed. The Second World War had largely been seen as a »good« struggle, which could (at least in public) be associated with an unproblematic distinction between *goed* and *fout*. More importantly, the Second World War was a struggle in which the suffering had not been in vain. The same could not be said about the Indonesian Revolution, which had ended with the loss of the former colony, the Dutch East Indies. What is more, the distinction between *goed* and *fout* was not straightforward in this case. Military intervention in Indonesia had already been called into question while the war was still being fought. Nevertheless, the military lobby proved stronger than these concerns.[15] The inclusion of the Dutch-Indonesian war of decolonisation in the official commemorations on 4 May was the first serious blot on the unanimity around the national commemoration day.

Starting in 1961, the Dutch Remembrance Day, originally instituted to honour the (active) victims of the Second World War, was no longer solely dedicated to this war, but to all wars in which the Netherlands had been involved since 1940. In this way, the Dutch national commemoration day came to resemble its counterparts in Great Britain, France or Belgium, where victims of the First and Second World War were collectively remembered on the same day. What did not yet change, however, in the Netherlands as elsewhere, is that memory culture in the first decades after the Second World War remained in the tradition of commemorating active victims, those who had »sacrificed« their lives for their country and

---

15   Iris van Ooijen/Ilse Raaijmakers: The Interaction between Postwar and Postcolonial Memory in the Netherlands, in: Journal of Genocide Research 14 (2012), no. 3–4, 463–483.

had not died »in vain«.[16] The Dutch followed patriotic and political rituals and rhetoric that were practiced in many European countries.[17]

III. Personal Suffering and Political Protest

From the 1960s onwards, the patriotic tide turned, as the Holocaust gradually began to take a more central place in the public memory of the Second World War. This was a process that again occurred simultaneously in many western European countries. Yet in the Netherlands the change in memory culture seems to have started slightly earlier. The 1960s had already seen a wider dissemination of the knowledge that the Nazis had murdered an incredibly high number of Dutch Jews – much higher than in other western European countries including Germany. In Dutch society there was an increasing interest in (and acknowledgement of) the suffering of the Jews during and after the war.

A series of events mark this change in Dutch memory culture. The Eichmann trial in Jerusalem (1961) was broadly covered by Dutch media, which alerted many Dutch people to the Jewish suffering. In 1962, the memorial site *Hollandsche Schouwburg* (Dutch theatre) in Amsterdam opened its doors as the first national monument dedicated specifically to Jewish war victims. The Nazis had used this former theatre as a deportation centre. Jews had been imprisoned here before they were transferred to *Durchgangslager Westerbork* or sometimes other camps. The third significant event, which is given most importance in the relevant historiography, is the publication of the deeply influential book *Ondergang* (literally, »Downfall«; translated into English in 1969 as »The Destruction of the Dutch Jews«). The author was Jacques Presser, a professor in Dutch history at the University of Amsterdam and a Jewish survivor himself. Published in 1965, the book sold over 140,000 copies within a year. Many people also watched the popular TV-series *De Bezetting* (The Occupation) that was broadcast between 1960 and 1965 on Dutch television and subsequently repeated many times. This TV-series tended to affirm the patriotic narrative of oppression and resistance, but significantly it also paid attention to the persecution and destruction of the Jews, as well as to personal

---

16 Manfred Hettling/Jörg Echternkamp (eds.): Gefallenengedenken im globalen Vergleich. Nationale Tradition, politische Legitimation und Individualisierung der Erinnerung, München 2013.
17 Van Vree: Auschwitz and the Origins, 203.

suffering in general, especially by introducing eyewitness accounts.[18] The process of increasing acknowledgment of individual suffering continued in the 1970s. As in Norway, the broadcasting of the American TV-miniseries »Holocaust« in 1979 was a key event that increased the awareness of the prosecution of the Jews. This TV-series had a huge impact on the debate about the Holocaust in the Netherlands as well, but it did not have the catalysing effect on memory culture as it had in Norway.[19] It was rather an illustrative event in a memory shift that was already underway.

In the 1960s and 1970s, the representation of the Second World War gradually started to change from the heroic and nationalistic notion of oppression and resistance into an image that focused more on senseless (passive) suffering – with the persecution and extermination in the concentration camps as icons – and on individual harm. The Dutch political class and society realised that many war victims still struggled with psychological and physical problems due to their dreadful experiences. »War trauma« became a central notion. Thus, new welfare provisions for some war victims were introduced, such as the »Victims of Persecution Benefits Act«[20] of 1972. In the framework of the new memory culture, the memories and feelings of survivors and other first generation victims were accorded a prominent role – their voices acquired authoritative status in many memory debates. Acknowledgment of and respect for the passive victims in addition to the active victims was increasingly regarded as common sense. This change has been characterised as a shift from a political to a psychological narrative. The war was now no longer primarily interpreted in terms of national suffering and of fellow countrymen who had died »for our freedom«. Rather it came to be seen as a period that had caused harm and hardship to many individuals who often are still scarred by their experiences.[21]

In the guidelines for the 4 May commemorations, this shift in Dutch memory culture of the Second World War was also visible. The new specification for those

---

18   Blom: Suffering as a Warning, 66–88; Van Vree: In de schaduw van Auschwitz, 80–86; Rob van Ginkel: Rondom de stilte. Herdenkingscultuur in Nederland, Amsterdam 2011, 379–392.
19   Bjarte Bruland/Mats Tangestuens: The Norwegian Holocaust. Changing Views and Representations, in: Scandinavian Journal of History 36 (2011), no. 5, 587–604.
20   Wet Uitkering Vervolgingsslachtoffers.
21   Jolande Withuis/Annet Mooij: From Totalitarianism to Trauma. A Paradigm Change in the Netherlands, in: ibid. (eds.): The Politics of War Trauma. The Aftermath of World War II in Eleven European Countries, Amsterdam 2010, 193–215.

that were to be remembered in the celebrations, introduced in 1961, were further amended in 1966 by adding one phrase. From that year on, the commemoration also explicitly referred to »all those, who died because of acts of war or terror«.[22] This was an indirect reference to the Jewish and other passive victims. The commission had changed the phrasing, it reported to the government, because it had been pointed out to them that the overwhelming majority of Jews had not fallen »in the interest of the Kingdom«, but rather had been murdered because of their descent.[23] That the commission explicitly explained their reasoning illustrates the change in thinking about the war in the Netherlands at the time. Again, this was a gradual process that took many years before it became dominant in Dutch memory culture – as of then, it only merited a sub-clause in the guidelines. During many commemorations on 4 May, at least until the late twentieth century and sometimes even at present, the patriotic rhetoric of the immediate post-war period has retained a strong influence. Yet from the late-1960s onwards, the passive victims have not been absent from the commemorative stage, and the organisers have persistently increased their prominence.

These changes were naturally linked to the social and cultural upheaval of the 1960s. A growing awareness of the persecution of the Jews was related to and interacted with the protest of a new generation that was born after the Second World War. The »baby boomers« were raised in prosperity and more interested in post-material values than their parents. One of the sacred cows that the protesters attacked was the patriotic narrative about the war. The resistance myth was the main target of criticism. Many in the protest generation held a more critical view of the Dutch war past, choosing rather to highlight collaboration. They confronted the administrative elites with their behaviour during the war, leading to numerous heated debates. As a result, the memory of the Second World War became highly politicised; the war was used as political weapon to criticise the present. As Dutch historian Frank van Vree has stressed: »The war became a source for political and moral criticism to establish positive proof of the inner weakness of the prevailing social and political system and its ›petty-bourgeois‹ mentality.«[24] But this did not lead to a change in the fundamental moral framework of interpreting the war in terms of *goed* and *fout*, as another famous Dutch historian J.C.H. Blom has

---

22 NL-HaNA, Prime minister's Cabinet, 2.03.01, 2338, guidelines CNH 1966.
23 NL-HaNA, Prime minister's Cabinet, 2.03.01, 2338, letter CNH to prime minister, 2 February 1966.
24 Van Vree: Auschwitz and the Origins, 209–210.

argued: »It is striking that the innovators, who wanted to overturn so many old values, did not oppose the basic consensus on the war.«²⁵ It is merely that they identified a lot more *fout* – not that they started to see more shades of grey.

The protest generation experimented with alternative ways of commemorating the war – ways that were more openly political manifestations. »Alternative commemorations« were organised to protest against worldwide injustices like racism and the oppression of minorities. The annual commemorations on 4 May were used to position oneself against human rights violations in Indonesia, Greece, Spain, Chile, Brazil, Angola or South Africa. In the same vein, others seized the opportunity of 4 May to denounce the dire housing shortage in the Netherlands. These concerns seem rather far removed from the direct memory of the Second World War, but such was indeed the intention. For the activists themselves, the commemorations were not only to remember the war dead, but also meant to have an impact on current issues. Initially, the alternative commemorations existed parallel to the official celebrations of 4 May, but slowly the former started to enter into the mainstream of Dutch memory culture. This development was again reflected in the guidelines for Remembrance Day. In 1970, another sentence was added to the 1966 formula: »It is advisable that the National Commemoration should also comprise, insofar as possible, a reflection on the present and the future of our country and people.«²⁶

Approximately a decade later, the influence of the protest generation and alternative commemorations had become even clearer with the addition of yet another sentence: »The commemorations are also an appeal to everyone's individual responsibility in today's society with regard to oppression, racism and intolerance.«²⁷ Thus, whilst the 1970 guidelines made no specific suggestions as to what the preferred lessons for the present and future during the commemorations of 4 May were to be, this was formalised in greater detail in the early 1980s. The commemorations were to contribute in the fight against oppression, racism and intolerance. These were causes that used to be associated more with left-wing social movements and action groups, but by the 1980s they had become accepted targets among large groups in society. Moreover, the idea that the memory of the Second World War was to be »actualised« became a common sense notion. In order to connect with the post-war generations, many people saw the need to »translate«

---

25   Blom: Suffering as a Warning, 67.
26   NL-HaNA, Prime minister's Cabinet, 2.03.01, 2338, guidelines CNH 1970.
27   NL-HaNA, Prime minister's Cabinet, 2.03.01, 8605, guidelines CNH 1981.

war memory into a present-day message. The government took an active role in this process of »actualising« by making this process an official policy field. It provided information and funded many initiatives throughout the country. The field of education on the Second World War in particular turned into a booming business. What is more, it was finally decided to make the commemorations of 4 May a government responsibility. Until that year, surprisingly, starting with Jan Drop's *coup* in 1946, the »National Commemorations« had remained under the supervision of a formally independent civil society initiative.

Over the course of a few decades, the traditional patriotic memory culture, centred on clearly defined active victims, had transformed into a more pluriform and critical discourse, focusing on different groups of victims and more generally on such issues as injustice and oppression. The particular groups of resistance fighters and (Allied) soldiers made room for wider categories of war victims and more universal war lessons on 4 May. At the same time, Dutch memory culture became increasingly differentiated and open to new voices. Especially in the 1980s, Dutch society witnessed more groups promoting their own agenda, more diverse commemorations, more monuments, as well as new categories of victims asserting themselves. They joined forces to lobby for their recognition in an official capacity, for instance, in such organisations as the »Foundation for Civilian War Victims«[28] (1981) or the »Association of Children of the Japanese Occupation and the *Bersiap* 1941–1949«[29] (1988). In general, the victims of the war in the former Dutch colony attracted more attention. In 1988, they received their own national monument and commemoration day on 15 August, the anniversary of the Japanese surrender. Likewise, »victims« of collaboration started to organise as well: the children of fascist party members of the *Nationaal-Socialistische Beweging* had their *Stichting Werkgroep Erkenning* (1981, Foundation Working Group Recognition). Thus, the flipside of the widespread respect for and acknowledgment of war victims in society also became visible: victim groups were specified in ever more minute detail, frequently giving rise to rivalry and competition between them.

In any case, the grand patriotic myth of oppression and resistance had lost its integrative power, making way for a narrative of suffering, with one central feature:

---

28 Stichting Burger-Oorlogsgetroffenen.
29 Vereniging Kinderen uit de Japanse Bezetting en de Bersiap 1941–1949. The *Bersiap* refers to the chaotic period in the Dutch-Indonesian war, in which many Dutch and Eurasian civilians were killed at the hands of Indonesians (para)-military groups.

the dominant place of the Holocaust. The deportation and murder of the Jews became the key experience of the Second World War.[30]

IV. Beyond *Goed* and *Fout* and the International Impact

Many of the memory trends that started in the 1960s have not yet come to a conclusion. The Holocaust has increasingly been considered the most important and radical event in the context of the Second World War, even of the twentieth century in general, but its specific position within the commemorations continues to be debated. There are, however, also some further transformations that have taken place since the fall of the Berlin Wall. In the 1990s, the call for a more critical perspective of the behaviour of the Dutch during the occupation period became more widespread. The moral framework of *goed* and *fout* itself was criticised for being too black and white. Hence, an insight that had become common in historiography already by the 1980s only entered the public debate in the 1990s, often presented as taboo breaking. The dichotomy of the evil and guilty Germans, on the one side, and the good and innocent Dutchmen, on the other, was questioned. Narratives of shame and guilt became more prominent in public discourse. Queen Beatrix, for instance, spoke in front of the Knesset during her state visit to Israel in 1995. She started out by making reference to the »courageous and sometimes successful resistance«. »But«, she continued, »we also know that they were the exceptional ones, that the people of the Netherlands could not prevent the destruction of their Jewish fellow citizens«.[31] In July of that same year, this new interpretation was thrown into sharp relief, as Dutch UN-peacekeepers stood passively by during the massacre of thousands of Muslim men in the Bosnian town of Srebrenica. In the public debate over these events, the narrative of war was interpreted as not only revolving around victims and perpetrators, but involving a category of bystanders as well. Parallels between Srebrenica and the Second World War were easily made, also in this respect.

This more critical perspective on the Second World War was central in various heated memory debates, for example, on the question of whether German representatives should be invited to commemorations on 4 May or to the national

---

30 Van Vree: Auschwitz and the Origins, 210.
31 Beatrix. Koningin der Nederlanden: Voor het behoud van de menselijkheid. Vier redevoeringen van Koningin Beatrix, Amsterdam 1995, 29.

liberation day celebrations on 5 May. Already in the 1990s a passionate discussion raged over the question of whether the Dutch should invite West German Chancellor Helmut Kohl to the ceremony on 4 May 1995. Advocates of a joint Dutch-German commemoration thought this would do justice to present-day international relations in Europe. The former enemy, Germany had turned into an ally in a united Europe. According to the proponents, 4 May would be the ideal occasion to stress post-war European successes like European reconciliation, integration and co-operation. Aversion to this plan was so intense, however, especially among contemporaries of the Second World War, that the government quickly abandoned the idea. Their perspective on the war was still dominant. A joint commemoration would deeply offend war victims who deserved to be the focus of attention. The overall feeling in 1994–1995 was that if these victims were not yet ready to commemorate in the presence of German representatives, Dutch society should respect this.[32] More than 15 years later, the situation had changed. Many contemporaries had passed away in the meantime and the invitation to German President Joachim Gauck to deliver a speech on 5 May 2012 in the Netherlands did not cause major outrage. A joint commemoration on 4 May, however, remains a taboo, as both the heated discussions in 2009–2010 as well as the Vorden incident of 2012 demonstrate.[33]

Another development traceable in the commemorations since 1989 is that Dutch memory culture became more and more internationally oriented and influenced by developments abroad. The fall of the Berlin Wall has made former Nazi concentration camps and war memories in Eastern Europe accessible for mass tourism. European integration has also impacted on the memory of the Second World War. In the interpretation that was given to the war, Europe came to play a more prominent role. European cooperation and reconciliation were more often highlighted during commemorations as important lessons to be learned and celebrated. Developments at home such as the growing importance of the Holocaust in the memory culture of the Second World War were further strengthened by the international context. For instance, the Netherlands participated in the Task Force for International Cooperation on Holocaust Education, Remembrance and

---

32 Ilse Raaijmakers: A new European myth? The debate about Dutch-German commemorations of the Second World War in the Netherlands, in: K.Thijs/R. Haude (eds.): Grenzfälle. Transfer und Konflikt zwischen Deutschland, Belgien und den Niederlanden im 20. Jahrhundert, Heidelberg 2013, 213–230.
33 Maud van de Reijt: Zestig jaar herrie om twee minuten stilte. Hoe wij steeds meer doden gingen herdenken, Amsterdam 2010, 10–14.

Research (ITF, known since January 2013 as the International Holocaust Remembrance Alliance, IHRA). From 2005 onwards, Holocaust Remembrance Day is commemorated every year in the Netherlands, mainly at universities as well as at the Auschwitz memorial in Amsterdam. Moreover, attention to the suffering of the Jews in many countries has become a vehicle for a more internationalised way of remembering the Second World War – the Holocaust as a transnational phenomenon. Since 1989, the Second World War has thus been given an increasingly international, European or even universal meaning, in the Netherlands as elsewhere.[34] This development continues until today, as was clearly demonstrated during Gauck's visit on 5 May 2012 when he referred to »Europe« and its blessings numerous times in his speech. Yet simultaneously, the more universalistic interpretation of the Second World War has started to cause increasing discomfort in some sections of the population, especially representatives of victim groups.

V. Conclusion: Between the Particular and the Universal

On the occasion of 4 May 2012, the 15-year-old Dutch pupil Auke de Leeuw wrote a poem about his great-uncle after whom he had been named. It was called *Foute keuze* (Wrong Choice) – the great-uncle in question had died as a Waffen SS volunteer on the Eastern Front. In the closing line the teenager wrote that his uncle »should not be forgotten«.[35] The poem was selected by the National Committee 4 and 5 May to be recited during the National Commemoration ceremony on 4 May in Amsterdam. It did not come to that. Fierce protests made the organisation decide to withdraw the poem from the programme.

May 2012 was thus in many ways a tumultuous remembrance month. The debates about the commemoration of German soldiers in Vorden or SS volunteers in Amsterdam reveal unease with recent developments in Dutch memory culture. The more self-critical perspective of the war has blurred the distinction between victims and perpetrators, between *goed* and *fout*. It has given way to a more nuanced view of the Second World War, but on the occasion of the national commemoration days this sometimes causes discomfort. If we can no longer distinguish between *goed*

---

34 Although less so in eastern Europe, see: Arnd Bauerkämper: Das umstrittene Gedächtnis. Die Erinnerung an Nationalsozialismus, Faschismus und Krieg in Europa seit 1945, Paderborn 2012.
35 Auke Siebe Dirk: Foute Keuze, NRC online, last access: 9 May 2014, <http://www.nrc.nl/nieuws/2012/04/26/maker-omstreden-gedicht-ik-heb-niemand-willen-kwetsen/>.

and *fout*, who, then, is to be remembered on 4 May? This uncertainty explains some of the fierce debates that have raged in the Netherlands in recent years.

These days, uniform official guidelines are no longer provided to all municipalities, but there is still a national template for 4 May. It defines who is to be remembered on this day: »During the National Commemoration on 4 May we commemorate all – civilians or soldiers – who died or were killed in the Kingdom of the Netherlands or wherever in the world since the Second World War broke out, in war situations or during peace operations.«[36] The »actualising« rhetoric from the 1980s has disappeared. »Peace operations« of course refers to more recent war experiences under the flags of the United Nations or NATO. In the early 1990s the wording that those to be commemorated should have died »in the interest of the Kingdom« was dropped. This has broadened the definition and left room for multiple interpretations. The verbatim text, interpreted literally, therefore reads that all war victims fall under this definition, including those who could be regarded as *fout*. After all, they died in war situations as well. But as the 2012 events illustrate, not everyone favours such a broad interpretation.

The recent criticism makes the circle round. The Dutch started with a very narrow definition of whom to remember: (Allied) soldiers and resistance fighters. This category of victims gradually became more inclusive and at the same time partly moved away from the Second World War by focusing on injustices in the present. There is currently a broad definition, leaving room for alternative interpretations. But as a reaction, some Dutch citizens have once again started to ask for more clarity. In their view, it should be indisputably clear who is in – and excluded from the commemorations of 4 May. It illustrates the importance of public remembrances as a moment in which the Dutch postulate and confirm a collective identity.

In the process of giving meaning to memory there is a tension between the particular and the universal. Particular and universal interpretations of the war have been like a pendulum, swinging back and forth between extremes, with many combinations in-between. They are not necessarily contrasting, but the Dutch have thus far lacked a vision or a formula for a national memory culture that combines both particularistic and universal elements. This tension between the particular and the universal, between exclusion and inclusion, is perhaps characteristic of memory cultures in democracies in general. It is a challenging task for all democratic countries to find a balance.

---

36 Memorandum National Committee 4 and 5 May, last access: 9 May 2014, <http://www.4en5mei.nl/4_en_5_mei/nationale_herdenking/wie_herdenken_we>.

III.
Narratives of the Past in Historiography, Education and Museums

Gunnar D. Hatlehol
In Command of History?
Historians, Memory Culture and German
War Crimes against Foreign Prisoners in Norway

I. Introduction

During the Second World War, Norway fared much better than many other countries under German occupation. Nevertheless, the German occupiers committed acts, including war crimes, during these war years which were without comparison the most radical ever carried out by a foreign power on Norwegian soil. The sheer scale of the war crimes committed in Europe was illustrated by the fact that 80,000 Germans were named on the list of suspected German war criminals which the Supreme Headquarters, Allied Expeditionary Forces (SHAEF), had prepared by the end of the war in May 1945. When the Allied Expeditionary Corps arrived in Norway to oversee the disarmament of the German occupying forces, the hunt for war criminals got underway. In connection with this effort, carried out by the War Crimes Investigation Branch, 1,622 Germans were arrested.[1] While 10,000 Norwegian citizens were killed during the war, 16,000 foreign prisoners died in prisoner of war camps in Norway, many of them the result of war crimes. The largest group of victims consisted of 13,000 Soviet prisoners of war. The other victims were British military personnel, Yugoslav prisoners, Polish, Czech, German and French forced labourers, and also German military convicts.[2]

In order to determine what the war cost Norway, to hold perpetrators accountable and clarify political questions regarding the German invasion and occupation, a number of historians began working on various topics related to the history of Norway from 1940 to 1945. This community of historians grew over time. At

---

1   Berit Nøkleby: Krigsforbrytelser. Brudd på krigens lov i 1940–1945, Oslo 2004, 23–25.
2   War Crimes in Norway. Report 21.3.1946 from War Crimes Investigation Branch, Norway. Riksarkivet, Riksadvokatens krigsforbryterarkiv, Da box 41.

the same time, public interest in the Norwegian wartime experiences remained strong.[3]

This article aims to examine how Norwegian historians became interested in foreign prisoners in Norway in general, and the war crimes committed against them by the German occupying forces in particular. What kind of interest have they shown towards the subject and in what ways did this influence their depictions of Norway's recent war history? And moreover – to which extent have these historical writings been influenced by the fact that the history of Norway during the Second World War is intertwined with those of other countries, as the arrival and treatment of foreign prisoners in Norway so vividly exemplified?

Furthermore, I want to see whether the historians' research results on the subject have made an impact on the general historical awareness of Norwegians. I will discuss whether Norwegian historians have managed to influence the public commemorations of the war and German war crimes. Have Norwegian historians been able to affect and influence the space afforded to foreign war victims in the Norwegian collective memory of the occupation? Or, would it be more accurate to say that it is the historians who have been affected by Norway's wider memory culture? In other words – what kind of interaction has existed between the research conducted by Norwegian historians and Norwegian memory culture?

II. Historiography

The Norwegian community of professional historians was very small immediately after the war, with scholarly positions limited to five professorships and docents at the University of Oslo and a professorship at Norway's Teacher College.[4] There were no other research institutions offering career prospects for historians during this initial post-war period, which strongly limited the amount of historical research that could have been published. The foundation for the study of the Norwegian occupation history was provided by the state-appointed Investigative Commission of 1945, which was meant to examine the circumstances that led to the German invasion and subjugation of Norway and the establishment of a

---

3   See Ole Kristian Grimnes: Occupation and Collective Memory in Norway, in: Stig Ekman & Nils Edling (ed.): War Experience, Self Image and National Identity. The Second World War as Myth and History, Stockholm 1997, 131–141.
4   Sivert Langholm: The Infrastructure of History, in: William H. Hubbard et al. (eds.): Making a Historical Culture. Historiography in Norway, Oslo 1995, 90.

German occupation government in the country, particularly with the objective of determining whether the Norwegian political authorities had acted in a questionable manner.[5] Professor Sverre Steen at the University of Oslo played a key role in the shaping of key parts of the Investigative Commission's final report. He subsequently became the chief editor of Norway's three-volume edition *Norges Krig* (»Norway's War«), which was published in the years between 1947 and 1950. With contributions from thirty individuals, of whom only five were trained historians, the work showed signs of having been written for an audience with firsthand experience of the occupation and with the events still fresh in their memory. The history depicted was that of the Norwegians, particularly those Norwegians who on 8 May 1945 welcomed the German defeat. A community of »us« versus »them« was cultivated. Aside from the Norwegians, the other prominent parties in the history were the Germans and the British.

Only one of the collection's entire 2,350 pages was devoted to foreign victims of German war crimes in Norway. In this modest space, the abuse and executions of Yugoslav prisoners in camps in Northern Norway were depicted. It would appear that the source for this entry is the report from a war crimes case against 33 Germans who were extradited from Norway to Yugoslavia and put on trial in Belgrade in 1946, but without the trial being referred to as anything other than »the process in Yugoslavia«. The time, location and basis for the trial, which was the subject of modest coverage in the Norwegian media, remained completely unaccounted for. Soviet prisoners of war were mentioned only twice, and then under the generic term »Eastern Europeans«. Their living conditions were illustrated with two images instead of text. The accompanying caption to one of the photographs states that the camps »were often inhumanely primitive«.[6]

The author of the contribution, Haakon Holmboe, then promptly returned to the subject of the Norwegians themselves, noting, »Norwegian political prisoners only endured such experiences in the concentration camps in Germany.« He then continues with a description of Grini prison camp, which in total takes up 30 pages of the relevant volume. Holmboe mentions that prisoners from 18 other nations were held in the camp, but dedicates less than one page to them. He does, however, make it clear that the treatment of foreign prisoners at Grini was even harsher than for the Norwegian prisoners. He suggests that some Norwegians' attitudes

---

5   Helge Sivertsen (ed.): Innstilling fra Undersøkelseskommisjonen av 1945, Oslo 2010.
6   Author's translation. Haakon Holmboe: De som ble tatt, in: Sverre Steen (ed.): Norges Krig, vol 3, Oslo 1950, 446.

towards the foreign prisoners went beyond just plain indifference: »One cannot deny that the Germans' contempt for and brutality towards the foreigners spread to a number of the Norwegian prisoners, who eventually became accustomed to accepting the Germans' view of the foreigners – especially Eastern Europeans – as inferior.«[7]

Sverre Steen's subsequent research project about the occupation, conducted within the institutional framework of the newly established »Institute for Norwegian Historical Research«, resulted in his supervision of three Ph.D. dissertations, all of which were subsequently published as books. Magne Skodvin's *Striden om okkupasjonsstyret i Norge fram til 25. september 1940* (1956), »The Struggle Regarding the Occupation Régime in Norway until 25 September 1940« and Thomas Christian Wyller's *Nyordning og Motstand: En framstilling og en analyse av organisasjonenes politiske funksjon under den tyske okkupasjonen 25.9.1940–25.9.1942* (1958), »New Order and Resistance: A Depiction and Analysis of the Organisations' Political Role during the German Occupation 25.9.1940–25.9.1942« dealt with topics peripheral to the issue of German war crimes.[8] However, the third dissertation, *Hjemmestyrkene: Hovedtrekk av den militære motstanden under okkupasjonen* (1959), »The Resistance: Characteristics of the Military Resistance during the Occupation«, by Sverre Kjeldstadli, went far beyond its initial narrow focus, mainly through describing the wider context of the resistance movement's activities, as well as the mentality of the opposing side. The work was limited, however, to depicting war crimes committed against Norwegians and Britons, as these had their origins in the operations by both the resistance movement and the Allied forces against the German occupation forces in Norway.

Already early on in the project, Steen returned to the research interests he had pursued before the war, and following the completion of Kjeldstadli's work, he withdrew completely from the historical research community that he had founded. Thomas Wyller, for his part, returned to his original career as a political scientist, and his subsequent academic career led him in other scholarly directions. Kjeldstadli died suddenly in 1961, just as he had begun working on completing a follow-up to the dissertation about the resistance movement.[9] Only Magne

---

7 Holmboe, 466.
8 Øystein Sørensen: Forskningen om krigen i Norge, in: Nytt Norsk Tidsskrift 6 (1989), 42.
9 The notes from his work on the second volume of *Hjemmestyrkene* would suggest that Kjeldstadli intended to describe the ordeals of the Soviet prisoners of war in some detail. See Sverre Kjeldstadli's private papers at the Norwegian Resistance Museum, NHM 187 box 48.

Skodvin remained active in the field; he subsequently became the focal point of the historical research community dealing with the occupation, and eventually the field's undisputed leading expert.

Skodvin became the leader of the Research Group for Contemporary History (*Samtidshistorisk Forskningsgruppe*), consisting of a circle of younger historians, and started the project »Norway and the Second World War« in 1968. The project was the most ambitious historical research initiative pertaining to World War II in Norway until then, and produced a number of anthologies and dissertations. It disbanded, however, when the Norwegian Research Council for General Science suspended funding in the mid-1970s.[10] A third research group, led by Rolf Danielsen and Stein Ugelvik Larsen, was at the same time established at the University of Bergen, but limited itself to an interdisciplinary study of various aspects of the Norwegian Nazi Party Nasjonal Samling in the years 1933–1945, which resulted in the release of an anthology, before this project was also to suffer a quiet death.[11]

Unlike other countries that had experienced German occupation, such as the Netherlands and Denmark, but also in contrast to Sweden, which had avoided being drawn into the war, the Norwegian government seemed to be rather uninterested in providing financial support to historical research on the war. Norwegian research institutions, which had increased in number in the meantime, were not prepared to give priority to occupation studies. German war crimes in particular, and the foreign prisoners and prisoners of war in general, thus remained neglected themes in the Norwegian historiography. While the occupying power's criminal policies towards foreigners were generally acknowledged and understood, and were in any case something that a substantial number of the Norwegian adult population had experienced first-hand, they remained a topic that failed to interest Norwegian historians. Yet, there were a number of freelance writers and journalists who since the 1950s had published books that provided more detailed accounts of the foreign prisoners' ordeals in Norway. For a lengthy period, these books remained the only secondary sources of knowledge on the subject of German war crimes committed against foreign prisoners in Norway.

---

10 Berit Nøkleby: Okkupasjonshistorien – Et minefelt, in: Guri Hjeltnes et al. (ed.): Det elegante uromoment. Hans Fredrik Dahl og offentligheten, Oslo 2009, 90.
11 Rolf Danielsen & Stein Ugelvik Larsen: Fra idé til dom. Noen trekk fra utviklingen av Nasjonal Samling, Bergen 1976.

A milestone in the Norwegian historiography of the war is the book series *Norge i krig* (»Norway at War«), published in a total of eight volumes between 1984 and 1987. This remains the latest comprehensive history of Norway during the Second World War. All the contributions to the series were formulated by historians, but were written and presented as a popular scientific study, aimed at the broadest possible audience, without any citations and even lacking a bibliography, despite the authors' expressed wishes to supplement the volumes with such material.[12] The publications revealed that there had been a significant development among Norwegian historians over the passing decades. In the words of the work's main consultant Bjarne Gran, there should be now »room for those who feel excluded«.[13] Gran did not specifically mention the foreign war victims among the excluded groups, but historians went on to make these groups more visible and let them assume a more integrated, if still far from comprehensive place in the historical war narrative. Three volumes of *Norge i krig* (nos. 3, 5 and 8), each of them to varying degrees based on original research, tried to depict the war crimes committed against foreign prisoners in greater detail. Among the contributions that stand out is the account by Guri Hjeltnes of the working and living conditions of the Soviet and Yugoslav prisoners of war at the so-called Blood Road. The text left the reader in no doubt as to the enormous differences between the lives and treatment of Norwegian and foreign prisoners. The prison camps for the Yugoslavs were collectively described as »pure extermination camps with a brutality on par with the worst that the Germans had established in Poland. In the Beisfjord camp, for example, 300 men were massacred in late July 1942. Among the approximately 900 Yugoslavs who were brought to Beisfjord around Midsummer 1942, only 150 were alive three to four months later.«[14] One of the other authors, Tim Greve, situated the war crimes in Norway into a broader international context and set himself apart by becoming the first historian to discuss the understanding of the war crime concept, a discussion that in Norway had previously been left to the lawyers.[15]

Historical perspectives on the war years broadened in the 1980s and 1990s. Historians then became interested in the war experiences of a number of previously

---

12   Synne Corell: Krigens ettertid. Okkupasjonshistorien i norske historiebøker, Oslo 2010, 116–117.
13   Corell, 122.
14   Guri Hjeltnes: Norge i krig, bind 5. Hverdagsliv, Oslo 1986, 76.
15   Tim Greve: Norge i krig, bind 3. Verdenskrig, Oslo 1985, 103–104; Johs. Andenæs: Det vanskelige oppgjøret. Rettsoppgjøret etter okkupasjonen, Oslo 1979, 210.

marginalised groups, such as the children of German soldiers, the Norwegian girlfriends of German soldiers, sailors in the merchant navy, but also partisans, members of Communist resistance groups, as well as Norwegian Jews and the Holocaust victims. Debates on which direction future research on the history of the occupation should take were usually heated.[16] Soviet and other foreign prisoners, however, still remained marginalised groups in historical research. No comprehensive study of German war crimes had been conducted. And while the Polish historian Emilia Denkiewicz-Szczepaniak wrote about Polish prisoners and forced labourers in Norway, and the Serbian historian Ljubo Mladenović chronicled the history of Yugoslav prisoners in Norway, neither of their books, published in their native countries in 1998 and 1991, respectively, were translated into Norwegian. The international impact of their research was minimal.

At the turn of the millennium, the book series *Norge i krig* remained the only attempt by Norwegian historians to expand on Norwegian war history studies, albeit modestly, so as to include foreign prisoners and victims of war crimes. A master's thesis, undertaken by Birgit Koch in 1988, on Soviet, Yugoslav and Polish prisoners of war remained the only major academic historical contribution.[17] Professor of History Odd-Bjørn Fure linked the historians' lack of interest in the topic to a presumed fear of involvement. He was open to the idea that the marginalisation of the foreign war victims in historical depictions reflected an unconscious attitude amongst Norwegians that the suffering of war victims did not concern them, especially in light of the patriotic fervour that had swept over the country immediately after the war as the collective war memory was being created. According to Fure, the history of the foreign prisoners ought to gain a central place in the narrative of the occupation years in Norway. They represented an imported version of »the catastrophic experience of occupation among Eastern Europeans« to Norway, and typified a local approach to understanding the brutal character of Nazi occupation policies in Eastern Europe: »Representations of Norwegian occupation history that fail to incorporate the treatment of Slavic prisoners are not simply incomplete. They also lack essential perspectives on the overall war and occupation experience.«[18]

---

16   Susanne Maerz: Okkupasjonstidens lange skygger. Fortidsbearbeidelse i Norge som identitetsdiskurs, Oslo 2010, 251–257.
17   Birgit Koch: De sovjetiske, polske og jugoslaviske krigsfanger i tysk fangenskap i Norge 1941–1945, University of Oslo 1988.
18   Odd Bjørn Fure: Norsk okkupasjonshistorie. Konsensus, berøringsangst og tabuisering, in Stein Ugelvik Larsen (ed.): I krigens kjølvann. Nye sider ved norsk krigshistorie

III. The Memory Culture and Politics of Memory

In the initial years after the war, German war crimes in Norway and the fate of the foreign prisoners in Norway regularly made headlines in Norwegian newspapers.[19] This helped foster a collective awareness of the issue. The victims were buried in far more dignified way than during the war years and laid to rest in cemeteries set aside for that purpose. In the vicinity of these cemeteries, a number of monuments honouring the victims were constructed. On the sites of several war crimes, memorials were also erected shortly after the war. By and large, however, the memorials, often linked to cemeteries, focused on the prisoners who had perished, while the story of the war crimes that caused their deaths usually ended up in the background.

The Norwegian-Yugoslav film *Blodveien* (»The Blood Road«), which was released in 1955 and dealt with Yugoslav prisoners in an unnamed prison camp, became a popular cultural approach to the memory of this group, but for decades was the only Norwegian film that depicted the German war crimes against foreign prisoners. The *Norsk-Jugoslavisk Samband* (Norwegian-Yugoslavian Association) arose in consequence of Yugoslav prisoners' experiences in Norway during the war, and the feeling that a mutual bond of friendship had emerged between both countries as a result. One of the association's objectives was to make known the abuse Yugoslavs had been subjected to by the Germans in Norway.[20] However, the association has only modestly pursued its aims since its establishment and attracted little public attention.

Ultimately, Norwegian public commemorations of war crimes and the mention of foreign prisoners became mostly limited to wreath-laying ceremonies during the anniversary of Liberation Day on 8 May.[21] It was only on this day that it became natural to hold regular commemorations related to Norway's experience of the

---

og etterkrigstid, Oslo 1999, 39.
19 Bjørn Knutsen: Erindringen om de østeuropeiske fangene i Norge. En drøfting av realhistorie versus erindringshistorie med vekt på historisk bevissthet og kollektiv erindring. Master thesis in history, University of Bergen/Bergen University College 2001, 66–73.
20 Edhem Čamo: Jugoslavisk-Norsk Sambands virksomhet, in: Ljubo Mladenović (ed.): Norge – Jugoslavia, Beograd 1974, 374.
21 Based on a review of various Norwegian newspapers, such as *Aftenposten*, *Dagbladet*, *Bergens Tidende*, and *Adresseavisen* and their coverage of the 8 May celebrations in the years 1953–1967.

Second World War. On significant anniversary years, the German invasion of Norway on 9 April also became the object of prominent official commemorations. Remembering the actual invasion itself, however, left little scope for remembering the foreign victims, given that they were brought to Norway at a later stage of the war.[22]

As both cemeteries and monuments connected to foreign prisoners were located in remote localities, commemorations of the war crimes held there did not easily arouse the interest of national or regional media outlets, and thus remained more or less unknown to the majority of the Norwegian populace. In the speeches given at the Norwegian Liberation Day celebrations, references to the foreign war victims in Norway were to a greater extent omitted. War victims in general were occasionally mentioned, however, if including a reference to their plight might serve to illustrate the criminal nature of the Nazi regime and the moral dimension of the Norwegian resistance.[23] Essentially, it was the self-sacrifice and active struggle against the occupiers by the Norwegian resistance that was highlighted. Focus was on the Norwegian aspects of the war and the Norwegian experience of occupation. The only prisoners included in the official commemorations in Oslo on the 25th anniversary of the liberation in 1970 were Norwegians who had been held captive in Germany during the war.[24]

The situation was somewhat different in those areas where the local population had lived in close proximity to foreign prisoners and thus to sites where war crimes had been perpetrated. In the county of Nordland the density of prison camps was particularly high.[25] Troms and Finnmark also had a relatively large number of foreign prisoners, if compared to the counties' population. Yet during the 25th anniversary celebrations, no particular emphasis was placed on the war crimes committed in Nordland. Even in Northern Norway, the suffering of Soviet and Yugoslav prisoners was pushed into the background in favour of a focus on

---

22   Berit Nøkleby: Skutt blir den ... Tysk bruk av dødsstraff i Norge 1940–1945, Oslo 1996, 34.
23   *Aftenposten*, 8 May 1970.
24   Bjørn Knutsen: »Erindringen om de østeuropeiske fangene i Norge. En drøfting av realhistorie versus erindringshistorie med vekt på historisk bevissthet og kollektiv erindring.« Master thesis in history, University of Bergen/Bergen University College 2001, 66–73.
25   Kristian Ottosen: Arbeits- und Konzentrationslager in Norwegen 1940–1945, in: Robert Bohn et al. (ed.): Neutralität und totalitäre Aggression, Stuttgart 1991, 363–368.

the liberation of the prisoners and the challenges involved in trying to take care of them shortly after their release.[26]

In 1985, at the 40th anniversary of the liberation, there were some minor indications that a change in attitude was underway towards the surviving foreign victims of the German occupation. On the occasion marking 8 May, fifty Yugoslavs who had been imprisoned in Norway during the war were invited to Oslo.[27] During the previous 20 years, the wreath-laying ceremonies at the cemetery in Oslo for Soviet prisoners of war was included in the Liberation Day programme of events, albeit under the auspices of the Soviet embassy, and this was to continue in the subsequent years.[28]

The speeches given on Liberation Day were characterised by the manner in which they were written by Norwegians for a Norwegian audience. The fact that the war had also affected other nationalities than the Norwegians was communicated through general formulations that obscured the very different fate suffered by those other nationalities. Such was the case, for example, when Prime Minister Kåre Willoch gave a speech on Liberation Day in 1985:

> *»We need to be reminded that solidarity makes us stronger. As we once again go out into everyday life, we should not forget what has happened. We look back to remember and give thanks, but also to deepen the experiences that we will pass on to the younger generation. We will preserve these experiences as an indispensable foundation in our efforts to build and secure the future.«*[29]

This Norwegian-centred focus continued to be the main theme for the Liberation Day commemoration in Oslo five years later. »We honour the fallen, both the 42 who fell at this location, and the nearly 11,000 other Norwegian men and women who did not experience the days of liberation,« declared Kristian Ottosen, who himself had been a concentration camp prisoner in Germany, at one of the wreath-laying ceremonies on that day.[30]

By 8 May 1995, however, the surviving foreign prisoners had become integrated into events on the site of Falstad prison camp,[31] and would remain so in subse-

---

26   *Nordlands Fremtid* 6 May 1970.
27   *Aftenposten*, 7 May 1985.
28   *Verdens Gang*, 7 May 1965.
29   *Aftenposten*, 9 May 1985.
30   *Aftenposten*, 9 May 1990.
31   Press release by *Norsk Telegrambyrå*, 7 May 1995.

quent years. Judging from the press coverage, the commemorations of the 50th year anniversary of the liberation were substantially more important than those for its 25th anniversary. For all that, however, the press did not display a clearly greater awareness of the former Eastern European prisoners. The limited attention they did receive was primarily thanks to contributions by readers and news stories in which individual Norwegian witnesses could make themselves heard. In other articles, the focus remained on Norwegians in Grini prison camp and Norwegian prisoners in German war camps.

Even in museums, foreign prisoners and victims of war crimes were initially treated as a marginalised group. They received most coverage in the permanent exhibition at Norway's Resistance Museum, which opened in 1970. Here, a single poster with the title »Foreign Prisoners« described how conditions in German prison camps in Norway seemed to have been considerably worse for Soviet and other Eastern European prisoners.[32]

This situation would change after the end of the Cold War. The Red Cross War Memorial Museum in Narvik was for a long time dedicated to the military aspect of the war history associated with the town and the surrounding area. Yet towards the middle of the 1990s, its focus shifted in the direction of the history of the county's prisoners. Rana Museum had already in 1985 begun the transformation from a local village museum to a museum oriented towards war history, through an exhibition depicting resistance activity in the locality. As the first such institution in the country, it began with efforts to preserve traces of prisoner camps in 1986. In the 1990s, the museum actively worked to unearth monuments that were displaced when the Soviet war graves were removed.[33] The museum also changed its professional profile and developed into a centre dedicated to telling the history of slave labourers working on the construction of the Nordland railway line.[34]

---

32 Author's conversations with Ivar Kraglund and Arnfinn Moland. For the history of the museum, see: Frode Færøy: *Norges Hjemmefrontmuseum – I stiftelsens år* (Oslo, 1997), 81–86.
33 Authors conversation with Thor Helge Eidsaune, 30 April 2013. The Soviet war graves were moved as part of »Operation Asphalt,« which aimed at having the Soviet war cemeteries concentrated in as few cemeteries in Norway as possible due to the fear of Soviet espionage. See Marianne Neerland Soleim: *Sovjetiske krigsfanger i Norge 1941–1945. Antall, organisering og repatriering*, unpublished PhD thesis, University of Tromsø 2004, 445–454.
34 Information provided to the author by Thor Helge Eidsaune, 30 April 2013.

This partial reorientation of the profile of an established museum must be seen as reflecting the growing interest in the wartime history of foreign prisoners.

The number of museums that tried to transmit Norway's wartime history grew throughout the 1990s, and devoted a larger space specifically for German war crimes. This development happened swiftly and within a surprisingly short timespan. The Blood Road Museum opened just before the liberation anniversary in 1995. Its exhibitions were organised according to an overall theme consisting of several sub-themes, each with a different approach to the working and living conditions of foreign prisoners.[35] In 1996, the Perspective Museum was established in Tromsø in order to present an exhibition over the following two years dealing with the ordeal facing Soviet prisoners of war in Troms county, with particular emphasis on the varying conditions in the camps. The description of war crimes ran like a common thread throughout the exhibition. A year later, the Trondenes Historical Centre opened – located in an area known for its German coastal artillery fort, but also for prison camps where some of the most serious war crimes were committed.[36] The Centre's communication activities initially emphasised the Middle Ages, but after two years they, too, directed focus towards the site's wartime and prisoner history, and work on an exhibition about the Soviet prisoners of war began.[37] Another institution that followed the precedent given by the museums in Narvik and Rana was the South Varanger Museum. In 1997, the museum, which dates back to 1964, moved into larger premises outside Kirkenes, and then opened new permanent exhibitions with a stronger profile on war history, emphasising the foreign prisoners' history. Archive collections related to prisoner history were created by the museum, albeit on a very modest scale.[38] The Reconstruction Museum, which opened in Hammerfest in 1998, offered comprehensive documentation of one of the most extensive German war crimes committed on Norwegian territory, namely, the destruction of Finnmark and northern Troms and the forced expulsion of the local population. The museum, however, also indicated ambitions to make known the history of foreign prisoners on Norwegian soil.

Further south, the Falstad Museum was established in 1995 on the site of a former German prison camp. After a modest beginning, an initiative began five

35 Odd Storteig: Blodveien i Saltdal. Krigsfangenes historie, Rognan 1997, 22–23.
36 War Crimes in Norway. Report 21 March 1946 from War Crimes Investigation Branch, Norway.
37 *Nordlys*, 3 February 1999.
38 Informations provided to the author by Steinar I. Johansen, 17 Descember 2012; Johan B. Siira and Erik Bolstad: Krigshistorisk materiale. Oversikt, Kirkenes 2011.

months later at county and municipal level to create the Falstad Centre Foundation, with the aim of creating a teaching and research centre to document the history of the prisoners. The war crimes committed at Falstad prison camp would serve as a basis and background for working on topics related to international law and human rights issues. Right from the outset it became clear that the international dimension needed to be shown and that the victims from the Soviet Union and Yugoslavia at Falstad would be given much focus.[39]

In 1998, the North Sea Traffic Museum in Telavåg opened at the site of another German war crime in Norway, and eventually saw its role to convey the history of prisoners in Western Norway.[40] The Arkivet Foundation was established in 1999 in Kristiansand and opened to the public two years later. This was also an educational and research centre, where peace-building and conflict studies were included in its mission statement. The Foundation moved into a house that during the occupation had served as headquarters for the security apparatus in Kristiansand. Its location made it natural for the Foundation to direct much of its scientific focus on the occupation period and thereby the topic of German war crimes.[41] After prolonged discussions about what ought to be done with Vidkun Quisling's residence during the occupation, Villa Grande on Bygdøy – the property belonged to the Norwegian state – it was decided in 2001 to set it up as a place of research and documentation under the name The Center for Studies of Holocaust and Religious Minorities.[42] Its activities were similar to those at the Falstad Centre and the Arkivet Foundation, but more extensive in scope. The international aspect of Norwegian prisoner history was not neglected by the historians employed by the Center, even though its exhibitions were mainly devoted to the conditions among Norway's Jews during the Second World War.[43]

---

39   *Adresseavisen*, 22 May 2000. The Falstad Centre was officially opened in 2006, see Leiv Sem: For oss er Falstad det norske holocaust, Oslo, 2009.
40   Trond Risto Nilssen og Jon Reitan: Falstadarkivet. En beskrivelse av samlingens innhold 1941–1945, Levanger 2002, 38.
41   *Aftenposten*, 11 May 2000.
42   *Aftenposten*, 2 February 2001.
43   Author's conversations with Terje Emberland and Sigurd Sørlie, 30 January 2012.

IV. Historians and Memory Culture 1950–2000: A Connection?

What connections might be traced between the depictions of foreign prisoners in the works of historians and the wider memory culture of Norway? As noted previously, foreign war victims were accorded common respect in the form of wreath laying at existing memorial sites, but were otherwise less visible during official commemorations of the war and the occupation years in Norway. They were in any case not given the attention one might expect given the fact that well over half of those who fell as victims during the German occupation were foreign nationals. The way the theme was treated was reminiscent of the historians' reluctant attitude toward becoming involved in a topic that appeared particularly sinister. The burgeoning interest in the foreign prisoners in the middle of the 1980s, however, corresponded with Norwegian historians devoting more attention to this group in their scholarly works. The heightened public attention can perhaps be viewed in connection with the historians' increased emphasis on the occupation years as a period of suffering. Norwegian historians were, however, not active in debates dealing with the management of war memorials, and also did not appear in public commemorations as speakers. Historians could, in the best case, hope to exert influence insofar as future speechwriters would read their publications. Aside from what I've mentioned, the connections between Norwegian historiography and Norwegian memory culture are difficult to trace, given the lack of research. However, historians have often been frustrated by their lack of impact on memory culture. This is also the case in celebrations for the Norwegian Constitution of 1814, where there appears to be a significant gap between the research findings that the historians conveyed through their publications and the discussion of the basis for the Constitution's creation as communicated in public speeches to commemorate the occasion.[44]

There is no exhaustive research on the position of foreign prisoners and war crime victims in Norwegian cultural history, but if we assume that historians have only been able to exercise a limited influence on how German war crimes committed in Norway have been understood and remembered, the question naturally arises as to what led to this predicament? The answer may lie in a combination of several factors. First, as previously mentioned, the number of historians engaged in studies of Norway during the Second World War has remained low, and besides

---

44 Lars Roar Langslet: Christian Frederik. Konge av Norge 1814, Oslo 1998, 207.

they have had their personal priorities. Second, the published literature often lacked an international perspective, and consequently overlooked the fact that the history of Germany's occupation of Norway was also an integral part of an international history. Third, popular historical publications, mainly authored by journalists, have usually received considerably more attention than scholarly historical literature, resulting in a rift between academic historians and the public.[45]

In addition, the fact that every historian who decided to tackle the subject would have to confront serious obstacles cannot be overlooked. If the lack of funding had not already put an abrupt stop to the project, formidable tasks still lay ahead: The archival material was spread over large parts of Europe, and acquiring source material was made even more complicated by the fact that Soviet and Yugoslav archives had long been inaccessible to researchers interested in matters dealing with overseas cases.[46] The researchers would also require extensive lingual skills. Ultimately, there were relatively few historians, let alone Norwegians, who were fluent in languages like Russian, Serbo-Croat or Polish.

The Cold War also played a role. In the scenario that another major war was to break out in Europe, the Soviet Union would in all likelihood be the next country to invade Norway. Norwegian connections with the Soviets were all the more cautious due to these tensions, to such an extent that Soviet war graves were relocated and regrouped so as to be converged in a smaller number of locations, in order to limit the movement of Soviet citizens within Norway. As for the Soviet authorities, they would not grant former Soviet prisoners of war in Norway permission to revisit the country. In the minds of the Norwegian public, the route to oblivion was even shorter.

In addition, if we look beyond the historians' lack of participation in official commemorations, questions may be asked about whether Norwegian historians actually tried to influence, directly or indirectly, how the memory of Norway during the Second World War is manifested in Norwegian public discourse. In 1997, Odd-Bjørn Fure described how Norwegian university historians as a collective group, after having previously played a more active role in social and cultural life, gradually withdrew over a period of several decades from the public domain and returned to academic circles.

---

45 Odd Bjørn Fure: Kampen mot glemselen. Kunnskapsvakuum i mediesamfunnet, Oslo 1997, 46.
46 The Russian archives were opened to foreign researchers after the dissolution of the Soviet Union, but gradually became less accessible after the mid-1990s, and has since come across as even less so. See, for instance, Soleim: 2004, 6.

V. After the Millennium: Reorientation and Integration

The current trend in historical research seems to be to illuminate thus far neglected actors and themes in the Norwegian wartime history, a tendency that continues with undiminished strength after the turn of the millennium. More than ever, focus is now on war victims in Norway, including an increased interest in the topic of German war crimes in Norway. A crucial source for those working on this topic was the Director General of Public Prosecution's Criminal Archive at the National Archives. This archive had until recently been entirely overlooked by researchers.[47] But in preparation for the sixtieth anniversary of the liberation a Norwegian research project – *Å overkomme fortiden* (»Overcoming the Past«) – set out to study the legal proceedings in the wake of the German occupation, and to publish the results in five different publications.[48] It then became natural to examine more thoroughly those aspects of the proceedings that dealt with perpetrators who were prosecuted for crimes against foreign nationals.

In 2003, Berit Nøkleby completed the first academic historical study of the Gestapo in Norway, a study that, significantly enough, also represented the first fairly exhaustive history of the historical treatment of German war crimes committed against Norwegians, given that Gestapo officials were some of the main perpetrators of these crimes.[49] These same figures were also responsible for war crimes against foreign personnel, whether they were British and Allied soldiers, or Eastern European prisoners. A natural follow-up to this dissertation was for Nøkleby to get to work on a study of war crimes committed against non-Norwegians.[50] This was published in book form the following year under the title *Krigsforbrytelser: Brudd på krigens lov i Norge 1940–45* (»War Crimes: Violations of the Laws of War in Norway from 1940 to 1945«). The core of her sources was the Director General of Public Prosecution's Criminal Archive. However, the provenance of her sources, and the fact that Nøkleby's project was conducted within such a limited timeframe, meant that the investigation of war crimes and the subsequent legal processes was to become the central point in her treatment

---

47 This was largely due to the fact that the archive had been restricted for a period of 80 years. Consequently, access were limited to historical researchers working on a specific research project.
48 The initiators and project managers were Hans Fredrik Dahl, Øyvind Sørensen, Jon Elster, and Stein Ugelvik Larsen. *Bergens Tidende*, 6 September 2003.
49 Berit Nøkleby: Gestapo. Tysk politi i Norge 1940–1945, Oslo 2003.
50 Berit Nøkleby: Krigsforbrytelser. Brudd på krigens lov i Norge 1940–45, Oslo 2004, 7.

of the subject. This also meant that an exhaustive, definitive representation was lacking.[51] The bibliography at the end of the mostly archive-based book served only to emphasise the fact that Nøkleby had entered hitherto uncharted territory, and consequently advanced the general understanding of the topic. It was short, and included only book publications covering peripheral topics.[52]

Subsequently, several publications followed that in various ways elaborated on the picture painted by Nøkleby. One of them was Marianne Neerland Soleim's doctoral thesis, *Sovjetiske krigsfanger i Norge 1941–1945: Antall, organisering og repatriering* (»Soviet Prisoners of War in Norway 1941–1945: Numbers, Organisation and Repatriation«), completed in 2004. Five years later it was also published in book form.[53] Based on archival studies, she explained why the Soviet prisoners of war were sent to Norway, but above all described their working and living conditions in occupied Norway, arguing that these were established by ideologically based beliefs about the war prisoners' racial value. The dissertation and the book contain the most comprehensive and detailed depictions of war crimes against prisoners of war to date.[54]

In the late 2000s, several attacks were directed towards historians' representation of the war history by commentators in the media. At Norwegian universities, research on war history had almost come to a halt.[55] However, a number of memorial centres have in the meantime emerged at historical locations, centres that to varying degrees are producing scholarly works. Such memorial centres, dedicated to »managing the past« are a well-known phenomenon on continental Europe, but are a relatively new feature of Norwegian memorial culture. A number of historians have also gained employment there, within education, communication and research. In this way, active memorials have been created, both managing existing knowledge and producing fresh insights. For the historians, these centres became platforms for conveying historical research to a wider audience. Since the same memorial institutions became centres for commemorations, which attracted

---

51 Such a study based on a broad utilisation of the diversity of archival sources both in Norway and abroad, has yet to appear. Nothing would suggest that it is even under preparation.
52 Berit Nøkleby, 2004, 188–192.
53 Marianne Neerland Soleim: Sovjetiske krigsfanger i Norge 1941–1945. Antall, organisering og repatriering Oslo 2009.
54 Magne Haugland: Do svidanija – på gjensyn! Dokumentarberetninger om sovjetiske krigsfanger, Sandnes 2008.
55 *Klassekampen*, 24 December 2008.

both larger and smaller crowds, the historians came in much closer contact than beforehand with audiences interested in the past. Still, the extent to which historians have discovered that they are able to influence the popular conception of history through their academic works and dissemination activities is a question requiring further study.

Robert Zimmermann
From Captivity to the Classroom
Educational Initiatives by Former Political Prisoners' Associations in Denmark and Norway since 1945

I. Introduction

After the 21-year old Danish girl Jannike had returned from a gathering of former political prisoners from Denmark and Norway, she wrote to the Danish prisoners' journal *Gestapofangen* in the autumn of 1973: »Can it really be possible that we young people don't show any interest in what happened during those years between 1940 and 1945? [...] Suddenly one day, we won't have them [the elderly] any longer, and what then? [...] Where are you, all you young people? Why don't you meet [with them]?«[1] Jannike's letter was subsequently published in the Norwegian prisoner's journal *Grini-Posten*.[2] Her entreaty was directed at two grievances in the early 1970s. The first was a lack of knowledge about the Second World War among younger people, and the second was their unwillingness to get in touch with war veterans. Her questions point to a challenge that became increasingly relevant for former victims of the German occupation: The Second World War and the dominant heroic narrative of the war veterans were losing their significance for the young generation thirty years after the end of the war – to the dismay of many former prisoners who had suffered in the German camps and prisons.

This anecdote points to the following key questions for this chapter: How did former political prisoners in Denmark and Norway confront the increasing loss of significance of their history among the younger generation? What initiatives did they take to get in contact with school children and the educational establishment? How did they adjust their pedagogical initiatives to the predominant zeitgeist during the post-war decades? How important had education or – as the former prisoners called it – »information activities« been in general?

---

1 Jannike: Strøtanker efter stævnet, in: Gestapofangen, 27 (1973), 7, p. 13. All translations by the author, unless otherwise noted.
2 Cf. Etter fangestevnet i Danmark, in: Grini-Posten 25 (1973), 4, p. 1.

The disappearance of the last living witnesses to the Second World War in general and survivors of the Holocaust in particular is imminent. Contemporary witnesses have become a source of concern and fascination in schools and TV-documentaries over recent years. However, the concept of the »contemporary witness« – a person who testifies about his or her own life story in public – is a barely thirty-year-old phenomenon.[3] Former detainees of the concentration camps are its archetype, in particular those Jews who survived the Nazi death camps. In the absence, however, of a large Jewish community in Norway and Denmark, political prisoners largely assumed the role of contemporary eye-witnesses in these Nordic countries. Due to their experiences, the prisoners became a symbol of resistance against the occupation regimes. According to this narrative, they suffered in the concentration and prison camps for their beliefs and actions.[4]

This chapter presents selected educational initiatives, their causes and consequences for the associations of political prisoners in Denmark and Norway. The investigation is restricted to activities that targeted school children and that brought former prisoners in contact with them. It concentrates on former detainees who organised themselves in post-war associations. The available source material does not allow for the consideration of the entire prison population – let alone veterans – in both Scandinavian countries.

Employing a comparative perspective, different approaches at various points in time will be presented, emphasising the variances and transnational linkages between the initiatives of Danish and Norwegian prisoner organisations. Private encounters cannot be taken in consideration due to methodological problems and the limited source base. Even the various prisoner associations had problems in tracking activities of their individual members who were not directly linked with their official programmes. One last constraint concerns the prisoners' actual stories, which they told in the classrooms. The available sources do not usually provide any records or other form of documentation of these early school visits. It is therefore impossible to trace any changes in the stories that they told to the students.[5] However, the sources do provide evidence of the ways in which Danish and Norwegian prisoner associations explained their efforts in the field of school

---

3   Martin Sabrow/Norbert Frei (eds.): Die Geburt des Zeitzeugen nach 1945, Göttingen 2012.
4   In the text I chose the male form to describe political prisoners. However, this also includes female prisoners, who were significantly smaller in numbers.
5   Anette Storeide: Fortelling om fangenskapet, Oslo 2007.

education since 1945. Those efforts will be at the centre of the diachronic comparison.

The major source materials are journals brought out by the prisoners' organisations.[6] In addition, the author gained access to the entire special archive of the largest Norwegian association, *Forening av politiske fanger 1940–1945* (Association of Political Prisoners 1940–1945), which is housed at *Riksarkivet* and the *Norges Hjemmefrontmuseum* (the Norwegian Resistance Museum) in Oslo.[7] Moreover, sources on Denmark, in particular the files of the *Landsforeningen Gestapofangerne* (National Association of Gestapo Prisoners) were at the author's disposal at *Frihedmuseet*, the Museum of the Danish Resistance in Copenhagen.[8] Due to limited sources, especially in Denmark, this study aims at an asymmetrical comparison, which presents transnational linkages.[9]

---

6 The major prisoner journals are *Gestapofangen* (1945–1977, founded as *Frøslevfangen*, renamed in 1949 and *Pigtraad* (1946–1978), which merged in 1978 with *Pigtraad-Gestapofangen* (1978–1995), in Denmark, and *Grini-Posten* in Norway. Cf. Jesper Vesterbæk: Fangetidsskrifter. Som erindringssted for historien om de danske koncentrationslejrfanger, unpublished M. A. thesis, University of Southern Denmark, Odense 2007.
7 Riksarkiv Oslo (RA), one part in private archive 1246 (PA 1246), the other part as yet unregistered; Archive of the Norges Hjemmefrontmuseum (NHM), loose collection, as yet unregistered. The RA and the NHM granted full access of the unregistered material to the author.
8 Frihedsmuseet Arkiv (FMA), section 46 Etterkrigsforeninger, folder 17 J. H. Barfod: »Gestapofangernes« foredrag på skolerne om besættelsestiden (in the following: FMA 46–17).
9 Arnd Bauerkämper: Wege zur europäischen Geschichte. Erträge und Perspektiven der vergleichs- und transfergeschichtlichen Forschung, in: Agnes Arndt/Joachim C. Häberlen/Christiane Reinecke (eds.): Vergleichen, verflechten, verwirren? Europäische Geschichtsschreibung zwischen Theorie und Praxis, Göttingen 2011, 33–60.

II. Educational Activities by Political Prisoners in Denmark

The first and only nationwide education initiative organised by a Danish prisoner association started as early as 1963. It was an immediate reaction to the results of a representative survey that had demonstrated a lack of knowledge on the history of the Second World War amongst Danish youth.[10] As a consequence, the prisoners' organisation *Landsforening Gestapofangerne* set up a school visit outreach programme. Its objective was to establish contacts with school pupils in order to keep the memory of the occupation alive. Erstwhile prisoners were to speak in front of higher-level students each year on the most important date of the Danish resistance calendar, namely 29 August, the day marking the anniversary of the uprising in August 1943. The organisers called it »the resistance movement's first major victory«[11], as it signalled the end of the official Danish collaboration policy and an increase in resistance activities. In the veterans' hindsight, 29 August 1943 was the day the majority of the Danes turned towards the active resistance movement, which previously had only been supported by a minority of the populace. Hence, the 20th anniversary of the uprising provided a fitting occasion for promoting the resistance story in school lectures that were initiated in 1963.

The instigator and central figure was Jørgen Barfod[12], head of the local Zealand branch of *Landsforening Gestapofangerne*. The former inmate of Neuengamme concentration camp and at that time teacher in Copenhagen took the leading role in the organisation and lobbied for the lectures by former resistance fighters in Danish schools. In order to motivate fellow club members to join his efforts, Barfod appealed to their sense of duty to keep the memory of their fallen comrades alive. He insisted that commemorating the dead and teaching the younger generation were deeply interrelated: »Can you imagine of any better way of commemorating our fallen comrades than by telling young people about their commitment

---

10 Unknown author: Bestemmer skolen de unges syn på besættelsestiden?, in: Pigtraad 18 (1963), 4, pp. 65–67.
11 Jørgen Barfod: Fortæl ungdommen om forholdene under besættelsen, in: Gestapofangen 17 (1963), 5, p. 4.
12 Jørgen Barfod (*1918) belonged to the Danish resistance group *Holger Danske* during World War II. Afterwards he became a historian and worked as teacher. He wrote several books on the occupation and on the prisoners. Barfod was leader of the prisoners' organisation *Landsforening Gestapofangerne*, the association *Sammenslutning af danske fanger fra frihedskampen* and *Frihedskampens Veteraner*. From 1971 to 1987 he was director of the Museum of Danish Resistance 1940–1945 in Copenhagen.

and [...] work, which they undertook in their struggle for the freedom of thought, belief and speech?«[13] At the same time, this statement reflects the self-image of the former political prisoners. They saw and presented themselves first and foremost as resistance fighters. During the entire school out-reach campaign, the Danish organisers never rated their time in captivity over their activities as resistance fighters. In fact, Ove Lembcke, a board member of *Landsforening Gestapofangerne*, claimed in a newspaper interview: »We no longer identify ourselves as prisoners, who sat in concentration camps.«[14] In this sense the Danish political prisoners are true advocates of the heroic resistance narrative of the Second World War, which prevailed not only in Denmark in the 1960s.

Nonetheless, Barfod always stressed that those veterans visiting schools were just ordinary citizens, whose intention was not to tell heroic tales in the classrooms. However, neither did they depict personal victim stories. Rather, the veterans explained to the students what it meant to live under a dictatorship and what the lack of democratic rights and sovereignty entailed. »It's our duty to continue our struggle for democracy, which we started during the occupation.«[15] By stressing their role as advocates for democracy, the organisers wanted to convince teachers and other veterans alike that their stories had a deeper meaning beyond a mere resistance narrative. The message of their lectures was directed at the everyday lives of young people, and addressed their future rather than merely harking back to the past. Furthermore, they constantly reiterated that the lectures were not meant to spread hatred against Germans, but rather against any kind of totalitarian regime. In hindsight, their storylines did not live up to these ideals. The reasons were manifold.

First, the resistance perspective of the German occupation – especially by those not involved in politics – was not widely accepted in the Danish society of the 1960s, a society permeated by Social Democracy. This rejection resulted from Denmark's unique occupation history, which had involved widespread collaboration by all major political parties (including the Social Democrats) under the most liberal regime of all Nazi occupied countries until August 1943 and in the following period of open resistance until liberation.[16] In contrast to the Norwegians, the

---

13   Jørgen Bardfod: Fortæl ungdommen, p. 5.
14   Unknown author: Der er datoer man aldrig glemmer, in: Gestapofangen 19 (1965), 9, p. 11. (Reprint of an article from *Randers Dagblad*)
15   Jørgen Barfod: Der er en opgave for os, in: Gestapofangen 17 (1963), 10, p. 2.
16   Cf. Claus Bundgård Christensen. Danmark besat – krig og hverdag 1940–45, Copenhagen 2009.

Danes were not so readily able to distinguish between »white« and »black«. Learning to choose what was »right« was therefore a core skill demanded by the veterans, an ability they set out to teach in their talks and lectures.[17] Thus, historian Nils Arne Sørensen has characterised the post-war Danish memory culture as a struggle between two conflicting narratives of the war experience. On the one hand, a broad consensus presented Denmark as a nation united in defiance – also known as the ›official narrative‹. And yet, a narrower »resistance narrative« stressed the opposition by most Danes, but depicted the collaborating establishment as traitors in cahoots with the Nazis.[18] At the beginning of the 1960s, the »official narrative« was increasingly called into question. The »resistance narrative« started gaining popularity especially amongst those younger Danes who opposed Denmark's accession to the European Common Market and the US involvement in Vietnam.[19] However, its sway was still restricted by the Danish elites and their »official« version. Such rivalry between different interpretations is stressed in a newsletter sent to all members of *Landsforening*. In this publication, Barfod underlined once again their affirmative approach: »It is [...] crucial that former resistance fighters furnish the necessary facts to these young people, because they alone can provide depictions with the proper content and in the right spirit. It is our duty to seek to counter this falsification of history, otherwise it will manifest itself, in a process that might already be underway.«[20]

Second, the organisers had no influence on how the various veterans would perform in a classroom setting. There was no particular mentoring or training programme to prepare them for the task. However, the trained historian Jørgen Barfod provided them with a manuscript which was to serve as a guideline to tell the story of the Danish resistance movement. The framework text included gaps, leaving space, as it were, for a personal account by the speaker. Notably, resistance activities were comprehensively described, whereas captivity in prisons and concentration camps was deliberately downplayed out of regard for the tender age of the listeners.[21] Like most of the speeches, the manuscript probably concentrated on efforts by the »good« Danes. The text was therefore structured in a

---

17 Unknown author: Se fremad, in: Gestapofangen 18 (1964), 3, p. 1.
18 Nils Arne Sørensen: Narrating the Second World War in Denmark since 1945, in: Contemporary European History 14 (2005), 3, 295–315.
19 Ibid., 305–311.
20 Jørgen Barfod: Skoleelver overalt i Danmark, 1964, in: FMA 46–17, folder 1963–1964.
21 Jørgen Barfod: Danmark under 2. verdenskrig, 1963, manuscript, in: FMA 46–17, folder 1963–1964.

straightforward way. Consequently, a closer look at the frequency of visits showed that many schools felt no obligation to invite the former political prisoners on a repeated basis every year.

Nonetheless, the out-reach campaign started well. As early as 1963, the veterans visited 65 schools in and around Copenhagen and obtained favourable press coverage. At the end of that year, *Landsforening's* Zealand division leader, Jørgen Barfod, became the new president of the entire organisation. Following his promotion, its educational activities were expanded. Thus, *Landsforening Gestapofangerne* extended their school visits nationwide in the second year. A total of 114 schools accepted the veterans' offers to visit either on, or around, 29 August. The initiative already reached its peak a year later in 1965 with over 140 school visits across the country, the majority of which were in Copenhagen. The lowest number of visits was registered on the isle of Funen and southern Jutland. Although the organisers extended their lectures to dates other than 29 August, interest had declined by the end of the decade.[22] Efforts were reduced after only five years. The list of schools that participated in 1967 reveals that 45 per cent of the schools had received the resistance fighters once, and 25 per cent of schools had welcomed them twice in the five years following 1963.[23] By contrast, only three out of a total of 207 schools had invited them on an annual basis.

Finally, the whole campaign faced near-permanent criticism from various parties including the Danish newspaper *Information*, which had been established as an illegal publication during the occupation years.[24] Most critics claimed that the veterans were using their school visits to bask in the glory of their past deeds as well as to stoke hatred against Germans. These accusations were repeatedly rejected in various newspaper and journal articles.[25] A central allegation by schoolteachers was that the former prisoners were too insistent in trying to obtain a commitment from the schools for visits on specific dates. Teachers gained the impression that

---

22   Other days include 16 September in memory of the founding of *Frihedsråd* (Freedom Council) in 1943; 19 September in memory of the action against the Danish police in 1944 and October 1 and 2 in memory of the action against the Jews in Denmark in 1943.
23   List of schools, FMA 46–17, folder IV 1969–70.
24   Cf. Letter to the editor by Leif Thomsen, Information, 6 September 1966.
25   Jørgen Barfod: Veteraner før og nu, FMA 46–17, folder 1965–1966; id.: Hvorfor nu?, in: Gestapofangen 20 (1966), 8, p. 197.

the prisoners were driven by self-interest.²⁶ Meanwhile, other veterans called for the matter to fade into oblivion by letting bygones be bygones, thereby questioning the lasting impact of the whole campaign. In fact, the organisers were unable to convince former resistance fighters not belonging to *Landsforening* to support their initiative. Even after various political prisoners' organisations had joined forces to establish *Sammenslutning af danske fanger fra frihedskampen 1940–1945* (Association of Danish Prisoners Fighting for Freedom 1940–1945) in 1967, the school visit programme was not revived.

Although *Landsforening Gestapofangerne* received much positive feedback from young people, demand for lectures steadily decreased. In 1969, Jørgen Barfod declared that the veterans would take a break for at least two years.²⁷ This was to mark the end of *Landsforening's* centrally organised school visit programme. At that point, only 56 schools showed any interest in welcoming the veterans.²⁸ Meanwhile, several schools had made separate agreements with individual eye-witnesses. By the time Barfod took over as director of the Danish Resistance Museum in 1971, school visits by former political prisoners were exclusively organised on such an individual basis. Over the following decades, the Danish prisoner journals occasionally reported on individual veterans who visited local schools telling their stories to young Danes, mostly on anniversaries related to the occupation.²⁹

III. Information Activities by Norwegian Prisoners' Associations

Unlike in Denmark, richer source material is available for investigating the »information activities« by former Norwegian political prisoners. Developments in Norway can be divided into two distinct periods, each of which represents a different stage both in terms of the frequency and intensity of activities by Norway's most prominent prisoners' association *Forening av politiske fanger 1940–45*, its prede-

---

26 Jørgen Barfod: Modstandsfolk på skolerne. Sammenslutnings foredrags-virksomhed, in: Gestapofangen 23 (1969), 7–8, p. 9.
27 Ibid.
28 Letter from Jørgen Barfod to the lecturers, February 1970, FMA-17, folder 1969–1970.
29 For instance, cf. Egon Havbo: Tidligere KZ-fanger lærer 7 klasse om besættelsen, in: Pigtraad-Gestapofangen 2 (1979), 4, p. 100; three-part series of articles De bærer frihedsfakler videre, in: Pigtraad-Gestapofangen 9 (1986), pp. 1–3, 10–14, 42–43, 67.

cessor, *Griniklubben* (Grini Club) and *Sachsenhausenfangenes Forening* (Association of Sachsenhausen Prisoners).[30]

Stage 1: Initial Attempts until the End of the 1970s

In the late 1950s, a close look at the history syllabus in Norwegian high schools reveals a stark deficit in the teaching of contemporary history. As in Denmark, the limited attention given to the history of the Second World War in Norwegian schools drove *Griniklubben* to send a petition to the Ministry of Education.[31] The former detainees made a clear point in their request. They stressed that the postwar generation was not in possession of sufficient knowledge concerning modern Norwegian history. Thus, they called for a special publication that was to be disseminated in every school and discussed in history classes. Politicians and the responsible Norwegian Education Council, *Undervisningsråd*, responded favourably.[32] Moreover, the initiative was also well received by the Danish resistance veterans who likewise deplored a similar lack of historical knowledge amongst younger Danes at that time. However, nothing came of their petition at first.[33]

It was to take another five years before the topic resurfaced. Highlighting the transnational connection, the debate was triggered by the publication of a textbook for secondary schools by the Danish teacher and former Dachau prisoner, Mogens Møller[34], in which he emphasised the Second World War. The newly established *Forening av politiske fanger 1940–45*, which brought together former

---

30 The Oslo-based unions of former political prisoners *Sachsenhausenfangenes Forening*, founded on 9 October 1945, and *Griniklubben*, established on 2 December 1945, merged in May 1962 to *Foreningen av politiske fanger 1940–1945* (in the following also *Foreningen*). Earlier attempts to establish a nationwide association of former political prisoners had not been successful. The author is meant to publish a doctoral thesis on Danish and Norwegian associations after 1945.
31 Unknown author: Skoleelevene må få undervisning im den siste krig og okkupasjonen, in: *Grini-Posten* 11 (1959), 2, p. 1.
32 Reply letters republished. Unknown author: Okkupasjonens historie for de høyere skoler, in: *Grini-Posten* 11 (1959), 3, p. 6.
33 Johannes Fosmark: Den moderne ungdom er uvidende om frihedskampen. Prisværdigt norsk initiative vil råde bod herpå, in: *Pigtraad* 14 (1959), 6, pp. 1–2.
34 Unknown author: Ny historie bog, der behandler besættelsestiden, modstandskampen og koncentrationslejrene, in: *Gestapofangen* 17 (1963), 11, pp. 6–7; cf. also *Grini-Posten* 15 (1963), 4, pp. 3–4.

prisoners and their families, seized the opportunity and once again demanded a similar publication be drafted for Norwegian schoolchildren.[35] This time round, they received support from the newspaper *Arbeiderbladet*, which interviewed a member of the Norwegian Education Council in 1964.[36] The Council reiterated its commitment to the idea. Nevertheless, its officials claimed that they needed a third party to write the textbook because neither the Council nor the Ministry had the necessary expertise and resources. The *Forening* regarded itself as a whistle-blower, who called for change, yet did not take the initiative at that juncture. Instead, they expected further action by political establishment and the Education Council. The *Grini-Posten* article duly closed with the words: »We are waiting for results.«[37]

It would take another twenty years before all veteran organisations received that special publication they had been clamouring for. In order to celebrate the fortieth anniversary of the liberation, the *Krigsinvalideforbund* and other veterans' organisations, including *Forening*, published a 56-page journal *Alt for Norge*[38] in 1985. Its circulation was 60,000 copies. Another comprehensive brochure entitled *Fritt Norge*[39] followed in 1995. Over 1.1 million copies were then distributed to every secondary school in Norway – an incredibly large number considering that the Norwegian population was just 4.3 million at the time. The reasons for this apparent success will become clearer in the following investigation of the next stage.

Stage 2: The Emergence of the Eye-witness in the 1980s

In the late 1970s and early 1980s, former political prisoners were confronted with new social and media developments that largely ran contrary to their interests. The rise of neo-fascist tendencies, not only in West Germany but also in Nor-

---

35 Unknown author: Skoleelevene må få undervisning im den siste krig og okkupasjonen!, in: Grini-Posten 16 (1964), 1, p. 3.
36 Cf. Nils Haave: Skoleelevene må få undervisning om den siste krig og okkupasjonen, in: Grini-Posten 16 (1964), 2, p. 3.
37 Ibid.
38 Krigsinvalideforbundet og Veteranorganisasjonene (eds.): Alt for Norge. 40 år etter, Oslo 1985.
39 Forsvarets Forum, Krigsinvalideforbundet, Krigsveteranorganisasjonene (eds.): Fritt Norge. Fra krig til fred, Oslo 1995.

way, became more pronounced as a result of growing youth unemployment.[40] For instance, in 1975 a small neo-fascist party called *Norsk Front* was founded whose membership largely consisted of young adults. Neo-Nazis attacked the communist parades on 1 May 1979 and the Mosque in Frogner in June 1985.[41] Furthermore, resistance memorials, such as the one at Vår Frelsers Gravlund in Oslo, were defiled repeatedly by groups or individuals with neo-fascist backgrounds. In addition, former members of the Norwegian Nazi party, the *Nasjonal Samling* were given the chance to air their beliefs to a wider audience with the help of a TV-documentary *I solkorsets tegn* (»In the Sign of the Sun Cross«, 1981) for the first time.[42] In this TV-series, former party members openly voiced their views on the Second World War and the occupation. Their apologetic accounts were not countered by any commentary in the documentary.[43] Former political prisoners were furious and complained directly to the Norwegian parliament, the *Storting*, and to the responsible Norwegian broadcast service, the NRK.[44] The former inmates demanded another series be broadcast that would provide »an unvarnished picture of what such a misguided ideology can result in«[45]. Both the resurgence of neo-fascist ideology and the public appearance of erstwhile pro-Nazis strongly contradicted the Norwegian prisoners' understanding of a democratic society. Unlike in their earlier protests, they took the initiative for change this time round.

This occurred at a time when membership of *Forening av politiske fanger 1940–45* had reached a historic all-time low with less than 270 members in the mid-1970s – barely a quarter of their initial peak in 1946.[46] They were no longer attracting former prisoners, partly due to the settlements regarding compensation claims and victim pensions that were widely regarded as satisfactory, and partly

---

40 Unknown author: Nynazisme er i full swing, in: Grini-Posten 32 (1981), 1, p. 1.
41 Cf. Tore Bjørgo: »Nynazisme«, in: Store norske leksikon, <http://snl.no/nynazisme>, last access: 27 January 2014; Henrik Lunde: Nynazisme, HL-Senteret, <http://www.hlsenteret.no/kunnskapsbasen/folkemord/folkemord-under-nazismen/ettertid/nynazisme>, last access: 27 January 2014.
42 The Sun Cross was the Norwegian equivalent to the swastika.
43 Karen-Margrethe Baltzrud: I lys av solkorset. Historien om en fjernsynsserie: »I solkorsets tegn«, sendt 1981, unpublished M. A. thesis, University of Oslo, 2004.
44 Krigsdeltakerforbundet, Foreningen av politiske fanger 1940–45: »I solkorsets tegn« – et krav til NRK, in: Grini-Posten 32 (1981), 2, p. 2.
45 Ibid.
46 The figures are taken from the annual reports from Forening av politiske fanger 1940–45, cf. RA, PA-1246/A/L0001-6.

because of internal conflicts dating back to the establishment of the common association in 1962. Overall, there was a lack of tasks and motives to which they could devote themselves, similar to their engagement for compensation claims during the 1950s and 1960s.

A development to their advantage was, however, the increasing media interest in their harrowing tales. Whereas heroic stories of military resistance had dominated the basic narrative on the Second World War in the 1950s and 1960s, the constellation started to change in light of new publications and films. The Norwegian Jew Herman Sachnowitz, who authored *Det angår også deg*[47] (»It also concerns you«) about his experiences in Auschwitz, is just one notable example. Others include biographies by former concentration camp detainees who had subsequently made a career in politics, such as former Norwegian Prime Ministers Einar Gerhardsen and Trygve Bratteli.[48] These books stand at the forefront of a shift of perception, in which captivity was no longer a source of shame, but of pride.[49] Thus, the opportunities open to former Norwegian prisoners differed markedly from those of their Danish counterparts twenty years earlier. Moreover, a large anti-nuclear and peace movement was just emerging whose demands for peace and disarmament were complementary to the beliefs of the former prisoners.

As in Denmark, the Norwegian prisoners' commitment for better historical education in schools depended on annual commemoration days such as 8 May, the anniversary of Norway's liberation in 1945. Commemoration speeches usually ended with an obligatory warning against oblivion and an appeal for civic engagement. For instance, the President of *Forening*, Leif Nordstrand, made the following plea in 1975:

> »*We can forgive, but never forget the lessons of war. […] In particular, we have to engage with our children and grandchildren not just by telling them heroic tales, but rather by making it clear to them that the legal principles we fought for during the war are the only durable foundation that mankind can build on*

---

47   Herman Sachnowitz: Det angår også deg, Oslo 1976.
48   Einar Gerhardsen: Felleskap i krig og fred, Oslo 1970; Trygve Bratteli: Fange i natt og tåke, Oslo 1980.
49   Jean-Michel Chaumont: Die Konkurrenz der Opfer, Lüneburg 2001, S. 217–218.

so as to survive. This is our message to our offspring and one that our vigorous and bright youth will understand, because these are universal values.«[50]

This appeal was primarily aimed at the younger generation. But could the veterans' stories strike a chord when the audience consisted chiefly of their peers? The TV-series *I solkorsets tegn* was an essential trigger for action.[51] The former prisoners turned their attention to schools in their neighbourhoods, mainly in the vicinity of Oslo. They offered to visit the schools free of charge to talk about their war experiences. The number of visits increased steadily over the course of the next few years. In 1980, only a few individual visits took place. In the following year, the board of *Forening* established an *opplysingskomité* (information committee) to oversee the coordination, recruitment and implementation of the information activities. Unfortunately, exact data on the programme are unavailable. But figures in *Forening's* annual reports offer some clues. In 1982, a total of eight members visited ten schools. The number increased to 16 schools in 1983 and to 32 in 1989 in the Oslo area alone.[52] Yet the Association was unable to exactly track the activities of their members nationwide. Nonetheless, the board of *Forening* was quite satisfied with the outcome of these initial attempts. They informed their members in 1982: »The school visits have been a success and were met with positive reactions from pupils and teachers alike. […] Our work on this [school visits] has gained a bigger and deeper meaning, too.«[53] In fact, the Association changed its statutes in April 1983 in order to incorporate this new field of activity. Along with general objectives such as working in support of all former political prisoners and their families, the new statutes stated the following: »The Association shall […] protect the memory of the victims of our fight for freedom by commemorating at memorials and by informing Norwegian youth about National Socialism's violation of freedom and human dignity.«[54]

School visits by former prisoners were arranged according to a regular procedure. Between two and five members participated at each visit and often spoke in

---

50 Formann Leif Nordstrand i Foreningen av politiske fanger 1940–1945. Hilsingstale på 30 års fest for dannelsen av Norske fangers forening, 8 december 1975, in: Grini-Posten 28 (1976), 1, p. 1.
51 Unknown author: En takk til krigsveteranene (sakset fra skoleavisa »furulusa«), in: Grini-Posten 33 (1982), 3, p. 5.
52 Cf. footnote 23.
53 Styret: »Vi er på offensiven!«, in: Grini-Posten 33 (1982), 3, p. 4.
54 Statues of Foreningen av politiske fanger 1940–45, 12 April 1983, RA PA-1246/D/L0011.

the largest auditorium available in the school in front of several classes and for a few hours. Each witness dealt with a specific topic.[55] Among the prisoners active in these events were also prominent public figures such as former Prime Minister Einar Gerhardsen in 1982; this underlines the importance of the programme.[56]

Not only former prisoners participated, but also many other veterans who had been involved in the Norwegian resistance movement during the occupation. In their speeches, the former prisoners tried to appeal to the emotions of their young audience by telling personal anecdotes and using slides and photographs, as recommended in the guidelines by the *Krigsinvalideforbundet*, Norway's largest veteran association in 1980.[57] These recommendations were created specifically for veterans, presenting them with a master plan of how to structure and deliver their presentations. In contrast to the Danish manuscript described earlier, the Norwegian guidelines did not give precise instructions on the actual story to be told, but rather contained a diverse list of keywords. Particularly interesting is the suggestion that the personal stories were to be related to current events in order to emphasise their contemporary relevance. Students should experience a »living history lesson« centred around the slogan *aldrig mer*, literally »never again«. In fact, the former prisoners had appropriated for their own ends the common warning *aldri mer 9. april* that had spread after the surprise German invasion of Norway in 1940 – a warning whose aim was used in certain quarters to justify the abandonment of Norway's policy of neutrality and to support higher defence spending as well as its membership of NATO. This was replaced by a new slogan for the educational campaign of the veterans' association: *Aldri mer nazisme, aldri mer fascisme, aldri mer krig* (»Never again Nazism, never again fascism, never again war«).[58]

The former prisoners' message was purely pacifistic. As stressed in the 1975 commemoration speech, children should always strive to prevent war, as well as all to combat tendencies towards fascism and Nazism. Here, their aims contradicted not only those of the Norwegian veterans of the military resistance, who promoted NATO membership and higher defence spending, but also the objectives of their Danish peers in their out-reach campaign of twenty years earlier. Such differences

---

55 For instance, unknown author: En takk til krigsveteranene (sakset fra skoleavisa »furulusa«), in: Grini-Posten 33 (1982), 3, p. 5.
56 Unknown author: Alværn-kveld på ungdomsskolen, in: Grini-Posten 32 (1981), 3, p. 3.
57 Disposisjonsplan for foredrag (kåserier m. m.) om krigen, krigsopplevelser o. l., August 1980, RA PA-1246/E/L0003.
58 Appeal to Norwegian and history teacher, April 1986, RA PA-1246/E/L0001.

between veteran groups had an influence on their respective information activities. While veterans of the military resistance *Milorg* focused on sabotage and other resistance activities involving military action, the political prisoners emphasised civil resistance and daily life during the occupation, as well as life in captivity.

In the view of the prisoners, the younger generation – who were often thought of as being unaware – had to ingrain future generations with »the truth about the Nazi regime«[59]. At the beginning of their work in schools the veterans often referred to themselves as *sannhetsvitne fra krigen*[60] (»truth witnesses to the war«). Later on, they adopted the more self-reflective term *tidsvitne* (»contemporary witness«) to refer to themselves. Through their accounts of the war, school children were to learn about »the fundamental values and principles of law, which were already followed by the Norwegian resistance movement between 1940 and 1945«[61]. This very general statement can be found repeatedly in *Forening's* documents, such as their statutes, without any specific discussion. From a historiographical perspective, this formulation was controversial, as it assumed that the entire resistance movement was homogeneous. Differences between civilian and military resistance, not forgetting between communists and royalists, were disregarded. Instead, references to the values and principles of the resistance movement adhered to the established national consensus narrative, which presented the resistance as a struggle of the good Norwegians against the »others«.[62]

The ways prisoners' narratives transformed over the years – from heroic accounts of resistance to a more universal approach – can be seen in an open letter to all teachers published in *Grini-Posten* in 1984. The former prisoners argued:

---

59   Stig Vanberg: IRK-konferansen, in: Grini-Posten 44 (1993), 3, p. 2.
60   Meeting protocol of Samarbeidsutvalget av Krigsveteranforeninger (cooperation committee of war veteran organisations), 25 October 1988, RA PA-1246/D/L0011.
61   Inquiry for financial support to city of Oslo, March 1981, RA PA-1246/E/L0001.
62   Cf. Anne Eriksen: Det var noe annet under krigen, Oslo 1995; Clemens Maier: Making Memories. The Politics of Remembrance in Postwar Norway and Denmark, European University Institute Florence 2007, 47–58, URL: <http://cadmus.eui.eu/bitstream/handle/1814/6996/2007_07_Maier.pdf?sequence=1>; Ole Kristian Grimnes: Occupation and Collective Memory in Norway, in: Stig Ekman/Nils Edling (eds.): War Experience, Self Image and National Identity. The Second World War as Myth and History, Stockholm 1997, 130–148; Claudia Lenz: Haushaltspflicht und Widerstand. Erzählungen norwegischer Frauen über die deutsche Besatzung 1940–1945 im Lichte nationaler Vergangenheitskonstruktionen, Tübingen 2003, 88–95.

»We know from experience that there can be different history lessons to those schoolchildren are used to [hearing]. *Now, don't believe that those are stories about heroes and heroism. No, it is the truth about what dictatorship and war means for all human beings. This is the history of the struggle for human dignity and human rights.«*[63]

The adaption of the victim narrative is clearly discernible in that quote. Considering the on-going discourse about the Holocaust, the commitment of the resistance veterans to Amnesty International and their close bonds to the Red Cross, they linked their accounts increasingly to the universalistic human rights narrative. Thereby, the former prisoners presented themselves as a group of individuals who knew what it meant to have their basic human rights denied. As human rights advocates, they adapted this dominant narrative at a time when the United Nations' Convention against Torture was signed in December 1984. Another statement demonstrates how the prisoners connected the resistance narrative with universal messages that go beyond the context of the Second World War. As the prisoners emphasised in an application for financial support to the city of Oslo: »Our information activities are first and foremost aimed at disseminating our experiences about the resistance fight between 1940 and 1945, and the fundamental democratic values and the basic human rights that we fought for.«[64]. Their narrative gradually evolved from heroic resistance fighters to being advocates of human rights, due to their experience in Nazi concentration camps.

Within a few short years, the prisoners' information activities revitalised the Association. Following years of decline, membership figures rose rapidly. In 1982 alone, the Association attracted over a hundred new members. By 1985, it had already doubled and the number peaked in 1988/89.[65] The rapid expansion of the Association's activities also led to an increase in support for their journal *Grini-Posten*. Though it was not published in 1980 due to a lack of funding, *Forening* was already able to raise its circulation from 600 to 950 copies as early as 1982.[66] The content and character of the periodical also changed. In addition to the usual stories about commemorations, compensation and welfare issues, an increasing number of articles on biographical stories and historical

---

63 Egil Wennemo: Til lærerne!, in: Grini-Posten 35 (1984), 3, p. 4.
64 Søknad om støtte for 1988, 17 December 1987, RA PA-1246/E/L0001.
65 Cf. footnote 23.
66 Øivind Hansen: *Grini-Posten*, in: Grini-Posten 33 (1982), 4, p. 4.

overviews were published. *Grini-Posten* also served as an advertising agency that was to attract the attention of history teachers. With the incisive plea »we desire more contact with the young – more co-operation with the teachers«[67], the journal promoted the educational activities of the veterans' association. The former prisoners expressed their desire to expand their work and get in touch with those veterans nationwide who might like to talk with school children in their neighbourhoods. More specifically, the information committee asked members to contact Folk high schools[68] (*folkehøyskoler*) and pedagogical colleges. Expanding the audience to older students and prospective teachers became the main goal. All in all, over 250 schools were contacted and subsequently provided with their journal free of charge in the mid-1980s. Short statements by the commissioned prisoners themselves or extracts from letters to the editor from students and teachers were to convince the readership of the success of the information campaign.

The educational activities of veterans' organisations also opened up new sources of funding. They received subsidies for their information campaign from the Norwegian Confederation of Trade Unions (*Landsorganisasjonen*) as well as from the cultural office of the Oslo municipality from 1981 to 2004. In order to receive continuing financial support, the Association had to re-apply each year. In their applications, the veterans always stressed their role as eye-witnesses and advocates of human rights values to children.

Other areas of the Association's activities were influenced by their educational commitment, too. In particular, entire school classes joined the commemorations on 8 May and assisted in organising events.[69] However, most young people were prevented by statute from becoming members of *Forening av politiske fanger 1940–45*, since membership was restricted to former inmates and their descendants.

The Norwegian Association saw its first significant upsurge in connection with the commemorations for the end of the war in 1985. The prisoners' stories received increasing attention in the media around 9 April and 8 May – the two key anniversaries. Moreover, the Association soon increased the numbers of school visits, expanding their venues to include military academies and public clubs. They had

---

67 Henriette Bie Lorentzen: Vi ønsker mer kontakt med ungdommen – mer samarbeid med lærerne, in: Grini-Posten 35 (1984), 1, p. 4.
68 Folk high schools are institutions for adult education that generally do not give academic degrees. The concept is based on the ideas of the Danish philosopher and writer Nikolaj F. S. Grundtvig (1783–1872).
69 Øivind Hansen: Minnestund på Vor Frelsers gravlund, 8. mai, in: Grini-Posten 34 (1983), 3, p. 3.

no longer only slide-shows at their disposal, but also a travelling exhibition and a restored »White Bus« from the corresponding rescue mission in March and April 1945 in co-operation with the Norwegian Red Cross.[70]

The largest and most important step in the prisoners' more professional approach was their roles as eye-witnesses and guides on the journeys organised by the Foundation *Hvite Busser til Auschwitz* (White Buses to Auschwitz).[71] Founded in 1992, the Foundation arranged school trips for 14- and 15-year old pupils to former concentration camps on continental Europe. During those trips the pupils together with at least one former prisoner usually visited the two most important camps for Norwegians: Auschwitz and Sachsenhausen.[72] These increasingly popular trips were meant to instil the teenagers with democratic values, and teach them about human rights and tolerance for other cultures and religions. In short, the school children and students became acquainted with the most essential components of today's universalistic narrative. The political prisoners served as key witnesses, who expressed these values and messages through their individual stories on the journey. Due to the lack of a large Jewish community, their testimonies were the Norwegian equivalent of the universalistic Holocaust narrative. According to Kyrre Kverndokk, the memorial practice was to focus on the Norwegian aspect of the history of concentration camps. Kverndokk argued: »When it comes to the Jewish Holocaust, it is by no means forgotten, but it is not as dominating in the ritual praxis as the memory of the Norwegian political prisoners. Hence, the universalistic Holocaust narrative is performed through a Norwegian memory narrative.«[73] In sum, these former political prisoners managed to intensify and professionalise their approach to information activities, to present themselves not only as advocates of their individual stories, but also to serve as representatives

---

70 The White Buses refer to a programme undertaken by the Swedish Red Cross and the Danish government in March and April 1945 to rescue Scandinavian concentration camp inmates and prisoners and bring back them to neutral Sweden. Cf. Wrochem, Oliver von (ed.): Skandinavien im Zweiten Weltkrieg und die Rettungsaktion Weiße Busse. Ereignisse und Erinnerung, Berlin 2012.

71 Stiftelsen Hvite Busser til Auschwitz, URL: <http://www.hvitebusser.no>, last access: 4 April 2014.

72 Over 90 per cent of the 767 Jews deported from Norway were killed in Auschwitz. The majority of Norwegian political prisoners outside of Norway were detained in Sachsenhausen (in total approximately 2,500).

73 Kyrre Kverndokk: Pilegrim, turist og elev. Norsk skoleturer til døds- og konsentrasjonsleirer, Linköping 2007, 256.

of universal values. Contrary to the evidence, a Norwegian political prisoner as contemporary witness in Auschwitz served as an icon that was to represent the universalistic Holocaust narrative.

IV. Conclusion

In both Denmark and Norway, former prisoners set up educational initiatives when they realised that younger generations were growing up in increasing ignorance about important events in recent history that had been biographical ruptures for many veterans. Motivated by the conviction that their struggles in the resistance movement and for survival in concentration camps had legitimised them to serve as eye-witnesses, the prisoners established contact with students through school lectures. The term *sannhetsvitne* (»truth witness«), used by Norwegian political prisoners, refers to this claim and role.

Unlike their Norwegian peers, the Danish former political prisoners in the *Landsforening Gestapofangerne* had already been organising school lectures in the 1960s. Yet the Danish prisoners failed to ingrain their information activities with an attractive narrative with universal values. Jørgen Barfod and his fellows focused exclusively – and possibly excessively so – on the commemoration of days of resistance such as 29 August. Their accounts were deeply rooted in the dominant heroic narrative of the immediate post-war decades in Denmark.

Neither the Danish nor the Norwegian prisoners preached at the expense of others. Hatred of Germans was to be resisted in order to ensure peaceful post-war co-operation with their former occupier. Nonetheless, the Danish memory culture was too heterogeneous to fully embrace the resisters' perspective on the occupation 25 years after the end of the war. Thus, the Danish initiative faced harsh criticism from various sides. By contrast, the narrative of their Norwegian peers was rooted in a less contested memory culture, due to a much lesser degree of official co-operation during the occupation and a clearer black and white dichotomy of »good Norwegians« and »evil others«.

The Norwegian Prisoners' Association *Forening av politiske fanger 1940–45* managed to expand their activities gradually, starting in the early 1980s. They were helped in their endeavours by the favourable political climate resulting from the rise of the peace movement. They also altered their narrative towards a victim's perspective, which was combined with pacifistic values as well as a focus on democratic and human rights. Hence, they have become an actor in modern history education, in which contemporary relevance is crucial.[74] By telling their stories, the former political prisoners urged their young listeners to carry on their memories. Thus, their message would prevail and continue to exert influence after the prisoners' deaths. The former Norwegian detainees hereby reframed the universalistic narrative of the Holocaust, and they adapted it to the specific Norwegian memory culture. In particular, political prisoners were highlighted instead of the Jews. This transition has not been a profound change, but rather a subtle transformation, which has stuck with the former political prisoners as the main reference group, due to the sparsity of Jewish survivors in Norway.

The early educational initiatives in both countries were to a certain extent transnationally entangled. In Norway, prisoners pressurised the National Education Council to publish a textbook for the history curriculum after learning of a similar publication in Denmark. This initiative was well received amongst their Danish peers. On the Danish side, Jørgen Barfod, during their annual joint meeting, tried to encourage the Norwegians to take part in their school visit programme.[75] The urge for »*norske tilstander*«[76] (»Norwegian conditions«) has always been a central call for Danish resistance fighters. Moreover, both countries followed each other's initiatives through their respective journals and publications. The mutual reception and selective transfers point to the transnational dimension of commemorations despite the distinctly national specifics in Norway's and Denmark's memory cultures, respectively.

Jannike, who wrote that desperate letter to the Danish *Gestapofangen* in 1973, was afraid that vital memories would be lost. Yet her fear that the story of the former political prisoners would vanish was unfounded. The members of the Norwegian Prisoners' Association certainly worked hard to become essential proponents

---

74 Peter Paul Schwarz: Zeit. Zeugen. Zeitzeugen. Zu Traditionen, Entwicklungslinien und Erscheinungsformen von Zeitzeugenschaft, in: Bildungswerk der Humanistischen Union NRW (ed.): Zeitzeugenarbeit zur DDR-Geschichte. Historische Entwicklungslinien – Konzepte – Bildungspraxis, Essen 2012, p. 8–46.
75 Letter from Jørgen Barfod to Johan Egeberg, 5 July 1964, RA PA-1246/E/L0002.
76 The term »norske tilstander« expresses the high esteem by Danes for the Norwegian resistance movement. Whereas Denmark capitulated within hours of the invasion by Nazi Germany on 9 April 1940, Norway kept fighting for nearly three months. The Norwegian king and government decided to leave their country and continue the struggle against the German occupation from exile, whereas the Danish king and government accepted the German terms of occupation. Cf. Gerda Gram: Norske tilstander. Norge under 2. verdenskrig, Odense 1986.

of modern history education on the Second World War and the occupation in Scandinavia as well as champions of universalistic concepts such as human rights and democracy.

Doreen Reinhold
Exhibiting the Second World War Now and Then
Narrative and Representation in
Norges Hjemmefrontmuseum and the
Senter for studier av Holocaust og livssynsminoriteter

During the 1990s, similar to developments in many European countries, the Norwegian memory culture of the Second World War began to change significantly.[1] Hitherto it had been dominated by a narrative which portrayed Norway during the occupation as a heroic ›nation-in-resistance‹ or as an ›illegal nation‹ that collectively resisted the German occupiers. This patriotic narrative was based on a very broad understanding of the term resistance. The Norwegian conception of the term includes both the military struggle to liberate Norway, referred to as *milorg*, as well as the civil resistance or *sivilorg*. Their understanding of the latter was mainly influenced by the notion of so-called *holdningskamp* (struggle for civic and democratic values), a term coined by King Haakon VII whereby he called upon his people to resist attacks on their values and morals by the German occupiers. After the war this broad and somewhat vague definition made it possible for Norwegian citizens who did not directly collaborate with the German occupiers or the Quisling regime to consider themselves as part of the collective resistance of the *holdningskamp*.[2] This essentially led to a division of the imagined community of

1 Cf. Günther Oesterle (ed.): Erinnerung, Gedächtnis, Wissen, Göttingen 2005.
2 Terje Halvorsen: Zwischen London und Berlin: Widerstand und Kollaboration in Norwegen 1940–45, in: R. Bohn/J. Elvert et al. (ed.): Neutralität und totalitäre Aggression. Nordeuropa und die Großmächte im Zweiten Weltkrieg, Stuttgart 1991, 337; Armin Lang: Die Besetzung Norwegens aus deutscher und norwegischer Sicht. Eine Typologie des Umgangs mit Invasion und Okkupation, in: W. Michalka (ed.): Der Zweite Weltkrieg. Analysen-Grundzüge-Forschungsbilanz, München 1990, 138–154; Claudia Lenz: Vom Widerstand zum Weltfrieden. Der Wandel nationaler und familiärer Konsenserzählungen über die Besatzungszeit in Norwegen, in: H. Welzer (ed.) Der Krieg der Erinnerung. Holocaust, Kollaboration und Widerstand im europäischen Gedächt-

Norwegian post-war society into »good« Norwegians, who were part of the resistance, and the »Quislingers« (referring to Vidkun Quisling, leader of the Nazi-style Norwegian *Nasjonal Samling*), who had betrayed their country by collaborating with the occupiers.[3] Anthropologist Anne Eriksen calls this fundamental division the »founding myth of modern Norway«.[4]

In this paper I will focus on how these changes and newly emerging tendencies in the public discourses about the Second World War are reflected in the Norwegian museum culture. Therefore, I will analyse and evaluate the exhibitions of the *Norges Hjemmefrontmuseum* and the *HL-senter*, as the two most important institutions for the Norwegian memory culture of the Second World War. Due to its origins, the *Hjemmefrontmuseum* is widely considered as the institution for the preservation of the patriotic narrative of the collective Norwegian resistance, while the newer *HL-senter* is usually perceived as its provocative, progressive counter-part. Upon closer observation, however, the exhibitions appear to be much more complex than this simple dichotomy might suggest. Based on a methodological framework developed by Henrietta Lidchi, I will first analyse the internal sequencing of the two exhibitions and the way they create and convey their narrative(s) concerning the Second World War. Building on that, I will evaluate my findings in light of the broader discourses about the Second World War within Norwegian society in the second part of this article. Thereby, I will focus on the developments within the Norwegian memory culture described above: To what extent can we identify elements of the patriotic narrative, newer progressive perspectives as well as universalistic tendencies in the museum exhibitions and how are those elements contextualised within the museum?

---

nis, Frankfurt am Main 2007, 42–43; Jörg Zägel: Vergangenheitsdiskurse in der Ostseeregion 1. Auseinandersetzung in den nordischen Staaten über Krieg, Völkermord, Diktatur, Besatzung und Vertreibung, Berlin 2007, 54.
3   Cf. Benedict Anderson: Imagined Communities: Reflections on the Origin and Spread of Nationalism, London 1991 [1983].
4   Anne Eriksen: Det var noe annet under krigen. 2. verdenskrig i norsk kollektivtradisjon, Oslo 1995, 163.

I. Introduction: The Second World War in the Norwegian Memory Culture

The opening of *Norges Hjemmefrontmuseum* (Norway's Resistance Museum) in 1970 on the occasion of the 25th anniversary of the liberation of Norway played a major role in the preservation and manifestation of the patriotic narrative in the Norwegian memory culture. The museum originated in the exhibition ›*Det illegale Norge*‹ (»The illegal Norway«) which was shown in 1945 and depicted the occupation from the perspective of the resistance movement, highlighting the activities of the *milorg*, in particular.[5] The *Hjemmefrontmuseum* maintained this focus on the patriotic narrative. According to its founding documents drafted by a group of former resistance activists, its goals were the accurate depiction of the war as well as the promotion of national and democratic values. The museum exhibition was never planned to be entirely neutral, but rather to accentuate patriotic aspects that were supposed to foster national values. Even today the *Hjemmefrontmuseum* is still considered as one of the most important preservers of the patriotic narrative.[6]

The dominance of the dichotomy of resistance and collaboration in the Norwegian memory culture marginalised all of those wartime experiences that did not fit into this rigid binary structure.[7] Despite an increasing number of scholars who criticised this mystified narrative of the occupation, it was not until the 1990s that the patriotic narrative lost its dominance on the Norwegian memory culture.[8] One important development during that time was the gradual inclusion of the Holocaust and the fate of the Norwegian Jews into the historiography of the Second World War. The single-most important cause for this change was a series

---

5 Frode Færøy: Norges Hjemmefrontmuseum – I stiftelses år, Oslo 1997, 10–12.
6 Maerz, 294–295.
7 Odd-Bjørn Fure: Norsk Okkupasjonshistorie: Konsensus, berøringsangst og tabuisering, in: Larsen, Stein Ugelvik (ed.): I krigens kjølvann. Nye sider ved norsk krigshistorie og etterkrigstid, Oslo 1999, 31–45; Susanne Maerz: Die langen Schatten der Besatzungszeit. »Vergangenheitsbewältigung« in Norwegen als Identitätsdiskurs, Freiburg 2008, 12–14; Synne Corell: The Solidity of National Narrative. The German Occupation in Norwegian History Culture, in: H. Stenius et al. (eds.): Skandinavian Narratives of the Second World War. National Historiographies Revisited, Lund 2011, 102–104.
8 For a detailed overview of the developments within the Norwegian memory culture from the post-war years until the 1990s cf. Stein Ugelvik Larsen: Innledning, in: Stein Ugelvik Larsen (ed.): I krigens kjølvann. Nye sider ved norsk krigshistorie og etterkrigstid, Oslo 1999, 9–30, and Maerz.

of articles published in 1995 by journalist Bjørn Westlie in the newspaper *Dagens Næringsliv*. In his articles, Westlie attested to the fact that Jewish property that had been confiscated during the occupation has never been adequately restituted after the war. The publication led to the establishment of a commission appointed in order to examine Westlie's claims. Notwithstanding its disintegration into two factions recommending contrasting courses of action to the government, the commission validated Westlie's accusations by stating that an estimated 110 million Norwegian crowns had never been paid out as compensation to Norwegian Jewish families. As a consequence the Norwegian parliament passed a resolution for the disbursement of 450 million Norwegian crowns, of which 200 million were allocated for individual restitution payments, while the rest was meant as a collective restitution to the Jews of Norway. A large part of the collective restitution was used for the establishment of the *Senter for studier av Holocaust og livssynsminoriteter* (Centre for the study of the Holocaust and religious minorities), abbreviated to *HL-senter*, which opened in 2001.[9]

The opening of the *HL-senter* is now considered an important manifestation of the changes within the Norwegian memory culture during the last twenty years in which marginalised and long-repressed aspects of the Second World War have entered the public discourses and have been gradually institutionalised within the Norwegian cultural memory. Although the patriotic narrative has not yet been entirely deconstructed and abandoned, a tendency towards a more diversified and multi-layered historiography of the occupation is observable. Some scholars have also detected a tendency towards a more universal narrative of the war with human rights – especially the 1948 Universal Declaration of the United Nations – as its focal point. This narrative advances the view that the Holocaust can be used as a paradigm to both explain previous and prevent future human rights violations. Thus, a tendency towards a universal narrative would mean that the Second World War and the Holocaust are progressively less understood as national tragedies, but rather as transnational or international phenomena.

---

9 Maerz, 219–246.

II. Poetics and Politics of Museum Exhibitions

In his book about the depiction of Jewish history and culture in museums, Jens Hoppe has emphasised: »Historical museums deal with the legacies of a society, which are threatened to disappear from the context of life due to changes in living conditions, but which are supposed to be preserved for the creation of meaning in the present or which re-appear as remnants of destroyed cultures [...]. The single objects in the permanent exhibitions are not only signs from the past but, moreover, refer to the present. The presentation of the exhibits only then in the museum leads to a creation of meaning for the cultural memory.«[10] According to this statement, museums are a product as well as an instrument of a society's cultural memory. They are not only a reflection of the narratives a society remembers, but they are also creating those narratives themselves. Thus, progressive museums have the capacity to introduce varying perspectives and a wide range of aspects, thereby diversifying a society's cultural memory.[11] By contrast, museums are also able to manifest and preserve a one-dimensional narrative which marginalises or distorts the memories of experiences that do not fit into the dominating single story.

In order to distinguish between those two functions of historical museums (to represent the past and to make it meaningful to the present), I will apply an analytical framework developed by Henrietta Lidchi. In her essay »The Poetics and Politics of Exhibiting and Other Cultures«, Lidchi makes the important distinction between the poetics of a museum exhibition and the politics of the museum as an institution.[12] She defines the poetics of an exhibition as »the practice of producing meaning through the internal ordering and conjunction of the separate but related components of an exhibition«.[13] In contrast, the politics of a museum

---

10 Jens Hoppe: Jüdische Geschichte und Kultur in Museen. Zur nichtjüdischen Museologie des Jüdischen in Deutschland, Münster 2002, 3.
11 Cf. Aleida Assmann: Der lange Schatten der Vergangenheit. Erinnerungspolitik und Geschichtspolitik, Bonn 2006; Aleida Assmann: Erinnerungsräume. Formen und Wandlungen des kulturellen Gedächtnisses, Munich 1999; Jan Assmann: Das kulturelle Gedächtnis. Schrift, Erinnerung und politische Identität in frühen Hochkulturen, Munich 1992.
12 Henrietta Lidchi: The Poetics and Politics of Exhibiting and Other Cultures, in: St. Hall (ed.): Representation. Cultural Representation and Signifying Practices, London, Thousand Oaks, New Delhi 1997, 152–208.
13 Ibid. 168.

are described as »the role of exhibitions/museums in the production of social knowledge«.[14] The latter is based on the notion that »museums appropriate and display objects for certain ends«[15] making use of the power of their institutional position. According to Lidchi, the museum thereby becomes »an arbiter of meaning«[16], changing or reinforcing discursive formations while simultaneously being influenced by these pre-existing discourses.

In her categorization Lidchi also distinguishes three different layers of meaning, which are important when analysing the poetics of an exhibition. According to her framework, the first layer is the individual object and the meaning it carries, which Lidchi defines as »presence«. The individual objects, moreover, work in conjunction with texts and the contexts in which they are placed. This layer is defined as »representation«. Finally, Lidchi describes a third layer, »presentation«, as »the overall arrangement and the techniques employed in an exhibition«.[17] This three level model offers the possibility of analysing the exhibition partially without, however, losing the focus on the broader context.

In order to turn the first layer of Lidchi's categorization into a workable framework for my analysis, I will differentiate between three different groups of objects that can be found in any museum exhibition:

1. Typical or representative objects which represent one of a kind to illustrate a whole group of similar objects.
2. Extraordinary objects that are included in the exhibition because they are exactly not one of a kind and, therefore, of extraordinary value and/or interest.
3. Iconographic objects which are expected to be so well known and easily decodeable for visitors that they are instantly understood and contextualised without the need for any further texts or other explanations.

However, when distinguishing between these three groups of objects it is crucial to bear in mind who this categorization is directed at, as this classification works differently for specific groups of visitors. In the *HL-senter*, for example, there is a room where illustrated tables of racial classifications and a set of instruments used to classify people into those alleged categories are displayed. These exhibits appear to be representational objects for a certain group of elderly visitors, who have seen

---

14 Lidchi, 184.
15 Ibid. 198.
16 Ibid.
17 Ibid. 174.

these instruments and racial classifications either directly in use or as illustrations in school books. To others, in particular younger visitors, these objects seem like curiosities from a distant past and are perceived as extraordinary rather than as typical items. Thus, the objects carry a different meaning, depending on the way they are integrated into the exhibition and depending on who perceives them, their prior knowledge, and life-experience.

III. The Presence of the Objects

In one of the first rooms at the exhibition in the *HL-senter*, a few objects which used to belong to Norwegian Jewish families are put on display, for instance a small mocha cup. It is both typical and extraordinary. It is extraordinary, because it illustrates the story of one specific family and their individual experiences during the Second World War. The cup belonged to the Steinfeld family from Ålesund, whose members were all murdered in Auschwitz, as we learn from the labels. Yet for a Norwegian visitor this cup is also typical in the sense that it could be found in any Norwegian home at that time. It is not specifically connected to Judaism or to the Jewishness of the family. In exhibiting this cup, the museum narrates the story of an average Norwegian family, as opposed to the image of exotic Jewish strangers, who perished during the Holocaust. This story, however, can only be decoded by and thus targeted at a certain group of recipients who are able to identify the mocha cup as a typical item of every-day use in Norway in the pre-war years. Looking at all the objects displayed in this section of the exhibition, such as a diary and an old-fashioned tool to wash the dishes, similar narratives can be identified. Hence, in the exhibition Jews are portrayed as average Norwegians who also happened to be Jewish. As there are hardly any specifically Jewish items, it is not the Jewishness, but the Norwegianness of the people that is accentuated in the exhibition. In addition, on the level of presence there is no significant distinction made between the different experiences of the individuals introduced during the time of the occupation. Jews who perished in the Holocaust, survived in hiding or were able to flee to Sweden are all depicted in the same manner.

In stark contrast to that, the only time we are introduced to what it meant to be a Jew in the *Hjemmefrontmuseum* is in the section about the concentration camps. There, two typical concentration camp prisoners' uniforms are put on display. No indications are given concerning a particular camp or to that they belonged to a specific person. They were chosen in order to illustrate the life in the camps rather generically. Visitors to the exhibition are not expected to know about the Holocaust, the camps or the uniforms before their museum visit and are, therefore, shown one typical example. The exhibits neither highlight the Jewishness nor the Norwegianness of the victims. Rather, they are displayed with their specific identity as concentration camp prisoners and, thereby, victims of German war crimes. The connection to Norway in general and Jewish life in Norway specifically, on the other hand, is kept vague.

In the *Hjemmefrontmuseum* typical objects have two distinct functions. Firstly, they introduce topics that are expected to be new for the recipient in a broad and generic way, as the concentration camp prisoner's uniforms show. Besides, objects which are presented as typical create a hierarchy between what is considered normal and extraordinary. A case in point would be the way resistance is illustrated in the museum. In several sections of the exhibition, we find various types of handguns and other weapons. One example is the section about the *Kompani Linge* (Norwegian Independent Company No. 1 – NORIC), a Norwegian military unit that served under the command of the British special operations unit. In this part of the exhibition, a large number of the same type of handguns is put on display. The exhibits are not explained individually on the labels or in the attached texts. The arrangement was presented in this manner in order to illustrate the normality of gun use in the resistance movement as opposed to every-day life experiences in times of peace. So as to contrast with that, an example of an extraordinary way of resisting is illustrated by a means of a shoe with a hole in its heel prepared in order to smuggle information. The museum seems to create a hierarchy between the military struggle, which is emphasised as the typical way of resistance by the sheer quantity of weapons present in the exhibition, and other forms of resistance, such as smuggling information and various, rather »soft« actions of the *holdningskamp*, which are then presented as curiosities.

In the *HL-senter*, extraordinary objects are mainly used in order to make the exhibition more interesting and varied. They introduce a few unusual cases and highlight certain aspects more prominently. Different from the extraordinary objects in the *Hjemmefrontmuseum*, they are not necessarily used as a contrast to that which is considered as the norm and therefore to be remembered. For instance, in the section about the exodus of Norwegian Jews to Sweden a backpack is displayed. From the labels, we learn that this backpack was used to carry a Jewish child over the border to Sweden, thus saving it from the Nazi persecution and possible murder. Doubtlessly, this backpack could also be perceived as a curiosity. But moreover, it illustrates how the extreme situation during the occupation and the threat towards the Jews prompted extraordinary rescue means. Hence, in this case the extraordinary object mirrors the unusual measures taken to rescue a child in an extreme situation. For certain groups of visitors, however, the backpack itself is also a typical object of every-day use in a specific time and place, namely, in Norway in the first half of the 20th century. For those observers the backpack thus holds a second layer of meaning emphasising once more the Norwegianness of the rescue operation, rather than the Jewishness. Observing how the very presence of the above cited examples impact upon the visitor, we can already distinguish a vast difference in the way in which two museums depict the different Norwegian experiences during the Second World War. While the *Hjemmefrontmuseum* highlights the military struggle of the Norwegian resistance against the German occupiers, the *HL-senter* focuses on the presence of the objects, illustrating the lives of average Norwegians categorised as being Jewish and for this reason fell victim to Nazi crimes. It is not so much the German evilness but rather a mind-set dominated by pseudo-scientific racism taken to extremes that is introduced as the cause for the crimes perpetrated by the Germans. In the *Hjemmefrontmuseum*, by contrast, the Germans are portrayed as military enemies who committed crimes against humanity in addition to their military atrocities.

We will take a closer look at this on the level of presentation later on. Let us presently examine the last category of objects introduced above: iconographic objects. Jury Lotman explains in his essay »The Structure of the Narrative Text« how icons function like narrative abbreviations.[18] They require an extended prior knowledge by the recipient in order to be de-codeable and understood. In addition, iconic or symbolic representations need to codify and save meaning in a rather simple way so that the abbreviated narrative is easily retrievable by the observer. Thus, they necessarily counteract the transmission of a complex and multi-layered narrative.

The Nazi flags displayed in the *Hjemmefrontmuseum*, for example, do not have a label, nor is there a text or any other form of explanation attached to them. Visitors are supposed to recognize the flag and the meaning of the swastika. The same applies to the photograph of Vidkun Quisling, which remains without explanation. This indicates that the museum, as it currently stands, is directed at an audience who already possess a prior knowledge of the history of the Second World War in Norway and who associate specific visual images with it. References to the patriotic narrative of the brave fight by the Norwegian resistance

---

18 Juri M. Lotman: The Structure of the Narrative Text, in: Mieke Bal (ed.): Narrative Theory. Critical Concepts in Literary and Cultural Studies, Vol. 1, London 2004 [1973], 20–24, 20.

against the German occupiers and the bitter betrayal by Quisling – symbolized by swastikas, numerous Norwegian flags and an iconic photograph of him – remain unexplained and therefore unchallenged in the presentation.

In the *HL-senter* exhibition, by contrast, we come across few iconographic objects that remain completely unexplained. Although icons such as the yellow star and a copy of *Mein Kampf* are included in the exhibition, all of these objects have an explanatory text attached to them. Visitors are not expected to have any prior knowledge about the occupation and the persecution of the Jews before entering the exhibition. They are even informed concerning the most basic facts about the Second World War and the crimes committed by the Nazis, and they are not required to decipher iconographic objects by themselves. Hence, the exhibition does not rely on a narrative manifested in the cultural memory in order to be understood. This enables the museum to potentially question and deconstruct existing interpretations of the dominating narratives by offering more complex explanations and a contextualisation for the iconographic objects that enable a variety of different readings. In order to evaluate whether the *HL-senter* has used its potential we will have to focus on the second layer Lidchi describes in her categorization – representation.

IV. Representation of the Objects

There are various ways to create meaning in a museum and contextualize the objects in a way they can be understood by visitors. In most cases, the objects are explained by texts on labels or tables alongside the glass cases. Sometimes graphics or charts are employed, as well as multi-media tools, video installations, or audio-guides. In the *Hjemmefrontmuseum*, we also find installations of various objects, miniature models and maps in order to place the exhibits in an understandable context. This variety of media employed on a representational level makes it difficult to coherently analyse and compare different exhibitions. This is why I will focus on two main aspects concerning the layer of representation: objectiveness and authenticity. First, I will evaluate, whether the representation of the objects is descriptive or interpretive. In other words, do the texts, labels, videos etc. state only facts about the objects shown (e. g. age, materials and place of origin) or, alternatively, do they offer explanations and interpretations in a broader context? Are the objects grouped together based on objective criteria, or do the arrangements make implicit suggestions as to how to evaluate and understand the exhibits? Given both of the exhibitions we are examining are to be found in historical museums (as opposed to ethnological museums or art exhibitions, for instance), they aim to explain historical processes, events and human activities rather than the objects themselves. Hence, descriptions which merely state facts about the actual objects are relatively rare. Rather, the exhibits are used to illustrate and exemplify the narratives and explanations of historical processes the museums strive to convey. The meaning of the objects becomes clear solely in the context of the exhibition.

As regards this issue, Bodo von Borries has stated that the »exhibits of a museum are fragmented and isolated from their real state in the past. They are relocated to a new (artificial) setting and thereby simultaneously depleted (made unreal). [...] In order for the exhibits to be perceived at least somewhat correctly, they need to be re-dimensioned and re-contextualized«[19]. The museums, moreover, choose certain objects to be included in the exhibition in order to represent erstwhile human activities: »...these actual bearers of history need to be made visible with the three-dimensional (museum) witnesses, which means they need to be (re)-constructed with their body techniques, and habitual ways of thinking, ways of lives, and their hopes for an afterlife.«[20] Thus, in the context of historical museums it is more important to analyse the authenticity of the re-contextualization and re-embedding of objects into a meaningful context rather than to distinguish between descriptions and interpretations.

Authenticity in that sense is not conceived as a normative factor. Rather, I am interested in why certain objects are placed in inauthentic or anachronistic settings. At the *HL-senter*, for example, two large video installations are included in the exhibition. The pictures and short film clips shown in the second installation are neither arranged in chronological order nor organized by location or any other recognisable ordering principle. Thus their re-contextualisation is highly inauthentic. Yet, this does not limit the impact the video installation has on the visitor. It is not designed to offer an accurate historical depiction of the Holocaust, but rather to create an uncanny feeling. The images appear to be chosen according to the emotional impact they might have on viewers. The non-observance of the chronological order functions as a means to make the impact on the viewer as powerful as possible.

---

19   Bodo von Borries: Präsentation und Rezeption von Geschichte im Museum, in: Geschichte in Wissenschaft und Unterricht, 6/7 (1997), 337–343, 337–338.
20   Ibid., 339.

In the *Hjemmefrontmuseum*, a large variety of media is utilised as explanatory tools in the exhibition. The main focus lies on information carriers, such as texts, documents, maps and so forth, which give the exhibition an objective appearance. However, parallel to this, lots of the objects and explanatory texts are placed within larger symbolic ensembles that are highly suggestive. An example is the prisoner's uniform from a concentration camp mentioned earlier. It has been placed in a setting resembling a normal prison, except for the barbed wire set on top of the regular prison bars. This setting, although based on and built around objective documents and representational objects, is by no means objective nor is it authentic. It is remarkable in itself that the Holocaust is included and problematized in a museum about the Norwegian resistance movement. However, as we have previously remarked, this section does not correlate the events with Norway, but it is connected to the overall topic of German war crimes. The highly suggestive representation of the objects is used to underline the cruelty of the German aggressor and, thereby, the heroism of the Norwegian resistance. The goal of the inauthentic re-contextualisation of the objects is to associate them with a setting the visitor is vaguely familiar with – a prison. Thereby, an uncanny feeling is created and the emotional impact, directed at condemning German cruelties, is enhanced. The installation thus serves the same purpose as the video installation at the *HL-senter*: to arouse emotions such as fear and anxiety in order to trigger empathy towards the victims and disgust towards the actions of the perpetrators. Apart from the installations, another example for this are the shapes of the vitrines used in the *Hjemmefrontmuseum*. The objects are not placed in traditional glass cases; rather, they are either embedded into larger ensembles, like the prisoners uniforms, or presented in vitrines behind metal frames in figurative shapes. By using their frames, like crosses, crooked pillars or posts, zigzag shaped holes that resemble burn holes or the image of an explosion in a comic book, the museum transmits an implicit evaluation of the objects on display.

Overall, the representations in the *Hjemmefrontmuseum* work on two distinct levels. First, texts, maps and similar information carriers offer facts about the objects displayed and, thereby, about the occupation and the resistance movement. Second, however, the exhibition is not only geared towards providing visitors with information but, moreover, also towards arousing emotional reactions. This second layer of meaning, implicitly conveyed through the inauthentic installations and the design choices, is supposed to emphasize the effect of the information supplied about the objects. The weapons shown in the section about the *Kompani Linge*, for instance, are placed in a vitrine shaped like an explosion in a comic book, which enhances the effect of the presence of the exhibits and the information given about the resistance of this company. The visitor is not only supposed to learn about but also emotionally react towards the objects shown in a way that is pre-determined by the museum. This leaves no room for further interpretation or alternative readings.

In the *HL-senter*, on the other hand, the entire permanent exhibition appears to be strangely divided between the authentic and factually illustrated texts, which resemble the pages of a school book, and the deeply suggestive, inauthentic video installations. Objective and suggestive, authentic and inauthentic representations are juxtaposed. As with the vitrines in the *Hjemmefrontmuseum*, the video installations are aimed at causing an emotional reaction. In contrast to the older museum, however, we also find more objective and neutral sections in the *HL-senter*. They are designed in a way that does not directly provoke an emotional reaction. Thus, the *HL-senter* appears to be slightly more prosaic and less suggestive than the *Hjemmefrontmuseum*. However, a marked tendency towards the emotionalisation of war experiences can be observed in both exhibitions. This limits the potential of the museums to create a diverse, multi-layered narrative of the war, because they suggest a highly specific emotional reaction from the visitor. Hence the narratives the museums convey are not communicated neutrally, but with an implicit evaluation and interpretation which does not allow for controversy or differing perspectives. As with the use of symbols or icons, the emotionalisation of museum exhibitions inevitably leads to an abbreviated and simplified narrative.

V. The Presentation in the Exhibitions

Symbols and emotionalisations cannot only be found on the level of representation, but also on the last layer Lidchi describes – the presentation or the overall design of the exhibition. The *Hjemmefrontmuseum* was constructed within the precincts of a building formerly known as *Dobbelte Batteri- og Bindingsverkhuset* (Double Artillery Battery and Half-timbered House) which is part of the *Akershusfestning* (Akershus fortress), a medieval fortress situated in the centre of Oslo.[21] Even these days, the fortress is used by the military, housing the Norwegian Ministry of Defence amongst others. Incorporating the museum into one of the buildings in the castle has a significant symbolic value for its depiction of the Second World War, as it positions the Norwegian resistance into the long tradi-

---

21   Færøy, 12.

tion of military defence. This emphasis is even further enhanced by the fact that the complex is still used as a military training ground. Its setting places the focus of the museum on the armed struggle of the resistance movement, as it calls the visitors' attention to this specific aspect of the Second World War, even before they enter the museum.

The building in which the *HL-senter* is housed has an equally high symbolic value for the institution. Though it held various different functions throughout its history, it is nowadays primarily known as *Villa Grande,* the former residence of Vidkun Quisling.[22] By placing a museum about the Holocaust into the villa of the former leader of the Norwegian Nazi party and iconic traitor Quisling, the museum reclaims the prerogative of interpretation over the meaning of this *lieu de mémoire*[23]. Unlike the *Hjemmefrontmuseum,* the *HL-senter* is not situated in the centre of Oslo, but on the Bygdøy peninsula, where several important Norwegian museums, such as the *Norsk Folkemuseum,* the *Norsk Maritimt Museum* or the *Fram-Museum,* can be found. Hence it is located in an area of the city well-known for being home to some of the most important museums in the country. Seen from this perspective, integrating *HL-senter* into the *Villa Grande* on Bygdøy was a brave but nonetheless risky choice. Firstly, the museum is expected to acquire a similar level of prominence as its famous neighbours. More importantly, however, it runs the danger of being overshadowed by the symbolic character of a building that attracts visitors not because of the exhibition being held there, but rather because of its famous erstwhile occupant. Just as in the *Hjemmefrontmuseum*, the visitor's attention is drawn towards a certain aspect of the history of the occupation. Unlike the former, however, the symbolism of the location does not mirror the museum's emphasis since Quisling and his role during the occupation do not feature prominently in the exhibition.

In the *Hjemmefrontmuseum,* the exhibition is organised chronologically and clustered around diverse topics within this chronological order. This is made transparent to the visitor by means of a guiding system that consists of large calendar sheets signifying the dates of the events depicted. The museum attempts in this way to narrate the story of the occupation from beginning to end. It starts with a section named *Forespillet* (»prelude«) spanning the years 1938 to 1940 by displaying newspaper articles about political developments in Europe and the beginning

---

22 Helge Maria Erikson: Mål og mening, in: Arkitektur N 2 (2009), 13–29, 20.
23 Cf. Pierre Nora: Realms of memory: the construction of the French past, New York 1997.

of the war; it culminates with the liberation of Norway 1945 in the section *Fem års okkupasjon er over*« (»Five years of occupation are over«). In the *HL*-senter, the exhibition is organised around four key words: *stigmatisering* (»stigmatisation«), *eksklusjon* (»exclusion«), *tilintetgjørelse* (»annihilation«) and *refleksjon* (»reflection«) which are communicated – albeit slightly less obvious for the visitor – as large letterings on the wall at the beginning of each of the sections. With its overall design choices, the exhibition is less coherent than the one in the *Hjemmefrontmuseum*. The emphasis is on the fact that the museum does not display a coherent narrative but rather several different aspects of a process. The exhibition neither communicates a specific date as a starting point for this process nor a definite ending. It starts, as mentioned previously, with the introduction of several Norwegian Jewish families and the illustration of the emergence of racism as a pseudo-science at the turn of the century. It ends with two rooms of merely symbolic importance. The first one is a very bright room where the names of all the Norwegian Holocaust victims have been written. They completely cover all four white walls of the room. The exhibition's final room has been integrated into Quisling's former dining room, which is dominated by its wooden panelling. In the middle of this room we find an unevenly shaped installation of mirrored partitions, forming a small room in itself. Inside this installation space short videos and images of past and present human rights violations are shown, with the intention to »encourage [...] visitors to contemplate on the meaning of the Holocaust in contemporary society«.[24] These two rooms accentuate the imperative to remember and learn from the Holocaust in the name of the victims, and serve as a lesson and reference point for contemporary and future genocides and human rights violations. In contrast to that, such a clear reference to the present and the future is not made in the *Hjemmefrontmuseum*. The exhibition culminates with the depiction of the liberation of Norway and the re-opening of the Norwegian parliament symbolising the re-establishing of the democratic system in 1945.

The room lay-out in both exhibitions is strikingly similar. Both predetermine a fixed path the visitor is obliged to follow. This path ushers the visitor through a suite of rooms that become progressively darker and narrower. Ultimately, in both cases, one has to go down a staircase to an even darker and narrower floor. In the last part of the exhibition, the visitor is led upstairs again and ends his walk in a large, bright room. This path is highly symbolic in the way it reflects the nar-

---

24 Description from the official information leaflet on the permanent exhibition published by *HL-senter*, English version.

rative(s) of the war both museums intend to convey. In the *Hjemmefrontmuseum* this symbolism underlines the overall narrative of the exhibition: It alludes to an unforeseen and unusual time of darkness that was overcome through the courageous acts of the Norwegian resistance movement, which eventually led to the ending of the occupation and brighter prospects for the future. In the *HL*-senter, a similar narrative can be read through the symbolism of the room arrangements and the use of lighting throughout the exhibition space. The Second World War and the Holocaust are perceived as an anomalous time of symbolic darkness which is eventually overcome and superseded by a brighter future. This symbolism, however, counteracts the narrative conveyed on all other layers of meaning at the exhibition. As mentioned previously, the exhibition begins with the depiction of escalating racism throughout Europe at the beginning of the century and culminates with a reference to the crimes and human rights violations committed today. Neither the Second World War nor the Holocaust are introduced as sudden and unexpected outbursts of evil but rather as a consequence of a process that originated with developments at the beginning of the 20th century and one that has not entirely completed its course.

VI. The Politics of the Museums

This brings us to the second part of Lidchi's framework: the politics of the exhibitions. In this ultimate section of my chapter, I will summarise and evaluate my findings from the analysis of the poetics of the exhibitions in light of broader discourses about the remembrance and the commemoration of the Second World War in Norway. As we have seen, the two museum exhibitions are far from being one-dimensional. The different layers of meaning within the exhibitions do not necessarily convey the same narrative; sometimes they complement each other, in some cases they underline or emphasise certain aspects and sometimes they even contradict each other. Therefore, the two museums do not form a simple dichotomy of reactionary and progressive or multi-dimensional and simplified narratives. Rather, their juxtaposition reveals the spectrum of perspectives and developments within different stages of the Norwegian memory culture.

The *Hjemmefrontmuseum* opened in 1970 and has not made any significant changes to its exhibition ever since.[25] When the museum was established, the

---

25 Færøy, 53.

patriotic narrative still strongly dominated Norwegian discourses about cultural memory of the Second World War.[26] In this context, the *Hjemmefrontmuseum* can be understood as a child of its time. In the analysis of the poetics of the exhibition we have found numerous allusions to the patriotic narrative on almost all layers of meaning, especially in the way the heroism of the resistance movement is highlighted in contrast to the viciousness of the German occupiers. Nonetheless the museum offers visitors a lot of background information on the Second World War in general and the occupation of Norway specifically. It is less the objects shown or the information provided through texts and maps but the way the exhibition transmits implicit and explicit evaluations and interpretations in light of the patriotic narrative that makes it appear rather problematic from a contemporary perspective. The main focus of the museum is the armed resistance, as we have seen when analysing the presence of certain objects, the design of the vitrines and the location of the museum as a part of *Akershusfestningen*. With this strong focus on the armed branch of the Norwegian resistance movement the museum differs slightly from the patriotic narrative with its emphasis on the *holdningskamp* as a collective resistance of all Norwegians that equally contributed to the victory over the Germans.

As regards the recent shift in in the Norwegian memory culture, however, the inclusion of the persecutions of Jews and the Holocaust into the exhibition is most remarkable. With its depiction of this aspect of the Second World War the museum is ahead of its time as neither the Holocaust in general nor the fate of the Norwegian Jews in particular were a part of the Norwegian memory culture in 1970.[27] Although highly suggestive and rather vague in its reference to Norway, the museum introduces the concentration camps, the persecution and mass murder of Jews from all over Europe as a crime of unimaginable proportions and separated from the military atrocities of the war. The section about the concentration camps is integrated into a part of the exhibition that deals with German atrocities. Obviously, this part of the exhibition is to provoke an emotional reaction in the visitor towards the evilness of the German enemy, making the Norwegian resistance movement appear all the more righteous. Nevertheless, the classification of the human rights violations, such as the imprisonment and murder of Jews and the torture of Norwegian prisoners of war, as crimes far worse than the combat operations during the war anticipates the later shift towards a more universal, human rights-focused narrative. Moreover, in this part of the exhibition the *Hjem-*

26 Maerz, 119.
27 Ibid.

mefrontmuseum offers a more complex narrative than the simplistic dichotomy of good Norwegians resisting the German occupiers and their Norwegian helpers. By including the fate of the Jews, the exhibition highlights a group of people that does not fit into either category – this is a clear difference to the dominating patriotic perspective of the time.

All in all, however, the *Hjemmefrontmuseum* can be perceived as an example of the manifestation of the patriotic narrative into the cultural memory of the Second World War. Yet, as we have seen, the exhibition does not exclusively adhere with this perspective, offering a slightly more complex picture of the war than the dominating patriotic narrative of that time. A direct comparison of its exhibition to the relatively modern *HL-senter*, however, makes it appear very out-dated. Notwithstanding recent shifts in the memory culture, the new aspects about the war that have come to light and the gradual deconstruction of the dominating patriotic narrative, the museum has remained unaltered. In order to figure out how these changes have affected the Norwegian museum culture, I will therefore take a closer look at the politics of the *HL-senter*.

The opening of the Holocaust centre in 2005 was a direct result of the debates in the 1990s about the restitution for Norwegian Jews who were dispossessed during the war. It was established during a time in which the patriotic memory of the war had already been challenged by various historians due to the different hitherto repressed aspects of the war that came to light, for instance the fate of the *tyskerbarna* (children of Norwegian women and German soldiers), the Norwegian SS-volunteers, or the role of the Norwegian police in the deportation of the Jews. This gradual shift from the rather monolithic patriotic narrative towards a more complex, multi-layered understanding of the war has strongly influenced how the Second World War and the Holocaust are depicted in the *HL-senter*. The museum does not offer one specific narrative of the war but rather an overview of the developments that eventually led to the persecution and murder of the Jews in Norway. Furthermore, the war is not depicted as a sudden unexpected outburst of violence but introduced as the culmination of several developments, such as the emergence of racism on a pseudo-scientific basis and the rising nationalism all over Europe. Therefore, it is not particularly the German evilness that is introduced as the root cause for these events but the prevailing zeitgeist of the first half of the 20th century taken to extremes. The exhibition aims at uncovering the mechanisms that could eventually lead to the tragedy of the Holocaust and ends with a clear imperative not only to remember, but also prevent future genocides and human rights violations. Therewith, the exhibition shows a clear reference to the universal narrative of the war.

Simultaneously, we are introduced to various individual stories and memories of witnesses of the Holocaust. In this way the museum not only emphasises the universal significance of the mass murder of the Jews, but also offers a more diverse picture of events than the generic representations in the *Hjemmefrontmuseum*. What is most remarkable about this is the way Jews are portrayed as average Norwegians and, therefore, as an inherent part of the collective of the Norwegian society. This takes the inclusion of Jews into the narrative of the war by the *Hjemmefrontmuseum* one step further: The Holocaust is no longer depicted as an abstract tragedy, but as an integral component of Norwegian history. This is a radical change from the patriotic narrative of the war and its focus on the rigid dichotomy of the ›nation-in-resistance‹ and the Quislinger.

Despite the overall progressive and multi-layered portrayal of the events, however, a few allusions to the patriotic narrative as well as a number of highly suggestive elements can also be found in *HL-senter*. Especially the video installations and their highly emotionalised depiction of the German perpetrators are a recurrent reference to the patriotic narrative of evil Germans and good Norwegians. The same holds true for the use of light and darkness as well as the layout of the rooms which, as mentioned previously, constitute a direct contradiction to the overall narrative(s) of the exhibition. All in all, however, the *HL-senter*, in comparison to the *Hjemmefrontmuseum*, is by far the more progressive of the two museums incorporating elements of the universal narrative of the Second World War into the Norwegian museum culture and problematising a number of formerly unquestioned givens of the patriotic narrative of the war.

IV.
Sites of Memory

Tor Einar Fagerland
Between Patriotism and Universalism
Norwegian World War II Monuments
and Memorials 1990–2014 from
a Transnational Perspective

I. Introduction

In 1997, a memorial was unveiled in the centre of Trondheim depicting Cissi Klein, a Jewish girl who was murdered in Auschwitz-Birkenau in 1943. The sculpture of 13-year-old Cissi – sitting on a park bench outside the house she once lived in – is a quiet, yet emotional and powerful statement, especially given that this monument, created by Tore Bjørn Skjølsvik and Tone Ekwas, is one of the very first attempts in any Norwegian cityscape to address the fact that the Holocaust also took place in our country and within our communities.

In 2007, the governing board of the historic and symbolic site at Stiklestad decided that it was now time to undertake a partial excavation of a destroyed and hitherto buried monument built there by Norwegian Nazis during the war years. In accordance with a more critical, even self-critical and open-ended pedagogical approach, the intent was to use the fascist monument along with its destruction and silencing as a means to reflect upon the way the past has been used and abused. It was to be a platform to discuss problematic features of Norwegian nationalism and the handling of difficult aspects of the past in contemporary Norway. Well received in some quarters and heavily criticized in others, the plans quickly reached a deadlock and have remained so – to this day (2014).

The following article presents and analyses a selection of Norwegian monuments and memorials built or planned between 1990 and 2014 commemorating events, persons or addressing issues connected to World War II. My aim is to discuss some of the complexities in representing and interpreting World War II in Norwegian public spaces in post-Cold War Norway by placing these examples into a broader international and theoretical framework.

By way of the present discussion I will argue that examples such as Trondheim's sculpture of Cissi Klein, or the unresolved issue concerning the buried fascist monument at Stiklestad, in many ways reflect Norway's doubled-sided public memory of World War II. Partly, and in accordance with transnational trends, this present-day memory consists of a growing interest in new perspectives, new issues and new ways of dealing with the past, but partly also of a strong will to protect the main structures of established national narratives.

II. Memory and Identity: Towards a new Concept of Collective Memory

In 1882, the French philologist Ernest Renan observed that for a nation to become a nation, the population has not only to remember many things, but also to forget many things.[1] A collective amnesia, as much as a collective memory, is therefore a key element in the process of nation building.[2] From the end of the eighteenth century onwards, sites, monuments and physical traces representing shared victories (for the powerful states) and shared defeats and losses (for the less fortunate states) have been crucial tools in the development of national identities. The search for useful imagery and narratives of the past has been coupled with the exclusion of less desirable or usable images and narratives. In order to create a shared single identity, a multitude of other competing identities have to be forgotten. This held true throughout the nineteenth century as it did in late twentieth century Spain where the »pact of forgetting« (*pacto del olvido*) ensured that divisive issues surrounding the civil war did not disturb the transition to democracy.

Today, the breakdown of grand narratives at the end of the Cold War such as those of post-colonialism, or the post-traumatic situation after the Holocaust and the two World Wars (surfacing only gradually after a period of psychic paralysis and silence) in combination with the recent digital revolution, have all contributed to a renewed and acute interest in memory and the past. Over the last couple of decades, »memory« and »collective memory«, in particular, have been acknowledged as two of the leading concepts in cultural studies. In this expanding and interdisciplinary field of what is now labelled as »memory studies« the focus is

---

1   Adrian Forty/Susanne Küchler (eds.): The Art of Forgetting, Oxford 1999, 7–9.
2   See Adrian Forty/Susanne Küchler and Paul Connerton: How Modernity Forgets, Cambridge 2009.

increasingly placed on how we live with our memories, how they haunt us, and how we use and abuse them.[3]

This implies also a spatial shift in our understanding of memory dynamics. Traditionally, a nation's collective memory has been managed within the nation-state and with little attention accorded to the entanglements with other nations' memories. Today, the nation-state is no longer the only vessel for memory debates, and nations no longer construct their past in such a hermetic fashion. Instead, they find themselves increasingly under observation and subject to criticism by other nations. Memory and identity are therefore issues increasingly discussed in an international context.[4] While succeeding in keeping the civil war out of the collective memory throughout the 1980s and 1990s, the Spanish pact of forgetting has started to unravel in recent years, as spontaneous movements began to (literally) unearth the past. Mass graves from the civil war were dug up and calls were made for those executed during the war to be given memorials and proper burials. This culminated with the Historical Memory Law in 2007 that led to the final removal of most fascist monuments and, moreover, for official support to exhume the mass graves.[5] Similar eruptions of repressed traumas connected with the Third Reich were also experienced in Germany during the 1970s and 1980s as a reaction to the Adenauer policy of »normality at all costs« of the first post-war decades.[6] In France the memories of the Vichy regime (1940–1944) resurfaced in the 1970s as a reaction to the enduring post-war myth of an all-embracing French resistance against the German occupier.[7]

---

3 See Maurice Halbwachs: On Collective Memory, London 1992 [1925]; Aleida Assmann: Memory, Individual and Collective, in: R. E. Goodin/C. Tilly (eds.): The Oxford Handbook of Contextual Political Analysis, Oxford, 2008, 210–224; Aleida Assmann: Canon and Archive, in: A. Erll, A. Nünning (eds.): A Companion to Cultural Memory Studies, Berlin 2010, 97–108; Aleida Assmann/Sebastian Conrad: Memory in a Global Age. Discourses, Practices and Trajectories, Basingstoke 2010, 97–108.
4 Assmann/Conrad.
5 See Giles Tremlett, Ghosts of Spain: Travels Through a Country's Hidden Past, London 2006, and Paloma Aguilar: Memory and Amnesia: The Role of the Spanish Civil War in the Transition to Democracy, Oxford 2002.
6 Mary Fulbrook: German National Identity after the Holocaust, Cambridge 1999; Andreas Huyssen: Present Pasts. Urban Palimpsets and the Politics of Memory, Stanford 2003.
7 Susan Suleiman: Crisis of Memory and the Second World War, Harvard 2006.

The spread of a European discourse on guilt, especially with respect to the Holocaust, can be interpreted as a transnational synchronization of memory cultures. The European Union, for instance, encourages the development of a »memory without borders«. It does so, not as a unified supranational memory, but as a shared pan-European norm for dealing with the past where the emphasis on human rights and unity in diversity play a crucial part. Attitudes to heritage and memory are changing within a context of new »moral politics« emphasizing testimony, trauma and restitution. The problems of remembrance and restitution posed by the experiences of the Holocaust and World War II have been crucial in the reinterpretation of collective memory. Throughout Europe today people are being asked to remember what they formerly were taught to forget. Currently, memories of collective traumas are partly supplementing and partly replacing discredited national heritages. In the global public sphere the management of the past, or in German *Vergangenheitsbewältigung*, has been turned into an issue of global accountability.[8]

III. Memory and Representation

According to its Latin meaning monuments are »things that remind«, things to be transmitted to later generations. As discussed above, the »things« worthy of being remembered in public spaces have traditionally been images of a nation's great victories, more often than not in the figure of the powerful »general astride a horse«. In a clear, unequivocal and formal language, the traditional monument quintessentially represented how a historical event or personage should be interpreted. Classical monuments are therefore usually mounted on plinths, designed as such to be viewed from a distance. The monument is a public, tactile representation of values that transcend individual beliefs and interpretations. Its purpose is to remind us of the existence of something greater than ourselves.[9] In the former occupied Western European countries, the experience of World War II once again

---

8   Henry Rousso: Vichy Syndrome. History and Memory in France since 1944, Harvard 1991, and Jeffrey C. Alexander et al. (eds.): Cultural Trauma and Collective Identity, Berkeley 2004.
9   The Great War (1914–1918) was commemorated within the same type of unifying framework but the emphasis now changed into images of the heroism of the unknown soldiers and of the shared sufferings in the trenches. For commemorations of the Great War see Jay Winter: Sites of Memory, Sites of Mourning. The Great War in European

led to a demand for patriotic narratives; this time to compensate for the shock and humiliation of Nazi occupation. In the post-war years, World War II in general, and the resistance movement more specifically, thereby became the central metaphor for renewed national unity. In this, the cultural afterlife of World War II became a confirmation and even a strengthening of the belief and idea of an ethnic and cultural homogeneous national community.[10]

Today, however, the need for a unified vision of the past as found in patriotic narratives and in traditional monuments collides with the modern conviction that neither the past nor its meanings are ever just one thing.[11] A fundamental shift in the functions as well as of our perceptions of monuments has consequentially taken place; static and monologue-oriented monuments are being gradually supplemented or replaced by dynamic and dialogue-oriented memorial sites. In close interplay with the changed concept of collective memory, there has also been a fundamental change into a new type of commemorative space. Much like collective memory itself, these sites are evolving from being in the service of the nation-state to becoming places for a much broader exploration of the relationship between past and present, where different values and interpretations can meet and be negotiated.

The question on how to commemorate the Holocaust – in the land of its perpetrators – has for several decades been problematic in Germany.[12] Or, as the German artist Jochen Gerz puts it: »Faced with Germany's past, a number of people my age, even those too young to remember events, or born after the war,

Cultural History, Cambridge 1995, and Jay Winter: Remembering War. The Great War between History and Memory in the 20th Century, Yale 2006.

10   For France, Belgium and Netherland see Pieter Lagrou: The Legacy of Nazi-Occupation. Patriotic Memory and National Recovery in Western Europe 1945–1965, Cambridge 2000. For Norway, Anne Eriksen: Det var noen annet under krigen. 2. verdenskrig i norsk kollektivtradisjon, Oslo 1995, and for Denmark, Claus Bryld/Anette Warring: Besættelsestiden som kollektiv erindring. Historie- og traditionsforvaltning af krig og besættelse 1945–1997, Roskilde 1998, and John T. Lauridsen: Dansk nazisme 1930–45 og derefter, København 2002.

11   James E. Young: Memory and the Monument after 9/11, in: R. Crownshaw et al. (eds.): The Future of Memory, New York 2010, 77–92.

12   James E. Young: Texture of Memory, Yale 1993, 17–112, James E. Young: At Memory's Edge. After-Images of the Holocaust in contemporary Art and Architecture, Yale 2000, 90–151.

have always been conscious of not knowing exactly how to behave.«[13] As Gerz remarks: »Germany is a society marked by a sublime repression of its past, and the challenge is to find new ways of facing the repressed memory of the Third Reich which keeps coming back to haunt us.«[14] The solution for Gerz and other German artists of his generation has been to resort to the philosophy of the *Gegen-Denkmal*, or counter-monument. This position refuses to assign a singular meaning either to events or their memories, but instead through conceptual, sculptural and architectural forms returns the burden of memory to those who come searching for it.[15] Unlike traditional history and monuments, the counter-monument philosophy's aim is not to simplify or unify interpretations. Instead, the main objective of *Gegen-Denkmal* is to spur debate and reflection about the past itself, as well as to how contemporary society interprets and makes use of the past. A counter-monument is thus interrogative rather than authoritative, critical rather than self-exalting, challenging rather than reassuring, dynamic rather than static and complex rather than one-dimensional.

When Gerz was assigned the task of designing the »Harburg Monument against Fascism« in Hamburg, he was determined not to make a traditional monument.[16] Moreover, he was resolved not to create a space that reduced the viewer to a passive spectator. He rejected, therefore, the designated location, a beautiful park in Hamburg's city centre, in favour of a commercial centre in the suburb of Harburg. According to Gerz, this was a »normal ugly place«, where people could choose to like or hate the installation, but not to avoid it. On a simple lead-coated square column, passers-by could read:

»We invite the citizens of Harburg, and visitors to the town, to add their names here next to ours. In doing so, we commit ourselves to remain vigilant. As more and more names cover this 12-metre tall lead column, it will gradually be lowered into the ground. One day it will have disappeared completely, and the site of the Harburg monument against fascism will be empty. In the end, it is only we ourselves who can rise up against injustice.«

---

13   Quoted in Young. Memory's Edge, 120. See also <http://www.gerz.fr/deb/put_file.html?ident=11231abbe420596ea6e72d6510bff87d>.
14   Quoted in Young, Memory's Edge, 120. Jochen Gerz is one of the pioneers in what James Young labelled the counter-monument movement. For an overview of Gerz's works and the philosophical concepts behind them see, Jochen Gerz, Werkverzeichnis Band I–IV, Verlag für moderne Kunst, Nürnberg 1999–2011.
15   Young, Memory's Edge, 90–119.
16   Gerz, Werkverzeichnis, 15, 90–91.

The more actively visitors participated, the faster they covered each section with their signatures, and the sooner the monument disappeared. In 1993 the column disappeared into the ground, entrusting the people of Harburg with the responsibility to resist and to remember. The response to Gerz's monument was mixed. While the mayor of Hamburg pointed out that the whole spectacle cost more than the re-pavement of several kilometres of autobahn, the local newspaper regarded the engraved messages of approval, hatred, anger and stupidity as important and revealing fingerprints of the city.[17]

In 1997, a competition was launched inviting artists to propose ways to commemorate the Holocaust in Berlin, the capital of the re-united Germany.[18] Following several earlier failed attempts, the new memorial should reflect, and not conceal, the difficulties surrounding Germany's memorial debate. The new generation of German artists was especially invited to participate. In one of the submissions, Reinhard Matz and Rudolf Herz proposed to take one kilometre of autobahn and pave it with cobblestones, thereby slowing traffic down to 40 kilometres an hour, and mark this stretch as a »Memorial for Europe's Murdered Jews«. Instead of being a memory site detached from our daily lives, this designated stretch of autobahn would be a way of creating a space, which, briefly at least, forced people to look within themselves for memories. Even though this particular concept, or proposals from other young Germans artists were ultimately not selected, the inclusion of perspectives typifying the *Gegen-Denkmal* philosophy was a crucial element for the memorial process in Berlin.

The winning designs for the memorial in Berlin were a large sculpture by the American architect Peter Eisenman in tandem with an attached underground »Information Point« created by the German exhibition designer Dagmar von Wilcken. The memorial was opened in May 2005 and consists of 2,711 concrete stelae of varying heights. The 800 square-metre underground information centre contains of a series of chambers comprising of the Room of Families, the Room of Dimensions, the Room of Names and the Room of Places. The memorial is conceptually accessible and inaccessible at the same time. It neither directs nor instructs the visitor, but lets them find their own way through the memorial – and into their own memory. The addition of a documentation centre and the manner in which it is conceived has also created an interesting interplay and interpenetration between the site's commemorative dimension above ground and its historical

17 Young, Memory's Edge, 135–139.
18 Ibid, 184–223.

dimension below. Together with the field of stelae, the information centre reminds us of the memorial's dual mandate as a commemorative and informative space, as a site both of memory and history, each shaped by the other. The placing of this memorial in the heart of Berlin also signifies that it is not memorial space originally built by the killers themselves, as the concentration camp sites inevitably were. To build a memorial at a distance from the actual sites of extermination is therefore something more than merely a passive preservation of the past. Berlin's Holocaust Memorial embodies a deliberate attempt to remember and a strong statement that *memory must be created* for future generations, and not simply preserved. In 2008, *The New York Times* commented: »Most countries celebrate the best in their pasts; Germany unrelentingly promotes its worst.«[19] At the opening ceremony for the »Denkmal für die ermordeten Juden Europas« its architect, Peter Eisenman, noted: »It is clear that we won't have solved all the problems – architecture and exhibitions are not a panacea for evil – nor will we have satisfied all those present today, but this cannot have been our intention.«[20]

IV. Norway: Between Patriotic and Transnational Memory

In Norway, as elsewhere in Western Europe, a specific kind of patriotic memory became dominant in the first post-war decades.[21] In this narrative the focus was on national unity and resistance (both active and passive) against the German occupier, thus omitting problematic topics such as the role of Norwegian collaborators in the deportation of 772 Jews to Auschwitz. Although well documented in archive materials, for a long time the destiny of these Norwegians Jews left few visible traces in the Norwegian memorial landscape. However, this changed in the 1990s. First with the sculpture of the 13-year old Cissi Klein unveiled in Trondheim in 1997, and subsequently in 2000 in Oslo's harbour (Vippetangen) with a memorial created by Antony Gormley, which commemorated the Norwegian Jews deported on the *SS Donau* on 26 November 1942. These memorials can be seen as a reflection of the development of a new commemorative culture and a fresh awareness of the Holocaust as being much more than a side effect of global warfare. On the

---

19 New York Times, 29 January 2008.
20 Program for the opening ceremony, stiftung-denkmal.de, last access: 24 January 2014, <http://www.stiftung-denkmal.de/fileadmin/user_upload/projekte/oeffentlichkeitsarbeit/pdf/docu_10thMay_doublepage.pdf>.
21 See Lagrou, Eriksen.

international front, the year 1961 and the Eichmann trial are often regarded as the turning point in this respect, while on the national level the debate regarding compensation for Jewish victims of the Holocaust is, of course, of critical importance.²² At a local level in Trondheim in 1995 an alliance of local citizens and politicians and the Jewish community succeeded in re-naming the street outside the house Cissi Klein where grew up to »Cissi Kleins gate«. As part of the city's millennium anniversary in 1997, the same alliance was successful in getting private and public sponsors to fund the monument that was unveiled that year.

To be fair, a monument had also been erected in 1947 at the cemetery at Lademoen in Trondheim in memory of the 131 murdered Jews from the local Jewish community. The following year a monument in memory of the Jews who were deported from southern Norway and killed by the Nazis was unveiled at *Det Mosaiske Trossamfunds* graveyard in Helsfyr. Both monuments were designed by the sculptor Harald Isenstein, he himself a Jewish refugee who had to flee from Germany to Denmark and thereafter to Sweden. A cemetery, while generally accessible to the public, however, remains a rather enclosed space and private in character. The memorialisation of the Norwegian Holocaust in public parks, town squares and, as we shall also see, in the city streets from the 1990s onwards, therefore represents a distinct transformation in the Norwegian memorial landscape. After 2010 the locally initiated Cissi Klein memorial in Trondheim and the governmental initiated memorial in Oslo have been supplemented by a growing number of transnational stumbling stones (*Stolpersteine*) – small, cobblestone-sized memorials for individual victims of Nazism embedded in the sidewalks in front of buildings formerly inhabited by deported Jews. Today, in Oslo's memorial landscape there are 66 of these small reminders and warnings focusing on victims at a deeply local level.²³ In 2012, these stumbling stones were also installed in Trondheim, and in 2013 Stavanger, Mosjøen, Kristiansand, Elverum and Haugesund received their very own small, albeit powerful, reminders of the local impact

---

22 See Michael Rothberg, Multidirectional Memory. Remembering the Holocaust in the Age of Decolonization, Stanford 2009, 176–179, and Jødeboutvalgets utredning (NOU 1997:22).

23 Originally initiated and organized by the Jewish Museum in Oslo, the laying of new stones in Norway today are mainly both initiated and organized by local communities, museums and organisations. See, for example, Mosjøen in northern Norway: Vefsn kommune, last access: 8 May 2014, <http://jupiter.vefsn.kommune.no/application/getDocument?filid=1713803.0>. For general information about the project see the artist's webpage <http://www.stolpersteine.eu/en/>.

of the Holocaust. The first stumbling stones were installed by the German artist Gunter Demnig in Cologne in 1994, and today there are more than 43,500 of them embedded in more than a thousand different locations.[24] Thanks to their wide geographic spread and by their continually growing numbers, the *Stolpersteine* link individual destinies to the grotesque magnitude both in the scale and the numbers of victims of the Holocaust. By remembering a tragedy that affected the whole of Europe and by being a transnational phenomenon, these stones are an example of a broadening of the aims and interpretations of historical monuments in public spaces.

Julius Paltiel was one of only 34 Norwegian Jews to survive deportation. Upon returning to Trondheim after the war, he spent most of his time giving talks and classes against hatred, racism and extremism. After his death a group of local citizens began an initiative to raise a memorial in his honour and for his work for the common good and human dignity. In 2012, the city authorities launched a competition for the development of a public site called »Julius Paltiels plass«. The designated committee, who also functioned as a jury, emphasised in the guidelines that they wanted a dynamic memorial site and not a static monument. Moreover, they specified that the space should accommodate dialogue and a variety of activities. In short, »Julius Paltiels plass« should be a place for both memory of and reflection on a mass catastrophe, yet at the same time a space that is open to new life and novel activities for the common good.[25] In order to achieve this, the committee selected three groups (from 30 combined groups) consisting of both artists and landscape architects and gave them six months and 50,000 Norwegian crowns each to develop a concept to embody these goals.[26] Throughout the project period open seminars and work meetings were arranged between the committee and the groups of finalists, while a public presentation of the three

24 Stolpersteine.eu, last access: 8 May 2014, <http://www.stolpersteine.eu/en/>.
25 »Julius Paltiels plass«, Landskapsarkitektur.no, last access: 8 May 2014, <http://www.landskapsarkitektur.no/?nid=81216>. This part of the article is based on the project's webpage, <https://www.facebook.com/JuliusPaltielsPlass>, media coverage, an interview with the head of the Art Committee, Sidsel M. Bergh, and my own notes as an observer in meetings between the jury and the three selected finalists.
26 The three selected finalists were: 1. Marius Dahl and Jan Christensen (artists) working together with the architects Elin Sørensen and Erle Stenberg (Oslo/Trondheim), 2. The artists Marit Justine Haugen and Dan Zohar together with the architect Nina Wang (Trondheim/Oslo/Israel), 3. The architect company Nâv in cooperation with the artists Lars Ramberg and Johan Paju (Trondheim/Berlin/Stockholm).

final proposals was organised. In September 2013 the jurors selected the project named »Dialogue« by the group comprising of Marit Justine Haugen, Dan Zohar and Nina Wang for further development. The idea behind the winning project is to develop an outdoor space centred on a round table that is lit at all hours. The jurors found the proposed design suitable both as a space open for thought and reflection but also as an inviting and dynamic space open to the needs of a living urban environment. The project is due to be completed in 2015.

These memorial spaces, whether already constructed or in the planning stage, indicate how Norway's memory culture has become more pluralistic. Today, universalistic approaches supplement and in some cases replace the dominance of the resistance narrative, which in many ways culminated with the creation of the *Norges Hjemmefrontmuseum* (Norway's Resistance Museum) in 1970. This museum was dedicated to the resistance and the resistance veterans' narratives that almost exclusively shape its exhibits.[27] It still enjoys great prestige and popularity in Norway, drawing on average about 50,000 visitors annually.[28] Furthermore, in 2011, a sculpture of the famous resistance fighter Max Manus was unveiled near the museum, just at the tail end of a surge of interest that had begun in 2008 when a film about Manus became one of Norwegian cinema's biggest ever blockbusters. Both the monarchy, represented by the King and Queen of Norway, and the government, represented by the Secretary of Defence and the Minister of Cultural Affairs, attended the opening night of »Max Manus: Man of War«. The unveiling of the sculpture in 2011, the continuous prestige of the *Norges Hjemmefrontmuseum* as well as the attendance by official dignitaries at the première coupled with the popularity of the film itself, suggest that the traditional patriotic narrative of World War II still has an important role to play in contemporary Norway. In a series of interviews, for instance, the filmmakers repeatedly stated that they were humbled to be allowed to make the film, since these resistance fighters (Max Manus and his comrades), had made such great sacrifices for the nation. In the weeks following the opening night the actor who played the leading character, Aksel Hennie, repeatedly appeared alongside highly decorated war veterans like Gunnar »Kjakan« Sønsteby, in events celebrating Norway's war heroes, events

---

27 Frode Færøy: Norges Hjemmefrontmuseum – i stiftelsens år, Oslo 1997. 43–53.
28 »Kultur å forsvare« Om kulturvirksomheten i Forsvaret frem mot 2020, Regjeringen. no, last access: 8. May 2014, <http://www.regjeringen.no/nb/dep/fd/dok/regpubl/stmeld/2008-2009/stmeld-nr-33-2008-2009-/6/2.html?id=557293>.

that underlined the importance of their stories for future generations.²⁹ In both its narrative structure and public reception »Max Manus: Man of War«, echoes the 1957 success of the film *Ni Liv*. At that time, this film transformed both its director Arne Skouen and the leading actor Jack Fjelstad (playing another war hero, Jan Balsrud), into some kind of folk heroes, much like Aksel Hennie in 2008–2009.³⁰

These examples serve to further illustrate how established Norwegian narratives about World War II still have a lot of persuasiveness that can be re-activated, especially if challenged by alternative approaches and interpretations. Stiklestad in Mid-Norway is one of the nation's most important historical sites – and of memory. Its fame dates back to the year 1030 AD when St. Olav, the »eternal king« of Norway, was killed in a battle at the site. For almost one thousand years this has been an important site in the Norwegian memory landscape, hosting celebrations of Norway both as a unified kingdom and as a Christian nation. In the last year of the Nazi occupation of Norway, Quisling and his Norwegian collaboration regime built a huge monument on the site to celebrate their own fascist version of Norwegian history. Only a few weeks after liberation, the monument was demolished and all traces erased except for a nine-metre tall obelisk, which was too big and heavy to be removed. Erected by Norwegian fascists, and not by the German occupiers, the monument represents a difficult and ambiguous element in Norwegian war history. This aspect has made it a problematic part of Norway's past to include in the traditional way of remembrance. The buried monument has thus remained part of our un-spoken past, at both local and national level.

After 50 years of silence, the use of Stiklestad by the Norwegian fascists became the topic of several newspaper articles in 2005, thus bringing the buried obelisk back into the public eye. As a response, the board at the Stiklestad National Culture Centre appointed a task group to look into the possibilities of including the ambiguous and painful uses of the site in the pedagogical and ethical work at Stiklestad. The main conclusion of the group – of which the author of this text was a member – was that since the repressed memory of the fascist presence at Stiklestad had literally surfaced again, »the pact of silence«, lasting roughly from

---

29   Hanne Sørli: Min Historie? Et kulturminnefaglig refleksjonsgrunnlag for en fremtidig bautautstilling på Stiklestad. Master's thesis NTNU, Trondheim 2009.
30   Claudia Lenz: The Second World War in the Popular Culture of Memory in Norway, in: S. Paletschek (ed.): Popular Historiographies in the 19th and 20th Centuries. Cultural Meanings, Social Practices, Oxford 2011, 149–150.

1945 to 2005, no longer worked.[31] The question was therefore not if, but how to include this layer of meaning. The task group further suggested to produce a study exhibition at the site and to make a partial excavation of the buried obelisk. In accordance with a critical and open-ended pedagogical approach, the idea was to use the fascist monument, its destruction and the ensuing silence to reflect upon uses and abuses of the past and problematic aspects of Norwegian nationalism. Criticism of the plans came from both war veterans and former members of the Norwegian fascist party *Nasjonal Samling*, and received wide media coverage. Supporters of the project, however, found it difficult to get their message across, that re-erecting the monument was not, and was never meant to be, a part of the proposal. The question at stake was how to deal with the highly unwelcome spectre of fascism, especially at an almost sacred site in the Norwegian historical landscape. Furthermore, could and should the public and historical site of Stiklestad be used to confront the significance of this buried monument and thereby serve as a way of confronting the fact that even Norwegians were not immune to fascism and political extremism? This was an important issue for the task group in 2007, and some might find it even more urgent after the terror and violence of 22 July 2011. The proposals were partly well received and partly heavily criticized and remain as of present (2014) in a deadlock.

V. Conclusion

The relationship between our memories, on the one hand, and historical objects and places, on the other, is close but complex. In his seven-volume novel »In Search of Lost Time« (1913–1927), Marcel Proust tells the reader how the smell and taste of a Madeleine biscuit triggered a surge of memories from his childhood. Objects can most certainly trigger our memories and if combined with the real or seemingly, non-changeable quality of place, a feeling of closeness or connection with the past can indeed be strongly felt. Although World War II is now history and will never return, the places and the landscapes are still here, and are in many ways the same and can be (re)visited. This is the reason humans,

---

31 Tor Einar Fagerland/Trond Risto Nilssen: The Norwegian Fascist Monument at Stiklestad, in: H. Bjerg et al. (eds.): Historicizing the Uses of the Past. Scandinavian Perspectives on History Culture, Historical Consciousness and Didactics of History related to World War II, Bielefeld 2011, 77–90.

alone and together, throughout time have returned to places of specific historical significance in order to remember those who were at these places and to reminisce about what once happened there.

Physical traces are in different ways carriers of meaning, and there are various strategies as to how to deal with physical remnants from the past, especially if their meanings are ambiguous, or perhaps even painful. The wartime monument at Stiklestad could theoretically, therefore, have been designated for re-use in the Norwegian post-war society. Another solution would have been to re-use the monument, but to do so only after an alteration and the removal of elements at loggerheads with the values of Norwegian post-war society such as the fascist Sun Wheel symbol engraved on the obelisk. Instead, the chosen solution was total destruction, thereby using the strategy of iconoclasm. The principle of iconoclasm is that the removal of material and visible traces from the past will also eventually lead to a removal of the mental memory. In other words, if one cannot see it anymore, it no longer exists. With the erasing of the fascist monument, Stiklestad was cleansed and reclaimed as a site for the national unity so strongly promoted in the post-war years. Today, an expression of the place's symbolic value is still to be found in the play »The Story of Saint Olav« which since 1958 has attracted about 20,000 spectators a year.[32]

In her book »Purity and Danger«, the anthropologist Mary Douglas introduces the term »matter out of place«.[33] In every culture every object has its specific place, and our concepts of dirt and cleanliness are, according to Douglas, shaped by whether things are seen to be in their right place or not. A monument representing fascist ideals, according to most Norwegians both in 1945 and today, patently does not belong at a place like Stiklestad. The fascist monument at Stiklestad is therefore »matter out of place« in regard to both our conception of the historical site of Stiklestad and our conception of World War II. The buried obelisk is clearly an intruder which, to borrow Douglas's concept, pollutes a place which should be clean, and creates disorder and abnormality at a place where there should be order and purity. The use of the site by the Norwegian fascists has still not been included in the post-war version of the history of Stiklestad. The erstwhile presence of the

---

32 Spelet om Heilag Olav – spel i 60 år, Stiklestad.no, last access: 8 May 2014, <http://stiklestad.no/opplevelser/spelet-om-heilag-olav/>.
33 Mary Douglas: Purity and Danger. An Analysis of Concepts of Pollution and Taboo, London 1966.

Norwegian National Socialists and the buried obelisk remain as an invisible scar in the memorial landscape.

Nonetheless, as James E. Young reminds us, active memory work entails more than simply to visit, recognize and preserve physical sites, buildings and objects from the past. After all, focusing only on the preservation of physical reminders of the Holocaust such as concentration camps would inevitably – and in fact – protect and preserve memorial spaces designed mainly by the killers themselves. Instead, Young argues that *memory work* is just as much about designing purpose-made memorial sites, and thereby about affirming that memory must be created for future generations, and not simply preserved.[34] When the then 21-year old Maya Lin won the competition for the Vietnam Veterans Memorial in 1982, she clearly stated that she wanted to create a *place* and not a *thing*. The memorial consists of a V-shaped wall made of black granite that sinks into the ground. The names of all 52,272 identified American victims of the Vietnam War are etched into the wall. Patriotic or heroic symbols, on the other hand, are completely absent. As visitors, we are faced with our own image and those of other visitors reflected in the polished surface of the black granite wall. Visually, the Vietnam Veterans Memorial Wall, with its abstract forms, black mass and its impression of sinking into the ground, represents a sharp contrast to the plinth-based, vertical and figurative monuments in white marble that feature in many other monuments on the National Mall in Washington D. C. More importantly, however, is the site's dynamic ambiguity in which the etched 52,272 names represent as many different stories, and invite reflection around the complex effect the Vietnam War had upon tens of thousands of families, circles of friends, local communities and American society as a whole. It is a space open to different opinions and emotions in relation to a war associated with sorrow, division, defeat and shame, to which Maya Lin succeeded in giving a physical form. Over 120 million people have visited the Veterans Memorial Wall since its opening, and today it is regarded as an iconic »game changer« in the shift from monological monument culture to a dialogical culture of the memorial.[35]

According to Alice Greenwald, director at the 9/11 Memorial Museum at Ground Zero in New York, a modern memorial today is a social and cultural

---

34 Young, Memory's Edge, 199.
35 »It is still far and away the greatest memorial of modern times—the most beautiful, the most heart-wrenching, the most subtle, and the most powerful.« Vanity Fair: Reflected Grief, vanityfair.com, last access: 24.1.2014, <http://www.vanityfair.com/politics/2012/04/maya-lin-vietnam-wall-memorial>.

meeting place where we come together with our different individual and collective memories to address what it means to be a human being, and what it means to live in a complex, global community at the start of the 21st century.[36] It is precisely this use of public space as a cultural and social arena for negotiating identity, for diverging opinions to be held, and for dialogue that is the most prominent feature of how memorials are approached across much of the Western world today. They supplement and, in many cases, replace the traditional approach to monuments.[37] The formal expression of such memorial sites vary greatly, from Micha Ullman's modest, submerged spaces with empty bookshelves at Bebelplatz in Berlin to Peter Eisenman's 19,000 square metres *Denkmal für die ermordeten Juden Europas* in the same city. Ullman's site, which recalls the Nazis' book burning in 1933, is barely visible until one gets very close, and visitors must actively seek out the small glass surface and bend down so as to see what lies beneath. In contrast to monuments that are designed for passive spectatorship, the memorial site is an arena to experience, to act and to take individual responsibility – to be counted as a citizen and as a human being amongst others.[38]

When encountering Eisenman's Holocaust Memorial visitors also have to make active choices. There are no clear points indicating the beginning and the end – people have to find their own path. By wandering into the sculptural landscape, alone or together with others, every visitor becomes an integrated and organic part of the memorial, in the same way that a visitor can see his or her own reflection in the Vietnam Veterans Memorial Wall. It is no coincidence that these examples of memorial sites all commemorate victims of traumatic, complex and/ or shameful events. While the classical monument displays its force as a powerful representation of a simple and unambiguous message, the strength of these new types of memorial spaces resides in their ability to create shared experiences

---

36   Quote from conversation with Executive Director Alice Greenwald, New York City 25.5.2013. Before serving at the 9/11 National Memorial Museum, Greenwald served as Associate Museum Director at the United States Holocaust Memorial Museum in Washington D.C., a museum well-known for its universalistic human rights based approach.

37   The impact of Maya Lin's minimalistic and open-ended approach as well as the spread of stumbling stones all over Europa are only two of the many examples of the transnational dimension of this new memorial approach.

38   See: Das Mahnmal von Micha Ullman auf dem Bebelplatz in Berlin, buecherverbrennung33.de, last access: 24.1.2014, <http://www.buecherverbrennung33.de/mahnmal.html>.

that encourage reflection on questions that do not necessarily have such simple, straight-forward answers. It is, therefore, no coincidence that this new approach to using public space for remembrance dovetails with the more recent impacts of the Holocaust, decolonization, the truth and reconciliation after Apartheid, the end of the Cold War, and the War on Terror. This, in turn, has led to what cultural theorist Aleida Assmann calls »a change in the basic grammar of the construction of collective memory«, which signifies a shift from an unequivocal cause-and-effect model to a greater willingness to engage with the complexity and ambiguity of past events and our interpretations of them.[39]

When official memorials representing World War II and the Holocaust are created, the timespan since 1945 has added many new layers of potentially diverging opinions and interpretations, and many contemporary memorials therefore allow space for conflicting understandings to co-exist. The guiding principle behind such an approach is that remembering and commemorating is a process, and the memories can only be kept alive if this process is allowed to continue and not be frozen as a finished result. In the same way that we in democratic societies find ways to co-exist with differences, a democratic memorial will be a communal space where there is at once both room for various contemporary needs and the memories and interpretations of future generations.

German scholar Aleida Assmann divides cultural or collective memory into what she calls »canon« and »archive«.[40] In the »archive« are all kinds of knowledge and memories of the past that are produced and stored by historians, archive workers and others. In the »canon« we find those parts of the past that are in active use, for instance, at memorials or at historical sites, forming our concepts and master narratives of the past. In general, all new knowledge about the past is welcome into the archive as a form of latent or non-active memory. Here, our knowledge and understanding of the past is therefore constantly expanding. In the fixed master narratives of the canon, as represented in public spaces, changes are much less likely to occur. Whether new interpretations of Stiklestad or the occupation years will make their way into the canon is therefore a much more complex matter. If some version of the past has made its way into the canon it tends to stick because we get used to it over time, but also often because influential interest groups set on preserving the status quo prop it up. The interplay between canon and archive

---

39 Assmann, Memory, Individual and Collective, 219.
40 Assmann, Canon and Archive, 97–108.

is, however, highly interesting, and under the right circumstances fresh knowledge can spill over into the canon, thereby making room for new master narratives.

In this chapter I have addressed the physical and mental Norwegian landscape of memory as represented in a variety of public spaces between 1990 and 2014. Public space as a broad concept is here defined as those spaces and arenas accessible to the general public. This framework includes all types of physical sites and representations placed outdoors in our urban or rural surroundings, but in principle it might also include more enclosed environments like exhibitions and museums. My empirical examples are all connected to World War II and the varieties of ways issues from this period are represented and interpreted in post Cold War Norway. My principal assertion is that the Norwegian landscape of memory has been dotted in the last two decades with representations and interpretations that fit well into what Levy and Sznaider call »a new global memory«, or to what Aleida Assmann terms as a change in the basic grammar of cultural memory.[41] Moreover, I demonstrate that traditional or patriotic ways of commemoration World War II still have the power both to protect established narratives and to establish new versions thereof.

41 Daniel Levy/Natan Sznaider: Holocaust and Memory in the Global Age, Philadelphia 2005.

Leiv Sem
The Eastern Front Revisited
The Landscape of Memory in Norwegian Second World War Discourse

I. Introduction

On 25 June 1944, Soviet troops attacked two SS fortifications deep in the Karelian forests.[1] These fortifications were built on two hilltops, named Kaprolat and Hasselman after two German officers, and were defended by approximately 180 Norwegian SS-volunteers from the SS-Skijäger-Bataillon »Norwegen«. The battle was to be a bloody one, with a reported toll of 141 dead or missing Norwegians – and an unknown number of dead Soviet soldiers. These figures represent the heaviest casualties suffered by any Norwegian army unit in a single land battle in modern times.[2] No contemporary records exist of the battle aside from a few lines in the divisional records; no official records inform us of who was in charge, or how the men were deployed. If we want to know the particulars of the battle, we have to rely on eyewitness accounts by the survivors.[3]

Reconnaissance patrols had already observed Soviet scouts in the spring of 1944, and in the summer of the same year they could hear trees being felled and roads being built to bring in heavy equipment for use against them. They knew then that an attack was imminent. Realizing their positions were undermanned, they asked for reinforcements. However, the division command deemed this unnecessary, and the battalion therefore had to fend for themselves. They fortified their positions, strengthened the bunkers, deepened the trenches and built palisades. Meanwhile, they could hear the Soviets steadily approaching. On the

---

1 Terje Emberland/Matthew Kott: Himmlers Norge. Nordmenn i det storgermanske prosjekt, Oslo 2012, 391–393.
2 Svein Blindheim: Nordmenn under Hitlers fane. Dei norske frontkjemparane, Oslo 1977, 86.
3 Sven T. Arneberg: Tragedie i Karelen. Norske skijegere i den finske Fortsettelseskrigen 1941–44, Oslo 1993, 157.

evening of 24 June the men got extra provisions of food and even spirits. It was Midsummer's day in Karelia.

In the early morning of 25 June the assault began. The first attacks were directed at Kaprolat. The position was overrun and only a few escaped to the Hasselmann hill, where they made their final stand on the top of the hill. The entire SS-battalion was crushed under the heavy bombardments over the following two days. In the end a few men made a last desperate attempt by sprinting through the Soviet lines to the shores of Lake Kapanez, where they could swim across to friendly positions. On 27 June, forty men were reported as having escaped to join positions further back.[4] Eight men were reported to have hidden in a no-man's land for 12 days.[5] Some were captured and imprisoned in Soviet prisoner of war camps. Most of the prisoners died in the camps, and only a few returned home some nine years after the battle. Most of the soldiers, however, were killed, either directly in action or first wounded and subsequently executed on-site.[6]

This is a well-known storyline: it's a repeat of Thermopylae, Chanson de Roland, the Alamo or Little Bighorn. This extremely dramatic story displays all the characteristics of a classic or legendary narrative: a small unit making its last stand on a hilltop against overwhelming forces, betrayed or let down by their own. Even its timing has a literary flair: on Midsummer's Eve, that very time of year, according to folklore, nature's mythical powers peak – this battle has more poetic qualities than many works of fiction. Here, we have a battle ready-made for tradition, as close as possible to the prerequisites for a successful tale.[7] The *Nasjonal Samling*'s propaganda machinery recognized this and tried to create a narrative, adding extras with the soldiers shouting praise of Quisling and chanting NS anthems while being attacked, according to a newspaper article from 1944.[8] Nevertheless, despite all its dramaturgic qualities, mythical potential and the national socialist hyperbole, the story fell into oblivion. A handful of books recount the story of

---

4 Arneberg, 168.
5 Arneberg, 173.
6 Sigurd Senje: Glemt soldat. Historien om Ulf, norsk østfrontsoldat, ti år krigsfange i Sovjet, Oslo 1983. The book was re-published in 2008, this time using the volunteer's real name: Wolfgang Windingstad.
7 Bruce A. Rosenberg: Custer and the Epic of Defeat, Pennsylvania University Park 1975.
8 SS-skibataljon 'Norge's tapre innsats på Finskefronten, in: *Adresseavisen* 11 September 1944.

the battle of Kaprolat and Hasselmann, but for most Norwegians it has largely remained unknown.[9]

In this article I would like to discuss in what way, in what contexts and to what effect the Eastern Front is represented in current Norwegian commemorative culture of the Second World War. More specifically, I will look at the writing of mémoire literature describing Norwegian volunteers' experiences on the Eastern Front, and discuss how this genre may have influenced the way Eastern Front experiences and actions are understood and perceived in Norwegian commemorative culture today.

II. The Landscape of the Eastern Front in *Mémoire* Literature

The Norwegian historian Gunnar S. Sjaastad carried out a comprehensive and methodologically thorough survey of the statistics of the SS volunteers in 2006. He concluded that the total amount of Norwegian volunteers lay somewhere between 4,500 and 5,000 – of whom some 800 lost their lives.[10] These figures are vague and uncertain, which is characteristic of the extent of our knowledge on the subject.

The Eastern Front and the Norwegian SS-volunteers, or *frontkjempere*, which is the conventional Norwegian term, was as a theme seldom discussed in public debates during the first post-war decades. Public interest in this aspect of Norway's contribution to the war mirrored the interest it received during the post-war trials. From the strictly national perspective that reigned during those earlier post-war years, the volunteers' willingness to put on a Nazi uniform was more important than *what* they did while wearing it. It would also appear that the subject held scarcely any interest for scholars. The first scholarly treatises did not appear until the 1970s.[11] From the late 1980s a series of popular-historical or journalistic books brought the subject to the attention of a general audience. During recent years interest has risen greatly among professional historians, journalists and publishers

---

9   Leiv Sem: Norske slagmarker, in: C. Lenz/T. R. Nilssen (eds.): Fortiden i nåtiden. Nye veier i formidlingen av andre verdenskrigs historie, Oslo 2011, 93.
10 Gunnar Sverreson Sjåstad: Nordmenn i tysk krigsinnsats. En kvantitativ undersøkelse av frontkjemperne under den andre verdenskrig, (master thesis) University of Bergen, 2006, 88–89.
11 Hans Fredrik Dahl: Hva er fascisme? Et essay om fascismens historie og sosiologi, Oslo 1972; Svein Blindheim: Nordmenn under Hitlers fane. Dei norske frontkjemparane, Oslo 1977.

of mémoire literature. Today, the Eastern Front is no longer another peripheral theme in the discourse on the Second World War and the occupation, but very much at the centre of attention. One important contribution in this regard is the publications of the research project on »Norwegian Volunteers in the Waffen-SS«, a project initiated by the Norwegian government.[12] Norway's war, it is now generally conceded, reached far into the Steppes, into the Balkans and the Baltic states. At the same time, the movement is reciprocal: The experiences of the SS volunteers have been drawn into our contemporary life-world.

In the years prior to scholars taking any interest in the subject, the field was to a certain degree left open to the volunteers themselves to shape it their understanding of it. Apart from NS Police Minister Jonas Lie's memoirs of his experiences during the German campaign in the Balkans, which was published during the war,[13] the first book on the subject to be published was by former war reporter Karl Holter and titled *Frontkjempere*.[14] The first memoir written by an actual field soldier – by the name of Svein Halse – appeared in 1970.[15] Almost two decades later Halse published a sequel.[16] Since 1970, a number of similar books reached a Norwegian audience. It is hardly comes as a surprise that quite a few of the Norwegian SS-men have written and published their memoirs, especially given that many of these so-called *frontkjempere* were middle-class, well educated, relatively young, often energetic and with many years of productive life left – and who had some extraordinary experiences to cope with and impart.[17] It is somewhat more curious, however, that scholarly interest came so late in the day and had remained scarce for so long. As a result of this enduring lack of interest by professional scholars, a relatively large section of Norwegian literature dealing with the Eastern Front is *mémoire* literature, either autobiographical or written by a second party.[18]

---

12   Emberland/Kott: Himmlers Norge. Nordmenn i det storgermanske prosjekt, Oslo 2012.
13   Jonas Lie: Over Balkans syv blåner, Oslo 1942.
14   Karl Holter: Frontkjempere, Oslo 1951.
15   Svein Halse: I forreste linje. Krigsroman fra Leningradfronten bygget på egne opplevelser, Oslo 1970.
16   Svein Halse: Mot sammenbruddet. Norsk soldat på Østfronten 1943–45, Oslo 1989.
17   Sjåstad, esp. 115–118.
18   A brief survey of this literature is to be found in Sjåstad, 19–21. See also Stein Ugelvik Larsen: De skriver om seg selv. Frontkjemperne, NS-medlemmene og NS-barna. Dokumentarlitteraturen om dem på »den gale siden«, in: B. Birkeland/A.Kittang/S.U. Larsen/L.Longum (eds.): Nazismen og norsk litteratur, Oslo 1995.

Sometimes this second party is a relative.[19] More often, however, it is a journalist. Indeed, in Norway's case, several journalistic publications are considered among the most influential when it came to establishing the concept of the Eastern Front in the public's mind.[20] One recent important contribution is the 2009 book on Norwegian SS-volunteers killed in action, written by the journalist Eirik Veum.[21] Veum's account is rather typical of this category, both in the sense that he provides the SS veterans with an unmediated voice, and through his focus on providing the reader with graphic descriptions of the events. This book received wide attention and spurred intense public debate, but most of this debate centred on the author's decision to publish all the names and the available pictures of the SS men, while other aspects of the book were largely left un-debated.[22]

The body of *mémoire* texts on the Eastern Front, then, consists of a multiplicity of singular voices. Yet, it is also fairly homogenous and displays clearly recurring patterns, a matter I will discuss later. First, this is due to the fact that the authors themselves endured similar experiences. Though with slight variations in terms of background, they have undergone roughly the same political formation that led them to becoming volunteers; they shared the military and ideological training as well as the subsequent experiences on the frontlines. Naturally, this resulted in nearly identical storylines. Equally important, however, is the fact that the authors write in the same context of general condemnation of the actions portrayed in these narratives. The Norwegian folklorist Anne Eriksen contended that a collaborator had to accept guilt and show remorse over their deeds in order to be even heard in the Norwegian discourse on the Second World War.[23] This in essence decisively affects the way the narrative is structured and framed. One obvious example is how sensitive subjects are often omitted; another is the general tendency to justify one's own actions. In addition to these, however, there are subtler, less visible and more deeply hidden effects as well.

The strong standing of *mémoire* literature among the accounts of events on the Eastern Front poses questions as to what effect it has had on the general public's

---

19 E. g. Rolf Ivar Jordbruen: Helvete på jord. En frontkjempers historie, Oslo 2006.
20 See, for instance, Egil Ulateig: Dagbok frå ein rotnorsk nazist, Oslo 1987; Kjell Fjørtoft: Veien til Østfronten. Krigens mange ansikter, Oslo 1993; and Kjell Fjørtoft: De som tapte krigen, Oslo 1995.
21 Erik Veum: De som falt. Nordmenn som døde i tysk krigstjeneste, Oslo 2009.
22 Espen Søbye: Frontkjemperne falt, forfatterne snubler, in: Prosa, 05 (2009), 37–40.
23 Anne Eriksen: Det var noe annet under krigen. 2. verdenskrig i norsk kollektivtradisjon, Oslo 1995, 157.

understanding and conception of the issue. The exclusion of Soviet sources and perspectives and a local viewpoint is one part of the problem. The dominance of the perspective by the SS volunteers themselves is another – a factor that amplifies the former. One consequence is that those very facets of life on the front which the *frontkjempere* themselves prefer to stress such as military elitism, comradeship and so on have been allowed to dominate. Another consequence might be that all these personal narratives and *mémoire* literature perhaps dispose the reader to have a merely personal, subjective and atomized perspective of history on the front rather than a comprehensive overview, and that this, in some cases, might unwittingly cause the reader to adopt a perpetrator's point of view, or even to perceive the perpetrator as victim.

In the following paragraphs I will offer a general description of the *mémoire* books dealing with the Eastern Front. I cannot here do justice to all the nuances this literature holds, and my examples are set forth as indications of what I perceive to be as general trends in this genre. I will start by pointing out that some traits are carry-overs from wartime propaganda to the *mémoire* literature published in the post-war period. An illustration of this is the manner in which landscapes on the Eastern Front are depicted. In wartime propaganda, the landscape is often described along the following lines:

> »*Do you remember, comrade, the sparkling cold winter night when the Legion advanced towards the positions at Leningrad* […] *The Northern Lights were ablaze in the sky, casting light on the giant city ahead where we could see brick buildings in the bewitching half-light* [det trolske halvmørket].«[24]

Images such as these stressing topographical features reminding them of their homeland would have had a psychological impact on soldiers and readers alike. More importantly, they would also have a political effect in this context, namely, the function of legitimising the SS volunteers being where they were in the first place, thus establishing an identity between their homeland and this landscape.

Echoes of these claims are found in much more recent mémoire literature of the Norwegian *frontkjempere* marching towards their positions on the front:

24 Ulf Breien: Kamp og idé. Streif av Den norske Legions saga, Oslo 1943, in: Frontkjemperkontoret (publisher): Legionsminner. Trekk av Den norske Legions historie, unpag. In the original language (Norwegian), the final phrase is a reference to a quite distinctively Norwegian mythical creature, the troll, adding to the imposing national content. All excerpts translated by the author, unless stated otherwise.

»Here, snow covers the ground, a proper spruce wood alongside the road, and the villages are Nordic wooden buildings«.[25] Natural, cultural and topographical features are used to underpin the claim that such a landscape is part of the natural habitat of Nordic man. This is supplemented by the recurring motif of the SS men's alleged mastery of harsh conditions – the isolated forest areas, the barren mires, and the freezing winter landscapes. In addition to describing the men as competent soldiers and true heroes, these portrayals also serve to prove their right to colonise and control the territory. Another motif uncannily similar in the *mémoire* literature is the description of the enemy. Although slightly more aware of the risk of dehumanising their antagonists, the authors nevertheless often portray the enemy as some kind of a non-human mass, growing out of the landscape, swarming around the earth – »the Russian infantry came teeming like lemmings«, reports Arne, a veteran and central source in Frode Halle's book.[26] While the weapons used by the Norwegian SS-men are hailed as technological wonders, the enemy's guns are described as parts of their animalistic existence: barking guns, or whimpering and whining bullets. Another example: »The low streamlined T-34 panzers drive forward swarm-like over the open fields. Here, we see a lot of panzers and few ›brains‹«.[27] The enemies are included in the landscape, as features of the terrain the Norwegians are destined to dominate.

This continuity in the choice of motifs, figures and tropes might be symptomatic of a deeply rooted ideology. An alternative explanation might be along the lines of that which George Mosse and Paul Fussel pointed out: when confronted with the traumas and horrors of warfare, a soldier often turns to a common, familiar language, as a way to domesticate the threat and to exert some sort of control.[28]

In any case, when comparing wartime propaganda with mémoire texts, an ambiguity seeps out between the lines of the latter, and a sneaking uncertainty reveals itself. The cold grows just a bit too severe; the old familiar arctic light, for instance, proves in fact to be treacherous, guiding enemy bullets and so on. Indeed, ironically, the landscape itself transforms into the main antagonist.[29] Often the ambiguity between the familiar and the strange deepens, even to the point of

25 Frode Halle: Fra Finland til Kaukasus. Nordmenn på Østfronten 1941–1945, Oslo 1972, 126.
26 Halle, 57.
27 Halse, Mot sammenbruddet, 83.
28 George Mosse: Fallen Soldiers. Reshaping the Memory of the World Wars, Oxford 1990; Paul Fussell: The Great War and Modern Memory, New York 1975.
29 Halle, 33–39.

total collapse. Sometimes at ruptures during flashes of violence and existential insights, the true nature of the setting is revealed: Not only is it another country, it is another world, or, as in one of the most common formulations, a »hell on earth«:

> »*I crawl up and take a look over the position. Everything seems desolate and dead. It smells of death, gunpowder and hell. All that is left of the once great, noble pine trees are branchless and splintered trunks, reaching forth to heaven and calling for help against human madness.*«[30]

The propaganda narratives also at times refer to »infernal noise« and dramatically tell of hell breaking loose. But in *mémoire* literature, these are seldom figures of speech and clearly accorded a more literal meaning.

While this genre unquestionably carries over many of propaganda's salient features, it does, however, offer new approaches, and one of these is a shift in language from the heroic to the tragic. The NS movement used an overtly heroic, neo-national style in their newsletters, speeches, reports and books. As befitting this language, the protagonists are invariably active and in control of the game. In *mémoire* literature, this is often supplanted with the protagonist not being in control and at the mercy of others. On occasion these »others« are incompetent or ignorant superior officers, but more frequently they are the numerically vastly superior enemy, or the Russian landscape. The protagonist is reduced to being passive, manhandled, confined and coerced. In terms of content, motifs and themes, there are clear similarities between wartime propaganda and *mémoire* literature. These traits have the same function, a similar textual role, make identical claims and have the same implications. However, the narrative structure has changed, and the moral evaluations enveloping the motifs might also differ.

The narratives of the *mémoire* literature are rather conventional, and most of them share a common basic structure in three parts: The first sets out the background, giving reasons why the protagonist volunteered, describing his recruitment, education, and deployment. Generally, the middle part contains detailed and comprehensive descriptions of action on the front. The narratives often conclude with an account of his homecoming to his native Norway, being judged, and in some cases describing his life after having served his sentence. This coda serves the vital function of offering a moral evaluation of the narrated events. In this narrative structure, the experiences on the Eastern Front represent a sort of acid

---

30   Rolf Bergsten. Bare en liten visitt i helvete, Melhus 2008, 106.

bath or purgatory, where human shortcomings and sins are purged, and whereby one re-emerges as a whole and ideologically sound individual. However, there are variations as to what is meant by human weakness. Some narrators make concessions to the sentiments of the general public and its expectation for an expression of remorse; they realize they have strayed onto the wrong path and repent their choice of volunteering to the ranks of the SS.[31] Others position themselves in stiff resistance against such expectations of a *mea culpa*. Some might claim their stay confirmed their belief in the correctness of their choices, and, if anything, strengthened their moral fabric.[32] There are also cases where the experiences on the front are described as having moulded the men together in comradeship and unbreakable allegiance, an allegiance only strengthened by their post-war treatment in Norway.[33] In those cases where the narrative does not conclude with the authors repenting of their choices and actions, the narrators most likely have forsaken any hope of being understood and respected by the general public, and address instead a narrower circle. Either way, this narrative structure readily resembles a classical *Bildungsroman*: childhood, the Grand Tour, the homecoming as a richer and wiser human being with a lesson to tell. Given the nature and content of the descriptions of hell on earth at the battlefront, these narratives could also be said to feed on a particular kind of travel literature, that of spiritualist or religious vision, in the tradition of Dante.[34] Such a journey is a recurring theme in *mémoire* literature. As far back as antiquity travelling has had a strong symbolic importance, in addition to its more practical and functional aspects. It has been seen as having a transformative power, of connecting the »outer« journey with an »inner« one.[35] In literature, it might have the important function of setting the stage, of preparing the characters and the reader alike. And, last but not least, traveling itself sometimes functions as a way of closing past chapters, in the vein of »it happened elsewhere, I was another person back then ...«. In later years, as the Former Soviet territories became more accessible, there has been a tendency to

---

31 See e.g. Bergsten.
32 E.g. Arvid Bryne: Vi sloss for Norge. Frontkjemper og motstandsmann: fiender i krig, venner i fred, Oslo 2007.
33 Hans Gervik: Refleksjoner etter 50 år. Historien i et annet lys. Ved en tidligere frontkjemper, Torp 1994, 136; 177.
34 Trond Berg Eriksen: Reisen gjennom helvete. Dantes Inferno, Oslo 1994, 23.
35 Bjarne Rogan: »Traveller chic. Et kulturhistorisk blikk på reiser og turisme, ritual og ekspressivitet«, in A. B. Amundsen/A. Ohrvik/B. Hodne (eds.): Ritualer. Kulturhistoriske studier, Oslo 2006, 123.

copy these travels, thus establishing a kind of sub-genre of literature on the Eastern Front. Books, blogs, TV and radio documentaries, newspaper articles often undertake and describe similar journeys. These re-enactments closely mirror the original routes taken by the SS volunteers. The traveller takes symbolically part in their experiences – of course not necessarily endorsing their deeds.

In this admittedly rather confined structural perspective it is in some ways similar to the narratives of concentration camp survivors, who, with respect to their extreme experiences and insights into ultimate evil, might be said to have acquired an aura of the visionary seer of esoteric truths.[36] While the SS-volunteer could arguably be recognized as having been afforded insights into the human capacity to cope with extreme experiences, he would hardly be acknowledged as a seer of eternal truths in a similar vein to the concentration camp survivor. However, given his efforts to describe the infernal nature of his experience, we might discern a prayer for forgiveness, either arguing that all rules were dropped, rendering normal evaluations, criteria and considerations irrelevant, or that the SS-volunteers have already been through a cleansing fire, paying a heavy price for their mistakes and deserving absolution for their past sins.

Mémoire literature, then, reveals a wide spectrum of strategies and positions in relation to the hegemonic conception of the Second World War and the occupation. But, as mentioned previously, this is not a one-way negotiation. The other side also makes concessions. In order to discuss this negotiation, I would like to return to the case of the battle at Kaprolat and Hasselmann.

III. The Eastern Front Returns

For decades, a vivid memory existed in Norway of a place in distant and desolate Karelia, but this image was largely unknown beyond the small circle of survivors. Outside this small community there was a larger circle of relatives and those especially interested in Second World War history, for most of whom, however, Kaprolat and Hasselmann remained but distant place names. This was probably due to a combination of two factors, namely, a tacit understanding that this was a matter not to be discussed, and that the battlefield was for the most part inaccessible behind the Iron Curtain. Scarcely any efforts were made to raise questions

---

36 Leiv Sem: »For oss er Falstad det norske holocaust«. Ein diskursanalytisk studie av debatten om krigsminnestaden Falstad i 2003–2004, University of Oslo 2009, 145.

concerning the remains of dead Norwegians. The Norwegian authorities certainly did not raise any, while the Soviets, for their part, had no interest in locating these corpses. They had scarcely the resources for or an interest in finding them of their own accord. Nina Tumarkin, in her 1994 book »The Living and the Dead«, quotes a 1992 Russian assessment that the remains of approximately one million German soldiers were still on former Soviet territory.[37] Nevertheless, according to a book published in 1993 and penned by the Norwegian journalist Sven T. Arneberg, the area around Kaprolat and Hasselmann was searched for mines in 1956 by groups of locals and volunteers. At that time, they also uncovered the bodies of six non-Soviet persons.[38] This discovery, however, did not spur them on to undertake a more thorough search. Most of the dead were left lying where they fell, and were neither identified, retrieved nor formally buried even 60 years after their death. Their remains had just been left lying there. This landscape, strewn with human remains, has in a way thus been inscribed at once both with memory and a mark of forgetfulness.

In 2005, the Russian amateur battlefield archaeologist Andrey Lysenko came across a Norwegian book on the battle of Kaprolat and Hasselmann.[39] Though unable to read Norwegian, he nevertheless found a map in the book that aroused his interest. After having the book translated by an automatic online translation resource he then realized there was a battlefield on Russian soil, abandoned and unvisited since 1944 – a dream come true for a man with his particular interests. He set out to locate the site and was soon to unearth the remains of Norwegian soldiers. Upon finding them, he contacted the Norwegian authorities and media outlets.[40]

By doing this, Lysenko engendered a series of news reports that were published in the Norwegian press, in *Verdens Gang, Adresseavisen, Dagbladet* and others, most frequently during the years 2005–2008. This was accompanied by a public debate that would position the Eastern Front in the public mind to a degree and in a way that was quite new to many Norwegians. The corpses lay discarded in a terrain among rusting metal and disintegrating equipment, just as though they were garbage. Locals had been trawling the vicinity for war memorabilia such

---

37 Nina Tumarkin: The Living and the Dead, New York 1994, 14.
38 Arneberg, 259.
39 The book in question was written by Arneberg and published in 1993. All information in this paragraph stems from an interview with Lysenko by the author in June 2010.
40 »Her ligger hodeskaller etter norske soldater åpent i terrenget – 60 år etter kampene ved Kaprolat«, in: Verdens Gang 28 May 2005.

as weapons, helmets, dog tags and other objects the dead soldiers were wearing. These gravediggers had violated the dead soldiers' status as human beings and merely exploited them as »mines« for digging out valuables. Furthermore, given the soldiers' remains had been left exposed in open terrain, wild animals such as bears and wolves would feed on their corpses and move their body parts. That such images of abandoned corpses in a Russian forest deeply disturbed newspaper readers back in Norway is evident from the ensuing intense interest and public debate. As far as the Norwegian commemoration is concerned, Lysenko's action was an intervention aimed at reconnecting landscape with memory. In Norway, the authorities and the public had to engage with the difficult question of whether to identify the remains and to give them a decent burial, either on-site or by repatriating them.

The findings on that battlefield led a professor of political science, Stein Ugelvik Larsen, to organise an interdisciplinary project committee, and they applied for public funding for the identification, repatriation and burial of the remains. The initiative taken by the Kaprolat Committee stated as its objectives – and which were shared by many of the relatives of the fallen – to identify as many of the corpses as possible, to repatriate them and to accord them a proper burial.[41] They received some 125,000 Euros from Norway's Ministry of Foreign Affairs. This again led to a response, notably from some Holocaust survivors and members of Norway's Jewish community. A member of the Christian People's Party questioned the Foreign Minister in a parliamentary debate as to how he could justify this use of resources, not least because there still were missing resistance fighters. In his reply the Foreign Minister pointed out that although there was no obligation on the government to aid this undertaking, it had chosen to help the bereaved on purely humanitarian grounds. He stressed that the government's financial support was limited to a certain figure and with the sole purpose of DNA registration and to ensure that no corpses were left lying out in the open. Were the remains to be repatriated and interred, the costs would have to be paid for by the relatives themselves.[42]

---

41 Kaprolat Committee: World War II Combat Zone ›Kaprolat/Hasselmann‹ in Russian Karelia – proper recovery of remains after some 100 Norwegian SS volunteers perished in June 1944 – a Cross-disciplinary Ethical and Research Project, University of Bergen 2008, 3.

42 Minister of Foreign Affairs' Answer given during parliamentary questions, 7 December 2007, regjeringen.no, last access: 28 January 2014, <http://www.regjeringen.no/

This debate and coverage in the press clearly demonstrate both the vexing nature of the subject matter, and how deeply ambiguous the public remain when it comes to attitudes towards these men and their deeds. The choice of language in the debate concerning the *frontkjempere* and the landscape is the result of a difficult negotiation between different ways of perceiving these men, of a condemning view and a more understanding one. The end result is a marked ambivalence within some texts, and open disagreement between others. Let me cite a few examples. Editorial texts most often refer to the dead with the conventional Norwegian term *frontkjemper*, a term that until recently applied exclusively to Norwegian volunteers in the SS, and clearly bearing negative connotations. Occasionally, however, some newspapers instead referred to them as »soldiers on the front« (»*frontsoldater*«), a term devoid of negative associations, obviously in order to cleanse the debate of specific ideological content.[43] Their youth is constantly referred to and some articles repeat this like a mantra »young, dead men [...] boys [...] very young boys« (»*unge, døde menn* [...] *guttene* [...] *svært unge gutter*«).[44] Some articles stress this point more emphatically with phrases like »only three weeks after his twentieth birthday«.[45] Such references to the volunteers' youth thus underlines the tragedy and induces sympathy with those who have fallen, while at the same time serving an apologetic function, as their young age and lack of experience might explain or even excuse their errors.[46]

The manner in which their deaths are described leaves a deeply ambiguous impression. The most common choices of words are neutral, for instance, that they »died« or »fell« (in Norwegian, *stupte, satte livet til*, or *falt*). These words are rather neutral regarding not only the attitude towards the SS troops, but also towards their killers. However, »fell« is often fleshed out to »fell in battle« which adds a heroic note, or to »fell in bloody/vicious battle« which can be interpreted as both signifying heroism and victimization.[47] Some texts – albeit a clear minority – choose formulations such as that they »were utterly annihilated« which clearly posits the Norwegians as victims.[48] Some newspapers went even further and

nb/dokumentarkiv/stoltenberg-ii/ud/svar-til-stortinget/sporretimesporsmal/2007/oestfronten.html?id=494380>.
43 »Vil hente levninger av frontsoldater«, in: *Nationen* 17 January 2007.
44 »Vil ha frontkjemperne hjem i norsk jord«, in: *Bergens Tidene* 2 April 2006.
45 »Fikk svar etter 60 år«, in: *Verdens Gang* 30 May 2005.
46 See also Sigurd Sørlie's article in this volume.
47 »En oppfordring til likplyndring«, in: *Adresseavisen* 13 December 2006.
48 »Henter hjem frontkjempere«, in: *Aftenposten* 16 January 2007.

reported that they »were slaughtered«, using language that conjures up images of hapless and passive victims of outrageous acts of cruelty.[49] The fallen are also often represented by a few selected biographies and pictures, and introduced in terms of their relations with living and grieving Norwegians, as someone's son, brother or father, and feature captions such as: »The 85 year-old confers a central place on the wall to the photo of his brother Kåre in his youth.«[50]

In these texts of this specific debate, the survivors and the relatives of the fallen insist on seeing these men and their units as honourable, if naïve and misled in their youth, and claim that they are untainted by the war crimes perpetrated by other SS units elsewhere on the front. The *frontkjempere* are instead often described as the outright victims of Bolshevik warfare, of gravediggers, and ultimately of the unforgiving and uncompassionate Norwegian authorities. A certain unwillingness to see the big picture of what the Nazi war effort was about is as typical for the surviving SS-men as it is for the relatives. What is interesting to observe is how painstakingly careful even the writers of the newspaper texts are in entering into negotiations on any moral evaluation of their deeds. Admittedly, the texts cited here are collected from a rather specific context, dealing with the abandoned remains of dead Norwegians on foreign soil. It seems less likely that all of these formulations could have been used in texts or contexts where the discourse on the Holocaust is explicitly mobilised.

Another interesting feature of how the debate reaches out to the *frontkjempere* is the way the landscape itself, as it were, is being repatriated, renewing the old claim that this is a Norwegian landscape, even if this claim is given a wholly new content. The qualities of the landscape are related in great detail in words and illustrations alike, often stressing features strongly reminiscent of Norwegian landscapes such as heaths and birch forests with mires and streams. These descriptions both underline the resemblance with Norwegian scenery and suggest a kind of identity, in a way subscribing to the *frontkjemper's* own self-conception as being at home and well-adjusted to this landscape. At the same time, these close and thick descriptions work well to give this distant landscape a manifestly tangible quality for the Norwegian reader, planting the landscape firmly in a current Norwegian context. In this way, these reports enter negotiations into the meaning of the landscape, using various discursive resources to create a manifest object, a second degree landscape that is something more than a map or a name, thus mak-

---

49 »Vil ha frontkjemperne hjem i norsk jord«, in: *Bergens Tidene* 2 April 2006.
50 »Har ventet i 60 år«, in: *Adresseavisen* 12 December 2006.

ing it possible and indispensable for the Norwegian public to relate to it. Often the press articles are accompanied by illustrations depicting the remains of the fallen lying in the terrain, or an overview of the scene. This might be understood as a cultural commemorative praxis, but it is also an intervention of a memory-political nature, an assertive claim on the reality and actuality of this landscape for the Norwegian public. The way landscape is represented in the debate invokes a material landscape, and links this both to personal and collective memory and to moral obligations.

The relatively many travels undertaken during the course or in the wake of this debate has also contributed to the emergence of the new understanding, as described above. Several journalists, veterans, and relatives of veterans made the trip to the Kaprolat and Hasselmann hills. Many of these travels resulted in a kind of travelogue or *mémoire*. The various TV documentaries, travel blogs and newspaper reports often display an identical structure: They generally set out in detail the travellers' reports on journeys to these sites, often having only vague ideas about the landscape they are searching, and of what to expect. Gradually, however, the landscape becomes more real over the course of the journey, to the reporter and to his audience. With the aid of video footage, photography and verbal testimonies, great efforts are made to relate the topography's various qualities. The setting is meticulously situated with the help of detailed information, with reference to national borders and major topographical features. These journeys are expressions of a need and a wish to relate personally with the events, the landscape and the people involved – on both sides of the conflict. As such they are interesting and necessary steps in coming to terms with our past. However, the other aspect of travelling involves one turning away from the homely and to direct one's attention towards a far-off place. This pilgrimage expresses a need to communicate with these experiences, but it also underlines a sense of remoteness from them. The ritual of travelling could therefore also be regarded as an expression of the dubious attitude towards these experiences, communicating with the deep moral problems of the exploits and deeds of the SS men, and at the same time with the inherent fascination that might have been created and borne through the one-sided dominance of the auto-narratives.

IV. Conclusion

On the basis on what we have seen in this specific debate, we might insert Anne Eriksen's statement on the need for the collaborator to accept guilt and show remorse in order to be heard in the Norwegian discourse about the Second World War.[51] This might be so in most instances, but the SS volunteers are in some ways and to some extent an exception, and present a complicated case. While taking up arms and waging war in the service of the enemy has always been regarded a grave form of treason, the verdict on these men nevertheless have been coupled with a certain amount of understanding and respect, for they have been deemed, by some, as at least idealists and courageous traitors who allegedly enlisted to fight Bolshevism.[52] The men who perished in the Kaprolat and Hasselmann hills did indeed pay a high prize for their choices, and this might to a certain extent have redeemed them further, in the eyes of some of the contenders in the specific debate discussed above. Furthermore, we have observed a rising tendency in recent decades to acknowledge both the victims and the losers in historical events. Peter Novick has placed this tendency in relation to the growing concern for victims of the Holocaust.[53] Perhaps this general tendency, quite paradoxically, also has played a role in regarding the SS volunteers with a degree of sympathy.

However, there are clear limits to this understanding and sympathy for these particular losers, not least in contexts where the discourse of the Holocaust is explicitly mustered, with its corollary of a weakened national bias and increased weight on universal values. As in many other countries, the Norwegian discourse of the Second World War has undergone a transformation in recent decades, from an overwhelmingly national bias towards a more universally humanistic conception.[54] This has changed the status of the *frontkjempere*. References to their alleged idealism will henceforth be far less effective, since any reference to ideology will necessarily and inherently entail attention being afforded to other aspects of the Nazi's ideological project. The *frontkjempere* actively participated in the very defining act of the war: The war of extermination on other peoples. Regardless of their stance on Bolshevism, ideology is no longer a winning argument in the case of the SS men. Understanding and sympathy with the SS volunteers can only

---

51 Eriksen, 157.
52 See, for instance, Bryne.
53 Peter Novick: The Holocaust and Collective Memory. The American Experience, London 2001, 8.
54 Sem, »For oss er Falstad det norske holocaust«, 165–169.

make sense in an extremely limited context. In contexts without reference to programmatic genocide, one might indeed witness a reciprocal movement to the volunteer's adaptation to the demand for remorse. There is then a tendency or a possibility to pay more heed to the world-view of the SS volunteers. But once the discourse of Holocaust is mobilised to any extent, this possibility vanishes.[55] Instead of challenging the hegemonic discourse, another and simpler strategy is then used: individualising the victims, with an implicit appeal to see the person behind the history and the ideologies. This is partly an emphatic attempt to see them as human beings. At the same time, however, this threatens an outright disentanglement from the ideological context.

---

55   Sem, Norske slagmarker, 97.

V.
General Exclusion? Marginal Groups in Postwar Norway

Susanne Maerz
From Taboo to Compensation
Krigsbarn in Public Discourse
and Literature after 1945

I. Introduction

> »›*Your father*‹, *Rachel began hesitantly,* ›*your father was an ordinary man with black hair and blue eyes and broad shoulders. A fine man. He and your mother fell in love. He wasn't an ordinary soldier.*‹ *Rachel came to a stop. She shifted her glance to the stove, to see if it was drawing. But then it burst out of her, fast and decisively,* ›*but he was sent here to conquer us, so he was an enemy!*‹«[1]

With these words, which the Norwegian woman Rachel spoke to her young niece Tora on a small island in northern Norway in the 1950s, she broke the taboo to talk about Tora's father, Wilhelm, a German soldier sent to Norway during the German occupation in the Second World War. The above lines are quoted from Herbjørg Wassmo's novel »The House with the Blind Glass Windows«, published in Norway in 1981. With these words and with her novel about Tora, the Norwegian writer also broke the taboo of broaching the fate and especially the origins of the so-called *krigsbarn* (war children) with the Norwegian public. Hitherto, their fate and lives had been concealed. The more neutral and commonly used word *krigsbarn*, or the more specific but at the same time somehow discriminating word *tyskerbarn* (child of a German) are the two principle terms to identify the children of German soldiers and Norwegian women born during or shortly after the Second World War.[2] Norwegians also use the term *krigsbarn* when they refer or write about war children in other countries. Nevertheless, the term refers to the period

---

1   Herbjørg Wassmo: The House with the Blind Glass Windows, Seattle 1987, 67. Translated by Roseann Lloyd and Allen Simpson. Original title: Herbjørg Wassmo: Huset med den blinde glassveranda, Oslo 1981.
2   Considering that »war children« have lived in many occupied countries, I will not translate the Norwegian expression into English but use the Norwegian word *krigsbarn* in this chapter.

of German occupation from 1940 to 1945 and more specifically to the children of German soldiers and Norwegian women.

As Wassmo was the first Norwegian writer to break this taboo 36 years after the end of the Second World War, her novel has been the first of many steps in the process of coming to terms with the fate of the Norwegian war children and in creating a new narrative about the attitude towards them. This is a process to be observed not only in Norwegian literature, but also subsequently in its politics, research and society in general. In this paper I will take a look at these different narratives beginning with Wassmo's novel and culminating with the recent German-Norwegian film »Two Lives«[3] (2012).[4] As a second example of pertinent literary discourse, Jostein Gaarder's novel »The Solitaire Mystery«[5] will also be investigated. It was published in 1990, while the public was in the midst of the process of coming to terms with the fate of the *krigsbarn*. Moreover, I will include Lars Saabye Christensen's novel »The Half Brother«[6] (2001) to broaden my analysis.

The major reason I focus on literary discourse is that one of the novels I mentioned broke the taboo of speaking about the *krigsbarn*. Another basis for my choice is that literary »discourse« – using the term as Michel Foucault employs it – can generally, as well exemplified in this case, go contrary to the predominant discourse and thereby act as a door opener for fresh narratives. Literary discourse, however, can – again according to Foucault – also be one of many specialized discourses which simultaneously emerge and which refer to each other.[7] Gaarder's

---

3   Original title: *Zwei Leben* (»Two Lives«), Germany/Norway 2012, director: Georg Maas.
4   The historical background is based upon: Susanne Maerz: Die langen Schatten der Besatzungszeit. »Vergangenheitsbewältigung« in Norwegen als Identitätsdiskurs, Berlin 2008. Norwegian translation: Susanne Maerz: Okkupasjonstidens lange skygger. »Fortidsbearbeidelse« i Norge som identitetsdiskurs, Oslo 2010. The basis for the analysis of the novels by Wassmo and Gaarder is my chapter: Susanne Maerz: Stigma deutscher Vater. Die Verhandlung der Herkunft von norwegischen Kriegskindern in Herbjørg Wassmos Das Haus mit der blinden Glasveranda und Jostein Gaarders Das Kartengeheimnis, in: Constanze Gestrich/Thomas Mohnike (eds.): Faszination des Illegitimen. Alterität in Konstruktionen von Genealogie, Herkunft und Ursprünglichkeit in den skandinavischen Literaturen seit 1800, Würzburg 2007, 195–211.
5   I refer to the following translation: Jostein Gaarder: The Solitaire Mystery, London 1996. Translated by Sarah Jane Hails. Original: Jostein Gaarder: Kabalmysteriet, Oslo 1990.
6   Lars Saabye Christensen: The Half Brother, London 2004. Translated by Kenneth Steven. Original: Lars Saabye Christensen, Halvbroren, Oslo 2001.
7   I hereby follow the interpretation of Foucault proposed by Jürgen Link and Ursula Link-Heer: Jürgen Link/Ursula Link-Heer: Diskurs/Interdiskurs und Literatur-

novel »The Solitaire Mystery« is a case in point. Saabye Christensen's »The Half Brother« might be an in-between case and thus merits a special status. Given they have all been translated into several foreign languages, they are salient examples of the transnationalisation of these narratives. Before I delve into this literary analysis, however, I would like to begin with a short glimpse back in history.

II. The Situation of the *Krigsbarn* before 1981

From 1940 to 1945, between 30,000 and 50,000 Norwegian women – the so-called *tyskerjenter* (German war brides) – had intimate relationships with members of the German occupying forces.[8] Between 10,000 and 12,000 children were born as a result of these relationships.[9] Many of the women were punished after the war for their »horizontal treason« by having their hair cropped and being paraded through the streets. Many were also interned by the Norwegian authorities for their own safety, or so it was claimed. For many Norwegians, the war children were not only evidence of the women's failure and treason, but also remnants of a defeated enemy. Their presence was a reminder of the German troops who had been forced to withdraw. In 1945 these children were considered a major social problem that could threaten Norwegian society because Nazi blood was running through their veins.[10]

One reason for this mind-set was that these children had played a vital role in German demographic politics. These politics were dominated by racial con-

---

analyse, in: Zeitschrift für Literaturwissenschaft und Linguistik, 77 (1990), (88–99) 91, 92, 94 and 96.

8   The realm-archivar (riksarkivar) Kåre Olsen estimates that there were at least 30,000 to 40,000 so-called *tyskerjenter* (German Girls, Deutschenmädchen), cf. Kåre Olsen: Krigens barn. De norske krigsbarna og deres mødre, Oslo 1998, 13. The journalist Ebba Drolshagen estimates between 40,000 to 50,000 and relies on the statistician Dag Ellingsen, cf. Ebba D. Drolshagen: Nicht ungeschoren davongekommen. Die Geliebten der Wehrmachtsoldaten im besetzten Europa, Hamburg 1998, 94.

9   According to German *Lebensborn* statistics, some 8,000 children were registered. Their actual number is estimated to be at least 9,000. Kåre Olsen estimates the number, also taking the estimated number of unreported cases in account, to be between 10,000 and 12,000, cf. to all this numbers: Olsen, 68–72. Ebba Drolshagen reckoned that there were at least 12, 000. Cf. Ebba D. Drolshagen: Wehrmachtskinder. Auf der Suche nach dem nie gekannten Vater, München 2005, 289.

10 Cf. Drolshagen, Nicht ungeschoren, 67.

cepts that had been popular before and during the war, and not only in Germany. According to these racial theories, the Nordic race was especially valuable.[11] This was the reason the German-based *Lebensborn* organization established twelve children's homes in Norway, in which around 1,200 *krigsbarn* were born.[12] The *krigsbarn* were generally also assumed to have inherited the »traitorous character« of their mothers.[13] Arguments like these were bandied about immediately after the war.[14] Moreover, a commission set up to deal with the *krigsbarn* issue officially discussed how to proceed with these unwelcome offspring. Commission members made references to the prevailing fear in society about the influence of the children's German heritage. They argued that the influence of Nazi racial theories had provoked this fear in society.[15] This demonstrates that such racial thinking was also popular in Norway. But given the commission rejected these theories, this also underpins a different interpretation, namely, that this was not the dominant cast of mind in post-war Norway. After this period of public debate the *krigsbarn* were no longer a subject for discussion among the Norwegian public. As it happened, many *krigsbarn* did not even live in Norway. The majority of those who used to live with their German relatives or in the *Lebensborn* birth houses in Germany during the war had to subsequently move back to Norway. Thirty children who had lived in a *Lebensborn* house in Bremen were instead brought to Sweden for adoption and provided with fake identities without the knowledge of their Norwegian parents. The Norwegian authorities, however, were aware of this scheme.[16] Furthermore, thirty Norwegian children who had received permission to be put up for adoption and were living in the *Lebensborn* home »Sonnenwiese« near Leipzig were forced to stay there. Initially, the Soviet administrators and later the local authorities in the German Democratic Republic prevented them return-

---

11 Cf. Olsen, 75.
12 The Lebensborn-organization was founded by the German SS in 1935 as part of the »Rasse- und Siedlungshauptamt-SS« (SS Race and Settlement Main Office). Its aim was to safeguard and promote »racial purity« in the population. In the spring of 1941 the Lebensborn became active in Norway as well.
13 Cf. Drolshagen, Nicht ungeschoren, 67.
14 Cf. Ibid.
15 Cf. Olsen, 352.
16 Cf. Karen Lillian Fladberg: Norge ville ikke ha ham, in: *Dagsavisen*, 27 March 2000; Lars Kluge: »De stjal min sjanse til å treffe mamma«, in: *Aftenposten*, 25 April 2002; Lars Borgersrud: Overlatt til svenske myndigheter. De norske krigsbarn som ble sendt til Sverige i 1945, Oslo 2002, ed.: Institutt for Kulturstudier, Universitetet i Oslo.

ing home. The Norwegian authorities avoided adopting them. Moreover, the East German authorities took preventative measures to ensure that the children could not get in contact with their Norwegian relatives. Ludwig Bergmann, for example, thought that his Norwegian family were shunning him. In Norway, Bergmann was considered a »missing« person. He did not know about this until 1997, at which stage his biological mother was already dead. *Der Spiegel* exposed his and two other similar cases in 1997.[17]

The majority of *krigsbarn* grew up like all other Norwegian children in post-war Norway. A minority, however, were discriminated against due to their origins; they were maltreated or sexually abused. While some were unaware that their father was a German, others knew it, and some others suspected it. Some were reared only by their biological mother, others by their mother and a stepfather; others were raised by foster parents, while still others were handed over for adoption. »Both the women, who had mothered the children, and the children themselves were sometimes treated as criminals,«[18] writes the political scientist Stein Ugelvik Larsen. There was one thing, however, the *krigsbarn* all had in common: their paternal origins and the way they were treated while growing up was never mentioned or openly discussed in post-war Norway. Still, the writer Torborg Nedreaas (1906–1987) took up these mothers' destinies in his short stories shortly after the war.[19]

However, this silence surrounding the *krigsbarn* – who by this stage were young adults – eventually cracked as the patriotic narrative about the occupation period started to erode in the 1980s. This occurred not only in Norway but also in some other formerly occupied countries like the Netherlands. One reason for this was the emergence of a new generation who had been born during or shortly after the war and who over time became involved in science, politics, journalism and litera-

---

17 NN: »Das ist wirklich bodenlos.« Wie die DDR drei norwegischen »Lebensborn«-Kindern ihre Biographie raubte, *Der Spiegel* 25/1997, 74–85.
18 Stein Ugelvik Larsen: »Nachdem der Stein ins Wasser geworfen wurde. Die Rolle der Erinnerung in der historischen Rekonstruktion«, in: Claudia Lenz/Jens Schmidt/Oliver von Wrochem (eds.): Erinnerungskulturen im Dialog. Europäische Perspektiven auf die NS-Vergangenheit, Münster 2002, (33–45) 39. Original: »Sowohl die Frauen, die diese Kinder bekommen haben, als auch die Kinder selbst wurden manchmal wie Kriminelle behandelt.«
19 Cf. for example: »Kvinnlinger II« and »Achtung, gnädiges Fräulein«, that were published in the collection of short stories »Bak skapet står øksen« in 1945. They are also accessible in: Torborg Nedreaas: Noveller – og noen essays, Oslo 1995.

ture. Therefore, they looked at the whole war episode from a certain distance. They also started to take an interest in subjects that had hitherto been neglected. For instance, the TV-series *I solkorsets tegn* (»In the Sign of the Suncross«)[20], which was broadcasted on Norwegian television in 1981, presented the stories and mindset of average former members of the Norwegian Nazi party *Nasjonal Samling* for the first time to the general public. This documentary was to trigger intense debate. Furthermore, historians such as Øystein Sørensen, Nils Johan Ringdal and Hans Fredrik Dahl took embarked upon new areas of research, including the ideological foundations of the *Nasjonal Samling*.[21] Like these historians, the novelist Herbjørg Wassmo also belonged to this up-coming generation.

III. The Taboo Breaker: Herbjørg Wassmo's »House with the Blind Glass Windows«

Herbjørg Wassmo wrote her novel about the *krigsbarn* Tora in the literary tradition of social realism. She chronicles life on a small island in the Vesterålen archipelago in northern Norway in the 1950s, as seen from Tora's point of view. Most islanders lead rather poor lives; they fish to make a living or work in the local fish factory, as did Tora's mother Ingrid. While her mother works in the factory, her husband Henrik often sexually abuses the ten-year old girl. During the war Henrik had been hit in the shoulder by shrapnel, effectively rendering him an invalid. On top of that, he's an alcoholic, unemployed most of the time, and hates the Germans. He calls them »devils«[22] whenever he talks about the war. When abusing Tora, the sole »German« on the island, he is taking his revenge on its former occupiers.

The sexual abuse might be the worst aspect of her ordeal, but it's by no means the only way in which Tora suffers. She is often confronted with her German origins in her daily life; in the form of derogatory comments from her schoolmates or neighbours, or when she experiences that she and her mother are excluded

---

20 I solkorsets tegn, Norway 1981, editor-in-chief: Haagen Ringnes. He also belonged to the new generation.
21 Cf. Nils Johan Ringdal: Historie og moral, in: Dagbladet 11 November 1987; Hans Fredrik Dahl: Når kampen blir historie, in: Dagbladet 14 September 1988; Øystein Sørensen: Forskningen om krigen i Norge: Tradisjonelle og nye perspektiver, in: Nytt Norsk Tidsskrift 6 (1989), 40–58; Øystein Sørensen: Hitler eller Quisling. Ideologiske brytninger i Nasjonal Samling 1940–1945, Oslo ²1989.
22 Wassmo, 34.

from the local and thereby the national community. They participate neither in the Christmas celebrations nor the National Day celebrations on 17 May. And yet, Tora hardly knows anything about her German origins and what happened to her mother after the war. She only knows what the neighbours told her and invents her own stories from this scant knowledge. In Wassmo's words, she believed »[t]hey'd cut off her mother's hair because Tora was born during the war«.[23] She feels guilt for what her mother has done because she herself is the living evidence of such wrongdoing.

Neither is Tora aware that her father, the soldier Wilhelm, is dead. No one had ever told her that he was killed by the Germans or Norwegians at the end of the war. He had tried to run away with Ingrid, at first to friends in Oslo where Tora was born, and subsequently to his family in Berlin: »Mama never talks about the war. Aunt Rachel once hinted that Tora's birth had been the death of Grandma. This wasn't meant for Tora's ears, so she couldn't ask any more about it.«[24]

Her aunt Rachel is the first person to ever talk to Tora about her father. She is appalled to learn that Tora knows nothing about him, and so she breaks the taboo and reveals all about how Wilhelm and Ingrid fell in love. Rachel tells of a wartime romance between two young lovers. Nevertheless, she also mentions that Wilhelm belonged to the enemy. Tora does not care about that. However, her world falls asunder as she learns that her father is dead and her dream of a better life together with him in Berlin cannot be fulfilled.[25] The relationship between Tora and her mother also remains difficult. Ingrid still refuses to talk about Wilhelm, because she feels ashamed about their relationship and for having given birth to Tora. At least Rachel tries a to make Ingrid talk when she remarks: »You're the one who has got to tell her [Tora] how we've struggled our way through this problem together, and that she doesn't need to go around feeling ashamed of the father she would have had if things had gone the right way.«[26] But Rachel's attempt to have Ingrid open up to her daughter is without success. The lack of communication in this family, especially between mother and daughter, can be read as an example of the silence that prevailed in many Norwegian families and in society in general in the 1950s and thereafter.

23   Ibid, 35.
24   Ibid, 34.
25   Ibid, 67.
26   Ibid, 71.

The sexual abuse and maltreatment of children, especially of *krigsbarn*, that Wassmo describes in her novel frequently occurred in the 1950s, be it on a small island in northern Norway or elsewhere. After the novel's publication in 1981, Wassmo was praised for her evocative depiction of life on a small island at that time.[27] Yet, no one applauded her for taking up the *krigsbarn* issue. It might have been too early for such recognition. Thus, Sissel Lange-Nielsen, a reviewer with the *Aftenposten*, questions the attention the *tyskerjenter* received in the autumn of 1981: »The mother was so unwise to fall in love with a German during these five long years. Strangely enough, the same topic also appears in two other novels this autumn.«[28] That is the only comment Lange-Nielsen made on the »German warbride« topic. Moreover, the *krigsbarn* barely merit a reference: »Tora is growing up in the shadow of her mother's ›sin‹, and we, who lived through those times, know what kind of a shadow this was. Others could hardly understand.«[29] With these closing phrases, the reviewer claimed that everyone knew how *krigsbarn* had been treated. By implication, there was no need to write any more about it. She did not even try to figure out why the novelists broached the subject in the first place. Still, the silence surrounding the *krigsbarn* had been broken.

The second step in the process of coming to terms with the treatment of the *krigsbarn* was a radio programme four years later, in 1985. In this broadcast, the journalist Veslemøy Kjendsli re-told the story of the women who had had love relationships with German soldiers, and who were later interned on Hovedøya, an island in the Oslofjord, after the war. Encouraged by this radio programme, the *krigsbarn* themselves started to come out and tell their stories to the public rather than to their mothers, who had been despised as *tyskerjenter*. In the following

---

27   Cf. Sissel Lange-Nielsen: Får hun Nordisk Råds pris?, *Aftenposten*, 24 November 1981.
28   Ibid. Translated by the author. Original: »Moren var så uforstandig å forelske seg i en tysker i de fem lang årene. Det samme emnet går rart nok igjen i to andre romaner i høst.« One of the novels Lange-Nielsen might be referring to is »Little Ida« by Marit Paulsen and published in 1981. The plot is set during the war. Ida's mother works for the Germans and has an affair with a German SS-officer. Ida suffers because of this relationship, but the German is not her biological father. Therefore, I will not discuss Paulsen's novel here. Also the film »Løperjenten« by Vibeke Løkkeberg (1981) is sometimes mentioned in conjunction with Wassmo. Both tell of growing-up in social poverty soon after World War II. Løperjenten is set in Bergen in 1948. But the main character, the seven-year-old Kamilla, is not a *krigsbarn*.
29   Ibid. Original: »Tora vokser opp i skyggen av morens ›synd‹, og vi som levde den gangen, vet hvilken skygge det var. Andre kan knapt forstå.«

years, they published the first documentary novels about their lives, especially their adolescent years during the 1950s, or told their stories to the press or on TV.[30] One of them, Per Arne Löhr Meek, founded the Norwegian Wartime Children Association (*Norges Krigsbarnforbund*) in 1986.[31] Its aim has been to help *krigsbarn* locate their relatives and especially their biological fathers. Changes to the relevant Norwegian law concerning adoption in 1987 made this possible. According to the re-drafted law, all adopted children had henceforth the right to obtain information about their biological parents. Given that many *krigsbarn* had been adopted, many of them set out to look for their biological parents. During their search, they often were accompanied by journalists from newspapers, radio and TV stations, who reported on their individual outcomes and especially the initial meetings with their biological fathers. Thus, they gradually attracted public interest.

IV. From the Perspective of a New Generation: Gaarder's »The Solitaire Mystery«

When Jostein Gaarder's novel »The Solitaire Mystery« was published in Norway in 1990, the topic of the *krigbarn* was no longer considered a taboo among the Norwegian public. While Wassmo had helped to forge a new narrative, Gaarder could elaborate on the pre-existing one. In terms of Foucault's discourse theory, he could refer to the *krigsbarn* discourse already prevalent in Norwegian society. Thus, the way Gaarder writes about the fate of being a *krigsbarn* differs somewhat. Moreover, »The Solitaire Mystery« is written for children and adolescents as well as from the point of view of the younger generation. Like Wassmo's Tora, Gaarder's protagonist is also a child: the twelve year-old boy Hans Thomas. He is not, however, a *krigsbarn* but the son of one who has become an adult. In this novel told from Hans Thomas' perspective, he comes across his German grandfather apparently by coincidence. His grandfather, the former soldier Ludwig, was unknown to Hans Thomas and even to his father. They had never systematically searched for him. Yet, »The Solitaire Mystery« is not primarily acclaimed or even known for this aspect of the *krigsbarn* narrative. The novel is highly regarded principally for the way in which it raised philosophical questions and explained Greek

---

30   Cf. Olsen, 436.
31   Cf. Norges Krigsbarnforbund, last access: 20 December 2013, <http://www.nkbf.no>.

mythology in terms that children and adolescents could comprehend. Gaarder is thus taking the well-known *krigsbarn* narrative in order to create a new story and to modify it for a younger generation that increasingly raises questions about its own genealogy.

The plot is as follows: Hans Thomas and his father are travelling from Norway to Greece in order to look for Hans Thomas' mother who had run away. She had wanted to »find herself« and to work as a model. During his numerous cigarette breaks during the trip, his father embarks Hans Thomas on a philosophical journey. He asks him, for example, where the universe originates and often discusses similarly deep questions about Greek mythology. The third journey discussed in the novel is fantastic in nature. Hans Thomas undertakes this trip while reading a magic book that he had given by the baker Ludwig in a small village in Switzerland during a stopover on their way to Greece. Later, while reading the magic book, Hans Thomas discovers that Ludwig is his German grandfather and that he was officially registered as missing on the Eastern Front. This fantasy story thus helps to bring the family together.

The fact that Ludwig has survived the war is not the only difference to Wassmo's novel in which the German soldier is already dead. Unlike Wassmo, Gaarder openly introduces Hans Thomas' father as a *krigsbarn* at the outset. As in the prologue to a theatrical play, all those who appear in the book are briefly introduced. Under the headline »In This Story You Will Meet«, the father is described as »Dad, who grew up in Arendal as the illegitimate child of a German soldier, before running away to become a sailor«.[32] It is conspicuous that the father is first of all described as a *krigsbarn* – and not as a philosopher, as he would consider himself. It is also implied that growing up a *krigsbarn* is such a horrible experience that even running away to sea becomes understandable.

Already in the opening chapter, once father and son reach Germany, his father tells Hans Thomas about his origins as a *krigsbarn* during a cigarette break. And Hans Thomas then informs the reader: »You see, Dad is the illegitimate child of a German soldier. I'm no longer embarrassed to mention it, because I now know that these children can be just as good as other children. But it's easy for me to say that. I haven't felt the pain of growing up in a small southern Norwegian town without a father.«[33] The author does not give any further information about how his father grew up and how he suffered. This kind of knowledge is taken as

---

32   Gaarder, 3.
33   Ibid, 12.

being understood by the reader. It is remarkable that Hans Thomas even mentions the process of coming to terms with his father's bloodline. Since he declared he's no longer embarrassed, it becomes obvious that he went through a process that many other Norwegians – and probably even other Europeans as well – had to go through. At the same time, Gaarder describes an ideal process of dealing not with one's own, but with one father's origins. This is only possible because it is no longer a taboo to talk about the *krigsbarn* – unlike when »The House with the Blind Glass Windows« was initially published back in the early 1980s. Because his father has told Hans Thomas everything, he now can, in turn, inform his readers.

It is also astonishing how Hans Thomas tells the story about his grandparents. It makes the process of coming to terms with history transparent. He describes how his grandparents met: The German soldier Ludwig helped the 17-year-old Norwegian girl when her bike needed repairs.[34] He mentions that Ludwig was not a military man, but courteous and definitely no Nazi. But, she should not have let the occupier help her, Hans Thomas comments. He apologizes for her having fallen in love with a German soldier, though not for having continued dating him. He held the soldier responsible for the worst thing that ever befell his grandmother. At the time Ludwig did not know that his Norwegian girlfriend was pregnant. Hans Thomas' grandmother did not succeed in locating him when she went in search of him years later.

The protagonist discloses all this in a somewhat childlike and yet a distanced tone – as if it were common knowledge that such things happened. Moreover, talking in a pedagogical manner, he reveals how he came to accept his grandmother's supposed failure and describes his process of coming to terms with the story: »Neither Grandma nor Dad seeks to excuse what happened at Froland. The only thing you might question is the punishment. How many generations should be punished for a single offence? Naturally, Grandma must shoulder her part of the blame for getting pregnant, and that is something she'll never deny. For me, it's more difficult to accept that people believed it was right to punish the child, too.«[35]

The noteworthy fact about mentioning *krigsbarn* in »The Solitaire Mystery« is not that the mother remains morally guilty for her relationship with a German soldier. That was regarded as common sense by the public at the end of the 1980s. Rather, the remarkable thing about Gaarder's account is that a member of the second post-war generation questions the manner in which the *krigsbarn* were

---

34 Ibid, 12–14.
35 Ibid, 14.

treated. Gaarder's protagonist does not overtly criticise, but instead asks leading questions. Nevertheless, this approach was innovative for the beginning of the 1990s.

The 1990s ticked by between the appearance of »The Solitaire Mystery« and Lars Saabye Christensen's »The Half Brother«. During this intervening decade the process of dealing with the *krigsbarn* was not only dominated by reports of individual destinies but also of scandals that actually had or were supposed to have happened after the war.[36] It produced a ripple effect, for instance, when reports appeared in the media that in 1945 thirty *krigsbarn* were not repatriated to Norway from a *Lebensborn* house in Bremen. Instead they were provided with fake identities and brought to Sweden. In 1998, another accusation – which turned out to be untrue – attracted further attention: A newspaper article claimed that the *krigsbarn* never received any compensation in 1959, when Norway negotiated a bilateral agreement with West Germany.[37] The article ignored the fact that this agreement did not concern *krigsbarn*. Rather, its aim was to compensate former political prisoners who had been held in captivity by the Germans. Although *krigsbarn* had never been eligible for compensation, this debate immediately triggered a parliamentary decision to establish a research project on the subject.

Furthermore, the above-mentioned article sparked claims for financial compensation by the *krigsbarn*.[38] But in 1998, no politician, scientist or journalist supported these claims. A year later seven *krigsbarn* founded the Wartime Children Association Lebensborn (Krigsbarnforbundet Lebensborn).[39] Their goal was to sue the Norwegian authorities for financial compensation. More than 100 *krigsbarn* joined them in their efforts. Public opinion was to shift in favour of the *krigsbarn* after Kjell Magne Bondevik's New Year's address in 2000.[40] Prime Minister Bondevik apologized for the discrimination and unfairness the *krigsbarn* had had to endure since the war.[41]

---

36   The above-mentioned articles in *Der Spiegel* from1997 provide an example of this as well.
37   Cf. Lily Kalvø (NTB): Staten tok krigsbarnas penger, in: Dagsavisen 16 March 1998.
38   Cf. Lily Kalvø (NTB): – Må fram i samfunnsdebatten, in: *Dagsavisen*, 16 March 1998.
39   Cf. Krigsbarnforbundet Lebensborn, last access: 20 December 2013, <http://www.lebensbornnorway.org>.
40   NN: Anstendighet, in: *Aftenposten*, 23 February 2000; NN: Oppreisning – ikke forskning, in: *Dagsavisen*, 26 February 2000.
41   Cf. Gunnar Magnus: Bondeviks nyttårstale. Norge må være en fredsnasjon, in: *Aftenposten*, 2 January 2000.

V. Playing with the *Krigsbarn* Narrative: Saabye Christensen's »The Half Brother«

By the time Lars Saabye Christensen's »The Half Brother« was published in Norway in 2001, most Norwegians were well aware that many *krigsbarn* had suffered in post-war Norway and regretted the fact. It had become a common sense view that both compensation and research were long overdue – but neither of these processes had to date been completed. Nevertheless, it is not unsurprising that Saabye Christensen did something completely unlike Wassmo and Gaarder when he took up the *krigsbarn* narrative. To borrow Foucault's terminology, he employed the common *krigsbarn* discourse and arranged it in a new way. This is a typical feature of postmodern literature[42], to which »The Half Brother« belongs, as I see it. The plot is as follows: The narrator, the unsuccessful scriptwriter Barnum, who like his father is very short, tells the story of his family, starting with his great grandmother – called the Old One – and his grandmother Boletta, with whom he in addition to his mother Vera and his half-brother Fred grow up together in Oslo. This family tale ends with the early years of Vivian's and Barnum's son.[43] After a prologue dealing with his childhood and a short chapter touching on the present – a visit to the Berlin Film Festival where Barnum is drunk and destructive most of the time – he starts with the day that utterly changed his mother's life: 8 May 1945. On the very day Norway was liberated from the German occupying forces, Vera was raped in the drying loft by an unknown man. The only thing she noticed – apart from his bad smell – was that he was missing a finger. The Old One and Boletta worry about Vera, as they gradually discover what happened, and wonder who could have raped her, knowing that several people were hiding in the loft at the end of the war: »Let's hope it was a soldier,« his great-grandmother remarks, her voice becoming quieter. »A Norwegian soldier who couldn't come to terms with the war inside.«[44]

---

42 Cf. Ruth Mayer: Postmoderne/Postmodernismus, in: Ansgar Nünning (ed.): Metzler Lexikon Literatur- und Kulturtheorie, Stuttgart 2001, 544. Mayer stresses that postmodern literature is rather a field for experimentation than an authority for meaningfulness.
43 Vivian is married to Barnum, so the child is treated as though it were Barnum's child. But he knows that he cannot be the child's father due to his infertility. It is not mentioned whether Vivian is aware of this. Boletta and Vera don't allude to the fact.
44 Christensen, 99.

The scene in the loft with all its consequences is the key one – in a review in the Norwegian newspaper *Dagbladet*, it was even referred to as the novel's »*urscene*«[45] (»primal scene«). The rape utterly destroys Vera's life, because she cannot name the father of her child that is born nine months later, and ironically given the name Fred.[46] Neighbours presume the father is a German soldier and punish Vera for having had a relationship with the enemy by ignoring her.[47] And when Vera wants to have the child baptized, the Vicar asks: »You didn't engage in intercourse with the enemy?«[48] So, he also suspects her of being a *tyskerjente*.

While Vera is treated as a traitor, Fred is regarded as a child begotten by the enemy and marginalized accordingly. As an illegitimate child and an accused *krigsbarn*, he too becomes an outsider. However, it is never directly mentioned how he is treated. Saabye Christensen assumes the reader is familiar with what could have happened, so he does not need to go into detail. Certain indirect comments, however, make it clear. After the death of King Haakon VII, one of Barnum's classmates whispers to him: »The King isn't everyone's King.«[49] And it is obvious that the comment is directed at Fred. The word »bastard« written on the shed wall in the schoolyard is another example.[50] In the family circle, too, Fred is sometimes treated differently to Barnum, who due to his small size is also an outsider. Unlike Fred, Barnum is sent to dancing school. Barnum, who manages to get expelled and to make friends with his future wife Vivian and his subsequent manager Peder, asks Boletta why Fred doesn't also have to go to dancing school. She answers: »It's different with Fred. [...] he wasn't born to dance.«[51] Boletta's words are ambiguous, because she, Vera and the Old One do not treat Fred any differently to Barnum because of his descent. But they assume that an illegitimate child that might even be a *krigsbarn* should not be admitted to a dance school in post-war Norway. Fred is not only different because of his origins but also due to his character, which of course might have something to do with his bloodline. He is an angry and often rebellious boy who does not find his place in society.

However, the *krigsbarn* narrative does not play a major role in »The Half Brother«. It is never mentioned, particularly in the reviews and other articles. Nor

---

45 Øystein Rottem: En guddommelig komedie, in: *Dagbladet*, 1 September 2001.
46 *Fred* means »peace« in Norwegian.
47 Cf. Christensen, 153.
48 Ibid, 109.
49 Ibid, 203.
50 Cf. ibid, 218.
51 Ibid, 334.

is Christensen's literary work, for which he won several prizes[52], reputed for his treatment of this particular subject. This is not unsurprising for it is Barnum's life, especially his childhood and adolescence, that occupy centre stage in the novel: growing-up among three women, his friendship with Vivian and Peder, who are both outsiders, and the figure of Barnum's father Arnold Nilsen, who like Fred is continually on the prowl and prefers the magic world of imagination to reality, just as Barnum does. Nevertheless, Fred and his unknown origins are constantly present in the book – not least because he is an important figure for Barnum especially during his childhood, and for the fact that he could be the father of Vivian's son. Since it is never stated directly, it can only be assumed. Similarly, the reader has to guess who Fred's father might be. It could have been »a departing German soldier«[53], as suggested in a review in the *Guardian*. It might have been Arnold Nilsen. Evidence for this assumption is based on the fact that he was initially missing a finger on one hand following a childhood accident. This hand was subsequently totally mutilated during the war. At least this is the account Nilsen gave on several occasions, and what Barnum as the novel's narrator continually alludes to. Still, no one really knows if this is true or even questions the assertion.[54]

Given that it is unclear whether Fred is in fact a *krigsbarn* – though his neighbours and the vicar seem convinced of the fact, we cannot place these three novels – »The House with the Blind Glass Windows«, »The Solitaire Mystery«, and »The Half Brother« – in a direct line. Moreover, the likelihood of being a *krigsbarn* is not even a central topic in Saabye Christensen's family epic. It is remarkable, however, that he creates a new kind of story by deconstructing the *krigsbarn* narrative. It is quite ironic that it suffices to be accused of being a war child to be treated as one. In hindsight »The Half Brother« re-samples the final stages of the process of coming to terms with the *krigsbarn* issue, because Saabye Christensen is detaching the narrative from its historical background and playing with it. This is a typical feature of postmodernist works of literature. By arranging the narrative in a new way, the author is at the same time criticising society for its attitude towards *krigsbarn* and illegitimate children.

---

52 The most important one is the prestigious Nordic Council Literature Prize in 2002.
53 Paul Binding: Life's a Circus, in: *The Guardian*, 24 May 2003.
54 This interpretation is suggested between the lines by Elizabeth Blair in the study-guide of the Norwegian researchers and teachers association of North America (NORTANA), cf. <http://nortana.org/reading/the-half-brother/>.

VI. Conclusion: Debates about Compensation and the *Krigsbarn* since 2000

Since the turn of the millennium, news items concerning *krigsbarn* have mostly dealt with their demands for compensation and research funding. Moreover, the *krigsbarn* have continued to tell their stories in various media outlets. Most of these stories accompanied various lawsuits regarding their claims for compensation. In the summer of 2004, researchers finally presented their results and they were able to clarify the various accusations. More importantly, they also documented the circumstances under which many *krigsbarn* have had to grow up.[55]

In April 2005 the Norwegian Parliament finally adopted the regulation concerning financial compensation for *krigsbarn*. Although the political process of coming to terms with the *krigsbarn* culminated in 2005, they still appear in public, on TV, in books or in the press. Two current examples demonstrate how *krigsbarn* stories are still being told – both in »traditional« as well as in new ways, and not only in Norway but also in Germany. The traditional example is the new German translation of »The House with the Blind Glass Windows« by Gabriele Haefs, published in 2012.[56] Not only is the translation in itself remarkable, but also the decision to rename the German book title from the former literal translation of the Norwegian title into »*Deutschenkind*« (*tyskerbarn*, literally, »German child«). This rebranding reveals that the focus on the book has now changed, if compared to its initial release in 1981. It is a sign that the *krigsbarn* remain a topic of enduring interest – not only in Norway but also in Germany.

Another recent example of this change of perception is the German-Norwegian film production »Two Lives«[57]. It tells the story of the fictitious *krigsbarn* Katrine who was sent by the *Lebensborn* organization to Germany after her birth and grew up in the children's home »Sonnenwiese« near Leipzig after the war. When she

---

55 Cf. Lars Borgersrud: Staten og krigsbarna, Oslo 2004, edited by: Institutt for kulturstudier, Universitet i Oslo; Dag Ellingsen: Krigsbarnas levekår. En registerbasert undersøkelse, Oslo 2004, edited by Statistisk Sentralbyrå.
56 Herbjørg Wassmo: Deutschenkind, Hamburg 2012, vollst. überarb. deutsche Fassung von Gabriele Haefs auf Grundlage der Übersetzung von Ingrid Sack. Original title: Das Haus mit der blinden Glasveranda.
57 It premiered in Norwegian cinemas in 2012, one year earlier than in Germany. It tells a fictional story based on the previously unpublished novel »Eiszeiten« (»Times of Ice«) by the German author Hannelore Hippe. For further information cf. <www.filmweb.no/film/article910814.ece?facts=t> or: <www.zweileben-film.de/#start>.

was 25, Katrine escaped to Norway to live with her biological mother near Bergen. Or, that at least is the story she tells her that she is her missing daughter. After the fall of the Berlin Wall, Katrine is forced to tell the truth: She used to be an agent for the East-German *Staatssicherheit* (State Security Police, or Stasi) and was dispatched to Norway by the Stasi under the fake identity of the *krigsbarn* Katrine. After her dramatic escape and arrival in Norway, the Stasi killed the real Katrine. Unveiling the secret piecemeal, Katrine shocks the woman who assumed she was her real mother, her husband and her daughter with the true story. The film's plot is fictional but inspired by the scandal *Der Spiegel* unleashed in 1997 when it revealed the true live of Ludwig Bergmann. »Two Lives« is a blend of family saga and Cold-War-thriller, performed by Norwegian and German actors. Ultimately, the film is little concerned with historical accuracy and it remains unclear whether the Stasi dispatched agents with fake identities of *Lebensborn* children to Norway. What is remarkable about »Two Lives« is the transnational character of the film project, given that both Germans and Norwegians were involved, and thus both perspectives on the *krigsbarn* issue are evident.

In Norway, the film met with a mixed reception. In most reviews, only the plot's suspense and the performance by the Norwegian actress Liv Ullmann were singled out for praise. None of the reviews offered an evaluation as to whether or to what extent the film is historically relevant.[58] They only stressed that the film is based upon historical facts – the Stasi story is taken for granted – and the historical background is just cursorily mentioned.[59] Liv Ullmann was the only cast member to speak out in her interviews of her sorrow for how the *krigsbarn* and their mothers were treated.[60]

---

58 Inger Merete Hobbelstad: De Andres liv, *Dagbladet*, 18 October 2012; Ingvill Dybfest Dahl: Film: Uforløst spenningsidé, in Verdens Gang 18 October 2012; Mode Steinkjer: Knugende og sprikende, Dagsavisen 18 October 2012.
59 NTB: Liv Ullmann-film er tysk Oscar-kandidat, in: *Aftenposten*, 28 August 2013.
60 Frank Haugsbø: Liv Ullmann i vinden igjen – stor rolle i tysk-norsk familiedrama, *Verdens Gang* 15 December 2011; Øystein David Johansen: Liv Ullmann for opptatt til å tenke norsk film, *Verdens Gang*, 27 October 2012.

In Germany, the film was considered too complicated[61] or difficult to follow[62]. The major difference with reviews in Norway is that more details concerning the plot's historical background (*Lebensborn, krigsbarn*) are given, even if not always correctly. Reviewers either mention that the film is based on real-life occurrences[63] or they refer to *Der Spiegel* article in 1997 concerning Ludwig Bergmann's life story.[64]

So, what might be the historical use of this film? It definitely shows once more to what extent German and Norwegian history was interwoven in the post-war period. Furthermore, the German-Norwegian film project is – like the new Wassmo German translation – an example of the transnationalisation of dealing with the past and especially with the *krigsbarn*. In all likelihood, it is not the last example of its kind.

Because of its transnational character, »Two Lives« is a good example with which to draw a curve of the taboo surrounding the *krigsbarn* from the 1980s until today. It is a process that spans from outright taboo and culminates in transnationalisation. At a time new and formerly neglected stories were emerging and the patriotic narratives about the occupation period were being put aside, Wassmo was the first author to break the taboo surrounding the *krigsbarn*. To use Foucault's terminology, Wassmo's *krigsbarn* discourse was contrary to the predominant discourses that represented a shameful silence. Thus Wassmo's novel acted as a door opener for war children themselves to build upon a *krigsbarn* narrative by telling their stories in books, newspapers, on radio or TV. In contrast, Gaarder's novel »The Solitaire Mystery« could in 1990 already refer to a pre-existing narrative. Thus his novel was part of a specialized discourse. Furthermore, Gaarder added new points of view to the narrative when he recounted his *krigsbarn* story from the perspective of the next generation. And yet, at the same time he was reflecting the dominant narrative.

---

61 Cf. Birgit Roschy: Film »Zwei Leben«: Deutsche Vergangenheitsbewältigung am Fjord, in: *Zeit online* 18 September 2013. She also criticises the film for not being technically well made.

62 Cf. Christian Buß: Feind in deiner Familie, in: *Spiegel online*, last access: 16 September 2013, <http://www.spiegel.de/kultur/kino/deutscher-oscar-kandidat-zwei-leben-mit-juliane-koehler-a-921216.html>. He comprehensively praises the film.

63 Cf. Rainer Gansera: Deutscher Film »Zwei Leben« bei den Oscars Fluchtpunkt Norwegen, in: *Süddeutsche Zeitung*, 22 September 2013.

64 Cf. Christina Bylow: Von Hitler geraubt, von der Stasi missbraucht, *Berliner Zeitung*, 17 September 2013; Buß; Roschy.

From the middle of the 1990s until 2005, the political and scientific process of coming to terms with the past dominated the *krigsbarn* discourse. The feeling of being morally responsible for some of the darker sides of the occupation and feeling regret for this fact influenced narratives about the occupation such as the attitude towards the Norwegian Jews and the *krigsbarn*. This became apparent in Kjell Magne Bondevik's New Year's address in 2000.

This process of coming to terms with this aspect of Norwegian history involved authors going to such great lengths that it was possible to use the *krigsbarn* narrative in an ironical way and to play with it in the literary discourse. This is what Lars Saabye Christensen did in his novel »The Half Brother« in 2001. For the protagonist's brother, Fred, it sufficed to be considered as a *krigsbarn* to be treated as one. Describing that process, Saabye Christensen offers society a mirror with which it could examine itself and how it treated the *krigsbarn*.

Given that Saabye Christensen's novel – as indeed are Wassmo's and even more so Gaarder's – are not only read and discussed in Norway, but also abroad, they are examples for the transnational character of coming to terms with the past. Nevertheless, they do not bring up the *krigsbarn* topic in general but specifically in relation to Norwegian history. The political process of coming to terms with the *krigsbarn* that ultimately led to monetary compensation can also be seen as part of a transnational one. Also, other former occupied countries have tried to come to terms with how they treated »their« *krigsbarn*. In this political process Norway can be considered as a pioneer. Just like with the financial compensation for Norwegian Jews that the government voted to accept in 1999, Norway once again in 2005 paved the way forward in the manner it brought the political process of coming to terms with the *krigsbarn* to a close. Other processes such as those in the literary and filmic realms remain on going, and it will be interesting to see how they will evolve.

Sigurd Sørlie

From Misguided Idealists to *Genocidaires:*
The Waffen-SS Volunteers in Norwegian Memory Culture

I. Introduction

Since the mid-1990s, scholars from various disciplines have described how the predominant national memory of Norway's wartime history evolved into a mythical narrative after 1945. Allegedly, this narrative is a unifying and heroic tale, overwhelmingly painted in black and white, of the *good* Norwegians fighting the *evil* occupiers. To the extent that collaborators feature at all in this master narrative, they are, so it is argued, depicted as wicked, deceitful, morally inferior, criminal, cowardly, stupid and incompetent and essentially written out of the national community.[1] According to Anne Eriksen, one of the pioneers in the study of Norway's commemoration of the war, the conventions of the national narrative prescribed that adherents of Vidkun Quisling and his collaborationist party, the *Nasjonal Samling* (NS), should always be represented as traitors who had shown solidarity with evil, with the enemy, and with the cruelties of Nazi Germany, and that it was completely misleading to draw any attention to these people's thoughts, emotions, and points of view.[2]

This article deals with one particular group of collaborators and its role in Norway's »collective memory«, namely, the approximately 4,500 Norwegians who joined Germany's armed forces during World War Two.[3] The vast majority of

---

1 Anne Eriksen: Det var noe annet under krigen. 2. verdenskrig i norsk kollektivtradisjon, Oslo 1995, 54–55, 145–147; Susanne Maerz: Die langen Schatten der Besatzungszeit. 'Vergangenheitsbewältigung' in Norwegen als Identitätsdiskurs, Oslo 2010, 13.
2 Eriksen, 155.
3 The number of Norwegians who served in Germany's armed forces during World War Two tends to be greatly inflated in the literature. Statistics from the responsible body of the NS reveals that a total of 4,252 volunteers had been inducted into the Waffen-SS

these so-called *frontkjempere* (front fighters) served on the Eastern Front in units of the Waffen-SS, the military branch of the SS.[4] Along with women who engaged in sexual relations with Germans, this group is commonly regarded as the most despised of all Norwegian collaborators. Anne Eriksen claims that this group, according to the national narrative, »committed the ultimate betrayal of the male gender role«.[5] Clemens Maier, in his study of the politics of remembrance in post-war Norway and Denmark, maintains that the group was particularly detested and »totally ostracised among the public«.[6]

If these claims are correct, it should be expected that the Waffen-SS volunteers have been represented in a particularly unfavorable manner to the public after 1945. It also seems logical to assume that the historiography has been stressing the volunteers' treacherous and brutal character and complicity in National Socialist crimes, and ignoring or downplaying their personal and political motives, the hardships they suffered at the front, and their self-perception and memory after the war.

But was this really the case? This article examines the public perception and representation of the Waffen-SS volunteers in Norway, drawing particular attention to the following questions: How was the group perceived and represented during the first decades after 1945, before historians started to engage with the subject? What general trends can be observed in the historiography of these »front fighters« from its initial phase in the 1970s and until the present day? To what extent did the veterans of the Waffen-SS disseminate a uniform narrative of the war, and what impact did their interpretation(s) of the past have on historical

---

and the German navy by December 1944. Even if it is assumed that some volunteers were not registered by the NS, it seems unlikely that the actual figure exceeded 4,500: Tallmessig oppgave over norske krigsfrivillige, Bjørn Noreger til Førerens og Ministerpresidentens kanselli, Herr byråsjef Carlson, 4.12.1944, RA, S-1006/Db – 0034. Se også Gunnar Sverresson Sjåstad, Nordmenn i tysk krigsinnsats. En kvantitativ undersøkelse av frontkjemperne under den andre verdenskrig, hovedoppgave i historie, fall 2006, University of Bergen, 58.

4 For a recent and thorough analysis of the role of Norwegians in the Waffen-SS, see Terje Emberland/Matthew Kott: Himmlers Norge. Nordmenn i det storgermanske prosjekt, Oslo 2012.
5 Eriksen, 55.
6 Clemens Maier: Making Memories: The Politics of Remembrance in Post-War Norway and Denmark, PhD in History and Civilization, European University Institute 2007, 230.

writing and memory construction in general? To what extent did shifts in the historiography and remembrance of this aspect of the war reflect wider trends in the writing and understanding of history? And finally – what light may be shed on the existing research into Norway's remembrance of the war by the case of the Waffen-SS volunteers?

II. Initial Perceptions and Representations of the »Front Fighters«

In the years following the German occupation of Norway, those perceived as collaborators were prosecuted and sentenced as part of the country's legal purge. Parallel to the legal prosecution, these people were also subjected to widespread contempt, demonisation, and mockery. Public expressions of disdain and scorn were particularly rife in liberal and left-leaning newspapers, but the tendency to ascribe inherently negative qualities to former members of the NS or other collaborators, or to portray them as mentally defective or social misfits was evident even in art, literature, and academic publications.[7] Not surprisingly, similar stereotypes were applied to the Waffen-SS volunteers. One of Norway's leading psychiatrists, Gabriel Langfeldt, who chaired a research project on the mental state of Norwegian collaborators initiated shortly after the country had been liberated, described his meeting with a group of former Waffen-SS volunteers at Ilebu prison in the summer of 1945 as follows: »It was like looking at a group of ancient human beings; their scary look and often deformed faces and dysplastic body types were reminiscent of Lombroso's ›Criminal Man‹.«[8]

Yet, even though such notions of mental deviation and inferiority might have remained widespread for decades after 1945, many Norwegians openly expressed a far more nuanced and sympathetic view of the former NS members and collaborators. Contrary to Eriksen and Maier's claims, this was particularly true for those who had served in the Waffen-SS. There was an apparent tendency to distinguish between »front fighters« on the one hand, and other collaborators on the other, and to adopt a more favourable approach to the former, often stressing the volunteers' young age, misguided »idealism«, and willingness to make sacrifices for

---

7 Nina Drolsum Kroglund: Hitlers norske hjelpere, Oslo 2010, 285–290.
8 Cited in Kroglund, 287–288. Translation by the author.

their cause.⁹ The impression that most people had a more positive perception of the »front fighters« than of other categories of collaborators is also confirmed by public opinion polls conducted shortly after the war.¹⁰ Although the comparatively positive assessment of the volunteers might have already evolved during the war, it was not publicly articulated until the legal purge sparked public controversy in the immediate post-war period.¹¹

One of those who gradually came to see the group in a completely different light was the psychiatrist Gabriel Langfeldt. In 1947, approximately two years after his aforementioned statement, he wrote the following passage in the Norwegian periodical *Samtiden*:

*»I have met some of these young ›front fighters‹, and more decent boys are hard to find. There is a minority who have committed minor offences, but the majority of them are young, decent people who, due to youthful fanaticism and enthusiasm for an idea, have ended up on the wrong side.«*¹²

Another psychiatrist, Harald Frøshaug, who served as prison medical officer at Ilebu prison – which housed the largest group of convicted collaborators – and

---

9   See below. An additional indication of this tendency can also be found in Frode Halle: Fra Finland til Kaukasus. Nordmenn på østfronten 1941–1945, Oslo 1972, 5. Some judges also explicitly gave positive assessments of the group during the legal purge: Riksarkivet (Oslo), L-sak, Nordre Jarlsberg politikammer, Anr. 273/45, Document nr. 18.

10 In March 1946, 3,000 Norwegians were asked to comment on the sentences meted out to various categories of collaborators prosecuted as part of the legal purge. The respondents expressed a more lenient attitude towards »front fighters« than to the other groups in question: Asbjørn Jaklin: De dødsdømte. 25 menn. 25 dødsdømte. Ett oppgjør, Oslo 2012, 306–307.

11 The claim that there was a tendency to adopt a more favourable approach to the »front fighters« than to other groups of collaborators already during the war has been made both by academic historians and former Waffen-SS volunteers: Tim Greve, Verdenskrig, in: M. Skodvin (ed.), Norge i krig, vol. 3, Oslo 1984, 175; Bjørn Lindstad: Den frivillige. En frontkjemper forteller sin historie, Oslo 2010, 27–28. The Norwegian novelist Ronald Fangen also hints at this tendency in a novel published shortly after the country's liberation: Ronald Fangen: En lysets engel. Beretningen om to norske gutter som falt i krigen, Oslo 1945, 335.

12 Gabriel Langfeldt: Tilbake til samfunnet, in: Samtiden 3 (1947), 169–178. Translation by the author.

participated in Langfeldt's research program on Norwegian collaborators, painted a very favourable picture of the Waffen-SS volunteers in two journal articles published in 1947 and 1955 respectively.[13] In a lecture held in 1947, Frøshaug left no doubt as to his approving attitude of this category of prisoner: »It immediately became clear to me that this group consisted of those with positive character traits and that it was of critical importance to learn how to understand them in order to facilitate the reintegration into society of these most valuable compatriots who had gone astray.«[14]

Johan Scharffenberg, another psychiatrist and a prominent public figure, criticised aspects of the legal purge and expressed particular sympathy for the Waffen-SS volunteers. In a newspaper article published in February 1947, he admitted that there were opportunists, psychopaths and adventurers among those who had volunteered to serve with the German forces, but also claimed that many »undoubtedly had believed, genuinely and naively, that they were fighting for Norway«.[15] Moreover, he suggested that the joint factors of anti-Soviet and anti-Bolshevist sentiments and the widespread sympathy with Finland following the Winter War of 1939–40 helped explain why many Norwegians had joined the Waffen-SS. He also drew attention to the volunteers' young age and rhetorically asked whether it was reasonable to expect more from this group than from the members of parliament, who had been willing to suspend the King and depose the government in the summer of 1940. In conclusion, Scharffenberg called for a general amnesty for all those who »thought they had been fighting for Norway«.[16]

Other prominent public figures expressed similar views. In 1947, Arne Næss, professor of philosophy and one of Norway's leading post-war intellectuals, who himself had been involved in resistance activities during the occupation, brought together former members of the resistance and former »front fighters« for a seminar at the University of Oslo. The aim was to clarify why the groups had ended up on opposing sides during the conflict. Næss later stressed that it was a »project

---

13   Harald Frøshaug: The Young »Patriots«, in: Acta Psychiatrica Scandinavica 22 (1947), 556–567; A Social-Psychiatric Examination of Young Front-Combattants, in: Acta Psychiatrica Scandinavica, 30 (1955), 443–465.
14   Harald Frøshaug, unpublished manuscript, 9 October 1947. Copy in possession of the author.
15   Espen Søbye: En mann fra forgangne århundrer. Overlege Johan Scharffenbergs liv og virke 1869–1965. En arkivstudie, Oslo 2010, 745.
16   Ibid., 745–746. Translation by the author.

of understanding«: He wanted to understand the »front fighters« – not to judge them.[17]

Johannes Andenæs, who had been imprisoned during parts of the war and worked as a consultant in the Office of the Director of Public Prosecutions in 1945, and who later became one of Norway's leading professors of criminal law, also expressed sympathy with the Waffen-SS volunteers. In the fall of 1945 he wrote as follows in the Labour Party newspaper *Arbeiderbladet*:

»*We call all these people traitors. But what resemblance is there between Quisling, this Norwegian officer, on the one hand, who conspires with a foreign power in the military occupation of his fatherland and later assists it in the suppression of his own compatriots for years, and, on the other hand, the 17 year-old who, filled with adventurousness and confused patriotism, and convinced that he is taking part in something big, volunteers to ›fight against communism‹«.*[18]

Andenæs' favourable perception of the volunteers seems to have been shared by other leading lawyers, including Judge Erik Solem, a prominent member of the civil resistance during the war and a key figure in the legal purge, and who, for example, presided over the case against Vidkun Quisling. Solem completely changed his opinion of the Waffen-SS volunteers in the winter of 1945/46, allegedly stating that he respected them for their spirit of self-sacrifice.[19]

On at least one occasion, the Waffen-SS volunteers were even mentioned with sympathy during a parliamentary debate. In January 1952, according to a newspaper review, a representative of the Agrarian Party rhetorically asked: »Who did the right thing – he who volunteered for service on the Eastern Front and put his life at risk, or he who volunteered for labour for the Germans? He who took part on the

17 Ingerid Hagen: Oppgjørets time. Om landssvikoppgjørets skyggesider, Oslo 2009, 7.
18 Cited in Johs. Andenæs: Det vanskelige oppgjøret, Oslo 1979 (3rd edn 1998), 88. Translation by the author.
19 H. O. Christophersen, Vintersolhverv 1944–45, *Aftenposten*, 2 January 1970; Letter from Johs. Andenæs to Odd Brunsvik, 27 August 1996, cited in Leif-Runar Forsth: For ære, folk og fedreland. Den norske legions historie. Unpublished manuscript. Copy in the Center for Studies of the Holocaust and Religious Minorities (HL-senteret, Oslo), Waffen-SS Collection (WSS), Acb.

Eastern Front fought for what we today spend billions on.«[20] What the Agrarian Party MP had in mind was of course the Cold War.

Sympathy could also be found within the Norwegian officer corps. Major Einar Sagen, a retired officer who in 1946 published a critical book about Norway's wartime Prime Minister Johan Nygaardsvold, regarded it as a huge mistake to put the »front fighters« behind bars: »As War Minister I would have said: ›Welcome home to Norway‹ and stretched out my hand to those who had done nothing worse than to fight in good faith on the wrong front.«[21] A stronger expression of sympathy within the officer corps can be found in the only collection of texts published by the volunteers themselves. The book *Fra Finland til Kaukasus* (»From Finland to the Caucasus«) was edited by the former SS-Sturmbannführer Frode Halle and published in 1972 with a foreword by Major-general Wilhelm Hansteen. The latter was not just any general. He had served as commander-in-chief of the Norwegian Armed Forces during much of the war and later held several key positions in Norway's post-war defence, including Inspector General of the Home Guard, head of the Independent Norwegian Brigade Group in Germany, Commander of the Norwegian Army, and Commander of Nato's Allied Land Forces Norway.[22] Hansteen's foreword signalled forgiveness and respect rather than mercilessness and contempt:

> »Whether we like it or not, this forms part of the complete history of our country's wartime fate. […]. During the war it was natural for us on the other side […] to consider those compatriots who wanted to fight with the enemy as particularly harmful. […]. But when the war ended in victory for our side and our country once again became free, and since so many years have passed since then, the kind of indulgence towards a beaten enemy that makes itself felt in other contexts must find its parallel in our relation to the front fighters. Some things must also be entered on the plus-side of the ledger, since these men were willing to accept all the hardships and sufferings of life on the front and even sacrifice their life for what they believed in.«[23]

20 Bunkholt (b) vil ha en kommisjon og revisjon, *Aftenposten*, 21 January 1952. Translation by the author.
21 Einar Sagen, cited in Kroglund, 419–420. Translation by the author.
22 Olav Riste, Norsk Biografisk Leksikon, last access: 8 April 2014, <http://nbl.snl.no/Wilhelm_Hansteen/utdypning>.
23 Foreword by Major-general Wilhelm Hansteen, in: Halle, Fra Finland til Kaukasus. Translation by the author.

Neither Halle's book nor Hansteen's foreword seem to have stirred public controversy. In a review of the book in the newspaper *VG* the former resistance and press veteran Asbjørn Barlaup wrote that he could not see any reason why it should not have been published. He even praised it for being »sober, unsentimental and free from polemics« and added, »it made up a page that belongs to the history of those unhappy years ...«[24] Barlaup also noted that the volunteers »experienced such disappointment and suffering [...] that there were probably those who would ask whether they should have been spared the years of imprisonment« after the war.[25] Barlaup's only critical comments related to one of the contributors who questioned whether he and other volunteers had in fact done anything wrong by joining Germany's forces, and to the absence of a thorough and self-critical discussion of why the volunteers chose to enlist in the first place. After all, what he as a reader was searching for in such a book was first and foremost to understand the »motivation for their voluntary participation for Germany on the Eastern Front«.[26]

In conclusion, it can be established that several leading scholars, intellectuals, officers and journalists, many of whom had taken part in the Norwegian resistance or armed forces in exile during the war, expressed a nuanced and often favourable impression of the Waffen-SS volunteers. Although the evidence is insufficient to make any generalisations as to how the majority of the population perceived the group, the above examples seem to confirm that a sympathetic approach was far from uncommon. Even Robert Savosnick, one of the 34 Norwegian Jews who had survived the Nazi death camps during World War Two, expressed a sense of respect for the volunteers when interviewed in connection with the controversial TV documentary *I solkorsets tegn* (»In the Sign of the Suncross«), which was televised by the NRK (The Norwegian Broadcasting Corporation) in 1981. Though he doubted that they had not been aware of the on-going mass murder on the Jews, Savosnick said of the volunteers: »In a sense I respect the front fighters, they were idealists who fought for a cause and wanted to sacrifice their lives.«[27] Irrespective of how widespread such views were, there is no doubt that the »front fighters« were perceived with more sympathy than other categories of collaborators. Hence, the claim that this group was particularly despised does not stand up to scrutiny.

24   Asbjørn Barlaup, Nordmenn på østfronten, *VG*, 8 January 1973.
25   Ibid.
26   Ibid. Translation by the author.
27   Haagen Ringnes: I skyggen av solkorset. Notater fra en fjernsynsserie, Oslo 1981, 63.

III. Contested Histories: the Veterans' Version of the War

Particularly from the 1970s onwards, Norwegian veterans of the Waffen-SS became increasingly active in disseminating their own memory of the war to the public. While some published books or articles, others gave oral or written testimony to scholars, journalists and authors, or they assisted them in other ways.[28] Although the veterans hardly communicated a completely consistent and uniform narrative, their accounts tended to share certain characteristics.

While an overwhelming majority claimed to have volunteered for »idealistic« reasons, above all to fight communism and the Soviet regime, to support Finland, and to help build a strong and independent Norway, a minority maintained that they ended up in the Waffen-SS for non-political reasons. However, hardly anyone admits to have been driven by a general sympathy for National Socialism – at least if this is equated with »German Nazism«.[29]

Whereas some devoted much attention to the prevalent military and political context, thereby trying to justify their own role, others focused on everyday life in the training camps, at the front, on leave, or in prison camps during and after

---

[28] The first significant publication from the Norwegian veterans of the Waffen-SS was Frode Halle's anthology in 1972. Later during the same decade several veterans gave interviews or assisted Svein Blindheim in connection with his dissertational work on history. Blindheim's dissertation was later published in book form. Svein Blindheim: Frontkjemperbevegelsen, hovedoppgave i historie, University of Oslo, 1974; Svein Blindheim: Nordmenn under Hitlers fane. Dei norske frontkjemparane, Oslo 1977. Above all, Blindheim was assisted by the former SS-Untersturmführer Bjørn Østring. See Arvid Bryne: Vi sloss for Norge. Frontkjemper og motstandsmann – fiender i krig, venner i fred, Oslo 2007, 9. A former member of the Freiwilligen-Legion Norwegen, Eivind Saxlund, was interviewed on the NRK in 1979: Karen-Margrethe Baltzrud: I lys av solkorset. Historien om en fjernsynsserie: »I solkorsets tegn«, sendt 1981, hovedoppgave i historie, University of Oslo, 2004, 50. Three former Waffen-SS volunteers were also among the interviewees in the TV series *I solkorsets tegn*: Ringnes, 45–48.

[29] Halle, 9, 63; Ringnes, 45–47; Knut Steenstrup: Dilemma. Opplevelser, minner og meninger – med små fakta om store fraser, Oslo 1989, 112, 122; Per R. Johansen: Frontkjemper, Oslo 1992, 24–27, 49; Sven T. Arneberg: Tragedie i Karelen. Norske skijegere i den finske fortsetteleskrigen 1941–44, Oslo 1993, 25–45; Kjell Fjørtoft: Veien til Østfronten. Krigens mange ansikter, Oslo 1993, 74; Egil Ulateig: Veien mot undergangen. Historien om de norske frontkjemperne, Lesja 2002, 47–58; Bryne, 11; Rolf Ursin: Et tilbakeblikk. En samling beretninger fra krigs- og etterkrigstiden, Evje 2009, 23–24.

the war. Like in soldiers' oral histories in general, themes such as fighting, bravery, joy, comradeship, hardship and suffering featured prominently in their accounts.

On the other hand, the ideological character of the Waffen-SS and the war in the East was normally either downplayed or rejected outright. Reflecting an international trend among veterans of the Waffen-SS, the vast majority of the Norwegians left the impression that they had served in a mainly, if not purely, *military* organisation and taken part in a rather conventional *military* campaign.[30] Themes such as ideological instruction and rituals, National Socialist beliefs, demonising images of the enemy, mistreatment of prisoners and civilians and the exploitation of the civilian population gained little or no attention.[31]

Omission and denial was particularly striking when it came to the question of complicity in the crimes of the Nazi regime. Whereas the majority avoided the subject altogether, several explicitly denied any knowledge of and complicity in the atrocities.[32] According to the latter group, the Waffen-SS was institutionally detached from other parts of the SS, and neither they nor their units had anything to do with the mass murder of the Jews or other such cruelties. These criminal activities, they argued, were committed by special killing squads behind the front-lines, and were completely unknown to them until after the war.[33] To the extent that they saw any signs of atrocities, these were normally committed by the enemy.[34] Rather than taking part in atrocities, they tried to soothe the hunger and suffering in the occupied areas, behaved considerately, and sometimes even developed warm relations with the civilian population.[35]

There is no doubt that the volunteers left a skewed impression of their own motives, attitudes, and experiences, as well as of the character of the Waffen-SS and the war in the East. First, even if the majority had been driven by anti-com-

---

30 E. g. Hans Gervik: Refleksjoner etter 50 år, Torp 1994, 172; Johansen, 46.
31 The above-mentioned aspects were, for example, hardly touched upon at all in Halle. However, an apparent change can be observed in some of the more recent publications, whether written by veterans or on basis of their written or oral testimony. See, for example, Ulateig, Veien, 102–112; Rolf Ivar Jordbruen: Helvete på jord. En frontkjempers historie, Oslo 2006, 65, 71, 106; Knut Flovik Thoresen: En verden i flammer. Frontkjemperne Bjarne Dramstads egen historie, Oslo 2010, 47; Lindstad, 34–36.
32 Silence was the predominant feature until the early 2000s. See Halle.
33 Cf. Steenstrup, 114, 123–125; Johansen, 45–47; Gervik, 136, 257; Ursin, 318–319.
34 Steenstrup, 115–116; Johansen, 48–49; Ursin, 25.
35 Gervik, 135; Johansen, 51; Ulateig, Veien, 65; Sven T. Arneberg: Legionærene. Nordmenn i skyttergravskrig ved Leningrad 1942–43, Lillehammer 2004, 78.

munism, sympathy with Finland, and nationalist sentiments, such motives were normally inextricably interwoven with other elements of National Socialist ideology, including notions of racism and anti-Semitism. In other words, they did not merely volunteer to fight communism, help neighbouring Finland, and secure Norway's independence, but also to ensure the realisation of a National Socialist order.[36] Second, the Waffen-SS constituted an integral part of Himmler's SS organisation and was permeated by its beliefs and values.[37] Third, there is no doubt that a significant share of the volunteers came to embrace the SS *Weltanschauung* to a very considerable extent.[38] Finally, rather than a traditional military campaign, Germany's war in the East was a war of extermination, and the Waffen-SS was deeply complicit in the crimes of the Nazi regime.[39] When all the evidence is taken into account, there is no doubt that a significant number of the Norwegian volunteers either heard rumours of atrocities, were witnesses to them or participated in them directly.[40]

IV. Historical Accounts until the late 1990s

Already in the 1970s, when the first historians started to engage with the subject, there were good reasons to question the reliability of the veterans' accounts. It could hardly come as a surprise to any critical historian that many former volunteers tried to justify their decision to enlist in the Waffen-SS by pointing to motives that were likely to find understanding amongst their compatriots after

---

36 Indicated already in Blindheim, Nordmenn, 144, 154–156.
37 Bernd Wegner: Hitlers politische Soldaten: Die Waffen- SS 1933–1945, Paderborn 1981 (9th ed., 2010), 84–103, 135–138; Frederik Müllers: Elite des »Führers«? Mentalitäten im subalternen Führungspersonal von Waffen-SS und Fallschirmjägertruppe 1944/45, Berlin 2012, 83–86.
38 Indicated already in Blindheim, Nordmenn, 176–177.
39 On the criminal character of the German War in the East, see, for example, Geoffrey P. Megargee: War of Annihilation: Combat and Genocide on the Eastern Front, 1941, Lanham 2006. On the complicity of front units of the Waffen-SS in the crimes of the Nazi regime: Jean-Luc Leleu: La Waffen-SS. Soldats politiques en guerre, Paris 2007, 772–808; Sönke Neitzel: Des Forschens noch wert? Anmerkungen zur Operationsgeschichte der Waffen-SS, in: Militärgeschichtliche Zeitschrift 61 (2002), 419–426; George H. Stein: The Waffen-SS: Hitler's Elite Guard at War 1939–1945, Ithaca 1966, 250–281.
40 E. g. Emberland/Kott, 236–237, 270–271.

the war. Moreover, from the second half of the 1960s it was well documented that the Waffen-SS remained an integral part of Himmler's »Black Corps« throughout the war, that it retained an ethos that was distinctly National Socialist, and that it was deeply complicit in the crimes of the Nazi regime.[41] Still, much of the historical writing on the subject came to rely heavily on post-war accounts by former members of the Waffen-SS.

The first scholarly book on Norwegians in the Waffen-SS was authored by Svein Blindheim and published in 1977 with the title *Nordmenn under Hitlers fane* (»Norwegians under Hitler's Banner«).[42] Blindheim, who was a highly decorated veteran of the Norwegian resistance and the Norwegian Independent Company Nr. 1 (*Kompani Linge*), a section of the British covert operations agency SOE (Special Operations Executive), set out to explore the origins and deployment history of the various volunteer formations and to analyse the group's socio-demographic composition and motives for enlistment.[43] In much the same vein as the notabilities mentioned earlier in this article, Blindheim's approach was marked by empathy and a genuine desire to uncover the volunteers' true motives. Although he did not fail to recognise that some sort of National Socialist sympathy was normally a precondition for enlistment, he concluded that the desire to take part in the »crusade against Bolshevism« was the single most important motivating factor, and that the volunteers were »idealists« who were convinced that they served their country in the best possible manner.[44] He even equated the group's motives with his own, stating that the »basic attitude of the front fighters must have been just as patriotic as that of the ›true believers‹ who served as volunteers in *Kompani Linge*«.[45] It should be added that Blindheim, who was by no means consistently uncritical of the volunteers, maintained that their patriotism had rested on false premises and that they had tried to establish a National Socialist dictatorship.[46] However, the book still left the impression that patriotism and anti-communism had been the volunteers' primary motives, and, in fact, even Blindheim himself

---

41   Stein, 250–294.
42   Blindheim, Nordmenn. The book was a slightly revised version of his *hovedoppgave* (equivalent of an MA-thesis) in history, which had been submitted at the University of Oslo a few years earlier (Blindheim, Frontkjemperbevegelsen).
43   Blindheim, Nordmenn, 8. For more information on Svein Blindheim's activities during the war, Bryne.
44   Blindheim, Nordmenn, 8, 144, 150, 154–156.
45   Ibid., 8. Translation by the author.
46   Ibid., 161, 189.

gradually tended to forget his initial reservations, stating, for example, the following in a newspaper interview in the early 1990s: »The front fighters believed in what they fought for, just like I did on the opposing side. The majority of them were no more Nazis than I was.«[47]

Arguably, the book's most striking flaw was its tendency to reproduce the image of the Waffen-SS as a more or less purely military organisation with little or no responsibility for the crimes of the Nazi regime.[48] Consequently, the book did not discuss whether Norwegian volunteers had witnessed or been involved in atrocities. This is all the more astonishing as Blindheim was well aware of George Stein's »The Waffen-SS: Hitler's Elite Guard at War«, the first scholarly monograph on the subject, which convincingly rebutted the apologetic myth of the »clean« Waffen-SS and even linked one of its units, the Division »Wiking«, with hundreds of Norwegians in its ranks, to a massacre.[49] Blindheim referred explicitly to Stein's book in an attempt to justify his false claim that the Waffen-SS had committed no more crimes than any other military organisation. Comparing the relevant parts of the two texts, it becomes clear that Blindheim confused Stein's own conclusion, that the Waffen-SS had been deeply complicit in Himmler's murderous policies, with a quote by the convicted war criminal and former SS officer Kurt Meyer, who claimed that the armed SS could only be blamed for a single war crime, namely, the massacre of 642 civilians in Oradour-sur-Glane in June 1944.[50] Although it is hard to conceive that Blindheim deliberately misrepresented the historical evidence, it seems equally hard to understand how the mistake could be the result of sheer sloppiness.[51] Regardless of whether we interpret Blindheim's conduct as an exceptional case of poor scholarship or as a case of intentional manipulation of historical records, his exoneration of the Waffen-SS should be understood in the context of his sympathetic approach to the volunteers and his corresponding distrust of the »victors«, who, in his eyes, had made unjustified efforts to criminalise the military branch of the SS after the war.[52]

During the 1980s, 1990s and early 2000s the subject received scant attention from academic historians. Thus, Blindheim's account remained the only

---

47 Frontkjemperne vil bli hedret, VG, 9 July 1993. Translation by the author.
48 Blindheim, Nordmenn, 12, 14–16, 159, 212 (footnote 108).
49 Stein, 272.
50 Blindheim, Nordmenn, 159, 212 (footnote 108); Stein, 255.
51 For a more thorough argument on this point, I refer to my articles in the newspaper *Dag og Tid*, 16 May 2013, 21 June 2013 and 5 July 2013.
52 Blindheim, Nordmenn, 12.

major scholarly reference, while it was mainly left to the Waffen-SS veterans and non-scholarly authors to shed further light on this part of Norway's wartime history. We have already seen how veterans gave a biased version of events. Popularised documentary books were important both in drawing attention to the subject and in significantly expanding our historical knowledge of the phenomenon.[53] While also adding new pieces to the contextual picture, the genre's primary concern was the volunteers' motives and individual experiences. Some accounts even challenged aspects of the veterans' narrative, for example by presenting evidence of anti-Semitism, of knowledge of the Holocaust, and of involvement in atrocities.[54] Yet the genre was never fully detached from the apologetic discourse. There was a strong tendency to stress motives such as patriotism, anti-communism, and sympathy with Finland, while similarly downplaying the broader ideological context.[55] Moreover, the authors continued to present the Waffen-SS as a purely military organisation, and drew a sharp distinction between the armed SS and other parts of the »Black Order«.[56] To the extent that they acknowledged that Norwegians had been involved in atrocities, they maintained that these were isolated incidents and that the conduct of the Waffen-SS generally conformed with the law of war.[57] In most accounts by non-academic historians during this period, the issue of war crimes was completely ignored.[58]

The few scholars who broached the subject as a sub-theme in their books or articles found it equally hard to break free from Blindheim's legacy. With limited room for elaboration, the academic accounts tended to focus on establishing basic facts regarding the planning, recruitment, and deployment of Norwegian volun-

---

53 Egil Ulateig: Dagbok frå ein rotnorsk nazist, Oslo 1987; Arneberg, Tragedie; Fjørtoft, Østfronten; Fjørtoft, De som tapte krigen, Oslo 1995; Ulateig, Veien; Arneberg, Legionærene.
54 Ulateig, Dagbok, 166–167, 226–227; Fjørtoft, Østfronten, 227–229; Ulateig, Veien, 63, 85, 103–112.
55 Arneberg, Tragedie, 25–45; Fjørtoft, Østfronten, 74; Ulateig, Veien, 47–58.
56 Ulateig, Dagbok, 218–219; Fjørtoft, Østfronten, 48.
57 E. g. Ulateig, Dagbok, 218–219; Ulateig, Veien, 101–112; Ulateig, Vis meg avsløringene om frontkjemperne!, *Aftenposten*, 20 November 2004.
58 For example, Johan Jensen: De nære årene. Norske kvinner og menn forteller om krigen, Oslo 1986, 155–163; Erling Rønneberg: Dei ville like gjerne levt som vi!, in: A. Skartveit (ed.): Vi valgte det vi ikke kjente. Norske krigsdeltagere om dengang og nå, Oslo 1995, 178–185; Randolf Alnæs: Frontkjempere. Kristiansundere på Østfronten og i Finland under den 2. verdenskrig, Kristiansund 1999.

teer units. However, there continued to be an apparent concern with the question of why Norwegians enlisted in the first instance. Just as previously, the analyses reflected genuine curiosity and even compassion, drawing attention to such factors as youth, social pressure, adventurousness, and – above all – »idealism«. To the extent that the authors elaborated on the content of this »idealism«, they stressed anti-communism, sympathy with Finland and nationalism, whereas the impact of National Socialist ideology was largely disregarded.[59] Anti-communism tended to be particularly emphasised. For example, in a book on Norwegian National Socialism and the NS party, written by three leading experts in the early 1980s, it was claimed that most volunteers were motivated »by a desire to fight against Marxism«.[60] Tim Greve, in his contribution to the major multi-volume work *Norge i krig*, also maintains that many found the ideological indoctrination »tedious« after induction into the Waffen-SS – thus leaving the impression that few of the volunteers had been ideologically committed.[61]

With regards to the character of the Waffen-SS and the war in the East, however, Greve was the only scholar to indicate that the volunteers could have been involved in atrocities as part of their military service.[62] Whereas the majority simply ignored the issue, political scientist Stein Ugelvik Larsen, in an anthology on Nazism and Norwegian literature published in 1995, echoed Blindheim's claim

---

59 Greve, 175; Hans Fredrik Dahl et al. (eds.): Norsk krigsleksikon 1940–45, Oslo 1995, 124–125; Stein Ugelvik Larsen: De skriver om seg selv. Frontkjemperne, NS-medlemmene og NS-barna. Dokumentarlitteraturen om dem på »den gale siden«, in: B. Birkeland et al. (eds.): Nazismen og norsk litteratur, Oslo 1995 (1st ed., 1975), 213–215; Berit Nøkleby and Guri Hjeltnes: Barn under krigen, Oslo 2000, 206.

60 Hans Fredrik Dahl/Bernt Hagtvet/Guri Hjeltnes: Den norske nasjonalsosialismen. Nasjonal Samling 1933–1945 i tekst og bilder, Oslo 1982, 96. In a newspaper interview in 1993, commenting on an initiative to raise a memorial in Finland to honour a group of volunteers who fell in East Karelia in 1944, historian Hans Fredrik Dahl, one of the authors of the book, stated that »anti-communism [was the] predominant motive of Norwegians who volunteered to the Eastern Front.« According to the article, he also stated: »Maybe the ›front fighters‹ did not fight on such a wrong side after all.« See Frontkjemperne vil bli hedret, *Aftenposten*, 9 July 1993.

61 Greve, 168, 174–175.

62 Ibid., 160, 168. On at least one occasion it was also claimed in the media that Norwegian Waffen-SS volunteers had been complicit in the mass killings by members of the SS and police forces: Nils Rømming, *Dagbladet*, 28 December 1996.

from the 1970s that the Waffen-SS was a purely military organisation that had not committed any more crimes than the Allies.[63]

V. Critical Turn: Atrocities Take Centre Stage

Only around the turn of the millennium did the approach to the volunteers and their role in World War Two begin to evolve in a markedly more critical direction.

In an article published in 1998, Norwegian historian Odd-Bjørn Fure drew attention to several sensitive and traumatic aspects of Norway's wartime experience that up until then had received little or no attention by the country's historical profession. One of the aspects that, according to him, deserved more careful scrutiny was the Norwegian NS regime's contribution to Nazi Germany's war on the Eastern Front. As Fure rightly observed, it had for several years been widely known that not only units of the SS but even regular Wehrmacht formations had taken part in mass atrocities in the East. However, hardly anything was known about the conduct of the thousands of Norwegians who had served in the Waffen-SS. Future research should therefore, he argued, focus on the volunteers' role in this savage war, including the mass killings of non-combatants.[64]

Fure's calls were partly heeded by the author Egil Ulateig, who devoted an entire chapter to the issue of atrocities in his book *Veien mot undergangen*, published in 2002. Ulateig's account left no doubt that Norwegians who served with the SS-Division »Wiking« during the summer of 1941 witnessed killings of civilians and POWs, and he even passed on testimony from individuals who claimed to

---

63 Larsen, 197. For accounts in which the issue is not dealt with, see Dahl et al. (eds), *Norsk krigsleksikon*; Nøkleby/Hjeltnes; Hans Fredrik Dahl, En fører for fall. Oslo 1992.
64 Odd-Bjørn Fure, Krigen. Konsensus og fortielse, *Dagbladet*, 8 May 1998. An extended version of the article was later published in a scholarly anthology: Fure, Norsk okkupasjonshistorie. Konsensus, berøringsangst og tabuisering, in: S. U. Larsen (ed.): I krigens kjølvann. Nye sider ved norsk krigshistorie og etterkrigstid, Oslo 1999, 33–34. In 2001, Ivo de Figueiredo, in a comprehensive article on the historiography of the Norwegian Waffen-SS volunteers, questioned Blindheim's tendency to reject the possibility that the »front fighters« could have been involved in atrocities. He also mentioned this aspect along with several others that deserved further scholarly attention. Ivo de Figueiredo, De norske frontkjemperne – hva litteraturen sier og veien videre, in: Historisk tidsskrift 4 (2001), 8, 15. Also available at <http://www.ivodefigueiredo.no/Artikler/Frontkjempere.htm>.

have refused to take part in executions. However, he concluded, »not one single piece of evidence exists that Norwegians partook in war crimes in Ukraine in the opening days of the war.«[65] He even left the impression that most, if not all, allegations of atrocities by the SS-Division »Wiking« were unfounded.[66]

Still, the book had important repercussions. In November 2004, inspired by Ulateig's book, the NRK presented further evidence of atrocities committed by the SS-Division »Wiking« in Western Ukraine during the summer of 1941.[67] The material, which for the most part was derived from scholarly historians, stirred a heated debate on the complicity of Norwegian volunteers in war crimes and crimes against humanity. Whereas Ulateig vehemently rejected that this information was a reason to revise his previous conclusions, others, including historians Terje Emberland and Bernt Rougthvedt, found it highly likely that at least some Norwegians had been involved in atrocities.[68] Emberland and Rougthvedt had just published a biography of the radical Nazi and Waffen-SS volunteer Per Imerslund, who served with the SS-Division »Wiking«. According to their findings, the division had left a trail of blood as it advanced through Ukraine in the summer and fall of 1941.[69]

Despite Emberland's and Roughthvedt's contributions, the controversy confirmed that Norwegian historians were suffering from an almost complete lack of knowledge regarding the volunteers' service on the Eastern Front. Confirming this fact, Norway's Justice Minister Odd-Einar Dørum shortly afterwards initiated a government-funded research project to shed light on the subject. The Center for Studies of the Holocaust and Religious Minorities (*HL-senteret*) in Oslo was given the task of carrying out the project.[70]

---

65   Ulateig, Veien, 111.
66   Ibid.
67   The journalist Eirik Veum, who was responsible for the news item, explicitly stated in the research report that Ulateig's book was an important source of inspiration: Eirik Veum, Nordmenn i Waffen-SS – bødler eller frontkjempere? Copy in possession of the author.
68   For instance, Egil Ulateig, Vis meg avsløringene om frontkjemperne!, *Aftenposten*, 20 November 2004; Terje Emberland/Bernt Rougthvedt, Norske Waffen-SS-frivillige og folkemord, *Aftenposten*, 23 November 2004.
69   Terje Emberland/Bernt Rougthvedt: Det ariske idol. Forfatteren, eventyreren og nazisten Per Imerslund, Oslo 2004, 370–378.
70   Odd-Bjørn Fure/Rolf Hobson/Matthew Kott, Hva skjedde med frontkjemperne i øst? *Aftenposten*, 3 September 2005.

The debate also stimulated others to engage with the topic. Thus, the following years saw a wave of new published and unpublished works on the volunteers, and even if most were not primarily concerned with the group's complicity in atrocities, questions concerning ideological indoctrination, brutality, and knowledge of and complicity in crimes had suddenly become common themes in scholarly as well as non-scholarly literature.[71] Whenever the issue of the Waffen-SS volunteers made its way into the news media, the question of atrocities was often at the centre of attention.[72]

In 2006, Egil Ulateig published *Jakten på massemorderne* (»The Hunt for the Mass Murderers«), which was completely devoted to this question. Drawing on insights developed over decades of close relations with Norwegian veterans of the Waffen-SS, as well as on source material compiled over many years of extensive work on the subject, he was able to present a detailed and intriguing account. Although unable to provide direct and convincing evidence of Norwegian participation in war crimes, the book left the impression that this almost certainly had happened.[73]

Six years later, in 2012, Terje Emberland and Matthew Kott published *Himmlers Norge* (»Himmler's Norway«), the first monograph produced as part of the aforementioned government-funded research project on Norwegians in the Waffen-SS. Compared with all previous accounts, the authors adopted a very broad approach, seeking to understand the recruitment of Norwegians and the various unit histories in light of Himmler's wider racial-political ambitions. The book also confirms the impression that the Waffen-SS units were pervaded by National Socialist ideals and values, and concludes that a significant number of Norwegian volunteers were involved in atrocities, either directly or indirectly. Many were also involved in the persecution of Jews and other groups on Norwegian soil.[74]

---

71 Jordbruen, 65, 71, 106; Ulateig: Jakten på massemorderne. En dokumentarbok, Lesja 2006; Bjørn Westlie: Fars krig, Oslo 2008; Thoresen, 47, 140–145; Eirik Veum: De som falt. Nordmenn drept i tysk krigstjeneste, Oslo 2009, 31–35, 307–315; Vegard Sæther: »En av oss«. Norske frontkjempere i krig og fred, Oslo 2010, 94–95, 347–348; Lindstad, 34–36; Emberland/Kott.
72 E.g. Ja, vi drepte jøder, *Adresseavisen*, 22 October 2013; Sårt og brutalt om far, *Dagbladet*, 15 September 2008; Nordmenn var krigsforbrytere, *Aftenposten*, 18 August 2009; Frontkjemperne deltok i ufattelige grusomheter, *Dagbladet*, 1 November 2006.
73 Ulateig, Jakten.
74 Emberland/Kott, 235–237, 358–359.

Even if a far more critical perspective has gained widespread acceptance after the millennium, the tendency of uncritically commemorating the volunteers as patriotic idealists has proven highly resilient. Probably the most illuminating example is Arvid Bryne's *Vi sloss for Norge* (»We Fought for Norway«), a double biography of Svein Blindheim and the former SS-Untersturmführer Bjørn Østring. In his book, the author equates the two protagonists' motives and ideals in an even more uncritical fashion than Blindheim had done three decades previously in *Nordmenn under Hitlers fane*:

»When Bjørn Østring fought at the Leningrad front, he fought on Germany's side against the Soviet Union. But he also saw it as a fight for Norway against communist aggression. Østring fought with the Norwegian flag on his chest, at the risk of his own life, for our national values and Norway's independence.«[75]

VI. From Misguided Idealists to *Genocidaires*: Explanations and Implications

The claim that Waffen-SS volunteers were seen as evil, deceitful, and inferior after 1945, that there was no interest in their thoughts, emotions, and points of view, and that the group, compared with other categories of collaborators, was particularly despised by the public, is utterly unfounded. From a very early stage there was an apparent tendency to adopt a balanced and sympathetic approach to the volunteers in the public discourse. Later, as scholars and non-scholars started to engage with the topic, many were easily convinced by the post-war testimony of the veterans, often ending up reproducing their apologetic claims and perspectives. Moreover, in stark contrast to explicit assumptions in the memory literature, hardly any theme gained as much attention in the historiography and public debate on the topic as the motives and experiences of the volunteers themselves.

How might this sense of sympathy and – sometimes – naivety be explained? The evidence suggests that many perceived the volunteers, or at least the majority of them, as young and unselfish idealists who had been victims of social pressure and circumstances, and who paid a very high price for their fateful decision to enlist in the Waffen-SS. Far from being completely unfounded, this impression was

---

75   Bryne, 11. Translation by the author. See also Harry Ellingsen: Regiment Norge. Historien om en norsk frontkjemperenhet, Oslo 2011, 220.

well-fitted to evoke sympathy. Moreover, the volunteers did not easily conform to the image of the deceitful and opportunistic traitor, as they had mostly been committed nationalists who had put their life at risk for a higher cause. Thus, in accordance with the predominant patriotic narrative of the first post-war decades, it was not unnatural to perceive them as »good Norwegians« who had been led astray. It is highly likely that the emergence of the Cold War made the public more inclined to view the volunteers and their conduct during the war with sympathy, as anti-Soviet sentiments probably made many people receptive to the argument that the »front fighters« had enlisted to save Europe from the communist threat. Waffen-SS veterans from Norway and elsewhere were also able to exert significant influence on public opinion, indirectly by assisting historians and journalists, and directly by disseminating their own narratives through written publications and interviews. The extent to which this alternative discourse affected the national memorial culture should not be underestimated, particularly since many scholarly and non-scholarly historians were – at least from a current perspective – strikingly uncritical of the volunteers' accounts.[76] Undoubtedly, the popular notion that the Wehrmacht had not generally been complicit in the crimes of the Third Reich, combined with a lack of scholarly expertise on the topic in Norway, facilitated the acceptance of the veterans' approach.

Why was the tendency to commemorate the Norwegian Waffen-SS volunteers as misguided idealists who had been »soldiers like all the others«[77] challenged by a more critical discourse in the late 1990s and early 2000s? The fact that scholarly historians took a greater interest in the subject during this period may in itself have contributed to the shift. However, even if scholars normally tend to adopt a more critical and analytical approach than non-scholarly writers, this was – as we have seen – not always the case with regards to this particular topic. Neither was it self-evident that scholars who adopted a more critical perspective would choose to focus on atrocities rather than, say, the volunteers' motives.

76 An illuminating example is the following passage in Svein Blindheim's book *Nordmenn under Hitlers fane*: »The idea that the Waffen-SS was any more criminal than other military organizations is impossible to determine from my material and the discussions I have had with volunteers, etc.« This quote clearly indicates that Blindheim assigned a lot of credibility to the volunteers' accounts, even when they commented on the issue of atrocities. Blindheim, Nordmenn, 15. See also Ulateig, Jakten, 24–25.
77 The concept was introduced by the former SS-Oberstgruppenführer Paul Hausser in his apologetic book of 1961: Paul Hausser: Soldaten wie andere auch. Der Weg der Waffen-SS, Osnabrück 1966.

The critical turn should therefore be understood in terms of other and more specific factors, some of which are closely intertwined with each other. Arguably, the most important factor seems to have been the enhanced awareness regarding the Wehrmacht's complicity in the crimes of the Third Reich. As Odd-Bjørn Fure noted in his 1998 article, massacres had constituted an integral part of Germany's campaign in the East.[78] And if ordinary Wehrmacht units had been involved in atrocities on a significant scale, why should this not also have been the case with the notorious formations of the armed SS? And if many ordinary Germans took part, were there any reasons to assume that Norwegians did not? It also seems likely that the augmented concern with the Holocaust in Norwegian memory culture during the same period, which reflected a broader international trend, contributed to this shift. Moreover, it may also be argued that the shift was influenced by the wider trend towards a more »universalistic« approach to history. Whereas the national perspective that dominated historical writing and public historical debates during the first post-war decades was well suited to maintain the uncritical discourse with its strong focus on the volunteers' motives – of whether or not they had volunteered for patriotic reasons –, the »universalistic« approach encouraged researchers and others to shift the centre of attention to the group's involvement in crimes committed beyond Norway's borders. Furthermore, the change was clearly stimulated by research published abroad, for example, on several case studies of Danes in the Waffen-SS.[79] Finally, as already noted above, certain non-scholarly authors and journalists played an important role in triggering public debate and, in turn, in promoting research, as well as in disseminating new findings and approaches to a popular audience.[80]

The new and more critical approach has undoubtedly helped to correct and complete the historical record regarding Norwegians who served in the Waffen-SS during the Second World War. Yet it does not mean that the shift has had no

---

78 Fure, Okkupasjonshistorie, 34.
79 E. g. Claus Bundgård/Niels Bo Poulsen/Peter Scharff Smith: Under hagekors og Dannebrog. Danskere i Waffen SS 1940–45, Copenhagen 1998. Case studies of Waffen-SS atrocities in particular areas in Eastern Europe should also be mentioned. Cf. Bernd Boll, Złoczów, July 1941: The Wehrmacht and the Beginning of the Holocaust in Galicia. From a Criticism of Photographs to a Revision of the Past, in: O. Bartov/ A. Grossmann/M. Nolan (eds): Crimes of War: Guilt and Denial in the Twentieth Century, New York 2002, 61–99.
80 For example, Ulateig, Dagbok; Ulateig, Veien; Ulateig, Jakten; Veum, Nordmenn; Westlie, Fars krig.

drawbacks. For example, it may be argued that the strong focus on participation in atrocities has left many with the impression that the massacring of non-combatants belonged to the volunteers' daily routines, while the vast majority of them in fact belonged to units that principally served military functions and seem to have carried out relatively few crimes. Even if the traditional image of the misguided »idealist« who served as a regular soldier in an ordinary military organisation is misleading, it does not mean that it should simply be replaced by that of the genocidaire. There are, however, indications that this has to some extent been the case, not in the historical writing, but in the popular mind.

If Anne Eriksen and others have misrepresented the role of the »front fighters« in Norwegian memory, what implications should this have for our general assessment of the so-called »national narrative«, as it has been outlined in numerous scholarly and popular accounts in recent years? Let there be no doubt: Anne Eriksen's pioneering study *Det var noe annet under krigen*, published back in the mid-1990s, added considerably to our understanding of how the war and the occupation was commemorated in Norway, and subsequent studies have shed further light on the subject. Some of the conclusions drawn in these studies are hardly contested. For example, not many would today reject that there has been a strong tendency to understand the occupation within a national framework and to focus on what was perceived as nationally memorable aspects of the war. Themes that did not fit easily into this approach, such as specific forms of collaboration and the arrest and deportation of the Jewish minority, were for a long time largely ignored in the public discourse.

Still, the case of the Waffen-SS volunteers shows that the commemoration of Norway's collaborators has been far more complex than assumed in the above-mentioned studies. The volunteers were not generally detested or represented as inferior or evil, and the claim that they were particularly despised and »committed the ultimate betrayal of the male gender role« is not only false, but rests on no evidence whatsoever. It is hard to avoid the impression that such claims at least partly derive from the apologetic discourse by the Waffen-SS veterans, and that these notions were accepted without reservations simply because they fitted easily into the theory of the existence of a mythical Manichean national narrative. This begs the question of whether other and more essential arguments and perspectives have been based on equally scant evidence, and whether some of the studies even suffer from more systematic biases. It could be argued that the striking contrast in Anne Eriksen's book between, on the one hand, a critical and often ironic approach to the so-called »national narrative«, and the almost complete lack of critical examination of oppositional discourses, on the other, is an example of the latter. However, it must be left to future research to judge the extent to which this and other studies of Norway's remembrance of the war simply replaced one mythical narrative with another.

The Authors

Arnd Bauerkämper, Professor of Modern European History at the *Freie Universität Berlin*. Studied History and English at the Universities of Bielefeld, Oxford and Göttingen. Selected publications: Der *Faschismus in Europa 1918–1945* (Stuttgart 2006); *Die Sozialgeschichte der DDR* (Munich 2005), *Das umstrittene Gedächtnis. Die Erinnerung an Nationalsozialismus, Faschismus und Krieg in Europa seit 1945* (Paderborn 2012).

Steffen Bruendel, Research Director of the Research Center for Historical Humanities at the *Goethe-Universität Frankfurt am Main*. Studied History and Public Law at the Universities of Freiburg, London (QMC) and Bielefeld. From 2006 to 2013 he was Programme Director of the E.ON Scholarship Fund. Selected publications: *Zeitenwende 1914. Künstler, Dichter und Denker im Ersten Weltkrieg* (Munich 2014); *Volksgemeinschaft oder Volksstaat. Die »Ideen von 1914« und die Neuordnung Deutschlands im Ersten Weltkrieg* (Berlin 2003).

Tor Einar Fagerland, Associate Professor and Chair, Department of History, The Norwegian University of Science and Technology, Trondheim. Research focus is on the Norwegian culture of memory. Since 2012 leader of a project addressing the terror attacks on July 22 2011 in Oslo/Utøya. This work includes advisory tasks on the national July 22 memorials and of the Labour Youth League on their return to Utøya.

Odd-Bjørn Fure, Professor Emeritus Senior Dr. Philos. Researcher at Center for Studies of Holocaust and Religious Minorities. Studied at the University of Bergen, Dr. Philos. in 1984, Professor in Modern History at the University of Bergen, Director of Center for Studies of Holocaust and Religious Minorities. Research stays in Zürich, Paris, Freiburg and Berlin. Selected publications: *Mellomkrigstid 1920–1940*. Vol. 3 Norsk utenrikspolitikks historie (Oslo 1996); *Norsk okkupasjonshistorie. Konsensus, berøringsangst og tabuisering*, in: Stein Ugelvik Larsen (ed.): I krigens kjølvann (Oslo 1999); *Tilintetgjørelsen av de europeiske jødene*, in: Nytt Norsk Tidsskrift 2/2002.

Gunnar D. Hatlehol, PhD Fellow in History at the Norwegian University of Science and Technology, Trondheim. Studied History and Anthropology at the University of Bergen. The subject of his PhD thesis is Organisation Todt's forced laborers in Norway during the Second World War. Selected publications: *I vente på skipsrederen. Hjemmevirksomheten til Hilmar Rekstens rederi 1940–1945* (Bergen 2011). He is also currently preparing publication of a history of the Norwegian Shipowners Mutual War Risks Insurance Association, 1945–2010.

Øystein Hetland, PhD candidate in History at the Center for Studies of the Holocaust and Religious Minorities, Oslo. Studied Political Science and History at the University of Trondheim. Selected publication: *Kva visste Nasjonal Samling om Holocaust?* (Oslo 2012).

Claudia Lenz, Head of Research at the European Wergeland Centre and Associate professor at the Norwegian University for Science and Technology. Studied Philosophy, Psychology and Political Science at the University of Hamburg, followed by a PhD in Political Science at the same university. Selected publication: *Historicising the uses of the past – Comparative Scandinavian perspectives on history culture, historical consciousness and didactics of history related to World War II* (Bielefeld 2011, co-edited with Helle Bjerg and Erik Thorstensen).

Susanne Maerz, editor at the magazine »Wirtschaft im Südwesten« in Freiburg, studied History, Scandinavian Studies and German Literature at the Universities of Freiburg and Bergen. Selected publications: *Die langen Schatten der Besatzungszeit. »Vergangenheitsbewältigung« in Norwegen als Identitätsdiskurs* (Berlin 2008), *Okkupasjonstidens lange skygger. Fortidsbearbeidelse i Norge som identitetsdiskur* (Oslo 2010).

Ilse Raaijmakers, PhD candidate at Maastricht University, studied History, European Studies and German Language and Culture at the Universities of Utrecht, Vienna and Amsterdam. Selected publication: *Competitive or multidirectional memory? The interaction between postwar and postcolonial memory in the Netherlands*, Journal of Genocide Research 14.3–4 (2012): 463–483 (with Iris van Ooijen).

Doreen Reinhold, PhD candidate at the Department of Northern European Studies, Humboldt-University Berlin, studied European Studies at the University of Bremen, University of Bergen and University College London.

The Authors

Jon Reitan, Historian and Deputy Director of the Falstad Centre in Norway. Selected publications: *Jödene fra Trondheim*, Trondheim: Tapir, 2005; *Falstad – nazileir og landssvikfengsel*, Trondheim 2008; »The Legacies of the Nazi Camps in Norway«, in: Wilfried Wiedermann et al. (eds.): *Landschaft und Gedächtnis* (Munich 2011).

Leiv Sem, Associate Professor in Norwegian literature at the Nord Trøndelag University College. PhD 2009 at the University of Oslo with a thesis on WWII commemoration in Norway. Selected publications: *Personal pain, national narrative. Commemorating an SS-camp*, in: Anne Eriksen/Jón Viðar Sigurdsson: Negotiating pasts in the Nordic countries (Lund 2009); »Norske slagmarker«, in: Claudia Lenz/ Trond Risto Nilssen: Fortiden i nåtiden (Oslo 2011).

Sigurd Sørlie, Research Fellow at the Norwegian Institute for Defence Studies, studied History and Political Science at the Universities of Oslo and Exeter. Selected publication: *Norwegische Freiwillige in der Waffen-SS und die Herausforderungen der Integration*, in: Jan Erik Schulte et al. (eds.): Die Waffen-SS. Neue Forschungen (Paderborn 2014).

Iselin Theien, Advisor at the *Center for Studies of Holocaust and Religious Minorities* and a freelance writer, holds a PhD in Modern History from the University of Oxford and was a postdoctoral fellow in History at the University of Oslo. Selected publications: *Norwegian fascism 1933–40: The position of the Nasjonal Samling in Norwegian Politics* (D. Phil. thesis, Oxford University, 2001); *Organisert kjøpekraft: forbrukersamvirkets historie i Norge* (co-author, Oslo, 2006); *Sonja Wigert. Et dobbeltliv* (Oslo 2010).

Bjørn Westlie, Associated Professor University College of Oslo and Akershus (HIOA), former journalist now working as a historian and writer. PhD Candidate, University of Oslo. Selected publications: *Fars krig* (Oslo 2008); *Hitlers norske budbringere* (Oslo 2011).

Robert Zimmermann, PhD candidate in History at Freie Universität Berlin, studied Modern History, Political Science and Geography at the University of Technology Dresden and Agder University College Kristiansand. Visiting scholar at NTNU Trondheim and University of Oslo. Selected publications: »*The War in the North*« *and German Historiography since 1945*, in: Nytt blikk (2011), pp. 62–77; »*Auch norwegische Frauen und Männer Haben mit diesem schrecklichen Lager*

Bekanntschaft gemacht«. Das Konzentrationslager Mauthausen in der norwegischen Erinnerungskultur, in: Gerhard Botz et al. (eds.): Mauthausen überleben und erinnern, Vol. 3 (with Merethe Aagaard Jensen, in preparation).

Index of Names

A
Adenauer, Konrad 217
Adorno, Theodor 34, 94 f., 103
Akselsen, Olav 121
Alighieri, Dante 241
Andenæs, Johannes 126, 158, 278
Arendt, Hannah 34, 83
Arneberg, Sven T. 233 f., 243, 281 f., 286
Assmann, Aleida 21 ff., 63, 88, 108 f., 140, 197, 217, 231 f.,
Assmann, Jan 63

B
Balsrud, Jan 226
Barfod, Jørgen 173–178, 189 f.
Barlaup, Asbjørn 280
Barkan, Elazar 99, 110, 134
Barrett, John 39
Bauerkämper, Arnd 15 f., 36, 64, 149, 173, 297
Bauman, Zygmunt 34
Beatrix, Queen of the Netherlands 147
Beker, Avi 117 f.
Benkow, Jo 118
Bergmann, Ludwig 257, 269 f.
Blair, Tony 107
Blindheim, Svein 233, 235, 281, 283–288, 291 f.
Blom, J. C. H. 136 f., 139, 143 ff.
Bodnar, John 22 f.
Bondevik, Kjell Magne 14, 76, 80, 120, 122, 133, 264, 271

Borries, Bodo von 203
Brakstad, Ingjerd Veiden 127
Bratteli, Trygve 182
Breivik, Anders 79
Browning, Christopher R. 34, 98
Bruland, Bjarte 32, 77, 79, 96, 122 ff., 132 f., 143,
Bryne, Arvid 61, 77, 241, 248, 281, 284, 291

C
Cesarani, David 113
Chirac, Jacques 80
Clinton, Bill 107, 117
Corell, Synne 19, 44, 56, 71, 127, 158, 195
Cornelißen, Christoph 9 f., 16, 22, 63, 70 f., 73, 82

D
Dahl, Hans Fredrik 15, 157, 168, 235, 258, 287 f.
Danielsen, Rolf 46, 157
Dean, Martin 124, 127
Demnig, Gunter 224
Denkiewicz-Szczepaniak, Emilia 159
Dørum, Odd-Einar 289
Douglas, Mary 228
Drop, Jan 139, 146
Duckwitz, Georg Ferdinand 67

E
Eichmann, Adolf 34, 113, 142, 223
Eisenman, Peter 221 f., 230

Eizenstaat, Stuart 107
Ekwas, Tone 215
Emberland, Terje 53, 165, 233, 236, 274, 283, 289 f.
Eriksen, Anne 185, 194, 219, 222, 237, 248, 273 ff., 294, 299

F
Fagerland, Tor Einar 23, 35, 38, 72, 76, 227, 297
Falkanger, Thor 122 f.
Faremo, Grete 105 f., 120
Feinberg, Kai 130 ff., 134
Fjelstad, Jack 226
Folkvord, Erling 121
Foss, Per-Kristian 121 f.
Foucault, Michel 254, 261, 265, 270
Frank, Anne 93, 112
Frei, Norbert 24, 63, 65, 78, 172
Friedländer, Saul 106
Frøland, Hans Otto 14
Fure, Eli 122 f.
Fure, Odd-Bjørn 15, 23, 27 ff., 32, 36, 46 ff., 57, 60, 69, 114, 159, 167, 195, 288 f., 293, 297
Fussel, Paul 239

G
Gaarder, Jostein 39, 254, 261–265, 270 f.
Gahr Støre, Jonas 35, 96, 97–103, 111, 114
Gauck, Joachim 148 f.
Gaulle, Charles de 23
Gerhardsen, Einar 69, 182, 184
Gerz, Jochen 219 ff.
Ginio, Ruth 118
Gormley, Antony 222

Gran, Bjarne 158
Graver, Hans Petter 126
Greenwald, Alice 229 f.
Greve, Tim 158, 276, 287
Grimnes, Ole Kristian 58, 70 f., 79, 122 f., 154, 185
Gross, Jan Tomasz 81

H
Haakon VII. 30, 68, 70, 193, 266
Haefs, Gabriele 268
Halbwachs, Maurice 10, 63, 217
Halle, Frode 239, 276, 279–282
Hals, Anne 122
Halse, Svein 236, 239
Hansteen, Wilhelm 279 f.
Hamsun, Knut 74
Harper, Christopher S. 126
Hatlehol, Gunnar 37, 298
Haugen, Marit Justine 224 f.
Hayes, Peter 118, 129
Hedtoft, Hans 67
Hennie, Aksel 225 f.
Herz, Rudolf 221
Hilberg, Raul 34, 124
Himmler, Heinrich 53, 233, 236, 274, 283 ff., 290
Hitler, Adolf 9, 15, 27, 29, 52 ff., 68, 79, 81, 233, 235, 258, 270, 275, 281, 283 ff., 291 f., 299
Hjeltnes, Guri 40, 157 f., 287 f.
Holmboe, Haakon 155 f.
Holmila, Antero 119
Holte, Johan B. 13
Holter, Karl 236
Hoppe, Jens 197
Høybråten, Dagfinn 133 f.
Humlegård, Odd 105

I
Imerslund, Per 289
Isenstein, Harald 223

J
Jagland, Thorbjørn 133
Johansen, Per Ole 32, 113
Judt, Tony 22, 35, 109, 140

K
Keil, André 39
Kjeldstadli, Sverre 156
Kjendsli, Veslemøy 260
Klein, Cissi 215, 222 f.
Koch, Birgit 159
Kohl, Helmut 148
Kohn, Ervin 105
Koselleck, Reinhart 63, 65, 94
Kott, Matthew 53, 233, 236, 274, 283, 289 f.
Kverndokk, Kyrre 188
Kvist Geverts, Karin 119

L
Lagrou, Pieter 27, 30, 127, 138, 219, 222
Lange-Nielsen, Sissel 260
Langfeldt, Gabriel 275, 276 f.
Larsen, Stein Ugelvik 32, 57, 72, 157, 159, 168, 195, 236, 244, 257, 287 f., 297
Leeuw, Auke de 149
Leggewie, Claus 21
Lembcke, Ove 175
Lenz, Claudia 23, 25, 32, 34 f., 37, 67, 70–73, 76 f., 79, 81, 91, 185, 193, 226, 235, 257, 298, 299
Levin, Irene 131
Levy, Daniel 24, 78, 81, 84, 93 f., 232,

Lidchi, Henrietta 194, 197 f., 202, 205, 208
Lie, Jonas 236
Lilletun, Jon 121 f.
Lin, Maya 229 f.
Löhr Meek, Per Arne 261
Lombroso, Cesare 275
Lysenko, Andrey 243 f.

M
Maerz, Susanne 23, 39, 57, 60, 70 f., 74 ff., 81, 83, 159, 195 f., 209, 253 f., 273, 298
Maier, Clemens 71, 185, 274 f.
Mannerheim, Carl 67
Manus, Max 78 f., 225 f.
Matz, Reinhard 221
Meier, Christian 12, 14
Meißner, Christoph 39
Mellbye, Ann Elisabeth 39
Meyer, Kurt 285
Milgram, Stanley 34
Mladenović, Ljubo 159 f.
Moeller, Robert W. 50
Møller, Mogens 179
Mosse, George 239

N
Nansen, Fridtjof 48
Næss, Arne 277
Nedreaas, Torborg 257
Nøkleby, Berit 153, 157, 161, 168 f., 287 f.
Nordseth-Tiller, Thomas 78
Nordstrand, Leif 182 f.
Novick, Peter 132, 248
Nygaardsvold, Johan 279

O
Østring, Bjørn 281, 291
Ottosen, Kristian 130, 161 f.

P
Paltiel, Julius 224
Persson, Göran 82, 107 f.
Plesansky, Bernard 130
Plesansky, Isak 130
Presser, Jacques 142
Proust, Marcel 227
Pryser, Tore 32

Q
Quisling, Vidkun 15, 19, 27, 48, 54, 68, 71 f., 123, 126, 165, 193 f., 201 f., 206 f., 211, 226, 234, 258, 273, 278

R
Raaijmakers, Ilse 33, 37, 103, 141, 148, 298
Raeder, Erich 27
Reinhold, Doreen 23, 37 f., 71, 78, 298
Reisel, Berit 32, 96, 119, 122 ff., 132 f.
Reitan, Jon 23, 31 f., 35, 37, 72, 79 f., 112 f., 165, 299
Renan, Ernst 216
Ribbentrop, Joachim von 68
Rieber-Mohn, Georg 126
Ringdal, Nils Johan 258
Rød, Knut 32, 75, 113, 126 f.
Rosenberg, Alfred 27, 54, 68
Rougthvedt, Bernt 289

S
Saabye Christensen, Lars 254 f., 264–267, 271
Sachnowitz, Herman 182
Sagen, Einar 279
Savosnick, Robert 280
Scharffenberg, Johan 277
Schjærve, Helge 125 ff.
Seip, Jens Arup 47
Sem, Leiv 23, 38, 165, 235, 242, 248 f., 299
Sender, Anne 132
Simensen, Jarle 12–15, 17
Sjaastad, Anders 122
Sjaastad, Gunnar S. 235
Skarpnes, Oluf 32, 122 f., 125, 128 f., 131–134
Skjølsvik, Tore Bjørn 215
Skodvin, Magne 156 f., 276
Skouen, Arne 226
Solheim, Erik 133 f.
Soleim, Marianne Neerland 58, 163, 167, 169
Sonia, Queen of Norway 76
Sønsteby, Gunnar 225
Sørensen, Øystein 15, 46, 156, 168, 258
Sørlie, Sigurd 23, 38, 77, 165, 245, 299
Stadelmann-Wenz, Elke 39
Stein, George 283 ff.
Steen, Sverre 155 f.
Støen, Ane Ingvild 39
Stoltenberg, Jens 20, 37, 76, 98, 100, 105 f., 111 f., 245
Støre, Jonas Gahr 35, 96–103, 111, 114
Sunde, Guri 122 f.
Sznaider, Natan 24, 78, 81, 93 f., 232

T
Terboven, Josef 27, 52 ff., 58, 68
Theien, Iselin 32, 37, 114, 126, 299
Thomassen, Petter 119 f.
Tito, Josip Broz 100

Tue, Anneken 13
Tumarkin, Nina 243

U
Ugelvik Larsen, Stein 57, 157, 159, 168, 195, 236, 244, 257, 287, 297
Ulateig, Egil 237, 281 f., 286, 288 ff., 292 f.
Ullman, Micha 230
Ullmann, Liv 269

V
Veum, Eirik 237, 289 f., 293
Vranitzky, Franz 80
Vree, Frank van 139 f., 142 ff., 147

W
Wang, Nina 224 f.
Wassmo, Herbjørg 39, 253 f., 258–262, 265, 268, 270 f.
Wedel, Count 72

Weizsäcker, Richard von 9
Westlie, Bjørn 32, 37, 114, 119 f., 122, 131, 133, 196, 290, 293, 299
Wetterstad, Roy 121 f.
Wiesel, Elie 118
Wieviorka, Anette 107
Wilcken, Dagmar von 221
Willoch, Kåre 162
Winter, Jay 118, 218 f.
Wolfrum, Edgar 16, 63
Wyller, Thomas Christian 55, 59, 156

Y
Young, James E. 219 ff., 229

Z
Ze'ev, Efrat Ben 118
Zimbardo, Philip 34
Zimmermann, Robert 23, 38, 299
Zohar, Dan 224 f.